INSIDERS' GUIDE®

OFF THE BEATEN PATH® SERIES

Off the
EIGHTH EDITION
Beaten Path®

hawaii

A GUIDE TO UNIQUE PLACES

SEAN PAGER
with
Sheryl Groden Pager

INSIDERS' GUIDE®

GUILFORD, CONNECTICUT
AN IMPRINT OF THE GLOBE PEQUOT PRESS

The prices and rates listed in this guidebook were confirmed at press time. We recommend, however, that you call establishments before traveling to obtain current information.

An additional note: All selections of lodgings and restaurants have been made by the author. No one can pay or be paid to be included in this book.

The detailed route maps provided in this guide should be used in conjunction with a road map. Distances indicated are approximate.

To buy books in quantity for corporate use or incentives, call **(800) 962–0973** or e-mail **premiums@GlobePequot.com.**

INSIDERS' GUIDE®

Text design by Linda Loiewski
Revisions for the Oahu and Kaua`i chapters in the eighth edition were contributed by Jill Dahlman.
Maps on pages iv, 2, 52, 134, 158, 170, and 228 by Equator Graphics © Morris Book Publishing, LLC. All other maps by Mary Ballachino.
Illustrations on pages 105, 177, and 236 © 1995 by Wren.
All other text illustrations by Daisy DePothod.
Spot photography throughout © James D. Watt/imagequestmarine.com

ISSN 1535-8313
ISBN 978-0-7627-4200-4

Manufactured in the United States of America
Eighth Edition/Second Printing

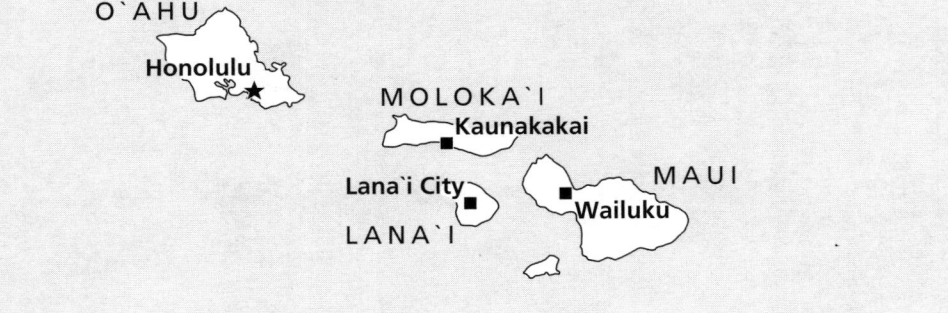

KAUA`I

Lihue

O`AHU

Honolulu

MOLOKA`I

Kaunakakai

Lana`i City

MAUI

Wailuku

LANA`I

Hilo

THE BIG ISLAND

Contents

Acknowledgments

As with any project of this scope, many individuals helped bring it to fruition. For whose *kokua* I am especially grateful, I include the Carolans on Kaua`i; the Shlachters on O`ahu; the Arensdorfs, Jim Grody, and Fern on Maui; Sol Kahoohalahala and John Graham on Lana`i; Jackie Horne, Patti Cook, Punahele Andrade, Kiko Johnston-Kitazawa, and Douglass Bartlett on the Big Island; Torrie Haurez on Moloka`i; Sheila Donnelly Associates; Becker Communications; Marisa Parker at Stryker Weiner Associates; Nathan Kam at McNeil Wilson; Connie Wright; Mary Paterson; Robert Bone; John Mink; Jackie Horne; Matt Cohen; Sheryl the patient; Devah the Goddess; Martha Yent; and Barbara and David Shideler. Thanks also to many others I met along the way who helped recharge my batteries with the spirit of aloha. To all of you, *mahalo a nui loa!*

Introduction

Welcome to Hawaii! These words are heard by the almost seven million tourists each year who storm the islands to roast themselves on Waikiki Beach and sip mai tais topped with paper parasols. Despite this annual onslaught, there remains a Hawaii that few tourists see and many hardly suspect exists. This book will take you there.

Bypass the tourist centers, and you can lose yourself in the midst of untouched natural beauty. You'll travel the back roads that tour buses cannot follow, or take to the hills on foot. Discover beaches empty of human footprints and remote valleys guarding sparkling waterfalls. Experience a Hawaii enriched by its diverse immigrant cultures and native Polynesian roots. You'll learn the legends of prehistoric temples, wander through royal palaces and missionary homes, shop in native craft shops, and sample exotic cuisines. All this awaits you in the Hawaii that lies off the beaten path.

A Setting of Superlatives

I have lived here almost all my life, and I'm still discovering new ways to appreciate Hawaii's charms. These islands boast the world's best surfing waves, the highest sea cliffs, the rainiest mountain peak, the largest and most active volcanoes, and the clearest night skies. They belong to the longest and most isolated archipelago in the world. More than 90 percent of the plants and animals living here are found nowhere else on the planet.

For all their beauty and wonder, the islands are newcomers as landforms go. They represent the peaks of enormous undersea volcanoes fueled by primeval fires welling up from deep within the earth. Because the ocean floor is shifting northwest over the underlying source of magma, the zone of active volcanism resembles a geological assembly line, with each island forming and then moving over to make way for its successors. The oldest islands, worn away by erosion and sinking under their own weight into the earth's mantle, have all but disappeared, while the youngest and largest island grows almost daily as eruptions continue to build new land, much to the delight of tourists lucky enough to witness this volcanic genesis.

Long before geology became a science, the ancient Hawaiians understood the natural forces governing their island home. Their legends told of the epic battle between Pele, the fire goddess, and her sister Na Maka o Ka Hai, goddess of the sea. Pele came to Hawaii to escape her older sister's wrath after she had stolen Na Maka's suitor. The sea goddess followed her and flooded the first shallow fire pits that Pele had dug. Pele moved from island to island, going southeast down the Hawaiian chain and building newer and taller mountains from the volcanic fires she summoned. Yet each time, the power of the ocean wore down Pele's island fortresses and drove her onward. Although her current home on the Big Island continues to grow, Pele knows that it too will have to be abandoned in time. Already, new undersea volcanoes farther southeast are rising to form the islands of the future.

Of the 132 volcanic peaks that rise above the highest tide, only the youngest 8 were large enough to be settled permanently by the early Hawaiians. Visitors today can explore six of these islands: Kaua`i, O`ahu, Moloka`i, Lana`i, Maui, and Hawai`i ("the Big Island"). Each maintains its own distinct identity. Even within the individual islands, you will marvel at the diversity of habitats. The most obvious contrasts are between windward (northeast) and leeward (southwest) coasts. Crossing a mountain barrier can bring you from rain forest into desert within the distance of a few miles. Weather patterns are also extremely localized. It rarely rains in one place for long, and it's almost always sunny somewhere.

Hawaii's human history is as unique as its natural setting. Polynesian voyagers in double-hulled canoes followed the stars from other Pacific islands across thousands of miles of open ocean to settle these lands more than 1,500 years ago. Although lacking metal, they developed a sophisticated culture governed by inflexible *kapu* (taboos). Elaborate *heiau* (temples) enshrined beautifully crafted *kii akua,* or tiki (idols), which accepted divine offerings from a grateful people.

The arrival of the English explorer Capt. James Cook in 1778 brought the archipelago into contact with the modern world. Western weapons enabled a Hawaii chieftain named Kamehameha to forge a unified kingdom, but Western diseases decimated his population. After his death, his son abandoned the old gods and ordered all the tiki destroyed in islandwide bonfires. Today only the stone foundations of the heiau remain as vestiges of a once flourishing civilization.

Missionaries soon arrived to convert the now godless people. Newly formed sugar plantations began to import laborers from around the world. Out of this immigrant pool grew a multiethnic society blending East and West. Now the fiftieth state in the Union, Hawaii is the only U.S. territory that was formerly a sovereign kingdom. Hawaii also remains one of the few places in the world where no ethnic group can claim a majority.

On the Practical Side

Heading off the beaten path in Hawaii can pose some special challenges. Most of the islands have a single main highway that hugs the coast. The Hawaii

Visitors and Convention Bureau (HVCB) has erected roadside marker signs styled in the shape of a Hawaiian warrior to designate the main points of interest. Green mile markers help you keep track of distances, but there are few street signs to guide you along secondary routes. Many places of interest can be reached only by unpaved roads. Because of liability risks, out-of-the-way sites often post discouraging signs while unofficially tolerating access. These artificial deterrents keep tourist hordes away from some of Hawaii's most memorable sights.

As an off-the-beaten-path traveler in Hawaii, you assume certain obligations. These are small islands, with fragile environments. Many of the sites described here rely on their inaccessibility as their only protection against abuse. Keep in mind that Hawaii's heiau and wilderness remain sacred sites to some, as you'll see by the offerings left (often a simple *ti* leaf wrapped around a rock).

Most people come here to bask in Hawaii's natural beauty, and, happily, the best parts are usually free. Natural attractions fall into two main categories: *mauka* (meaning "mountain"—you pronounce it maow-kah) and *makai* (meaning "ocean"—you pronounce it mah-kye). You'll hear these two words used frequently in the islands as directions, as you can almost always use one or the other as a convenient landmark. Going mauka (inland) often involves hiking, and Hawaii has some of the world's best trails. Depending on the season, you might be rewarded with guavas, passion fruit, mangos, mountain apples, and other exotic fruits that grow wild in the hills. You needn't worry about poisonous or predatory animals here, but other dangers exist. Volcanic soil and rock can often be treacherously crumbly and undergrowth impossibly thick. Illicit backwoods *pakalolo* (marijuana) patches can put unwary "trespassers" at risk. Stick to posted trails and you'll be fine. Bring mosquito repellant for wet valley hikes and flashlights to explore the occasional cave.

Going makai (seaward) eventually means hitting the beach. A simple rule: If a sign says BEACH PARK, you can usually expect facilities (but not necessarily a sandy beach). If it says just BEACH, the reverse is usually the case. Keep in mind that all of Hawaii's shoreline up to the highest high-water mark is public property. Public shoreline access, where possible, is required by law. Hawaii has an amazing variety of beaches, but again, the visitor should proceed cautiously. Depending on the season and location, surf and currents can make swimming unsafe. In particular, the northern and western shores of all islands are exposed to dangerous surf in winter. The well-fed reef sharks almost never attack humans in Hawaiian waters, but the occasional jellyfish or Portuguese man-of-war can sting painfully. Razor-sharp coral reefs will cut unprotected feet, and crevices may conceal spiny sea urchins and moray eels. Conditions change rapidly, so never turn your back on the ocean. Also, be aware that all marine mammals and sea turtles are protected by federal law, and visitors can be fined for disturbing their natural activity.

You shouldn't overlook Hawaii's cultural offerings, either. In many ways, the Aloha State is still a "foreign" country, and you may as well enjoy its differences. Wear a flower lei. Listen to a Hawaiian music station. Look for ethnic festivities listed in the local newspaper or check out the events calendar at www.gohawaii.com. Sample some exotic foods, and order out a local-style "plate lunch" to eat at a picnic. In addition to the islands' Polynesian heritage, Asian influences are especially strong. You'll find many Buddhist temples. Most of these temples welcome visitors, but they ask that you remove your shoes before entering. As for shopping, try the gift shops of the attractions listed throughout the guide. Many stock unusual items at very reasonable prices.

One of Hawaii's unadvertised charms is its rainbow people, who make up America's true melting pot. Almost everyone speaks English, but you might not feel sure of this when they're laying on the pidgin, a unique local dialect that incorporates foreign words, slang, and a singsong inflection. Although some locals feel threatened by the tourist industry and resent tourists, if you stay mellow and say "howzit" (hello), you'll still get a lot of aloha. The glossary defines a selection of Hawaiian words used in this guide; many terms are also explained in the text.

For offbeat accommodations, try one of the many bed-and-breakfast outfits (B&Bs). Besides the ones listed in this guide, you can book with several statewide agencies. Those with Internet access can find additional accommodation listings plus other useful visitor information at the following Web sites: www.gohawaii.com; www.planet-hawaii.com; www.alternative-hawaii.com; and www.bestplaceshawaii.com. *All Islands B&B* (263–2342; 800–542–0344; www .all-islands.com), *Hawaiian Islands B&B* (261–7895; 800–258–7895; www .lanikaibeachrentals.com), and *B&B Honolulu* (595–7533; 800–288–4666; www.hawaiibnb.com) are based on O`ahu. *B&B Hawaii* (822–7771; 800–733–1632; www.bandb-hawaii.com) is based on Kaua`i. *Hawaii's Best B&Bs* (263–3100; 800–262–9912; www.bestbnb.com) concentrates on upscale listings. If you want more rugged lodgings, camping is safe and practical on most islands. Contact the *Department of State Parks* (587–0300; 1151 Punchbowl Street, Honolulu 96813) to get the scoop on state campgrounds. For *county campgrounds,* get in touch with the particular island's department of parks and recreation. Contact Kaua`i's DPR (241–4463) at 4444 Rice Street, Lihue 96766; O`ahu's DPR (523–4527) at 650 South King Street, Honolulu 96813; Maui County's DPR (270–7389) at 700 Hali`a Nakoa Street, Unit 2, Wailuku 96793; and Hawai`i's DPR (961–8311) at 101 Pauahi Street, Suite 6, Hilo 96720. For additional camping options, see chapters on individual islands. Hostel accommodations are also available on most islands; see chapter listings.

The only regularly scheduled interisland transport is by air. The most extensive flight service is offered by **Aloha Airlines** (484–1111; 800–367–5250; www.alohaairlines.com) and its subsidiary, **Island Air** (484–2222; 800–323–3345; www.islandair.com), which serves smaller, secondary airports. **Hawaiian Air** (838–1555; 800–367–5320; www.hawaiianair.com) is the principal competitor. At press time, a new interisland airline, **Go!** (888–435–9462; www.iflygo.com), had commenced service between the four main islands.

Getting around on the islands themselves will require a rental car, except on O`ahu, where the bus system might be adequate. All the major national firms, as well as local independents, are represented on the larger islands. It is a competitive market, so call around. It also pays to ask your interisland airline for special fly-drive rates.

There are any number of commercial alternatives to driving that will take you off the beaten path—from submarine tours to mountain biking to kayaking. Space does not permit a full listing here, but most advertise in the free, weekly tourist publications available for all islands except Lana`i. Specially recommended are the highly informative **101 Things to Do** booklets for Kaua`i, O`ahu, Maui, and the Big Island; you'll find them at brochure racks throughout those islands; free. Hikers can take advantage of weekend Sierra Club outings on the four major islands. Write the Hawaii chapter office at P.O. Box 2577, Honolulu 96803; call 538–6616 for a statewide schedule; or visit www.hi.sierra club.org.

As for using the guide itself, you should note that it is written as a narrative, designed to be used on the scene. Attractions are listed geographically in the order you will encounter them, except within individual towns, where accommodations and restaurants are grouped together. Items of special interest appear in boldface italic type. Accommodation prices are based on a double room. Unless noted otherwise, the label "B&B" implies that continental breakfast is included.

So much for general advice from me. The rest is up to you. Good luck—and get ready for the memories!

Me ke aloha,

Sean Pager

Restaurant prices are given by category based on the cost of an average entree: Inexpensive—less than $10; moderate—$10 to $17; expensive—$18 to $25; and investment-caliber—more than $25.

Note that for all telephone numbers in Hawaii, the area code is (808).

MAP LEGEND

(For all maps except those on
pages iv, 2, 52, 134, 158, 170, and 228.)

Streets, highways

Unpaved drivable roads

Footpaths, trails

Rivers, streams

Kaua`i

Kaua`i stands apart from the other islands of Hawaii. The farthest north of the main islands, Kaua`i is the oldest geologically. Six million years have given erosive forces the time to sculpt its mountain slopes with a delicate scalpel. An eternity of waves has wreathed the island in a white lei of sand. Kaua`i is also the wettest Hawaiian island. Its central peak, Mount Wai`ale`ale ("overflowing waters"), holds the world's record for annual rainfall. The overflowing waters from such constant precipitation feed Kaua`i's seven full-fledged rivers, where other islands have mere streams. The unrivaled lushness of this "Garden Island" has lured Hollywood here to film countless motion pictures.

Kaua`i has always stood apart in human terms as well. The Kaua`i Channel is wider, deeper, and rougher than those between other islands. Scientists think Kaua`i and its nearest neighbor, Niihau, remained fairly isolated in ancient Hawaii. These were the only islands Kamehameha did not conquer. Two invasion fleets failed, one beaten back by storms, the next devastated by sickness. In the end, Kaua`i's King Kaumualii voluntarily acknowledged Kamehameha's sovereignty, but the islands remained a separate kingdom until his death.

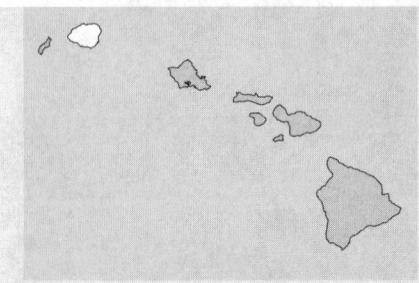

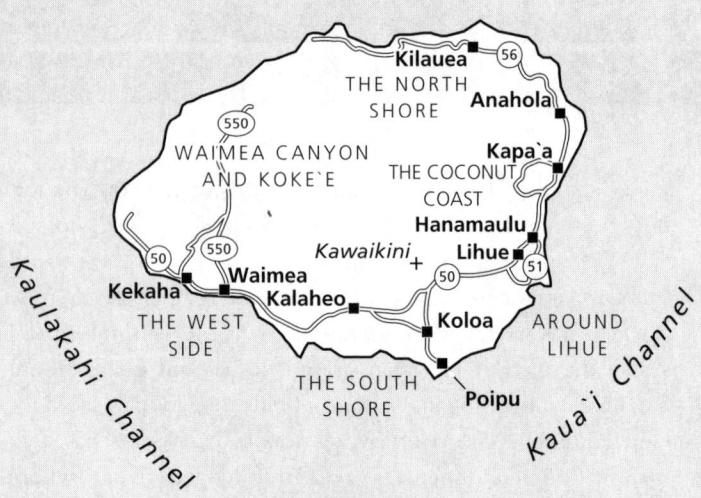

Kilauea

THE NORTH
SHORE

56

Anahola

550

WAIMEA CANYON
AND KOKE`E

Kapa`a

THE COCONUT
COAST

Hanamaulu

Kawaikini
+

Lihue

50

51

550

50

Kekaha

Waimea

Kalaheo

Koloa

AROUND
LIHUE

THE WEST
SIDE

Kaulakahi Channel

THE SOUTH
SHORE

Poipu

Kaua`i Channel

*PACIFIC
OCEAN*

N

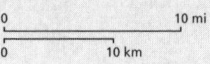

0   10 mi

0   10 km

Two main highways, Kaumualii (Route 50) and Kuhio (Route 56), reach like arms around the island, with a third main roadway branching off Route 50 to climb the inland heights of Koke'e State Park. Starting from Lihue, the central town, you can drive slightly more than 40 miles in each direction before running into the impassable barrier of the Na Pali Coast. Throughout your stay on Kaua'i, look for the Sunshine Farmers' Markets that rotate through the island towns six days a week. They combine local color with real bargains. Call 241–6390 for the current schedule.

A great way to go off the beaten path on Kaua'i is by paddling a kayak. Even novices can safely navigate the island's rivers to reach secluded waterfalls. Experienced ocean paddlers can explore sections of otherwise inaccessible coastline. Several local firms rent kayaks and supply racks to transport them. **Outfitters Kaua'i** (742–9667; 888–742–9887; www.outfitterskauai.com) in Poipu also rents bikes and leads hiking, biking, and kayaking tours. They have a permit for tours in Waimea Canyon and Koke'e and can supply detailed route maps for suggested activities. **Kayak Kaua'i** (826–9844 in Hanalei; 800–437–3507; www.kayak kauai.com) offers similar services on the North Shore and Coconut Coast.

Ecologist Dr. Carl Berg offers custom hiking tours tailored according to interest and ability at very reasonable rates. Call **Hawaiian Wildlife Tours** (639–2968; www.hawaiianwildlifetours.com). In addition, look in the local paper for listings of the Kaua'i Sierra Club's bimonthly outings. If hiking is out, contact **Aloha Kaua'i Tours** (245–6400; 800–452–1113; www.alohakauai tours.com). The air-conditioned vans allow passengers to see some of the island's scenic backcountry without the burden of sore feet. Full-day tours usually include hotel pickup and lunch for $125. They also do shorter excursions elsewhere on the island, including a snorkeling trip.

kaua'ifacts

Nickname: Garden Isle
Dimensions: 32 x 25 miles
Highest elevation:
Mt. Kawaikini (5,243 feet)
Population: 59,946 (2003)
Principal City: Lihue
Flower: Mokihana
Color: Purple

Around Lihue

Located on the southeastern corner of Kaua'i, Lihue serves as the county seat, the main air and sea port, and the midpoint from which highway mileage is numbered. Surrounded by sugarcane and hemmed in on all sides by mountains, Lihue town is relatively new as a settlement. The ancient Hawaiians usually bypassed this section of the coast, following instead an inland route behind the mountains. Sugar, centrality, and proximity to O'ahu conspired to put Lihue

kaua`itrivia

There are more miles of beach per coastline here than on any other island.

By law, no building here can be taller than a palm tree.

Kaua`i hosts the largest coffee plantation in Hawaii.

Kaua`i's Mount Wai`ale`ale is the wettest spot on earth.

Wailua River is the only navigable river in Hawaii.

Kaua`i's tropical beauty has been filmed in more than sixty Hollywood movies.

on the map. Recent tourist developments favoring other coasts have had the opposite effect.

At the junction of the two main highways, turn into Lihue on Rice Street, named for an early manager of the Lihue Sugar Plantation. Almost immediately on your left, the **Kaua`i Museum** (245–6931) stands behind an imposing classical facade. The well-organized exhibits within cover the story of Kaua`i from many angles. You can see photos of Niihau (as close as most people will ever get), study a model Hawaiian village, rattle a gourd, read excerpts from Captain Cook's log on "discovery" day, and even take a video tour, shot by helicopter, of the island's remote interior. The museum is open Monday through Friday 9:00 A.M. to 4:00 P.M. and Saturday 10:00 A.M. to 4:00 P.M. $7 admission fee.

On the next block, the 1913 former **County Building** reposes in a stately, royal palm-lined park. The **Kaua`i Historical Society** (245–3373) has its office inside, with books on island history and self-guiding "history maps" for sale. Open weekdays from 8:00 A.M. to 4:00 P.M. You can get state camping permits (274–3444) from the State Building behind the old county building for $5.00 per night ($10.00 for Na Pali Coast). Permits for the county's excellent campgrounds (241–4463; recpermits@kauai.gov) are issued for $3.00 per adult at the new cylindrical county building at the top end of Rice Street. Haleko Road runs west off Rice Street just inland of the museum, directly behind the now-silent Lihue sugar mill. On the way down, notice the **Haleko Shops** on the right, near the corner. Severely damaged in the 1992 hurricane, these four concrete remnants and ornate marble horse trough came from a plantation housing camp for German workers.

As a side trip, you can find the **Church of All Nations,** which these devout immigrants built atop "German Hill" on the other side of the mill. (An HVCB marker points up Ho`omana Road from Route 50.) This 1885 Lutheran church has an attractive baroque altar inside. But look more closely. The floor is actually bowed like the deck of a ship, with the pulpit the elevated forecastle and the balcony the quarterdeck. The church design symbolizes not only the ship that carried these immigrants to their new home but also the ship of faith that sustained them on their voyage.

Geography of Kaua`i

The oldest and northernmost of the Hawaiian Islands, Kaua`i ranks fourth by size and population. Built from a single massive volcano, the island has been eroded into a series of mountain ridges, valleys, and canyons. Its two central peaks usually remain shrouded in clouds. Of the two, Kawaikini is the highest at 5,243 feet, but Wai`ale`ale, 100 feet lower, holds the record for the world's highest annual rainfall. The island has 90 miles of coastline (much of it sandy beaches), 16 of which, along the spectacular Na Pali Coast, are inaccessible by road.

Continuing on Haleko Road past the mill takes you on a winding path through lush jungle. Take the next left onto Nawiliwili Drive, which skirts the cane fields on its way to the harbor. You'll pass a sign on your left marking **Grove Farm Homestead** (245–3202). Book well in advance for a tour of this historic estate. Often led by descendants of Kaua`i's plantation families who offer insider "gossip" about the past, the two-hour tours of Grove Farm are offered Monday, Wednesday, and Thursday at 10:00 A.M. and 1:00 P.M. for a $10 donation.

The homestead's founder, George Wilcox, was a son of missionaries. He raised tuition for his engineering degree by collecting bird guano to sell as fertilizer. After purchasing the dry land for next to nothing, Wilcox brought irrigation water from the mountains to create a profitable sugar plantation in 1864. A visit to Grove Farm provides a timeless glimpse of the plantation lifestyle he helped pioneer. Designed as a self-contained community, the beautifully maintained grounds still yield harvests of fruits and vegetables. Those who are game can taste raw coffee beans and macadamia nuts.

The Wilcoxes were true pack rats who collected much and threw away nothing. All the furnishings and personal possessions remain as if the inhabitants were due to return momentarily.

You'll also visit the spartan dwelling of the Moriwake family. Mrs. Moriwake, a picture bride from Japan, lived here with her family through fifty-two years of service as the Wilcoxes' laundress. A print of Mount Fuji on the wall provides a touch of the old country. The main house, built and furnished from beautiful native woods, is where George Wilcox lived with his brother Sam and Sam's family. Among the antique furniture, you'll find an embroidered settee that Helen Lehman, a longtime house guest, took ten years to complete.

To escape the family bustle, George later built himself a bachelor pad, designed with two bedrooms (winter and summer) draped with mosquito nets.

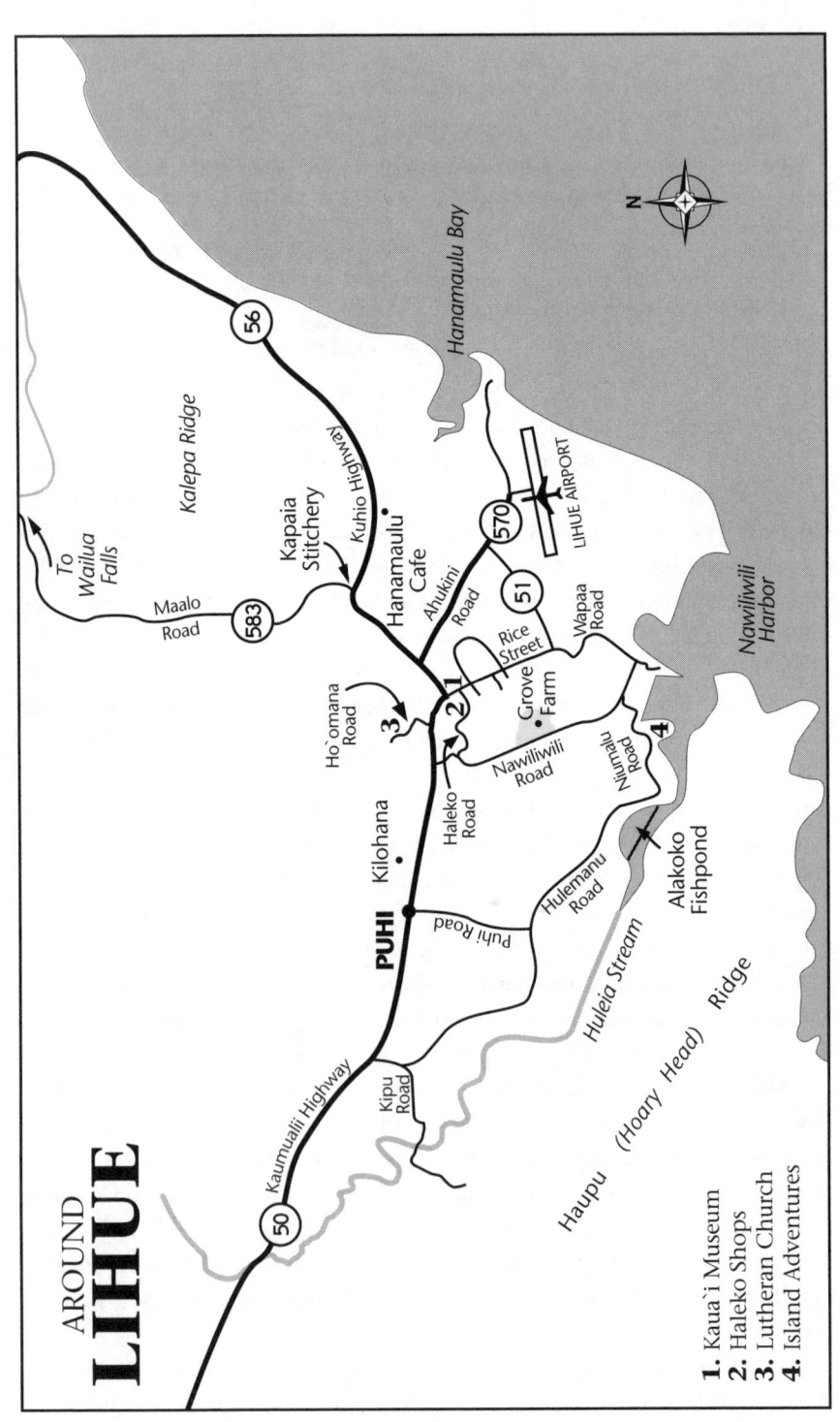

The unadorned rooms are almost bare of furnishings. Although a millionaire, the frugal mission son kept his fragments of soap in an old sardine can.

Nawiliwili Road continues down to its namesake harbor, Kaua`i's main shipping port ever since its completion in 1930. In your mind, try to screen out the heavy dock machinery and industrial warehouses and focus on the lovely setting of the bay, with the Haupu (or Hoary Head) Mountains closing in on its western edge. In the opposite direction, Nawiliwili Beach Park abuts Kalapaki Beach, the site of the Marriott. But you can enjoy the same views at considerably less cost by staying at the **Garden Island Inn** (245–7227; 800–648–0154; www.gardenislandinn.com), across the street from the beach park. The rooms show novel touches such as palm-pattern imprints in the ceiling plaster and original artwork by former "resident artist" Camile Fontaine. Bougainvillea drapes from the balconies, and floral gardens surrounding the inn include carp ponds. Owner Steve Layne works hard to make his guests' stay pleasant. With rooms from $90 to $145, the Garden Island Inn could be a real sleeper (no pun intended). If you just want a place to lay your head, try the **Tip Top Motel** (245–2333) at 3173 Akahi Street in Lihue. It's known locally for its bakery/cafe of the same name. Doubles start at $65.

Return to Nawiliwili Road and turn west onto Niumalu Road, 2 blocks above the harbor. Niumalu climbs behind a bulk-sugar warehouse and sidles along the cane fields. Pause at the unmarked turnout ahead for another view of the bay. The road then descends through the rustic Hawaiian village of Niumalu.

At Niumalu Park, turn right onto Hulemanu Road, which curves uphill again. About 0.5 mile farther, stop at the overlook to view **Alakoko Fishpond,** tucked below along a bend in Huleia Stream, backdropped by the rugged beauty of the Haupu Mountains. Alakoko is also known as Menehune Fishpond because of its legendary builders. A supposedly reclusive, pixielike people, the Menehune were said to be expert masons who performed miraculous construction feats overnight for payment in food. Menehune legends are part of the folklore throughout Hawaii, and theories vary as to their origin. The Tahitian word *manahune* means "slave." Some say the Menehune were an earlier people who became a hereditary caste of workers. The bird chatter you hear comes from **Huleia National Wildlife Refuge,** just upstream. **Island Adventures** (245–9662) leads kayak tours through the refuge twice daily. The half-day morning trip includes a waterfall swim, snacks, and a deli lunch for $89. The three-hour afternoon tour costs $59.

Hulemanu Road continues past the overlook, shadowing the Haupu Mountains as it cuts through green waves of endless cane. Turn right on Puhi Road to rejoin the highway. On your way back to town, you might visit **Kilohana** (245–5608), another restored plantation estate on the inland side of the highway. Gaylord Wilcox, the head of Grove Farm, brought renowned architect Mark Potter from O`ahu in 1935 to build his dream house. The name Kilohana means "not to be surpassed," and Potter made a strong bid to design and furnish a home worthy of this name. Stop at the main house to get a map of the thirty-five-acre estate and restored farm area. Or tour the grounds in style in an old-fashioned carriage drawn by Clydesdale horses. Hour-long "sugarcane" tours covering plantation history and modern sugar production are also offered on Monday, Tuesday, and Thursday at 11:00 A.M. and 2:00 P.M.; call 246–9529 to reserve. To learn more about Hawaii agriculture, past and future, hop a ride on the *Kauai Plantation Railway,* which will take you through an additional sixty acres in a progression from taro (the staple of ancient Hawaiians) to exotic fruit trees and other tropical niche crops that are replacing sugar. The railway plans to use refurbished vintage rail stock (including eventually a pair of historic steam engines used in Hawaii) for the trip and expects to charge about $20.

The inside of Kilohana is part museum and part boutiques specializing in Kaua`i-made wares. Kilohana's courtyard provides a romantic setting for alfresco dining at *Gaylords* (245–9593). Continental entrees come with vegetables and fruits from Kilohana's own gardens. Monday through Saturday a buffet breakfast is served 7:45 to 10:00 A.M. and lunch 11:00 A.M. to 3:00 P.M.; Sunday brunch 9:30 A.M. to 3:00 P.M. Expensive prices. Candlelight dinners are offered nightly 5:00 to 8:45 P.M. Reservations suggested. Investment-caliber.

Brief History of Kaua`i

Capt. James Cook's arrival on the west coast of Kaua`i in 1778 touched off a new era that would transform the Hawaiian Islands. A steady stream of Western ships followed in his footsteps, many of them anchoring at the protected Waimea harbor that Cook had described in his journals, making Kaua`i an early center of trade.

The separate political status retained by the island in the early days of the Hawaiian kingdom made it the focus of international intrigue, most notably by a German adventurer acting in the service of the Russian czar.

As the site of Hawaii's first commercial sugar plantation, Kaua`i was also at the forefront of another watershed, the birth of an industry that dominated the islands' socioeconomic landscape for more than a century. Strangely, sugar's successor, tourism, has come later to Kaua`i than to some of its neighbors, although the Garden Isle has long been the darling of Hollywood filmmakers. Kaua`i suffered widespread devastation at the hands of two hurricanes, Iwa in 1982 and Iniki in 1992, which further slowed development on the island.

Gaylord's also offers "Most Romantic Dinner" packages that include a private estate tour in a Clydesdale-drawn carriage ride ending at your own private table, where a bottle of sparkling wine and a special dinner menu await you, all for $239. Kilohana opens daily at 9:30 A.M.

Farther west on Route 50, shortly after Kauai Community College in the town of Puhi, is a small take-out restaurant, **Mark's Place** (245–2522), specializing in the local plate lunch with an upscale twist. Chef Mark Oyama teaches culinary arts at the college, and this is where he practices what he preaches. It is open Monday through Friday from 10:00 A.M. to 2:00 P.M. Inexpensive.

Back in town, dining options consist mostly of mom-and-pop restaurants serving ethnic cuisine in unadorned settings. Two blocks seaward of the County Building, off Rice, a number of eateries cluster around Kress Street. Disguised as a camp house kitchen with its trademark corrugated orange formica counter, **Hamura's Saimin,** 2956 Kress Street (245–3271), ladles out Kaua`i's best bowl of saimin (a Hawaiian-Japanese dish based on noodles in broth). Select your own add-ins to slurp with your noodles, find a stool to sit on, but heed the sign on the wall that says PLEASE DON'T PUT GUM UNDER THE COUNTER. Hamura's is open from 10:00 A.M. to 10:00 P.M. Inexpensive. In the same building, **Halo Halo Shave Ice** cranks out a fruity Filipino version of this Hawaiian frozen treat daily until 4:00 P.M.

Across from the County Building at 4491 Rice Street is **Oki's Diner** (245–5899), which is as local as they come. It serves up old-time favorites such as oxtail soup and chicken katsu, as well as housemade tropical syrups to douse your pancakes. Open 6:00 A.M. to midnight, and until 3:00 A.M. Thursday through Saturday.

Nearby, **Ma's Family Inc.,** at 4277 Halenani Street (245–3142) behind the Salvation Army Thrift Shop, serves hearty Hawaiian breakfasts and a famous tripe stew for lunch. Plantation workers used to stop here for an early-morning plate of *kalua* pig (steamed in an underground oven and shredded) with eggs and a free cup of coffee before heading for the cane fields. Note the laundered Calrose rice sacks covering unused tables. Open daily from 5:00 A.M. to 12:30 P.M. Monday through Friday, and to 11:30 A.M. on weekends. Inexpensive. The coffee is still free with meals. Another standby, only a block away at 2991 Umi Street, is **Kiibo's** (245–2650), for Japanese fare.

More Lihue eateries lie along Route 56, north of Rice Street. For those who like seafood, **Fish Express** (245–9918), at 3343 Kuhio Highway, across the street from the hospital, offers unbeatable values. Its tiny lunch counter serves gourmet fish specials: Choose from among the daily fresh-catch and organic selections prepared in intriguing ways, such as macadamia-nut-encrusted fish with lilikoi sauce or salmon lumpia over Kilauea greens. At a price less than

$8.00, you can't eat this well anywhere else on the island. (Fish-haters can sample Hawaiian plates instead.) The lunch counter operates Monday through Friday from 10:00 A.M. to 3:00 P.M. A more limited hot menu is served at other times. (The Oriental fried chicken and ginger shrimp are popular choices.) The deli counter also offers an impressive selection of poke, the local version of seafood salad made from (mostly raw) fish, seaweed, crab, or octopus. Fresh fish fillets are also available to grill for your own beachside barbecue. Open Monday through Saturday 10:00 A.M. to 6:00 P.M. and until 4:00 P.M. on Sunday.

For beachfront dining and live Hawaiian music, locals favor **Duke's Canoe Club** (246–9599), adjacent to the Marriott on Kalapaki Beach. Roaming aunties bearing guitars make the rounds in the upstairs restaurant, but the Barefoot Bar is where the music lingers, and if you are upstairs, you won't even know anything is going on below. The latter is open for lunch and dinner from 11:00 A.M. to 11:00 P.M. Inexpensive.

For a quick bite, the nearby **Kalapaki Beach Hut** (246–6330), across Rice Street from the shopping center, features Kaua`i-raised buffalo burgers and fresh-caught *ono* (fish) sandwiches. The upstairs dining room boasts a panoramic view of the bay. Open daily from 7:00 A.M. to 8:00 P.M. (Monday until 9:00 P.M.). Inexpensive.

If you want a taste of Asian luxury, visit the teahouse at **Hanamaulu Cafe** (245–2511), a yellow building just north and over the hill from Lihue on Route 56 across from the Shell station. The menu at this third-generation Kaua`i establishment includes Chinese dishes, but if you ask for the teahouse, you dine in traditional Japanese fashion, kneeling on futons and tatami mats in front of very low tables. The shoji-partitioned rooms open onto a Japanese garden and koi (carp) pond. Reservations recommended. Open Tuesday through Friday 9:00 A.M. to 1:00 P.M. and Tuesday through Sunday 4:30 to 8:30 P.M.

There are things to see on the way to Hanamaulu. One hill closer to Lihue, Route 56 passes through Kapaia, where you can stop to admire the handcrafted fabric creations at **Kapaia Stitchery** (245–2281), housed in a red plantation store. You will find everything from traditional kimonos to quilt-making kits—or choose your own fabric and have something custom-made. Open Monday through Saturday 9:00 A.M. to 5:00 P.M.

For a scenic jaunt inland, take Maalo Road uphill from the stitchery through 3 miles of sugarcane with steadily improving mountain views. At the end of the road, your reward is a bird's-eye view of mighty **Wailua Falls,** featured on the TV show *Fantasy Island.* Those feeling adventurous (and sure of foot) can leave their fellow tourists gawking at the lookout and head 100 yards back up the road. At the far edge of the second guardrail, a steep and very slippery trail leads down to the pool at the base of the falls. Wave to the people above as you back float.

If a waterfall dip sounds too old hat, how about rafting an inner tube down a mountain flume? Kaua`i Backcountry's **Mountain Tubing Adventures** (245–2506; 888–270–0555; www.kauaibackcountry.com) offers tube rides down a 2-mile stretch of a former sugar irrigation ditch not far from here. The forty-minute ride passes a few small rapids but is fairly tame; it goes through five tunnels totaling about a half mile in all; headlamps are provided. On the ride up to the ditch, you'll get to see some of the scenic backcountry the ditch traverses and learn the history of the plantation that the ditch once served. Part of a larger irrigation system that consisted of 51 miles of ditch in all, the flumes were built in the 1870s, largely by Chinese immigrants, many of whom had come from California after the Gold Rush fizzled. Because the ground was too brittle for dynamite, the tunnels were all dug by hand, with workers receiving 50 cents per day for this dangerous, backbreaking labor. After the tube ride, you get a picnic lunch by a mountain pool. The full experience lasts about three hours. Call for reservations; cost is $92. The same company also operates a zipline adventure as an aerial alternative for $110.

The South Shore

Departing west from the Lihue area, the Kaumualii Highway (Route 50) crosses through the Knudsen Gap between Kahili Ridge and the Haupu Range to enter the **Koloa District,** birthplace of the Hawaiian sugar industry. The word *koloa* is usually translated as "tall cane," for the region, blessed with ample irrigation and yearlong sunshine, has yielded bumper crops since antiquity.

Turn left onto Maluhia Road (Route 520), 5 miles west of Lihue, and head through the **Tree Tunnel,** a fragrant double row of overhanging eucalyptus trees planted in 1911. Continue through more exotic foliage, then sugarcane, as you descend upon Koloa Town, now known to tourists as Old Koloa Town. Maluhia Road ends at a "T" junction with Koloa Road. On the right-hand side as you enter town, a tiny anonymous park commemorates Hawaii's sugar heritage. Erected in 1985 for the 150th anniversary of commercial sugar production in Hawaii, a small concrete monument symbolizes an opened millstone. Inside, a set of bronze bas-relief carvings portrays the different ethnic groups that figured in sugar's past. Careful readers of the accompanying plaque will notice historical revisionism at work: Someone has taken the *haole* plantation manager, formerly represented on horseback, out of the scene entirely.

The plaque gives a brief overview of the sugar industry's evolution. The story begins with William Hooper, who arrived from Boston in 1833 at age twenty-four with little expertise in agriculture and no knowledge of Hawaii. Yet somehow he secured enough native cooperation to begin the first large-scale

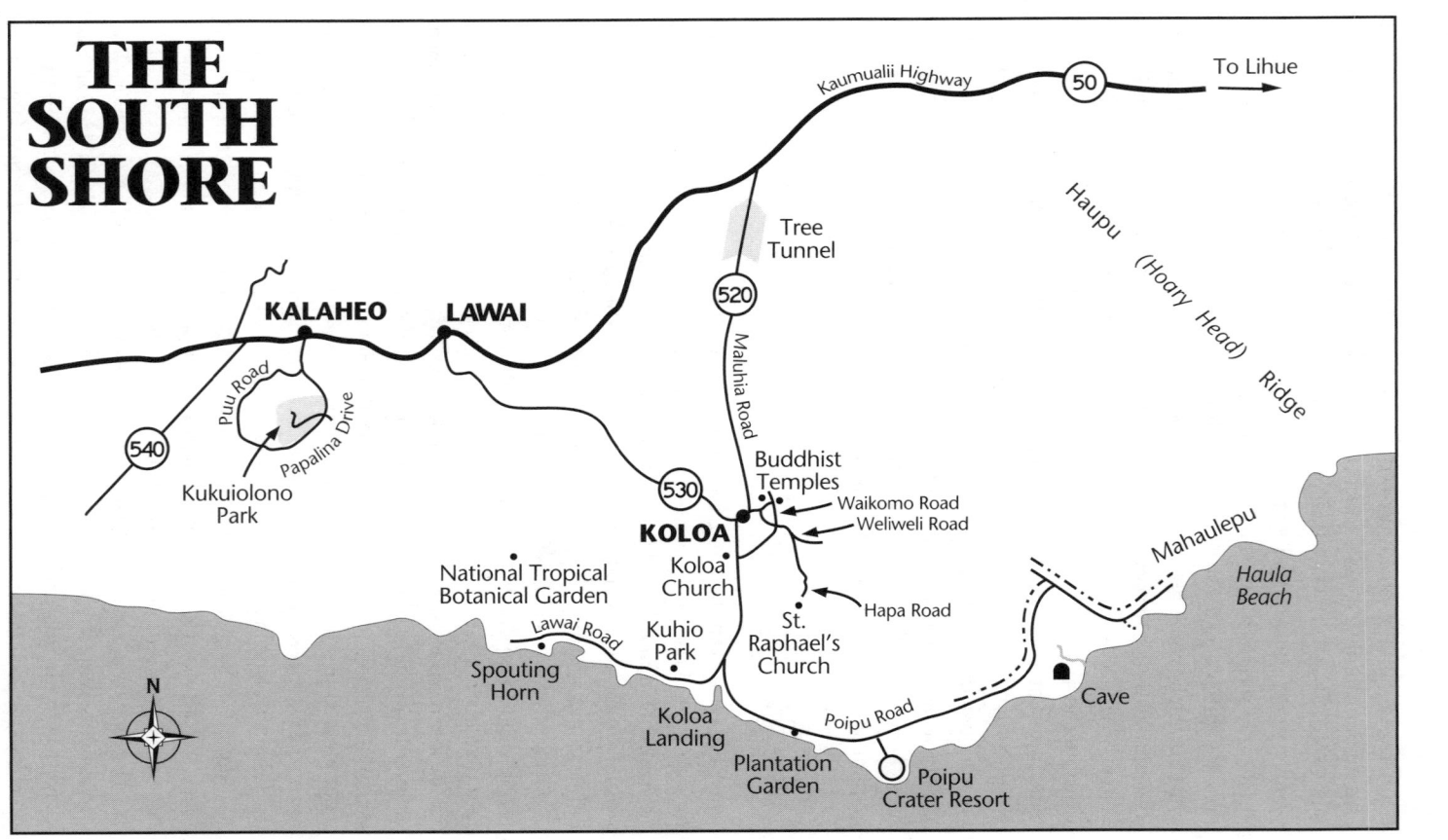

sugar plantation in the islands. The plaque neglects to mention that Hooper and his two partners became embroiled in an international investment scandal and went bankrupt. Despite such rocky beginnings, sugar went on to become Hawaii's dominant industry and the mainstay of its economy for almost a century. At one point, 60 percent of the island's electricity was generated by burning sugar by-products. In spite of this, labor costs and foreign subsidies have put sugar on the decline since World War II. The industry may well die where it began. Kaua'i's Gay & Robinson is one of two remaining sugar plantations in the state (the other is on Maui). Although the burning of leftover bagasse from harvested cane no longer contributes directly to the island grid, hydroelectric generators installed by the sugar industry continue to supply most of Kaua'i's electricity.

Near the monument, a small garden displays different varieties of sugarcane, and behind (partially engulfed by a banyan tree) stand the remains of the third mill built in Koloa.

Across Koloa Road from the park, the Yamamoto Store is the focus of more town history. On the sidewalk in front of the store stand cartoon-style sculptures by Maui artist Reems Mitchell, depicting a pair of Koloa old-timers, Toshi Freitas, the mechanic, and "Chinaman" Lickety Split. Wander into the courtyard behind the store to explore the **Koloa History Center,** a collection of exhibits and artifacts portraying aspects of plantation life, from the different immigrant groups housed in camps to the itinerant "drummers" and "shibai" artists who passed through the town hotel. You can also pick up a free brochure for the self-guided **Koloa Heritage Trail** to other south-shore spots of historical interest.

Koloa Fish Market (742–6199), just down the road at 5482 Koloa Road, serves a tasty Hawaiian plate lunch, with rotating multiethnic specialties, plus sushi and an assortment of poke waiting for the choosing behind its small deli counter. Open Monday through Friday 10:00 A.M. to 6:00 P.M. and Saturday 10:00 A.M. to 5:00 P.M. Inexpensive.

For a tour of Koloa's churches and temples, continue east on Koloa Road to the Big Save market at the corner. Craftspeople from Japan built the two Buddhist temples here in 1910 to cater to immigrant cane workers. The **Hongwanji Mission** has its temple behind the green YBA (Young Buddhists Association) Hall. Its carved roof and decorative metal inlays form a delicate black-on-white pattern. Around the corner, on Waikomo Road, **Jodo Mission** competes with two temples. The smaller original has an elaborate altar inside.

Turning from sutras to rosary beads, follow the signs to **St. Raphael's Church** from Koloa onto Weliweli Road (between Maluhia and Waikomo), then turn right onto Hapa Road to reach Kaua'i's oldest Catholic church. The

Jodo Mission

original Calvinist missionaries strove to exclude Catholicism, convincing their Hawaiian converts that papistry was "just another form of idolatry." Gunboat diplomacy by French warships brought an end to such discrimination.

Several church buildings lie scattered in this peaceful lot, bordered by cane fields, with Koloa's current mill smoking in the distance. The current church dates from 1866, but the graves of Portuguese immigrants in the cemetery are older. In the corner, behind the rectory, stands a beautiful ruinlike shrine built from black lava rocks arranged in steps and levels seemingly at random, highlighted by white marble statuary. The remains of the original 1841 church, rediscovered a century later in an adjacent field, have been shaped into a grotto accented by a giant cross.

Returning onto Weliweli Road, turn left onto Waikomo Road and notice the rickety plantation homes here, as yet untouched by the tourist traffic a few blocks over. Waikomo Road runs into Poipu Road and **Koloa Church,** which dates from 1837. The tall steeple of this New England–style edifice built by missionaries served as a landmark for whaling ships approaching port.

Turn left onto Poipu Road and bear left at the Y junction ahead to pass through Poipu Beach, an area thickly populated with plush hotels. A visual oddity among these is the **Poipu Crater Resort** (742–2000) off Pe`e Road, the tiny villas of which sprout like acne on the steep walls inside a crater formed by Kaua`i's last volcanic gasp. You might also visit **Kiahuna Plantation Resort** (742–6411), which engulfed the former Moir Garden. Plantation manager Hector Moir and his wife, Sandy, planted this attractive assortment of cacti and succulents suited to Poipu's arid climate back in 1938. In the center of the garden, the Moirs' plantation home has become **Plantation Gardens Restaurant** (742–2216; www.pgrestaurant.com). You can dine either at lanai tables facing the tiki torchlit gardens or in the elegant, old-fashioned interior. Open nightly 5:30 to 10:00 P.M. Expensive.

Poipu's most notable eatery, however, is the **Beach House** (742–1424; www.the-beach-house.com), at 5022 Lawai Road on the way to Spouting Horn. The stunning oceanfront location provides the perfect setting for the inventive Pacific Rim cuisine. Open daily 5:30 to 10:00 P.M. (October 1 to March 31), 6:00 to 10:00 P.M. (April 1 to September 30). Investment-caliber.

There is little point tarrying in crowded Poipu, though, when the coast is clearer farther on in **Mahaulepu.** Follow the main cane road extension from Poipu for almost 2 miles until you come to a stop sign at another major cane road. Turn right (following the utility poles) and continue another mile past the quarry. Check in at the guard station to sign a liability release. From here, various turnoffs lead to distinct beaches along the Mahaulepu coast. Mahaulepu means "falling together," referring to the remnants of Kamehameha's abortive 1796 invasion force that staggered ashore here to face a brutal ambush.

Start your exploring at the nearest beach access straight ahead and park at the stone barrier. Walk back toward Poipu until you reach the stream at the end of the beach, and follow the faint trail that runs through cane grass along the far bank. The trail continues a quarter mile inland and disappears into the mouth of a cave. You have to duck at the entrance, but the rest of the way is OK. Keep a hand above your head just in case, as you grope your way toward the light at the other side. Dense vines hang from the large opening here like a sixties bead curtain. And behind the curtain? A Chinese banyan in a natural courtyard of stone. As for the rest of Mahaulepu, you can play Robinson Crusoe, hunting for hidden footprints on a series of deserted beaches alternating with rocky outcrops. The farthest beach, **Haula,** cannot be reached by road; you have to hike a half mile east along low sea cliffs at the foot of the Haupu Mountain Range.

The Kaua'i Historical Society offers free, ninety-minute **archaeology tours** of Mahaulepu on the first and third Monday of the month; reserve ahead.

Retrace your steps to the Y junction at the entrance to Poipu Beach, where the right fork, Lawai Road, leads to attractions of its own. Tucked inside the Y is Koloa Landing, a narrow coastal inlet at the mouth of Waikono Stream. Nothing remains of this once-crowded port from whaling's heyday, but accommodation bargains cluster nearby. Book well in advance for any of these. **Poipu Bed & Breakfast** (742–1146; 800–808–2330; www.poipu-inn.com) offers cheery lodging in a colorfully restored plantation home with white trellis porches and antique carousel horses in every room. Rates run from $95 to $155. **Garden Isle Cottages** (742–6717; 800–742–6711; 2660 Puuholo Road, Koloa; www.oceancottages.com) overlook the water. Nestled in lush gardens, the self-contained units are decorated with the owners' original artwork. Studios begin at $159 (low season), $180 (high season), two-day minimum.

Koloa Landing Cottages (742–1470; 800–779–8773; www.koloalanding
cottages.com) nearby also have sumptuous gardens and similar amenities.
Rates range from $105 to $195.

For a truly oceanfront setting, continue down the coast to *Gloria's
Spouting Horn B&B* (742–6995; 888–742–6995; www.gloriasbedandbreakfast
.com), at 4464 Lawai Road. Here you can curl up in a hammock strung between
palm trees in the backyard and bask in the salt spray from the ocean at your
feet. Owners Gloria and Bob ("Mr. Gloria") Merkle lost the original Gloria's to
Hurricane Iniki. They rebuilt a dream house whose elegant, airy interior belies
its fortresslike engineering. The two upstairs rooms have the choicest views,
but honeymooners will want to nestle in the "love nest" below, featuring a
unique canopy bed fashioned from woven willow boughs. All rooms have
four-poster beds, private baths, and wet bars and cost $350 with a three-night
minimum; book well in advance. Full breakfast included. Children younger
than age fourteen discouraged.

The main scenic attraction along Lawai Road is the *Spouting Horn.*
Hidden behind the tour buses in the parking lot, this surf-driven geyser does
its best "thar she blows" imitation through a submerged lava tube. Rumor has
it that the spout went much higher before plantation owners dynamited the
opening to prevent salt sprays from damaging their crops. On the way to the
Spouting Horn, you'll pass another neglected park of historical interest. *Kuhio
Park* marks the birth site of Kaua`i's favorite son, Prince Jonah Kuhio
Kalanianaole, heir to the Hawaiian monarchy and one of Hawaii's first dele-
gates to Congress. The park also includes the remains of an ancient fishpond
and a small heiau.

At the end of Lawai Road, a 1920s plantation home serves as the visitor
center for the *National Tropical Botanical Garden* (742–2623). Reserve in
advance for one of the two tours per day for an experience that even non-green
thumbs will appreciate. Lawai Valley is a sunken oasis of tropical vegetation surrounded by former sugar land. The gardens are roughly segregated into botanical classes and beautifully landscaped around natural streambeds and hillsides.
Robert Allerton and his adopted son (some say homosexual lover), John, used
their Chicago mercantile fortune to create a tropical Eden here on an estate originally owned by Queen Emma. Emma herself was known as the first Hawaiian
monarch to cultivate a garden for aesthetic rather than functional purposes; she
began gardening at Lawai in 1870. The Allertons greatly expanded her efforts
throughout five decades in the twentieth century and were instrumental in
establishing the National Tropical Botanical Gardens under congressional char-
ter in 1964. The garden management now oversees the 286-acre property, which
is divided into the separate Allerton and McBryde Gardens.

The visitor center is open daily from 8:30 A.M. to 5:00 P.M. Guided walking tours of the **Allerton Garden** are offered four times daily except Sundays. The two-and-a-half-hour tours require advance reservations and are not for children under ten; the cost is $35. The Allerton Garden is a masterwork of landscape design. The formal geometry of the reflective pools and fountains blends harmoniously with the wildly tropical vegetation and exotic flowers, accented by art pieces from around the world. The adjacent **McBryde Garden** serves as the botanical gardens' research collection and contains some 270 different types of palms as well as a broad representation of Hawaiian flora, including endangered and endemic species. The garden sustained substantial flood damage in 2006; however, tours are scheduled to resume on Sundays only for $35. At other times, self-guided tours of McBryde are available for all ages without reservations; the cost is $20 for adults. The one-and-a-half-hour guided tours involve a 2-mile ride on a tram and at least 1.5 miles of walking on a gravel path up and down stairs. Along the way, you gain hands-on exposure to some of the world's most exotic tropical flora, including four different colors of hibiscus (white, red, yellow, orange) and the rarely seen brighamia, which looks like a cabbage on a bowling pin. The latter grows only on the edge of the remote sea cliffs of Kaua`i and Moloka`i. Driven to near extinction when the sphingid moth that used to pollinate its yellow/white, trumpet-shaped flowers itself became extinct, the brighamia survives only through the efforts of botanists, who must hand-pollinate each plant, often rappelling down steep rock faces to reach them.

Return along Lawai Road until it dead-ends at Koloa Road and turn left onto Route 530, which cuts west through rolling hills carpeted with sugarcane to rejoin the Kaumualii Highway at Lawai. These upland fields once grew pineapples, but by 1970 all had switched to sugar, a less labor-intensive crop. The old pineapple cannery has been converted to retail space near the junction with Route 50.

If you're hungry, a second location of Mark's Place (see the Lihue section) sits on Route 50 in Lawai, next to the Garden Island Mortuary. Open Monday through Friday from 10:00 A.M. to 7:00 P.M. Pizza-lovers will want to continue west to **Brick Oven Pizza** (332–8561), on the mountain side of Route 50 in Kalaheo. The freshly risen crusts brushed with garlic come laden with tummy-pleasing toppings. Open Tuesday through Sunday 11:00 A.M. to 10:00 P.M. Inexpensive to moderate. For a more elaborate dinner, **Pomodoro Italian Restaurant** (332–5945), just up the road upstairs in the Rainbow Shopping Plaza on the ocean side of Route 50, boasts housemade pastas, including a much-revered lasagna. Owned by pair of brothers from Salerno, Italy, it's open Monday through Saturday from 5:30 to 9:30 P.M. Expensive.

Turn left from the end of Route 530 to continue west on Route 50 to the town of Kalaheo. Turn left onto Papalina Drive near the center of town to enjoy the scenic vistas over the Lawai Valley and Poipu Coast on your way to **Kukuiolono Park.** This cool hilltop sanctuary includes a nine-hole public golf course and a small pseudo-Japanese garden. Follow the road up to the club-house for a panoramic view stretching all the way to Niihau. You can loop back to the highway on Puu Road.

The fields west of Kalaheo have been planted with coffee bushes as a replacement for sugar. Coffee's commercial history began in Hawaii on this island, and although the baton has since passed to the Big Island's Kona Coast as the industry center, the 3,400 acres here now constitute Hawaii's largest cof-fee plantation. You can learn more about island coffee (and sample the final product) by stopping at the **Kaua`i Coffee Visitor Center** (335–0813), just ahead on the left. Housed in two former sugar camp homes, the center has dis-plays on the plantation's sugar past as well as its coffee future. Open daily 9:00 A.M. to 5:00 P.M. Free.

The West Side

About 2 miles west of Kalaheo on Kaumualii Highway, be sure to stop at the **Hanapepe Valley Overlook** for a technicolor vision of red canyon walls ris-ing vertically above a tree-carpeted valley floor. Continue on Route 50, which curves around the mouth of the canyon to descend into Hanapepe town. A roadside sign welcomes you to KAUA`I'S BIGGEST LITTLE TOWN, part of an attempt to lure westbound tourists. Fortunately, they have not yet been too successful. To see for yourself, veer right beneath the bougainvillea-draped cliffs and park on Hanapepe Road.

Hanapepe has its share of history to relate. The valley you admired from above witnessed the bloody suppression of Kaua`i loyalists who revolted against the Kamehameha dynasty in 1824. A hundred years later, sixteen Filipino work-ers and four police officers were killed here during a plantation strike. But Hanapepe's main attraction springs from its vintage plantation shops, still infused with the rhythm of small-town life. Much of *The Thorn Birds* was filmed here.

Begin your walking tour at **Taro Ko Chips** (335–5586), a tiny one-room factory that Mr. and Mrs. S. Nagamine started as a retirement project. The taro they fry in their two woks comes from nearby valley fields that their son now tends. Open daily from 8:00 A.M. to 5:00 P.M. Next, you can explore a series of **art galleries** notable not so much for the originality of their work—you can judge that for yourself—as for the accessibility of the tenant-artists, many of whom paint in studios on the premises and are happy to discuss their work.

Most stay open Monday through Saturday. **Kaua`i Fine Arts** (332–8508) sells a different kind of artwork, though; it specializes in antique maps and prints.

You shouldn't overlook Hanapepe's more traditional vendors, either. Sample the spicy confections at the Crackseed Center or pop inside Yoshiura's General Store, known as the Mikado until World War II. And before you leave, have a swing on the rope bridge over Hanapepe River next to the old church. Continue on the road across the 1911 bridge farther downstream. From here, you can turn up Awawa Road into the valley for a scenic digression along the west canyon wall past sugarcane and taro fields. Distinctive for its large forked leaves, the taro plant served as the early Hawaiians' staple crop. They mashed its starchy roots to make poi and cooked the stem and leaves as vegetables. The Hawaiians believed that the taro plant grew from the grave of humankind's elder brother, who had died in infancy. Taro was their link to the land and their "staff of life." Out on the highway, galleries await, including some with "surfboard art." Friday evenings from 6:00 to 9:00 P.M., the town galleries host a free open house, with live music, hula, storytelling, and Hawaiian craft demonstrations.

Naturally, no self-respecting art town could long survive without a decent coffeehouse. In addition to hot java, tasty, albeit somewhat pricey, gourmet vegetarian and seafood lunches are served at **Hanapepe Cafe** (335–5011) Monday through Thursday 11:00 A.M. to 3:00 P.M. and on Friday from 11:00 A.M. to 2:00 P.M.; dinner is served on Friday from 6:00 to 9:00 P.M. Live music on Friday. Inexpensive to moderate. Lovers of Thai food should backtrack uphill from Hanapepe to **Toi's Thai Kitchen** (335–3111) in the Ele`ele Shopping Center. Open Tuesday through Saturday 10:30 A.M. to 2:00 P.M. and 5:30 to 9:00 P.M. Moderate.

Near the edge of town, turn left from the highway onto Lele Road, then right onto Lolokai Road to **Salt Pond Beach Park.** Besides offering a beautiful protected beach, the park abuts ancient salt ponds used to harvest sea salt. Rights of use pass through descent. Captain Cook got his salt here, and if you ask someone in the Hui Hana Paakai, which still operates these evaporative basins, you may be able to as well. State health department regulations prevent the "impure" salt from being sold commercially, but the impurities add flavor.

West of Hanapepe, a number of small, working sugar towns are strung along the highway. Looking out onto the horizon, the remote and mysterious islands of Niihau and uninhabited Lehua hover across Kaulakahi Channel. Owned by a missionary-descended ranching family, Niihau is the only private island in the state. The pure-blooded Hawaiians who live here still speak their native tongue and eke out a rustic existence tending the island ranch and gathering honey. Although residents remain free to come and go, uninvited visitors

THE WEST SIDE
AND WAIMEA CANYON AND KOKE`E

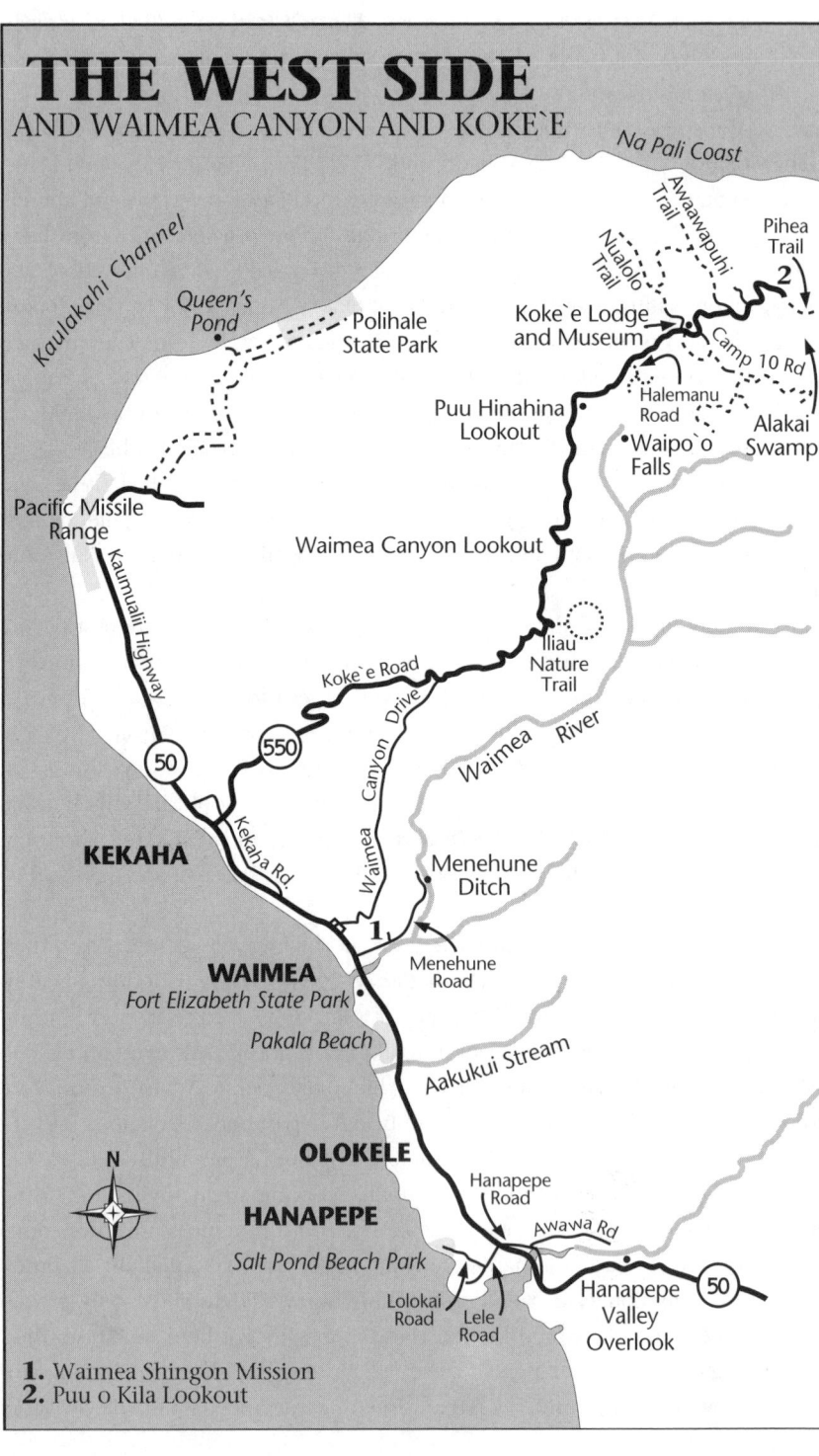

Na Pali Coast

Kaulakahi Channel

Queen's Pond

Polihale State Park

Pacific Missile Range

Kaumualii Highway

Waimea Canyon Lookout

Koke`e Road

Canyon Drive

Waimea

Awaawapuhi Trail

Nualolo Trail

Pihea Trail

2

Koke`e Lodge and Museum

Camp 10 Rd

Puu Hinahina Lookout

Halemanu Road

Alakai Swamp

•Waipo`o Falls

Iliau Nature Trail

Waimea River

50

550

KEKAHA

Kekaha Rd.

Menehune Ditch

1

WAIMEA
Fort Elizabeth State Park

Menehune Road

Pakala Beach

Aakukui Stream

N

OLOKELE

Hanapepe Road

HANAPEPE

Awawa Rd

Salt Pond Beach Park

Lolokai Road

Lele Road

Hanapepe Valley Overlook

50

1. Waimea Shingon Mission
2. Puu o Kila Lookout

are strictly forbidden. Niihau was also the only Hawaiian island "invaded" during the Pearl Harbor attack. A downed Japanese fighter pilot terrorized inhabitants until a large Hawaiian man, disregarding three bullet wounds, literally crushed the pilot with his bare hands.

Past the 18-mile marker in Kaumakani, the **Niihau Helicopter** office (335–3500) offers exclusive tours of the "Forbidden Isle," including a three-hour beach landing with swimming and snorkeling if weather permits. The half-day tours cost $325; reserve in advance. A half mile farther, turn left onto the main avenue of **Olokele.** Shaded by banyan and monkeypod trees, a procession of plantation management homes with old-fashioned lampposts culminates at the sugar refinery. **Gay & Robinson Sugar Co.** (335–2824), headquartered here, is the only plantation still operating on the island, one of two in the state and the largest private employer on the island. It offers tours for those interested in seeing a working plantation up close and personal. The two-hour bus tour follows the cane from field to mill. The main growing season runs from April through October, but the tour operates year-round twice daily Monday through Saturday and costs $34. A three-and-a-half-hour tour for $60 also visits scenic Olokele Canyon and includes lunch. Call to reserve a spot. The tour office at Olokele also has a small visitor center exhibiting various sugar paraphernalia, much of which was salvaged from closed plantations on the island, as well as displays on the industry. Open weekdays 8:00 A.M. to 4:00 P.M. and Saturday 11:00 A.M. to 3:00 P.M. Gay & Robinson also offers more adventurous all-terrain-vehicle and four-wheel-drive tours that include a dip in a remote mountain pool. At the 21-mile marker, **Pakala** boasts a famous surfing beach known as "Infinities" for its endless breaking waves. The unofficial access is via the cattle gate immediately past the bridge across Aakukui Stream. Look out for bulls in the pasture!

From here another 2 miles takes you to Waimea, once the largest settlement on this coast and a historical center of interest. Waimea Bay served as Kaua`i's first major port, beginning with two celebrated British vessels anchored offshore in 1778. A small marker in **Lucy Wright Park** marks the spot where Captain Cook first stepped ashore at 3:30 P.M. in January of that year, bringing Hawaii into contact with the modern world. This metal plaque and another modest statue in the center of town (cast from the original in Whitby, England, Cook's birthplace) constitute the sole acknowledgment of the historic visit by one of the world's greatest explorers and Hawaii's first tourist. Cook's journals became best sellers back in Europe. His description of Waimea Bay as a safe anchorage on Kaua`i made it the port of call for a steady stream of Western vessels crossing the Pacific. Waimea became the island's de facto capital as Kaua`i's ruling chiefs gathered here year-round to take advantage of the trading opportunities. Waimea Bay also witnessed the abduction of Kaua`i's King Kaumualii, when Kamehameha II invited him on what became a one-way sailing cruise to O`ahu in 1821. Ka`ahumanu, the queen regent, then forced both Kaumualii and his oldest son to marry her. These unorthodox tactics ensured Kaua`i's allegiance to the unified Hawaiian kingdom.

At the entrance to town, turn left into **Fort Elizabeth State Park** to absorb some more history. One of three forts on Kaua`i built by Georg Anton Schaeffer, a German adventurer acting in the service of the Russian czar, Fort Elizabeth dates from 1815. Schaeffer persuaded King Kaumualii to permit these outposts in defense of Russian trading interests. Other foreign powers objected, and the Kamehameha monarchy protested this bid by Kaumualii to bolster Kaua`i's autonomy. Schaeffer had overstepped himself, and in 1817, having fallen out of favor, he departed the islands for good. Hawaiian troops completed the construction and occupied the fort until 1864, when it was dismantled.

The fort's outer walls are still readily apparent, and a path leads through the main gate to the interior. Climb the steps to the battlements to gain a view of the coast. Inside the fort, various signs along the path label random piles of rubble or empty spaces, according to the architectural feature of the fort believed to have stood there. Look for dark green clumps of "sleeping grass" scattered around the parking lot and entrance sign. In reality a relative of the giant koa tree, the "grass" has tiny branches sprouting miniature purple-tinged leaves paired in two symmetric rows. Touching the leaves causes each pair to fold tightly closed as if curled up to sleep.

Cross the bridge across flood-prone Waimea River into town. Waimea means "reddish waters." Although Hawaiian legend ascribes the river's color to blood from an unjustly slain maiden, the ruddy water bleeds from a far greater wound—Waimea Canyon. Stop by the public library (338–6848) on the highway to pick up a copy of a self-guided walking tour of Waimea's historic buildings.

Highlights include the privately owned **Gulick-Rowell House,** begun in stone in 1829 by the Reverend Peter Gulick and completed with wooden porches and balconies seventeen years later by the Reverend George Rowell. This building is notable for its adaptation of New England designs to Hawaiian building materials and climate. Rowell, "the builder missionary," also completed the current **Waimea Foreign Church** in 1859 from sandstone cut nearby. The two buildings stand on Huakai Road 1 block on either side of Waimea Canyon Drive (Route 550).

Back on the highway, notice the open-wall frame of the old Waimea Mill. The damage predates Iniki to the earlier Hurricane Iwa in 1982. You'll find a third building by Rowell opposite the Big Save. After a personal dispute with the established mission, Rowell built **Waimea Hawaiian Church** for his breakaway congregation around 1865. Sunday services are conducted in Hawaiian.

Not included in the walking tour but worth a gander is the **Menehune Ditch,** part of an ancient irrigation system diverting the Waimea River to surrounding taro fields. Follow the HVCB warrior onto Menehune Road from the highway and drive about 1.3 miles, stopping where the cactus-draped cliffs crowd in on the river. What little remains of the ditch, sandwiched between the road and cliffs, may not impress you, but the significance of this still-functioning watercourse lies in its use of dressed lava stone, which some argue indicates more sophisticated masonry than the Hawaiians were known to have—hence the credit to the Menehunes.

On the way back, you will see taro fields on your right, which the ditch irrigates. A little farther on, follow the sign to **Waimea Shingon Mission** at the end of Pule Road, where a sci-fi vision confronts you. Rows of silver, conical-topped cylinders line the temple perimeter, illuminated by red shower-nozzle lights. In the corner, a multiplatform monument supported by these silver cylinders glistens like a wedding cake. Inscribed with Asian characters, each of these bizarre concrete blocks also houses a miniature statuette. These figurines are traditional in Shingon temples. Each represents one of the eighty-eight sins described in Buddhist sutras, and making the tour past all eighty-eight supposedly inoculates you against temptation. But what is unique about this shrine is the unusual shape and appearance of the containers in which the statuettes are housed. They were designed to mimic the appearance of missile shells. Gold-star mothers of Japanese-American soldiers who fought in World War II commissioned these monuments to honor their fallen sons. Ancient Hawaiian burial caves dot the cliffs above.

A unique way to experience plantation living is to stay at the **Waimea Plantation Cottages** (338–1625; 800–9–WAIMEA or 800–992–4632). Scattered among clusters of coconut trees in a huge garden lot bordering a silty black-sand beach on the west end of town, the cottages are renovated homes brought in from sugar camps all along the coast and furnished with understated charm. The resort was started by descendants of Hans Peter Faye, a Norwegian immigrant who rose to become one of the early sugar barons in the area. His original home at Mana now serves as the resort's administration building. Rates go from $175 to $240 for a one-bedroom cottage (9400 Kaumualii Highway; www.waimea-plantation.com).

To explore Waimea's heritage as a sugar town, consider taking the historical walking tour run by the **West Kaua`i Technology and Visitor Center** (338–1332). The tour explores the missionary stories as well as ancient and modern Waimea. The tour is free and is offered every Monday at 9:30 A.M., weather permitting. Call to reserve a spot.

If Waimea's sugar heritage lies increasingly in its past, the displays at the center chronicle the promise of a high-tech future. This state-of-the-art multimedia facility, located on the highway at the corner of Waimea Canyon Drive, is part of a campaign to attract technology companies to West Kaua`i. The exhibits describe the activities of some of these companies, which rent space at the center. But it has a much broader focus, covering technology used in the region from the days of the ancient Hawaiians to the present day's solar-powered aircraft tested at the nearby Pacific Missile Range. The center also holds classes in lei making on Friday at 9:30 A.M.; reservations required for the classes. Donation requested. The center has a wealth of visitor information on the island. Open Monday through Friday 9:30 A.M. to 5:00 P.M.

Back in town, shoppers will enjoy browsing through the inventory of **Collectibles and Fine Junque** (338–9855), opposite Waimea Hawaiian Church. You'll find everything from vintage plantation implements to fine china dinnerware. Open Monday, Tuesday, Thursday, and Friday 11:00 A.M. to 4:00 P.M. and Wednesday and Saturday 1:00 to 4:00 P.M. The hot climate on this side of the island makes it a great place to try shaved ice (a local version of snow cones), and Waimea has some of the best on the island at **Jojo's,** a colorful roadside shack. Choose from a variety of exotic flavorings, such as *li hing mui,* a tangy Chinese salty-sour candy made from preserved plums, or try *halo halo,* a kind of Filipino tropical smoothie. For local treats, stop by **Ishihara Market,** which serves take-out plate lunches from 10:00 A.M. to 2:00 P.M. and sells sushi and poke from the deli counter throughout the day. Open weekdays 6:00 A.M. to 8:30 P.M. and Saturday through Sunday 7:00 A.M. to 8:00 P.M.

For dinner, the town favorite is **Wrangler's Steak House** (338–1218), decorated in predictable Western style but with a much broader menu than the name suggests. Save room for the peach cobbler, which is baked to order—yum! Open Monday through Thursday 11:00 A.M. to 8:30 P.M., Friday 11:00 A.M. to 9:00 P.M., and Saturday 5:00 to 9:00 P.M. Moderate. The yuppie alternative is **Waimea Brewing Co.** (338–9733), located in the Waimea Plantation Cottages. It claims to be the "World's Western-Most Brewpub." Spacious lanai seating adds to the appeal. A moderately priced menu, including fresh-catch specials, is served daily 11:00 A.M. to 9:00 P.M. Live music Tuesday through Friday from 7:00 to 9:00 P.M.

If instead of taking Waimea Canyon Road up to its namesake you continue west, Route 50 leads next to Kekaha, the largest settlement on the west coast. Kekaha's giant mill sets the tone for this blue-collar community. Although the mill no longer operates, part of Kekaha Sugar's land has been bought by Gay & Robinson and remains in production. Just past the mill on Kekaha Road, the former post office building now houses Ray Nitta's **Westside Wood Designs** (337–1875). Unlike most artisans of his caliber who fashion objets d'art that never get used, Ray's shop is full of beautiful-yet-functional items, from canoe paddles to Zen Buddhist drums. He works mostly in native woods; variable hours.

From Kekaha north stretches an almost endless beach, but the park here has the only facilities before Polihale. Kekaha is also the turnoff for Koke'e Road, an alternate route to Waimea Canyon. Sticking to the coast, Route 50 continues as far as Mana and the Pacific Missile Firing Range at Barking Sands. In dry weather, a portion of the beach here sometimes emits "barking" sounds when you walk on it. Locals, however, say that "the dog stay old already" and has grown silent.

Just as the state highway ends and swings inland to connect with some closed military roads, a single-word sign, POLIHALE, designates the cane road access to **Polihale State Park.** The price you pay for admission here is 5 miles along a bumpy dirt road. Your reward is a beautiful desolate beach extending across windswept sand dunes as far as the eye can see.

About 3.5 miles in, the road approaches a large monkeypod tree fronting a scrub-covered hill with another sign indicating POLIHALE STRAIGHT AHEAD. If you turn left at the tree instead, the road leads seaward toward some enormous sand dunes. Park safely so as not to get your wheels stuck, and climb over the dunes to **Queen's Pond,** a reef-protected lagoon. This is the only part of Polihale Beach safe for swimming (in moderate surf). After a dip here, continue on to the state park at the end of the road.

As you drive the final miles past the camping area, the mountain ridges edge closer to the shoreline until they loom directly overhead. Beyond Polihale begins the Na Pali Coast, 16 miles of jagged cliffs plunging directly into the ocean. Hanging valleys, hidden sea caves, and ancient ruins lie shrouded in mystery—incomparable and all but impenetrable.

The park itself offers a pleasant setting with beach pavilions and picnic tables surrounded by native beach vegetation. The shrubbery bush covering the dunes here is beach naupaka. Because of its tolerance to salt spray, this is often the closest-growing plant to the ocean. Besides its stubby leaves and small white pods, naupaka is distinguished by its "half flowers" that appear to be missing petals on one side. A related variety, mountain naupaka, shares this trait and is found only atop the highest peaks. According to Hawaiian legend, the two represent parted lovers whose half-formed flowers reflect a single broken heart. Niihau and Lehua float serenely above the horizon, and if you scoop sand near the shoreline, you may find some of the tiny shells from which the famous Niihau necklaces are made.

Polihale means "home of the spirits." At the very edge of the beach, where it tapers off beneath the encroaching cliffline, an ancient heiau marks the site from which, according to Hawaiian belief, the souls of fallen warriors would depart the earth to the drumbeat of *kahuna* (priests). A sacred spring still bubbles beneath the sands nearby. Standing amid this desolate setting, the meager trappings of civilization that the park provides seem foreign to and dwarfed by the power of the natural splendor. Sunset at Polihale feels like the end of the world.

Waimea Canyon and Koke'e

The drive-by scenery in these adjacent state parks is unmatched in Hawaii. Waimea Canyon serves up eyefuls of choice canyon vistas along the 12-mile cleft in the island's west flank, while higher up Koke'e luxuriates in a cool, nontropical setting with breathtaking overlooks onto the Na Pali Coast. To get to these views, take Waimea Canyon Road, which offers the most scenic views on the way up from the highway merging into Koke'e Road near the entrance to the park. Stop at the first turnout once you climb above Waimea town for a view of the western coastline. A display board explains the changing land use of this region. As you continue on your way up, note the many dead or toppled trees left in Hurricane Iniki's wake.

Besides checking your gas gauge, it's a good idea to check the weather before embarking on the long haul up the canyon roads. Call the Koke'e Museum at 335–9975, or peer up the valley from Waimea and gauge the cloud cover. Most of the scenery lies at elevations between 3,000 and 4,000 feet. If the whole area appears fogged in, you may prefer to hang out on the beach or tour Waimea town and hope things clear up on top. As a rule, more clouds tend to gather as the day goes on. If the weather looks dicey, head straight to the Na Pali overlooks at the end, as they tend to cloud over first. If it does rain while you are up there, don't lose hope. Retreat to the **Lodge at Koke'e** (335–6061) for a cup of hot caffeine and let the trade winds do their work. You may witness some stunning rainbows to reward your patience.

Three designated canyon overlooks along the upper Koke'e Road fill their railings with gawking crowds. The **Waimea Canyon Lookout,** first at 11 miles in and 3,120 feet elevation, offers the most dramatic frontal view into the main canyon and its three tributaries. Mark Twain, who toured the Hawaiian Islands in his youth and got in first with the most quotable quotes, billed this "the Grand Canyon of the Pacific." While nowhere near as large as Arizona's famous hole, Waimea Canyon boasts a lusher climate that adds a vibrant green to the palette of reds, oranges, and browns used to paint its mainland counterpart.

Clouds float in and out of the 3,000-foot-deep gorge, redefining the landscape by shape and shadow and sometimes dissolving reality into mist. Helicopters make a less-welcome intrusion.

The next stop, at *Pu`u Ka Pele,* provides picnic tables and a side view of the canyon, while the third turnoff, at *Pu`u Hinahina,* features yet another angle as well as a separate view toward the coast and out to Niihau. The brightly colored wildfowl you see strutting and pecking in the parking lots are *moa,* descendants of the original Polynesian chickens brought to Hawaii. They are protected by park statute and fed by tourists, and their clucking and crowing are heard everywhere. In between these official lookouts, frequent bends in the highway provide space to safely pull over and find your own preferred vantage point.

An even better option is to take a hike. Anyone ambulatory can and *should* enjoy the ***Iliau Nature Trail,*** a 0.3-mile loop through sporadically labeled native vegetation leading to an impressive canyon overlook and a glimpse of Waialae Waterfall on the far rim. Look for the signposted Kukui trailhead just before the 9-mile point. The stars of the show here are the rare *iliau,* relatives of the silversword plants found on Haleakala and the Big Island that are unique to Kaua`i. These branchless plants topped with spiky leaves wait until the end of their life before erupting in hundreds of yellow blossoms. Branching off from the loop, the longer ***Kukui Trail*** drops 2,000 feet to connect with the extensive trail system and wilderness camps on the canyon floor.

A mile past the third posted canyon lookout, the NASA tracking facilities mark the boundary between Waimea and Koke`e Parks. The first right (Halemanu Road) leads to yet another canyon viewpoint (looking back down the canyon) as well as to trails to the Waipo`o Falls and beyond. Unpaved Halemanu Road is often unsuitable for conventional vehicles, but it's less than a mile hike to the lookout just off Halemanu to the right on the ***Cliff Trail.*** Branch left from the trail to the waterfalls for a dip in a refreshing pool surrounded by ginger.

From here on, the main highway moves away from the canyon rim and continues climbing to ***Kanalohulu Meadow,*** the center of Koke`e activity. The god Kanaloa supposedly fashioned this clearing to prevent malevolent forest sprites from preying on passersby. You can get a meal here at ***The Lodge at Koke`e*** (335–6061) from 9:00 A.M. to 3:30 P.M., including a delicious Portuguese bean soup and corn bread. The small gift shop inside the lodge features local artisans' handiwork. The lodge also rents comfortably equipped housekeeping cabins sleeping three to seven for $45. Early bookings are essential, especially for weekends and holidays (P.O. Box 367, Waimea 96796). ***Camp Sloggett,*** run by the YWCA (245–5959 for YWCA main office), rents space in its lodge and

Garden Isle Celluloid

Kaua'i's jagged green mountains and dazzling white beaches would stir any cinematographer's soul. So it's no surprise that the island has become Hollywood's venue of choice whenever a script calls for a tropical setting. Throughout the years, Kaua'i has doubled for Vietnam's rice paddies (*Uncommon Valor, Flight of the Intruder*), Costa Rican rain forest (*Jurassic Park*), African jungle (*Outbreak*), and even the Australian outback (*The Thorn Birds*). It served as Peter Pan's Never-Never Land (*Hook*), South Pacific's *Bali Hai*, television's *Fantasy Island,* and the original *Gilligan's Island.* The island has also put in more than a few appearances as itself. Elvis Presley got married at the Coco Palms in 1961's *Blue Hawaii* and returned to croon his way through two other movies set here. More recently, Nicolas Cage and Sarah Jessica Parker's *Honeymoon in Vegas* devolved into a Garden Isle romp. In all, Kaua'i has been filmed in more than sixty full-length motion pictures, beginning with 1933's *White Heat.* Stephen Spielberg alone has made four of them, including *Raiders of the Lost Ark.*

Almost any old-timer on the island can tell you stories about how John Wayne came drinking at the local saloon while filming *Donovan's Reef.* Or how Frank Sinatra nearly drowned at the beach in Wailua while making *None but the Brave.* With as many as three different movies under production at the same time in recent years and with so many celebrities owning vacation homes on Kaua'i's North Shore, island residents have become almost blasé about their Hollywood connection.

For visitors to Kaua'i, however, the chance to brush against movie history has proven a great selling point. The official *Kaua'i Visitors Bureau Map Guide* includes markers of thirty-nine different film locations for visitors to inspect. You can pick one up at the bureau's office at 4334 Rice Street in Lihue, or at many other locations around the island. Local bookstores and gift shops stock copies of *The Kaua'i Movie Book,* the definitive guide to moviemaking on the Garden Isle; it is full of photos and anecdotes about the shoots, as well as a map of their locations.

For those wanting help in reaching some of the more out-of-the-way sites (many of which are on private property), *Hawaii Movie Tours* (www.hawaiimovietour.com) provides a fully narrated tour service. Its fifteen-passenger vans are equipped with VCRs and surround sound, so you can see the actual scenes filmed at each location before you visit. You also learn a wealth of insider gossip about the goings-on behind the scenes and even sing show tunes from *South Pacific.* The five-and-a-half-hour tours run daily, beginning at 9:00 A.M., with lunch and hotel pickup included; they cost $95. Reserve in advance at 822–1192 or (800) 628–8432, as space is limited.

bunkhouse to groups for $20 per person, but you need a minimum of five people on weekdays and more on weekends. Linens not provided; reserve well in advance (YWCA, 3094 Elua Street, Lihue 96766). Tent camping is available on the property provided you make reservations with the caretaker (335–0710). Tent sites are also available throughout the park with a state permit.

Next to the lodge, the **Koke'e Museum** (335–9975), run by the Hui o Laka in honor of Laka, the goddess of the forest, offers hiking information and maps (including a giant 3-D topological map of West Kaua'i with all the trails marked). The two-room museum also crams in a wealth of natural-history lore. Well-organized exhibits touch on Hawaiiana, geology, and botany and display stuffed wildlife (including a ferocious boar's head). Be sure to strike the bell stone to hear a working example of these geologic curiosities used by the Hawaiians. Open daily 10:00 A.M. to 4:00 P.M. Volunteers also lead guided hikes between June and September on alternating weekends (call for schedule).

Outdoors enthusiasts will delight in Koke'e's many activities. Hunters (with a state permit) track pigs year-round. Frugivores descend upon Koke'e during late June and July for the Menthley plum season. The first Saturday of August kicks off trout season. Anglers can tackle rainbow trout (stocked annually) for the next sixteen days, then on weekends through September. Licenses are available at Koke'e Lodge.

The Camp 10 Road, the second right after the lodge, leads through 2 miles of sylvan splendor to picnic areas around the Sugi Grove. The latter half of the road usually requires four-wheel drive. Cedar, fir, eucalyptus, and even redwood trees line the forest paths here. At dusk, look for Hawaiian bats, the islands' only endemic mammal, fluttering from the treetops. From Sugi Grove, you can hike to some upper canyon vantage points. But for scenic destinations, most Koke'e trails head for ridgetop views above the Na Pali Coast or make soggy forays through the Alakai Swamp.

You can get a taste of both without departing pavement by continuing on Koke'e Road to the **Kalalau** and **Pu'u o Kila Lookouts.** Both overlook the lushly carpeted amphitheater of Kalalau Valley 4,000 feet below. Waterfalls spill silently down the razor-slashed walls. Kalalau Beach, the end point of the Na Pali coastal trail (see The North Shore), lies just beyond the left rim of the valley. Uninhabited since the 1920s, the hidden depths of the Kalalau radiate a remote and mysterious power. Here, in a real-life story immortalized by Jack London's pen, Ko'olau the Leper hid with his family to escape exile to Moloka'i. After World War II, Bernard Wheatley, "the Hermit of Kalalau," lived alone in the valley for more than ten years before disappearing.

From Puu o Kila, at the end of Koke'e Road, you can also scan the vast acreage of the **Alakai Swamp,** which stretches across the sunken volcanic basin of Kaua'i's original caldera. The remnant of an aborted road project designed to reach Hanalei extends from the lookout along the narrow ridge dividing Kalalau and the Alakai. Free yourself from human static (if not the inescapable buzz of helicopter sorties) by walking a short distance along **Pihea Track** and contemplating the changing angles into Kalalau Valley. Follow your nose to the spicy anise aroma of berries from the mokihana trees along this trail. Woven with the equally fragrant leaves of the maile vine, which grows here also, the combination forms Hawaii's most sacred lei. (If you find mokihana tree, look but don't touch; the tree's berry is extremely acidic and can burn bare skin.)

After a half mile, the "road" narrows; a trail continues to Pihea Overlook, then drops into the murky depths of the Alakai Swamp. The largest wetland area in Hawaii, the Alakai extends to the summit of Waialeale, absorbing the prodigious rainfall this peak attracts. The swamp provides refuge for countless endangered native birds, shielded from predators in the mire and, at 4,000 feet, out of range of mosquito-borne diseases. Keep your eyes peeled for the brilliant red *i`iwi* or, if you're lucky, the lime-green *nukupu`u*. Both have curved beaks; the latter exists only in the eastern Alakai. The almost totally endemic vegetation creates a unique moss-covered environment for hardy souls to explore, but be prepared for rain and mud. Fortunately, a newly built boardwalk bridges the worst patches of muck along the way.

If mud-soaked socks do not appeal, three somewhat drier trails branch off Koke`e Road between the lodge and the air guard station, descending parallel ridges to reach spectacular vantage points overlooking the Na Pali Coast. Here you can sit, deafened by silence, watching white tropical birds circle in search of nesting sites as mountain goats clamber along impossibly steep ledges. The two overlooks at the end of the **Awaawapuhi and Nualolo Trails** connect via a third trail. The combined 10-mile loop makes for one of the most stunning—and strenuous—day hikes in Hawaii. Recent rains (in 2006) have left some areas of the trail heavily eroded and damaged. The hike is not for those afraid of heights.

The Coconut Coast

Heading northeast from Lihue beyond Hanamaulu, the Kuhio Highway (Route 56) descends from the edge of the Kalepa Ridge and hugs the coast for the next 10 miles or so. The profusion of coconut trees dotting the golf course on your right makes it immediately obvious how the eastern shore acquired its nickname. Before you fast-forward on to the North Shore, take some time to explore the Wailua River Valley. One of the two most sacred areas in all Hawaii, this lush waterway was the residence of Kaua`i's *alii nui* rulers.

Start your tour on the coast at **Lydgate Park.** To get there, turn right onto Leho Road just past the Wailua Golf Course, then right again. The park borders a long, white-sand beach shaded by ironwood trees. Two lava-rock wading pools offer protection against the trade wind–borne swells that buffet the shore. At the far end of the beach road, just below the Aston Kaua`i Resort, scattered clusters of lava rocks mark the remains of *Hikini o Kala Heiau,* an ancient sanctuary at the mouth of the Wailua River. The heiau is one of seven strung along the river valley, culminating in an altar on the summit of Mount Waialeale. Keep in mind that when you look at these heiau, you're seeing only the stone foundations and walls. Kamehameha II abandoned the old religion in 1819. On his orders, all the wooden idols and altars in temples throughout the kingdom were burned to the ground. The few that survived are housed in museums. The heiau here was part of Hauola Place of Refuge. By reaching this peaceful spot, fugitives of old could gain sanctuary from their persecutors. Notice the small noni trees that grow amid the stones here. The pear-size noni fruits bulge like cancerous growths, starting off green and ripening to an unappetizing gray, translucent hue. The fruit has strong medicinal value and is used by some to control hypertension.

The next heiau of the Wailua seven lies hidden among the cane fields above the highway, but you can see numbers three and four by crossing the Wailua River and turning left from Kuhio Highway onto Kuamo`o Road (Route 580), an ancient roadway once forbidden to commoners. Royalty would beach their canoes and be carried, still seated, along the sacred path to their homes by the lagoon. On your right is the *Coco Palms Resort,* the granddaddy of island resorts, built around ancient fishponds where Queen Kapule, the island's last reigning monarch, once lived. An enormous stand of coconut trees encircles the grounds, remnants of an unsuccessful nineteenth-century copra plantation. The hotel itself has a grand history as a pioneer of Hawaiian resort kitsch, from clamshell washbasins to palm-frond chandeliers; it was featured in several Hollywood movies, including Elvis Presley's *Blue Hawaii.* Severely damaged by Hurricane Iniki in 1992, it has been closed ever since, but it is slated for redevelopment as a combined resort/condo project. Stay tuned.

Now on to the heiau. Only a short distance up the road, in Wailua River State Park, an HVCB warrior points to *Holoholo Ku Heiau,* an ancient temple of sacrifice. Some controversy exists as to the authenticity of the ruins. Queen Kapule is believed to have converted the structure into a pigpen. Notice the dense interlocking thickets of hau trees planted as a natural barrier around this sacred spot.

A few yards farther, you can visit another set of stones used for birth, not death. *Pohaku Hoohanau,* a large stone set against the hillside, marks the site where royal mothers came to give birth in a rustic shelter. Infants born here absorbed the *mana* (spiritual power) of this sacred spot. The umbilical cords were stashed in the adjacent *pohaku piko* following delivery. A special bell stone on the ridge above would be struck on the occasion of a royal birth, sounding the happy news across the valley.

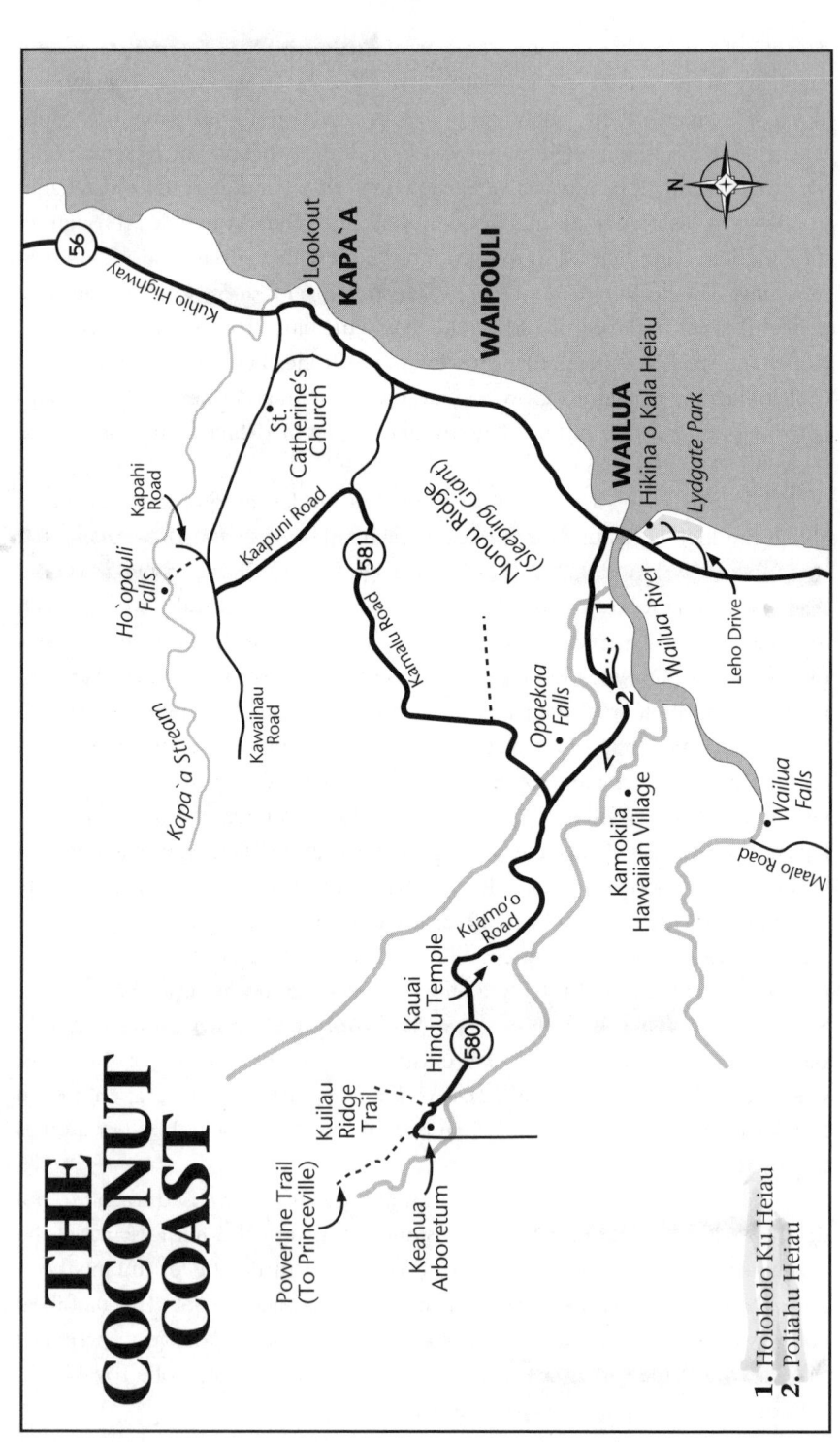

THE COCONUT COAST

Farther on, Kuamo'o Road begins to climb the ridge between the Wailua River and Opaekaa Stream. Be sure to stop at the scenic lookout on top to savor the sweeping view of Wailua Valley as you watch riverboats chug slowly upstream. The Wailua River is easily the most navigable river in the state—a Yankee vessel hid here from a Confederate warship during the Civil War. The boats you see today are ferrying tourists to the **Fern Grotto,** a natural rock cavity draped with maidenhair ferns. If you can, consider renting a kayak and paddling up on your own (see Introduction). If you do, you can also reach "secret" Ho'olalae Falls by hiking a short distance from the river (ask for directions when you rent your kayak). Interpretive signs at the lookout also identify the adjacent **Poliahu Heiau.** The dedication of this temple to Poliahu, the goddess of snow (who lives on the Big Island), is left unexplained.

Your next stop just ahead looks out above **Opaekaa Falls,** named for the tiny shrimp that frolic in the pools below. Once a year, while laying eggs, these shrimp dye the water and waterfall red. Walk across to the highway to treat yourself to yet another great view of the main valley. Near the riverbank below, you will see the thatched roofs of **Kamokila Hawaiian Village** (823–0559), an authentic re-creation of an ancient Hawaiian community. A self-guiding brochure explains the purpose of each structure. There may also be some craft demonstrations. It's very low-key, but genuine. Open Monday through Sunday 9:00 A.M. to 5:00 P.M., $5.00 admission. They also do outrigger canoe tours upriver for $30 as well as other kayaking and hiking tours.

Farther up Kuamo'o Road, the Wailua Valley gradually opens into Wailua Homesteads, a vast expanse of green pastures and scattered houses ringed by mountains. The cool, fresh air here brings a welcome respite from the coastal heat. To see a very different set of temples, turn left from Kuamo'o Road onto Kaholalele Road, one-quarter of a mile past the 4-mile marker, and go 1 block to the end of the road to reach **Kauai's Hindu Monastery** (822–4351; www .himalayanacademy.com), at 107 Kaholalele Road. This active cloistered community conducts a daily *puja* (purification ritual) at 9:00 A.M. in the Kadavul Temple, which visitors are welcome to join. Dedicated to Shiva, the temple houses a 700-pound crystal *shivalingam* at its center, while the surrounding iconography portrays other avatars of Shiva and his family, including Ganesha, Shiva's elephant-headed son, and Nandi, the bull on which Shiva rides. Taking photographs inside the temple is not permitted. Nearby, the massive white granite Iraivan temple is slowly taking form, built in traditional south Indian style from carved blocks imported from India. Visitors are welcome to visit the complex during daylight hours, and organized tours may be available. Modest dress is requested (no shorts or T-shirts).

For those wishing to spend the night amid this bucolic beauty, there is no shortage of bed-and-breakfasts to choose from. Among the most darling is ***Rosewood B&B*** (822–5216; 872 Kamalu Road; www.rosewoodkauai.com), which rents a charming upstairs room in the main house, a 110-year-old plantation home, for $85. The real finds, however, are the two private cottages situated on the professionally landscaped one-acre lot. The Victorian cottage earns its name with white-on-yellow gables and lattice trim. A flower-laden trellis fronts the lanai. Inside, it's a spacious two-bedroom duplex complete with a skylight and is fully equipped (including washer/dryer) and elegantly furnished. Smaller and more rustic, the Thatched Cottage has guess what kind of roof. Both cottages feature hot outside showers; they rent for $140 and $120 per day, respectively; three-night minimum stay. For those on a budget, three simply furnished bunkhouse rooms share a bathroom and rent for $45 to $55. Rosewood also books vacation rentals elsewhere on the island. Another fashion-magazine contender is ***Inn Paradise*** (822–2542; 6381 Makana Road; innparadisekauai.com). The three modern, tastefully furnished bed-and-breakfast suites are all in a single unit, which owners Major and Connie Inch originally built for their respective parents. The inn overlooks a three-and-a-half-acre property, complete with grazing horses and a rushing stream. Rates run from $70 to $95; three-day minimum stay. Also recommended is nearby ***Hale Lani*** (823–6434; www.halelani.com).

For something more rustic, ***Kakalina's B&B*** (822–2328; 800–662–4330; www.kakalina.com; info@kakalina.com) offers four studio *hale* on a three-acre working flower farm. The two newer units, Kolu and `Elua, have the nicest setup and go for $90 and $85, respectively. Those on tighter budgets will have to slum it in Kapa`a. ***Kaua`i International Hostel*** (823–6142), opposite the beach park, has dorm beds for $25 and private rooms for $60.

Kuamo`o Road continues to climb deeper into the island interior. At about 5 miles in, a sign warns that the road ahead is "unimproved," but it really is not that bad. You pass hillsides carpeted with maidenhair ferns, fragrant patches of yellow ginger, and other exotic flora. At about 6.5 miles from its start, the road crosses Keahua Stream, where you can park and stretch your legs in ***Keahua Arboretum.*** Although most of the plant labels have been lost, nature paths wind along the stream through open meadows and clusters of exotic trees. The Makaleha Mountains, Wailua's rear wall, loom fairly close by, and behind them, the twin peaks of Waialeale and Kawaikiu slash upward to skewer the clouds.

For those wishing to take in more of the scenery on foot, an excellent network of hiking trails begins near Keahua. The ***Kuilau Ridge Trail,*** one of the most scenic on Kaua`i, has its signposted trailhead on the right of the highway just before you cross Keahua Stream. The 2.1-mile (one-and-a-half-hour) jaunt through diverse vegetation and fruit winds along a steep ridge to reach a shelter-picnic site. Continue on a half mile farther to get the best views. More hardcore is the **Powerline Trail,** which starts at the end of the road and leads you on an all-day slog across the mountains to Princeville. On clear days the views are spectacular, but expect thigh-deep mud in patches.

On your way down from Keahua, take the turnoff left onto Route 581 (Kamalu Road), which winds through lush forest and rolling pastures behind Nounou Mountain. About 1.2 miles along, a sign on the right, opposite 1055 Kamulu, indicates the trailhead for the ascent up Nounou, better known as the Sleeping Giant. Hawaiian legend claims the mountain is really the overgrown body of the giant Nounou, whose recumbent form is best viewed from the coast. The trail travels 1.5 miles to Nounou's chin (about an hour's hike) and offers panoramic views from the top.

Route 581 continues for another couple of miles of mountain vistas before it swings toward the coast to rejoin the coastal highway near the center of Kapa'a, where an HCVB warrior designates the optimum viewing angle to make out the Sleeping Giant's shape, but you can see him from anywhere along the Coconut Coast. (Hint: Nounou's head rests on a pillow above Wailua, and his body stretches north.)

Kapa'a used to be a funky plantation town full of rickety buildings. Unfortunately, the infestation of tourists along this coast has transformed it into an endless sequence of shopping plazas and boutiques. To get a taste of the Kapa'a of old, those of a historical bent can take the **Kapa'a Walking Tour** (245–3373) offered by the Kaua'i Historical Society. The one-and-a-half-hour tour traces Kapa'a's roots as a Hawaiian fishing village and its subsequent plantation heritage that began with a sugar venture launched under royal patronage. Tours are offered Tuesday, Thursday, and Saturday at 10:00 A.M. and cost $15. Call to reserve.

Those traveling with kids may want to visit the **Kaua'i Children's Discovery Museum** (823–8222), under the whale tower of the Kaua'i Village Shopping Center. Many of the hands-on exhibits—covering everything from coral reefs and "deep-sea giants" to the island's ethnic diversity—bear on aspects of Kaua'i's environment and will be of interest to adults as well. Open Tuesday through Saturday 10:00 A.M. to 5:00 P.M. Admission is $5.00. If you're more interested in exploring the diversity of Kaua'i shopping, stop by the **Kaua'i Products Fair** (246–0988); look for the colored awnings of vendors along the highway. Open Thursday through Sunday 9:00 A.M. to 5:00 P.M.

When hunger beckons, you will find the Coconut Coast loaded with restaurants of all stripes strung along the highway. To eat as locals do, visit **Pono Market** (822–4581), at the southern edge of Kapa'a, for a take-out plate

The Twice-Buried Lantern

In a quiet corner of Kapa'a Ball Park, next to the highway, stands an enormous Japanese stone lantern with a curious past. The saga of this monument in many ways mirrors the evolving identity of the local Japanese community that built it in 1915, using leftover funds raised during the 1905 Russo-Japanese War. In addition to honoring Japanese soldiers who fought in that war, an inscription on the lantern's face commemorates the ascension of a new emperor to the Japanese throne. With its bombing of Pearl Harbor in 1941, Japan became public enemy number one. To protect it against vandals, the 25-foot-tall, sixteen-ton lantern was buried soon afterward, a precaution symbolic of efforts by local Japanese to hide ties to their motherland. After the war ended, the lantern remained forgotten underground until it was exposed accidentally in 1972. County officials turned to the local Japanese community for guidance, but no one stepped forward to take charge of this unwelcome relic from a bygone era, and the lantern was reburied soon afterward. However, by 1985, a new generation of Japanese Americans, led by then-mayor Tony Kunimura, sparked interest in the monument as a reminder of their heritage.

The lantern was unearthed for the second time and placed in a supportive brace, pending renovation. Donations for this purpose are sought by the historical society. Call 245-3373 for information.

lunch and poke; the *lau lau* (a sort of steamed Hawaiian tamale) and *manju* (a Japanese filled pastry) have a special following. Open Monday through Friday 6:00 A.M. to 6:00 P.M., Saturday 7:00 A.M. to 4:00 P.M. For a broader range of authentic Hawaiian staples, you might try the family-run ***Aloha Diner*** (822–3851), in the Waipouli Complex between Wailua and Kapaa. Open Tuesday through Saturday 10:30 A.M. to 2:30 P.M. and 5:30 to 8:30 P.M. Also in the same complex is ***KCL Barbeque*** (823–8168), which serves a local/Chinese menu. Both inexpensive.

For more sophisticated fare, ***Caffe Coco*** (822–7990), next to the Wailua Family Restaurant in Wailua, has cultivated the perfect tropical bungalow ambience. A pair of sisters renovated these 1930s Montgomery Ward prefab homes with tin roofs and clapboard walls. One runs the cafe, while the other sells Hawaiian nostalgia kitsch and artsy collectibles next door. Together they planted a wraparound garden full of exotic flowering tropicals and fern, so dense and lush that you can't even see the buildings from the road. Inside, the cafe displays artwork for sale and is full of idiosyncratic touches. Outside, an assortment of lawn chairs beckon for alfresco dining with live music most evenings, including belly dancing on Tuesdays and Hawaiian music and hula dancing on Friday. Locals complain that Pacific Rim cuisine can be variable and the service amateurish, but still come for the entertainment. Moderate; BYO alcohol ($5.00 corkage). Open Tuesday through Friday 11:00 A.M. to 9:00 P.M. and weekends 5:00 to 9:00 P.M. Another contender in the East Kaua`i dining scene is **Coconuts Island Style Grill** (823–8777), not to be confused with Caffe Coco above; it's on the mountain side of the highway, just after the Safeway. The decor features handmade coconut tables, colorful wall art, and leafy potted ferns, while hip island entrees such as Lobster Ravioli, Tempura Dip Ono, and Dragon Fire Ribs enliven the menu. Open Monday through Saturday 4:00 to 10:00 P.M. Happy Hour is from 4:00 to 6:00 P.M.—a perfect spot to spend time waiting for traffic to clear. Expensive.

Those with a yen for Japanese should visit **Restaurant Kintaro** (822–3341), across the street from Caffe Coco, where you can order either *teppan yaki* dishes prepared at your table or sushi and other delicacies from the kitchen. Open Monday through Saturday 5:30 to 9:30 P.M. Expensive. Thai food lovers locally split their votes between **The King and I** (822–1642) in Waipouli Plaza (open daily from 4:30 to 9:00 P.M.) and **Mema's** (823–0899) near Caffe Coco (open Monday through Friday for lunch from 11:15 A.M. to 2:00 P.M. and daily for dinner from 5:00 to 9:00 P.M.). Both are priced in the moderate range; the latter has the edge on decor but costs a little more.

Finally, tucked inside the Kauai Coast Resort behind the Coconut Marketplace is the **Hukilau Lanai Restaurant** (822–0600). This establishment is also owned by Gaylords Restaurant. Early birds who arrive before 6:00 P.M. can enjoy a special tasting menu that features six courses and five wines for $40 per person ($28 for food only). Open from 5:00 to 9:00 P.M., with live music nightly. Expensive to investment-caliber.

Those craving another waterfall-fed pond to frolic in can take Kawaihau Road off Kuhio Highway (near the north edge of town). On the way, you will pass **St. Catherine's Church,** which looks like an aircraft hangar but harbors beautiful murals by prominent local artists portraying Christian scenes in a Hawaiian and Asian idiom. Continue on for another 2 miles, then turn right onto Kapahi Road, which angles back to end at a dirt road. Follow this dirt road to a narrow trail and keep on the left fork as you zero in on the sound of the falls. Kapa`a Stream funnels over **Ho`opouli Falls** into a narrow steep-walled pool formed by an exposed lava tube.

The North Shore

Those striking "Bali Hai" peaks you've admired all the way from Lihue rise from the edge of the Anahola Mountains at the northern limit of the Coconut Coast. North of Kapa`a, Kealia Beach marks the beginning of undeveloped coastline; however, Kuhio Highway turns inland as it climbs over the Anahola

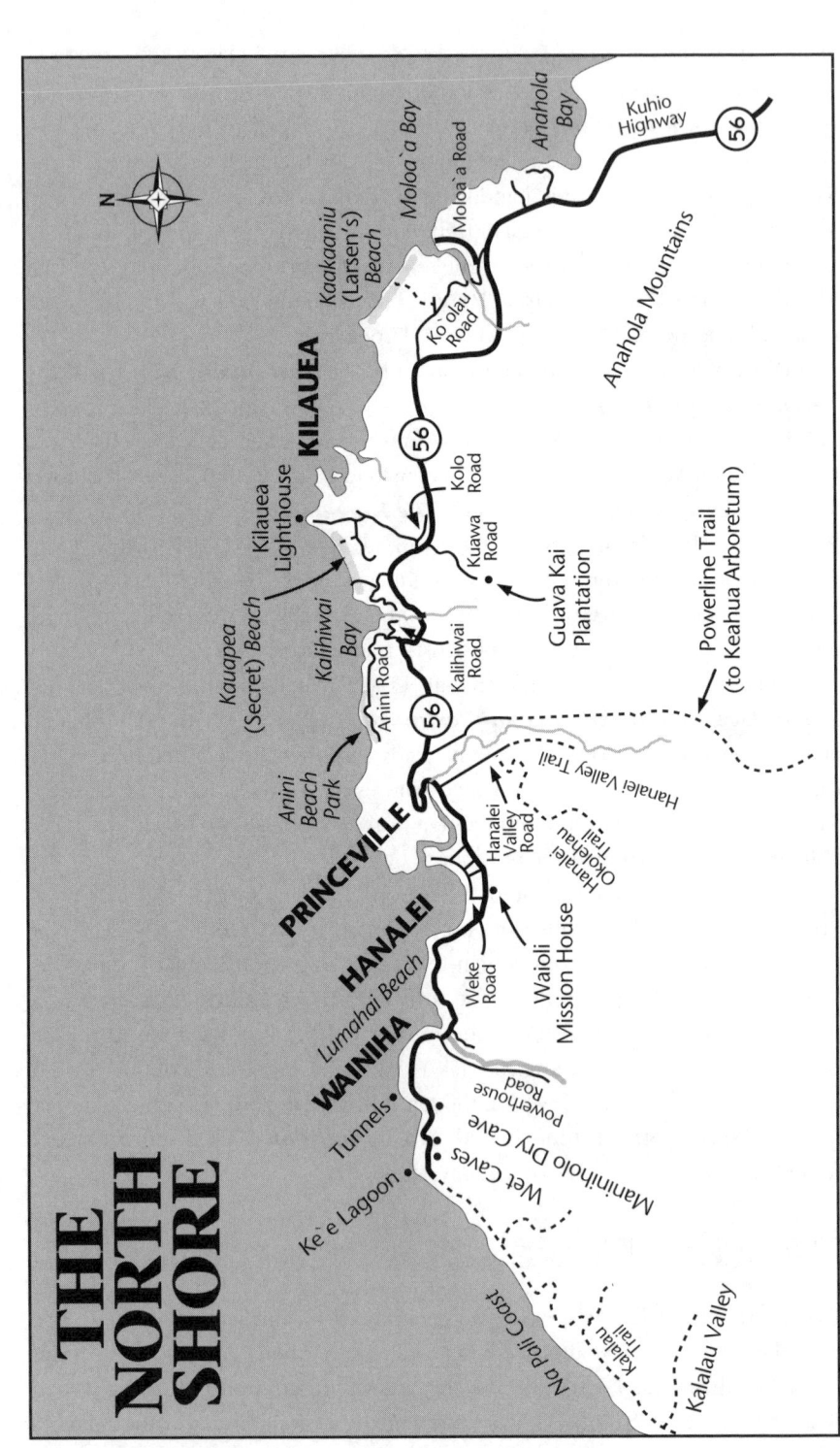

Mountains, leaving the beaches ahead hidden from tourist traffic. WARNING: With all North Shore beaches, extreme caution must be exercised while swimming. Dangerous currents form along the coast, and monstrous surf appears during winter.

After crossing the Anahola Mountains, you enter a vast clearing, but surprise, no sugarcane: The climate on the North Shore is too wet. Sugar has given way to niche farms such as the small papaya plantation about a half mile past the 16-mile marker. Turn right here onto Ko`olau Road to do some exploring. To reach secluded *Moloa`a Bay,* take the next right and follow bumpy Moloa`a Road to its end. Park and walk past the cluster of beach homes along the public right-of-way to the beach. Sheltered inside the steep walls of the bay, this beautiful curving strand is bisected by Moloa`a Stream. Windblown debris accumulates at the far end of the beach. You may get lucky and discover a Japanese fishing float, a hollow ball of glass that has floated thousands of miles across the Pacific.

To cool your thirst after your seaside frolics, you might stop *at Moloa`a Sunrise Fruit Stand* (822–1441), back at the turnoff from the highway, for a tropical fruit smoothie. Open Monday through Saturday 7:30 A.M. to 6:00 P.M. and Sunday 9:00 A.M. to 6:00 P.M.

Ko`olau Road winds uphill past Moloa`a to cross rolling pastureland. For diehards who thought Moloa`a wasn't deserted enough, turn back on the angled cane road on your right just more than a mile farther on Ko`olau Road, then take an immediate left. Follow this second dirt road to the end and hike the remaining half mile down to *Kaakaaniu* or *Larsen's Beach.* All this effort guarantees seclusion on a lovely stretch of shoreline that is a traditional harvesting site for *limu,* an edible seaweed. Ko`olau Road continues past an 1853 cemetery and affords ocean and mountain vistas before it rejoins Kuhio Highway.

At the 23-mile marker you reach the first real settlement on the North Shore, at Kilauea. A plantation town that refused to die, Kilauea now thrives on the tourist traffic lured by *Kilauea Lighthouse.* Turn right off the highway onto Kolo Road to enter town. You take the first left to reach the lighthouse, but before doing so, have a look at tiny *Christ Memorial Episcopal Church,* a charming lava-rock edifice set amid a peaceful garden and cemetery. Inside the church are some colorful stained-glass windows imported from England and a hand-carved altar fashioned by a parishioner, Mrs. William Hyde Rice. The present church dates from 1941, but many of the plots in the cemetery hark back to the original Congregational mission church. Farther along Kolo Road, *Saint Sylvester's Catholic Church* claims its share of attention for its innovative octagonal design. Inside, painted ceiling panels by Jean Charlot depict the Stations of the Cross.

At the end of the road, **_Kilauea Point National Wildlife Refuge_** (828–1413) surrounds the old lighthouse standing on Kaua`i's northernmost tip. Stop first at the visitor center to take in some information-packed displays on Pacific wildlife. You can then walk out to the end of the point and enjoy sweeping views along the coast in both directions while looking for the critters you've just read up on. Dolphins, green sea turtles, monk seals, and even humpback whales can all be spotted on occasion, as well as dozens of seabirds whirling overhead.

The old lighthouse is no longer used and is closed to visitors, but a separate set of displays tells the story of its rare "clamshell" lens. Designed by French physicist Augustin Fresnel in 1913, using thousands of fragile interlocking pieces, the four-ton lens beamed its light 20 miles out to sea. Volunteers lead informative and very scenic hikes along the cliffside terrain and native vegetation of adjacent Crater Hill. The refuge is open 10:00 A.M. to 4:00 P.M. daily. Admission is $3.00. On the way to the lighthouse, you'll pass the Kong Lung Center, a historic trading post turned tourist complex.

Across the road from the Kong Lung Center, **_Kilauea Fish Market_** (828–6244) offers the North Shore's best dining value. Gourmet plate lunch, including fresh fish specials, is served Monday through Saturday 11:00 A.M. to 8:00 P.M. Inexpensive to moderate.

If you don't know how to spot guavas in the wild, stop by the free visitor center at **_Guava Kai Plantation_** (828–6121). Backtrack on the highway to take Kuawa Road inland just east of the Kolo Road junction. Guavas have such a short shelf life that they aren't even sold in local supermarkets, but the yellow-pink fruit makes tasty juice. Open daily 9:00 A.M. to 5:00 P.M. A self-guided tour with a garden and nature walk is available, with free samples at the visitor center. On the way in, you will pass the **_Native Plant Propagators_** (828–1454). Owner Janet Graves grows only endemic and indigenous plants, those that existed on Kaua`i before humans arrived. You'll find such rarities here as the _ulei_ (Hawaiian rose), the only member of the rose family that lacks thorns. Open by appointment.

These gardens are but a prelude to the horticultural wonders of the newest kid on the block, **_Na`Aina Kai_** ("Lands by the Sea") (828–0525; www .naainakai.org), a twelve-acre tropical extravaganza, complete with a landscaped waterfall, a Japanese teahouse, a koi pond, and bronze statuary. The gardens consist of six major sections, from the bog house to the obligatory poinciana maze, as well as an "international desert," jungle rain forest, and beachside wetland. The landscaped plots are surrounded by 45 acres of exotic fruits and 110 acres of tropical hardwood forest—planted as a revenue source for the garden's future. There's also a whimsical childrens' garden for tots to explore. The gardens are open for guided tours twice daily on Tuesday through Thursday at 9:00 A.M. at 1:00 P.M. and once on Friday (morning only). Reservations recommended. The tours involve walking and/or riding in an open cart, and each emphasizes different aspects of the gardens. They range from ninety minutes to a five-hour walking tour and cost $25 to $70. Call for a complete schedule.

If you glanced along the western shoreline from Kilauea Point, you probably saw a wide patch of sandy beach. Getting there is another story. **Kauapea Beach** once bore the nickname Secret Beach because of its hidden access. The secret is out now, and there is no reason why you should not enjoy its charms. Take Kalihiwai Road, the first right past Kilauea, and then turn right again onto a dirt road. From the end of this road, you have a short (five-minute) hike down a very steep hill. Popular with alternative lifestyle types, Kauapea Beach at the bottom is much bigger than you might expect, but it is partitioned by lava-rock outcrops into cozy subsections. Although calmer in the summer, the beach is not recommended for swimming any time of year due to dangerous currents.

Michelle Hughes rents two **Secret Beach Hideaways** (828–2862; 800–820–2862; www.secretbeachkauai.com) on a thirty-five-acre plot directly above (and with private access to) Kauapea Beach. Custom-built with panoramic views from mountain to ocean and fully equipped, these one-bedroom cottages have all kinds of thoughtful touches and amenities you would never expect in a rental property, such as Japanese ceramic plates in an all-granite kitchen and double-head showers, which open onto a private garden and Jacuzzi. They rent for $550 per night. There is a $225 cleaning fee and $500 security deposit.

The more adventurous will appreciate the equally idyllic (and more affordable) **Jade Lily Pad** in nearby Moloa`a. This nicely equipped, two-bedroom house sits on stilts only minutes from the beach. To get there, you can paddle the pair of kayaks on the property downstream through a jungly bird sanctuary and soothe your aching muscles afterward in the outdoor hot tub. You need a four-wheel-drive vehicle to get here. The house rents for $250 per night, with a three-night minimum. There is a $150 cleaning fee. Book through Rosewood B&B (822–5216; www.rosewoodkauai.com).

Kalihiwai Road continues on through lush foliage and then curls around the mouth of beautiful **Kalihiwai Bay** to descend to yet another pristine North Shore beach. Children swing on a rope over the lagoon formed at the mouth of Kalihiwai Stream. Tidal waves in 1946 and 1957 twice flattened the entire valley. As a result, a broken circuit has left a second Kalihiwai Road joining the highway farther along.

On your way there, park at the scenic overlook near the 24-mile marker and walk onto the highway bridge to savor the tropical vision of Kalihiwai

Valley. The waterfall you see upstream can be reached by kayak or jeep trail. The trailhead begins at the next turnout a mile farther at the FALLING ROCKS sign. Bear left at the meadow. Past the bridge, turn onto the western branch of Kalihiwai Road, choosing the left fork (Anini Road) unless you want to admire Kalihiwai Bay from the other side. Anini Road passes some elegant beach homes (which may explain its good state of repair) on its way to *Anini Beach Park*, a huge, grassy expanse with the usual facilities. WARNING: One of the largest fringing reefs in Hawaii protects the coastline here, but dangerous currents still form in the winter, especially through Anini Channel, a gap in the reef where sailboarders romp on windy days. Beyond the beach park on the left, *Kaua`i Polo Club* attracts boisterous crowds to its Sunday afternoon matches from late April to September starting at 3:00 P.M. Polo, "the sport of kings," was popular among the island's plantation aristocracy. Anini Road hugs the shoreline for another mile, offering coastal views stretching from Kilauea Point to Princeville. A narrow beach lines its length.

Back on the highway, you next pass Princeville Resort. Built onto bluffs overlooking magnificent Hanalei Bay, the ultraluxury *Princeville Hotel* (826–9644; 800–826–4400) has perhaps the most scenic location of any in Hawaii. If you can't afford to stay here, the unbeatable view may be worth the price of a cup of coffee on the terrace. Rooms start at $500, but ask about their "escape rate." On Sunday the hotel does a free thirty-minute hula and chanting ceremony at 6:30 P.M. in the living room. A small gazebo nearby houses displays on Princeville's royal past.

Princeville Ranch (826–7669; 888–955–7669; www.adventureskauai.com) offers three outdoor adventures on private ranch land. You can hike and/or paddle your way to remote waterfalls or soar across jungle canyons on a zipline. The half-day outings cost between $79 and $125 and include lunch. Reserve in advance.

You can also explore Princeville's remote interior on your own by hiking the *Powerline Trail*, a rough, unpaved road that crosses the island to emerge at Keahua Arboretum in Wailua. The one-way trip takes several hours and can get very wet and muddy as you climb toward the rain-soaked summit. But if the weather's good, heading even a few miles in can yield spectacular views of mountain ridges and waterfalls. To reach the trailhead, turn inland at the Princeville Ranch onto Pooku Road, then drive 1.7 miles to the pavement's end; the trail follows the Hanalei River upstream.

On the other side of the highway from the Princeville entrance, be sure to stop at the *Hanalei Valley Overlook* on the left for one of the classic vistas in Hawaii. The Hanalei River emerges from the mouth of a deep valley and curves gently west through fields of taro toward Hanalei Bay. When it rains in the mountains, tiny waterfalls appear—local lore warns not to visit Hanalei when more than eight cascades are gushing, or you risk being stranded by flash floods. Most of the land before you belongs to the Hanalei National Wildlife Refuge. The Hanalei Valley has been farmed by different people throughout the years through a cycle of crops. Now, as a protected wildlife refuge, the land has reverted to the taro cultivation of ancient times in a cooperative venture whereby flooded taro fields, regulated by terracing, provide a favorable habitat for endangered wildfowl. Birders can study an illustrated placard to bone up on the different species they might encounter below. Almost 40 percent of all taro grown in Hawaii comes from the 917-acre refuge.

As the highway begins its descent to the valley floor, a wide strip around the first bend allows space to pull over and admire **Hanalei Bay** ("Crescent Bay"), the companion view to the valley overlook. Surfers stop here and check out the breakers through binoculars to decide which part of the bay to paddle out to below. Keen eyes may spot the buffalo that graze in Bill Mowry's farm in front of the bay; this meat is featured on local restaurant menus.

At the bottom of the hill, you reach the famous single-lane **Hanalei Bridge,** a symbolic gateway to the scenic wonders ahead. Mileage numbers are zeroed from this point, and as a practical benefit, weight restrictions prevent tour buses from crossing. The bridge is actually two-in-one: a 1912 Pratt truss bridge reinforced below by a late-1960s Warren pony truss. Additional one-lane bridges span the 10 miles of highway ahead, enforcing a slower pace of life. By custom, traffic on the bridge alternates, allowing cars gathered on the one side to clear while the other side waits to cross. Etiquette dictates that you wave to acknowledge other motorists' courtesy in yielding.

To explore the upper valley you saw from the overlook, turn left after the bridge onto Ohiki Road, which heads upriver through the taro fields/wildlife refuge. A turnoff just ahead to the right leads to an old cemetery. A little bit farther on, there's a parking lot where a quarter-mile nature loop leads to a recently discovered heiau. The steep powerline trail behind the cemetery serves as the beginning of the **Hanalei Okolehao Trail,** named for the *okolehao* liquor distilled from *ki* plants along this ridge during Prohibition. The 2.25-mile hike takes about two hours and offers great views of Hanalei Bay. Another mile and a half inland, the main road ends at the easier **Hanalei Valley Trail,** which heads 2 miles upstream through fruit trees and bamboo forests.

After the bridge, the Kuhio Highway follows the Hanalei River into Hanalei Town. Stop when you spot the soothing green of **Waioli Huiia Church** on your left. If you come by on Sunday morning, you will hear the church's famous choir fill the rafters with Hawaiian hymns. The building to the right, **Waioli Mission Hall,** built in 1841, housed the original congregation.

The real treat, however, awaits at the end of the long driveway between these two buildings. Park in the lot behind the Mission Hall to visit **Waioli Mission House** (245–3202), the 1837 residence of the Alexanders, the first missionaries on the North Shore. Restored in 1921 by three Wilcox sisters whose missionary grandparents succeeded the Alexander family here, the mission house is run by the same trust that oversees Grove Farm. Where Grove Farm portrays life during sugar's heyday, this Hanalei museum returns to an even earlier time for a glimpse at the lives of Bedford missionaries in "Owhyhee," as it was referred to back then. Docents lead tours of the property, revealing the stories behind its contents, while the letters and portraits on display chronicle the early inhabitants. The prefab house and most of the furniture (including a bed warmer!) were shipped around Cape Horn. A garden in back made this isolated mission self-sufficient in food supplies. Tours are offered Tuesday, Thursday, and Saturday from 9:00 A.M. to 3:00 P.M.; donations voluntary.

From the mission, take any road seaward and then turn right to backtrack along the bay to **Black Pot Beach Park** at the mouth of the Hanalei River. The park name honors a tradition of seaside festivities held on this spot in decades past. Local fishermen, visiting yacht crews, and anyone else who cared to join in would gather nightly to cook in a communal black pot. "Uncle" Henry Kalani Tai Hook, the unofficial mayor of Hanalei, set records with the enormous outdoor banquets he organized here. An old pier that juts offshore once served to load rice from the valley mill (note the faint rail tracks). Kids play on and around the crumbling pier, and swimming in these estuarine waters is the safest in the bay.

Most of the restaurants in Hanalei cater to tourists and price accordingly, so you might want to bring a picnic lunch. **Postcards Cafe** (826–1191), first in line as you enter town from Princeville, serves decent, albeit pricey, fish and veggie fare with some Pacific Rim touches in an old plantation-style house decorated with vintage photos and guess what else. Expensive to investment-caliber prices. Open for dinner daily 6:00

Waioli Mission Hall

to 9:30 P.M. **Hanalei Mixed Plate** (826–7888), in the Ching Young Center, offers moderately priced, ethnic island food, including $13 fresh-catch fish. Open daily 11:00 A.M. to 7:00 P.M. There's also **Neide's Salsa and Samba** (826–1851), open daily 11:30 A.M. to 2:30 P.M. and 5:00 to 9:00 P.M., for Brazilian/Mexican cooking and **Pizza Hanalei** (826–9494), open daily from noon to 9:00 P.M., for, well, you know . . . What Hanalei lacks in eateries it makes up for in its bars. **Tahiti Nui** (826–6277), on the highway in the center of town, is practically an institution. There's live traditional Hawaiian music on Sunday afternoons and live popular music most nights after 8:00 P.M. The place fills with raucous locals after the tourists have gone to bed, especially on Monday and Thursday karaoke nights. This South Seas watering hole dates from over forty years ago, when owner Louise Marston arrived as a war bride from Tahiti and fell in love with Hanalei. Polynesian architecture and decor run from floor to ceiling. The glass fishing-float lanterns and carved-coconut-stump barstools are especially nice touches. Bar dining is available. Also popular after dark is the **Hanalei Gourmet** (826–2524), a deli-bar housed in the restored 1926 Old Hanalei Schoolhouse across the street. Try the chicken salad in papaya boat. The deli is open daily from 8:00 A.M. to 9:00 P.M., with the bar staying open until 10:30 P.M. Live music four nights a week; moderate.

For those wishing to stay the night, Hanalei has a few options. **Faye Hanalei House and Cottage** can be rented from Waimea Plantation Cottages (338–1625). Originally a 1916 retreat belonging to the Faye sugar family, the simple but nicely renovated cottage portion of this three-acre beachfront estate books for $425 a night ($375 in low season). Not too far removed from the beach in its name is Carolyn Barnes's **Bed, Breakfast and Beach** (826–6111; hanaleibay@aol.com). Her three rooms, all with private baths, start at $95, but the Bali Hai suite with wraparound views of Hanalei Bay is worth the extra bucks at $150. There is a two- or three-night minimum stay.

You can also book a variety of rental properties, some owned by absentee celebrities, through **Hanalei NorthShore Properties,** P.O. Box 607, Hanalei 96714 (826–9622; 800–488–3336; www.rentalsonkauai.com).

As Route 56 climbs around the western edge of Hanalei Bay, the road widens at two pullout spaces, from which a steep, often muddy trail descends through the forest of *hala* trees to **Lumahai Beach.** This lovely strand starred in *South Pacific* as Nurses' Beach, where Mitzi Gaynor tried to "wash that man right out of my hair." Waters here are very treacherous, so best stick to the sand.

The highway next crosses Lumahai Stream to enter **Wainiha**—Valley, River, Bay, Beach, General Store. The latter is your last stop for provisions. WARNING: Wainiha quite appropriately means "unfriendly waters." Not only is the beach treacherous, but the river mouth is a nursery for baby sharks—so

Hanalei Rice Mill

Deep within the Hanalei National Wildlife Refuge, unobtrusively located on the banks of the Hanalei River, sits the state's only rice mill. Included on the National Register of Historic Places, the mill was built by a Chinese farmer in the late 1880s and came into the (Japanese) Haraguchi family in 1924. Rice was harvested here until the 1960s, when the rice industry collapsed, and the land reverted to taro. Having already rebuilt the mill once after a 1930 fire, the Haraguchi family never intended to restore the historic property twice more after it closed, but hurricanes Iwa and Iniki had other plans. The building and all its original equipment had stood in disarray until the early 1980s, when the family formed a nonprofit organization and slowly began moving toward restoration. Their efforts included taking an oral history from family patriarch Kayohei Haraguchi, who died shortly before Iwa demolished the building in 1982. The mill was fully restored and operating as an education center for schoolchildren when Iniki hit in 1992 and again leveled the structure. The family's homes and farm also were devastated, delaying further reconstruction efforts until 1996. Besides rebuilding the mill, workers also labored for months to restore the ancient equipment, which is now fully functional. It's the only such building of its kind in the state.

Now rebuilt, the facility is open to the public on a limited basis. Three-hour guided tours of the mill and surrounding refuge and taro *lo'i* are given on Wednesday at 10:00 A.M. The cost is $65 per person and includes a picnic lunch featuring locally grown taro; reservations required. Call 651–3399 (www.haraguchiricemill.org). If you can't make the tour, stop by the roadside informational kiosk at the entrance to Hanalei town (next to the Bike Doctor); the Hariguchis also own the adjacent Hanalei Taro & Juice stand, which sells a wide range of island produce and special taro smoothies.

steer clear. Consider turning inland onto Powerhouse Road to explore wide-mouthed Wainiha Valley, where an early census listed fifty-two residents as Menehunes. You'll pass the standard North Shore offerings of lush vegetation, waterfalls, and ancient taro terraces before ending up 2 miles in at the 1906 hydroelectric power station.

Back on the highway, the YMCA's *Camp Naue* (246–9090 for YMCA main office) lies at the 8-mile marker, spread over a choice beachfront lot. Often the site of community functions, the camp rents dorm bunks for $12 to those who can furnish their own bedding in between group bookings. No reservations are accepted, but call ahead to check availability.

After rounding a final curve, the highway crosses a small stream (and quite often vice versa) where, yawning open as if to swallow unwary motorists, **⟩ *Maniniholo (Dry) Cave*** appears on the left. Park at Haena Beach Park across the road to explore this cavernous chamber, named for the head fisherman of the Menehunes who lived here. Sinuous vines hang over the rim, and wild taro grows near the entrance. Inside, with the aid of a flashlight, you can follow a passage opening from the back left wall a good distance in before the ceiling becomes uncomfortably low. This ancient lava tube helped form the sea cave through which you entered. Haena Beach Park has facilities, but a nicer stretch of sand lies back around the bend toward Hanalei. Take the beach access road a quarter mile before Maniniholo Cave to *Tunnels,* a popular surfing spot with outstanding snorkeling during calm summer months. Sandlubbers can simply admire the mountain and ocean views.

Kuhio Highway presses on through lush vegetation darkened by the shadow of the mountains overhead. About a half mile past the 9-mile marker, on the mountain side of the road, you will see the entrance to *Limahuli Gardens* (826–1053), the North Shore satellite of the National Tropical Botanical Garden in Lawai, with an environmentally friendly visitor center intended to be visually compatible with its fabulous setting. The structure began as a 10-by-32-foot office trailer, which was transformed into a building resembling a historic, plantation-style home.

The center displays Hawaiian crafts and offers information about the environment and the garden, a seventeen-acre facility that features a large collection of rare and endangered native Hawaiian plants and many tropical species. The plantings here focus on ethnobotany. You can learn about the plants the ancient Hawaiians used in their daily life as you explore this spectacular valley setting via a three-quarter-mile loop trail. Black lava rock contours the green valley slopes in an age-old system of terraces built for taro. A coastal overlook offers stunning views. Guided tours are $15 (reserve in advance); self-guided, $10. Open Tuesday through Friday and Sunday 9:30 A.M. to 4:00 P.M.

Back on the highway, *Haena State Park* just ahead was the site of the infamous Taylor's Camp, a 1960s hippie community started by Liz's brother, Howard, whose free-living style did not include plumbing or waste disposal. State authorities eventually condemned the land. Park at the visitor parking area, cross the street, and take the short but steep trail ahead to the ledge overlooking *Waikapalae (Wet) Cave.* To get the full spelunking effect, you should ease your way down to the edge of the water. Daylight, tinted green by the foliage overhead, filters through the mouth of the cave, and the soundless water inside acquires an eerie blue hue.

A second wet cave, *Waikanaloa,* opens onto the highway just ahead. Peering inside, you can see through to a second chamber. The legend of Pele explains how these two caves became wet. It seems the volcano goddess dug her fire pits here when she came to Kaua'i in search of a home. Her sister, the ocean, flooded her out of Waikanaloa; Pele tried higher up at Waikapalae, but the ocean followed still. Defeated, Pele took her fires to O'ahu.

Lohiau's House or the Tale of Three Sisters

Countless hikers head into the Na Pali every day without noticing an archaeological site that the Kalalau Trail passes scarcely 50 feet from the trailhead. Just to the left of the trail, keen eyes will discern the vine-draped lava-rock foundation that is reputedly the site of Lohiau's house. Legends recount that Lohiau was a handsome chieftain associated with the hula halau at the nearby Ka Ulu o Laka temple. When the volcano goddess Pele arrived on Kaua`i, she was fleeing the wrath of her elder sister, a powerful ocean goddess. Hearing the sounds of the drums at Ka Ulu o Laka, Pele drew near to watch the ritual hula. With his graceful dancing, Lohiau won Pele's favor. They vowed to live together as man and wife.

Unfortunately, Pele's older sister, Na Maka o Ka Ha`i, had followed her to the island. When Pele attempted to dig for fire to build a home for her and her beloved, the ocean goddess rushed in with crashing waves to squelch Pele's fire. Pele's flooded fire pits remain known as the wet caves of Waikapalae and Waikanaloa. With a heavy heart, Pele had to leave Lohiau in quest of fire elsewhere. As she moved from island to island, Pele longed for her beloved mortal. When at last she settled on the Big Island, her volcanic fires secure in the mighty lava fortress she had built, she sent her younger sister, Hiiaka, to summon her paramour.

Lohiau had since died a lonely death, but Hiiaka was able to recover his spirit, trapped in a flower, and bring him back to life. The two then embarked on an arduous journey down the Hawaiian island chain, battling monsters and overcoming obstacles. Somewhere along the way the two fell in love, although neither dared to speak of it. When at last they came within sight of Halemaumau Crater, Pele's sacred fire pit on the Big Island of Hawai`i, the two embraced, as much from relief as repressed longing. Upon seeing them together, Pele's wrath overflowed. Torrents of fire gushed down the slopes, causing Lohiau to die a second death engulfed in molten lava. Pele's brothers pitied Lohiau and again brought him back to life. However, Hiiaka had vanished by then. Lohiau wandered aimlessly from island to island until at last he stumbled upon the hula heiau at Ka Ulu o Laka. A singing contest was in progress, and Lohiau recognized Hiiaka's voice. The two lovers embraced once more and returned to Haena to live happily ever after.

As you return to your car, keep your eye on the cliff-top peaks above the highway. These silent sentinels loom ever closer, choking off the road against the sea, until all at once it ends at Ke`e Beach; beyond lies only the remote Na Pali Coast and the start of the Kalalau Trail. ***Ke`e Beach,*** at the far end of the parking lot, provides ample reward for your perseverance in coming this far. Dominated by the spires of rock overhead and sheltered by a protective reef, this tiny cove offers excellent snorkeling in calm waters and is usually safe for a dip in moderate surf. Long stretches of hidden sandy beach extend around the right side of the lagoon. You can walk there or drive from the parking lot, but the swimming is less protected.

The left side of Ke`e Beach conceals secrets of its own. Follow the short sidewalk strip from the edge of the parking lot toward a narrow trail skirting the edge of the former Allerton estate, just above the rocky border of the lagoon. You get a magnificent glimpse of the endlessly silhouetted *pali* (cliffs) ahead that give this coast its name. Near the end of the point, the trail turns left and climbs steeply through vegetation to emerge in the clearing that was once **Ka Ulu o Laka Heiau,** dedicated to Laka, the patron of the hula (dance). The rocky remains of this ancient temple have weathered considerably, but you can still feel the power of the setting, hovering midway between mountain and ocean, encircled by jungle, at the very edge of civilization. The ancient Hawaiians held night rituals on this site, hurling special burning branches from the cliffs nearby in a natural display of fireworks. Hula *halau* still return today to leave offerings and rededicate their arts in this sacred spot. Casual visitors are requested to refrain from entering beyond the marked boundary.

Across the parking lot from Ke`e Beach begins the **Kalalau Trail,** Hawaii's most celebrated wilderness experience. Along the way, you take in magnificent scenery, lush tropical vegetation, dramatic seascapes, hidden valleys cloaked in mist, and, above all, the magnetic presence of *na pali,* the endless sea cliffs whose sheer edges the trail traverses. This is no cakewalk. To travel the full 11 miles along the Na Pali Coast to Kalalau Beach takes at least two days. There are numerous spur trails heading inland to explore. State camping permits are required. A popular day hike goes 2 miles to **Hanakapiai Beach** (swimming not recommended) and then an optional 2 miles upstream past ancient taro terraces and remnants of an 1890 coffee plantation to the 300-foot **Hanakapiai Falls** for a chilling plunge in the pool below.

Those with less time or stamina might consider hiking only a half mile in on the trail until you catch the first full glimpse of the Na Pali coastline spread out before you. You'll know when you're there. Finally, to explore the Na Pali Coast by catamaran or zodiac, call **Captain Andy/Captain Zodiak** (335–6833; 800–535–0830; www.napali.com).

Places to Stay in Kaua`i

HANALEI

Bed, Breakfast and Beach
826–6111
Comfortable rooms close to Hanalei Beach from $95.

KAPA`A

Inn Paradise
Coconut Coast
822–2542
This three-and-a-half-acre estate overflows with country charm. Rooms from $70.

Rosewood B&B
872 Kamalu Road
822–5216
www.rosewoodkauai.com
Offers a wide variety of lodging, all impeccably maintained, on a beautiful country estate. Rooms: $45 to $200.

KOLOA

Gloria's Spouting Horn B&B
4464 Lawai Beach Road
(Poipu Beach)
742–6995
www.gloriasbedandbreakfast.com

Offers elegant oceanfront lodging. Rooms with four-poster beds and Hawaiian quilts rent for $350.

LIHUE

Garden Island Inn
3445 Wilcox Road
245–7227, (800) 648–0154
www.gardenislandinn.com
Rates are $90 to $145.

WAIMEA

Waimea Plantation Cottages
9400 Kaumualii Highway
338–1625, (800) 9–WAIMEA
www.waimea-plantation.com
Charming individual cottage-type accommodations. Rates start at $175.

Places to Eat in Kaua`i

KAPA`A

Caffe Coco
4–369 Kuhio Highway
822–7990
Tasty food served in a romantic tropical bungalow ambience. Moderate.

LIHUE

Gaylords at Kilohana
3–2087 Kaumualii
245–9593
www.gaylordskauai.com
Continental entrees come with veggies and fruit grown on the property. Revered islandwide for the bountiful Sunday brunch. Expensive to investment-caliber.

Hamura's Saimin
2956 Kress Street
245–3271
Ladles out Kaua`i's best bowl of saimin. Open from 11:00 A.M. until late in the evening. Inexpensive.

POIPU

The Beach House Restaurant
5022 Lawai Road
742–1424
www.the-beach-house.com
Hawaiian regional cuisine served in a romantic oceanfront setting. Expensive to investment-caliber.

Roy's Poipu Bar & Grill
2360 Kiahuna
Plantation Drive
742–5000
Inventive Hawaiian regional cuisine. Open 5:30 to 9:30 P.M. Expensive to investment-caliber.

TO LEARN MORE ABOUT KAUA`I VISIT THE FOLLOWING WEB SITES:

www.trykauai.com

www.hshawaii.com

www.kauaivisitorsbureau.com

www.kauai-hawaii.com

O'ahu

With 80 percent of the state's population on this island, it's not surprising that O'ahu is commonly (if erroneously) translated as "the gathering place." The fact that the state capital resides here is almost redundant. On the other hand, officially, O'ahu itself does not exist anymore. The entire island belongs to the city and county of Honolulu, which also includes the uninhabited Leeward Islands that stretch a thousand miles northwest of Kaua'i, making it the largest "city" in the world. This semantic confusion only serves to underline the extent to which Honolulu dominates the islands.

Honolulu Harbor assured O'ahu commercial preeminence, and Pearl Harbor to the west made it a vital strategic asset as well. On the other side of Honolulu Harbor, Waikiki Beach gave O'ahu a jump start into tourism far ahead of the other islands. It still bears the brunt of Hawaii's visitors, and some say O'ahu is past its prime. This is grossly unfair. Honolulu has grown into a vibrant, culturally sophisticated city, and O'ahu, although undeniably more built up than its neighbors, still retains a scenic beauty rivaling the best in Hawaii. What's more, unlike most of the other islands, O'ahu has only one concentrated resort center along a single beach. Much of its shoreline remains public beach park. O'ahu boasts more miles

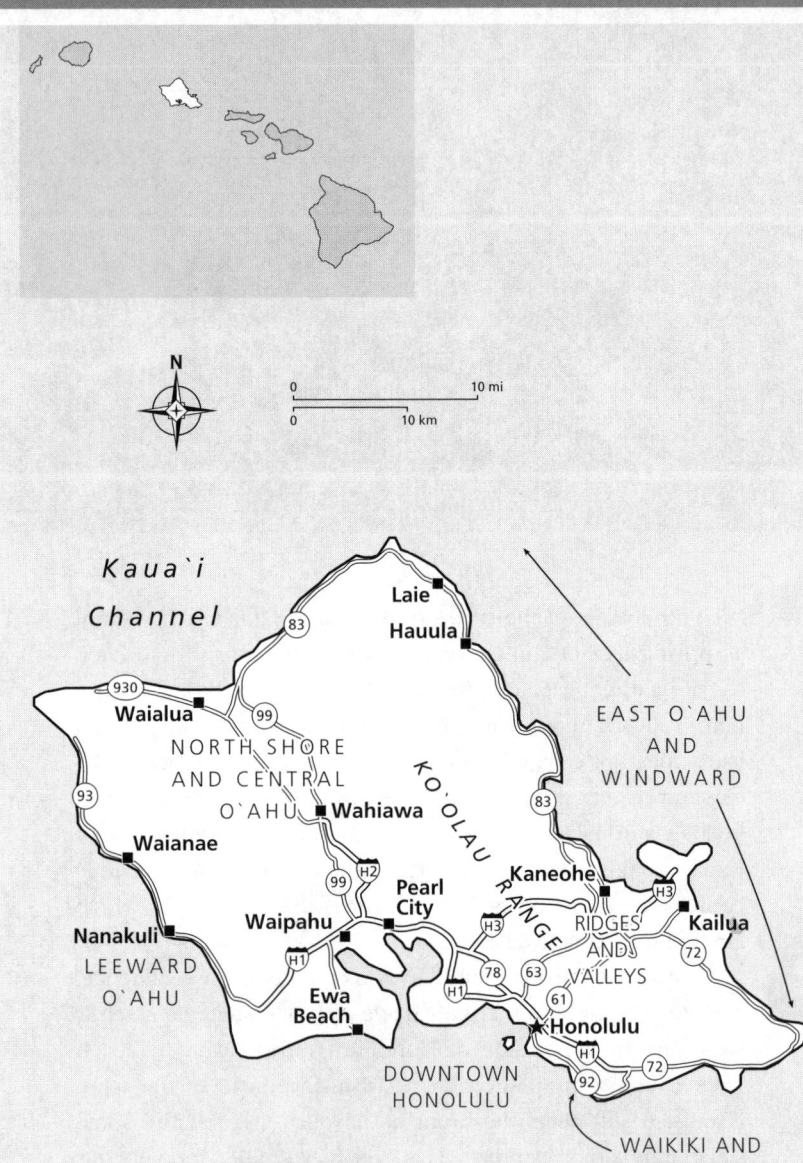

of swimming beaches than any other island, and its surfing beaches on the North Shore are unmatched anywhere.

Measuring 44 by 25 miles in a sort of squashed parallelogram, O'ahu rests on the overlapping slopes of two extinct volcanoes. Their heavily eroded remains extend as parallel mountain ranges running northwest to southeast. Urban Honolulu spreads along the southern shore, walled in by the Ko'olau Mountains, the younger and larger volcanic range.

Downtown Honolulu

The heart of historic Honolulu resides in its downtown area by the harbor. Downtown divides naturally into three sections, reflecting distinct stages in its development. The business district remains at the center, flanked by the enclaves of government and Chinatown. The scarcity of parking makes driving a burden, however. Consider taking TheBus (848–5555) or the slightly more expensive *Waikiki Trolley* (591–2561; 800–824–8804), which operates narrated tourist circuits throughout the city using old-style streetcars. Tickets may be purchased through any concierge desk.

Begin your tour where the town itself began—at the harbor waterfront. Water from Nunanu Stream prevented coral growth offshore, making this the only natural harbor on the islands. In 1792 William Brown, a British merchant captain, discovered this large protected harbor, which he named Fair Haven. Other merchants followed, first China clippers, then whalers. Local inhabitants

Brief History of O'ahu

In 1795 O'ahu bore witness to Kamehameha's final victory, a brutal conquest that made him supreme in the islands. A century later O'ahu also witnessed the overthrow of the monarchy that Kamehameha had established. But of all the landmark events of Hawaiian history, the Japanese attack on O'ahu's Pearl Harbor stands out. December 7, 1941, "a date which will live in infamy," changed the course of World War II and the postwar order that followed.

In other respects, too, O'ahu occupies center stage in Hawaii. For years the islands remained synonymous with Waikiki in the eyes of the world, and even today Waikiki receives the lion's share of visitors. The military presence at Pearl Harbor and other bases around O'ahu continue to provide an important source of revenue to the state's economy. Likewise, as the state capital and the only major urban population center, Honolulu dominates educational, cultural, and professional life in Hawaii. As the Pacific Rim continues to gain in economic and geopolitical significance, policy makers hope to capitalize on Honolulu's strategic mid-Pacific location.

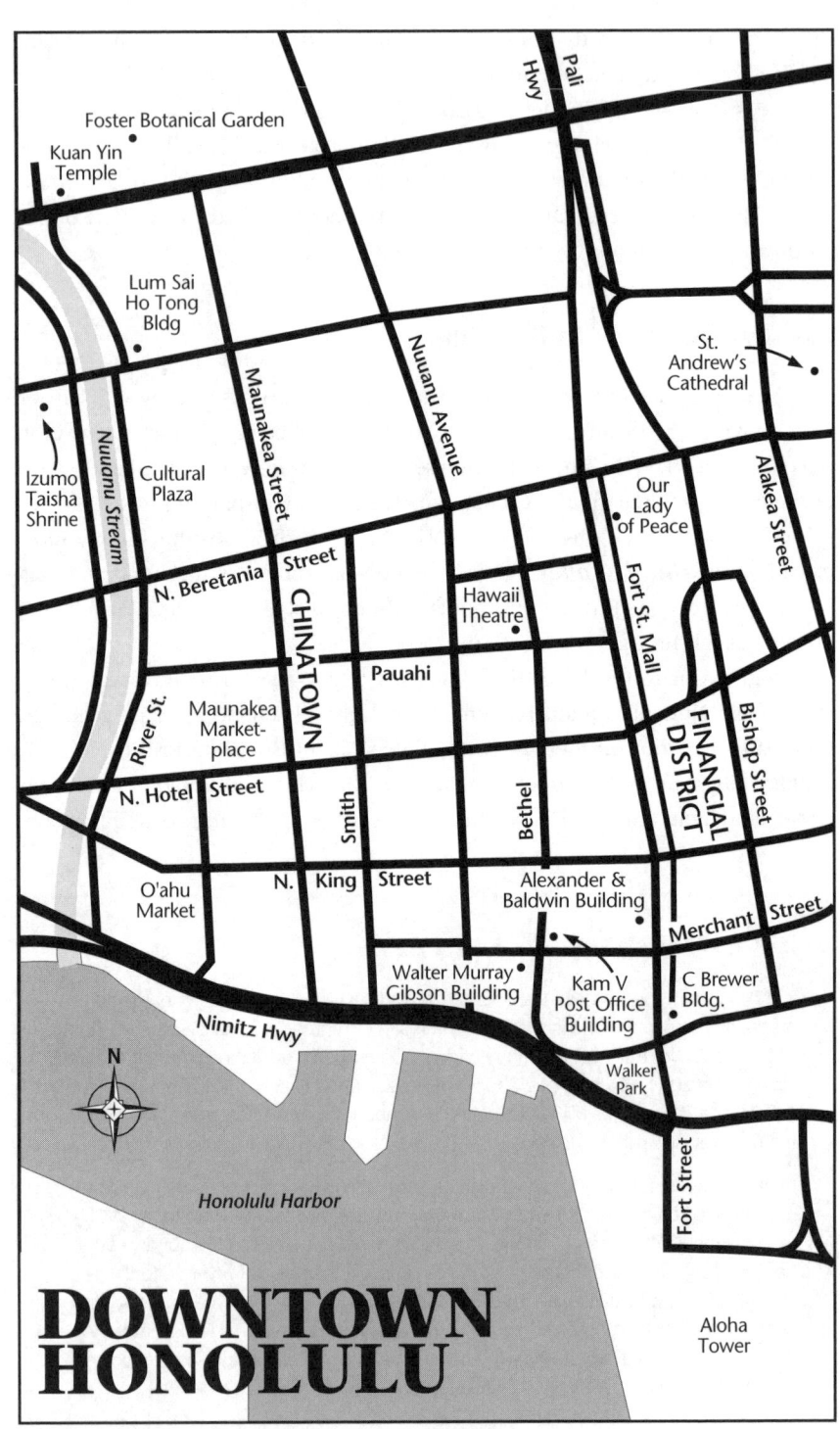

DOWNTOWN HONOLULU

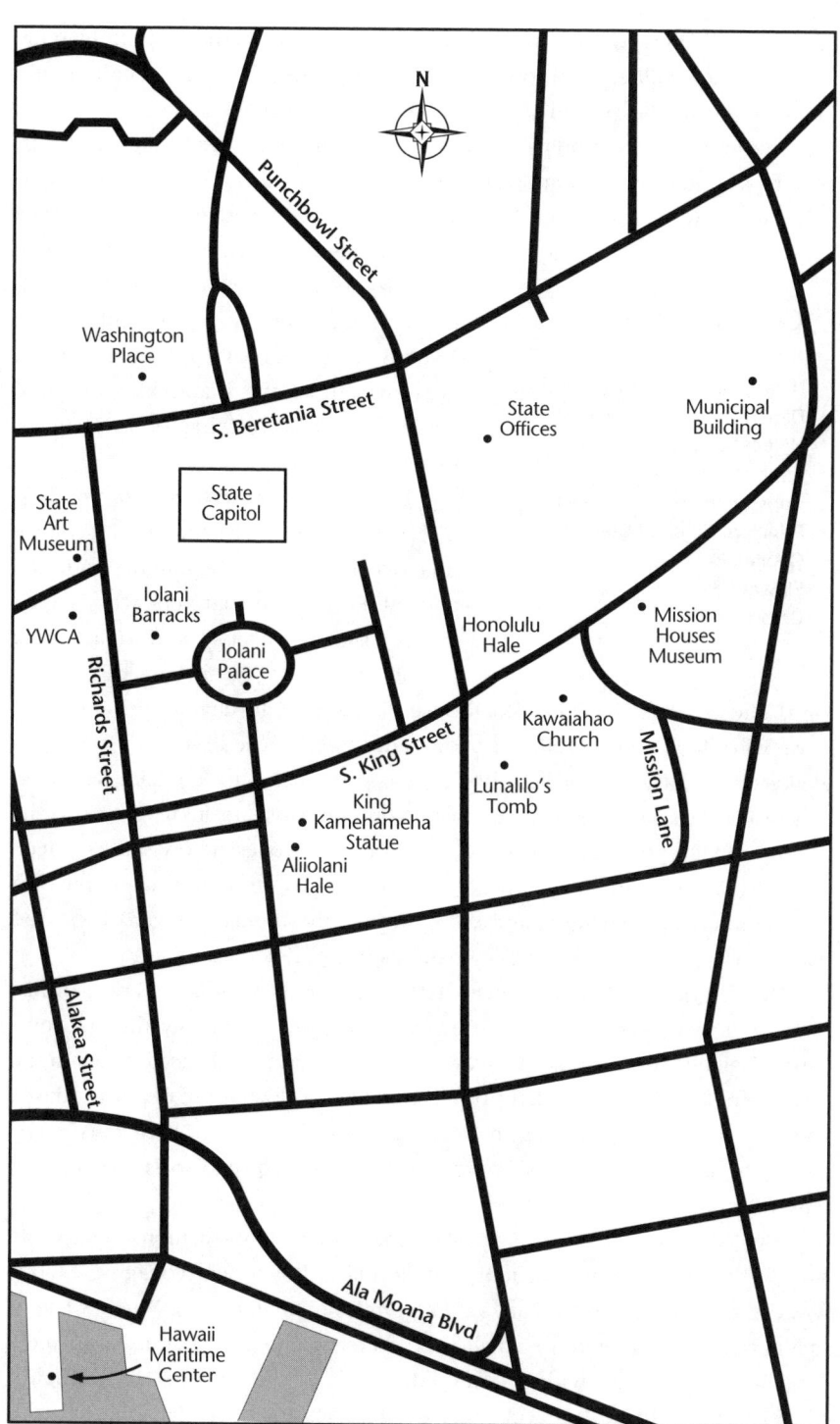

gathered to barter provisions and sandalwood, and Westerners began to settle as well. A new village arose on the hot, dusty plains inland of the harbor, taking for its name the Hawaiian translation of Fair Haven—Honolulu.

The growing community of *haoles* (foreigners) included all kinds of miscreants who jumped ship and caused trouble. Other menaces came from outside. French warships shelled Honolulu more than once, demanding tolerance of Catholics and lower tariffs on French champagne. A hotheaded British captain briefly took over the entire kingdom in 1843. Still, the harbor commerce brought great wealth to the island kingdom and made for a colorful chapter in Hawaii's maritime history.

o`ahu facts

Nickname: The Gathering Place
Dimensions: 44 x 25 miles
Highest elevation: Mount Ka`ala (4,020 feet)
Population: 896,019 (2002)
Principal City and State Capital: Honolulu
Flower: `Ilima
Color: Yellow

The ***Hawaii Maritime Center*** (536–6373) at Honolulu Harbor's Pier 7 explores this ocean heritage, beginning with the ancient Polynesian mariners who settled these distant islands and continuing through to the jet age that made tourism king. The center's Kalakaua Boathouse is designed to change the minds of those who think that museum is a four-letter word spelled b-o-r-e. Multimedia exhibits and snazzy decor help bring the subject matter to life. Life-size dioramas of Hawaii's maritime past take you from the cabins of luxury liners to the waterfront tattoo parlors of World War II. You can also learn how sharks played an important role in Hawaiian culture, admire a rare 46-foot skeleton of a female humpback whale, take a video tour of the remote Leeward isles, and play with hands-on ocean ecology exhibits. Free audiocassette tours.

Docked outside the boathouse are two important vessels in Hawaiian history. Built in Glasgow in 1878, the *Falls of Clyde* is reputedly the last four-masted sailing clipper afloat. Its worldwide travels included cargo duties in the Hawaiian Islands, but it ended up being used as a floating oil depot in Alaska and was slated for grounding in Seattle as a breakwater. Local citizens raised money to save it, and the *Falls* was restored and returned to Honolulu as a museum ship.

The adjacent *Hokule`a* ("star of gladness") has an even more remarkable story. This replica of the ancient double-hulled Polynesian voyaging canoes was the first to grace Hawaiian waters in more than 700 years. When Western sailors began to arrive in the Pacific, the secrets of ocean seafaring had largely been forgotten in the widely scattered islands of the "Polynesian Triangle." Western egos refused to accept that the Polynesians could have carried out such long-distance exploration centuries before the Vikings. In 1976 the *Hokule`a* silenced skeptics by retracing the ancient sea route from Hawaii to Tahiti relying solely on traditional methods of navigation. Members of the Polynesian Voyaging Society, who sail the *Hokule`a* and its successors, can tell you how they did it on their regularly scheduled tours of the canoe. (Unless the crew is in training, either the *Hokule`a* or one of its sister canoes is always docked here.) The Maritime Center is open daily from 8:30 A.M. to 5:00 P.M. The **Hokule`a** and the **Falls of Clyde** close at 5:00 P.M.; $7.50 admission.

To see some maritime history in the making, have a look at Pier 6, adjacent to the center, to see if the **Navatek I** (973–1311) is in port. This 140-foot vessel uses advanced SWATH technology based on twin hulls plus computer-controlled ballast to dramatically improve its stability and reduce the risk of seasickness on the commercial cruises it makes. Two-hour cruises cost $58 to $175. On the other side of the Maritime Center stands **Aloba Tower** (528–5700), built in 1926 as Honolulu's tallest building and remodeled in 1992 as part of a harborfront marketplace. The observation deck is open daily from 9:00 A.M. to 5:00 P.M. In former times the tower's four-sided clock face and single-word message greeted passengers arriving on Matson's weekly steamships from the mainland, Hawaii's only link to the outside world before the jet age.

A mural in the arrival hall recalls the pageantry of a 1930s "boat day." As island residents gathered, leis in hand, a flotilla of local craft would escort the steamer into dock while the Royal Hawaiian Band played, hula dancers swayed, and boys dived for tossed coins. The return of passenger cruise ships to Honolulu Harbor has prompted a revival of this tradition. Cruise ships dock at least twice a week (more during winter). The boats usually come in to port at 7:00 A.M. and leave port at 7:00 P.M. Contact the Aloha Tower Marketplace concierge (566–2333) for a daily schedule of boat dockings, events, and entertainment. Tours of the tower can also be arranged by advance request; free.

Olympic gold medalist Duke Kahanamoku set his first world record swimming in the water off Pier 8 in 1911. Mainland swimming officials refused to believe the unofficially clocked time. Their suspicions were briefly vindicated when Duke finished dead last in his first

o`ahutrivia

O'ahu is home to world-famous surfing beaches, the state capital, and a historic naval base.

Iolani Palace, located in downtown Honolulu, is the only royal palace in the United States.

More than 14,000 coral blocks were taken from offshore reefs to build Kawaiahao Church in 1836.

Jurisdictionally speaking, Honolulu is the largest "city" in the world.

mainland race. He'd never swum in water that cold and hadn't warmed up. In his next race, he broke his own world record and went on to compete in four Olympics, striking Olympic gold in 1912 and 1920.

A century earlier, Honolulu Fort occupied this spot, the focus of several tumultuous events. Today, the only reminder is a solitary cannon on Fort Street. Cross Nimitz Highway to reach *Walker Park,* where the cannon mingles with other historical relics from the area's past. Continue across Queen Street to the *C. Brewer Building.* Now home to the University of Phoenix, this 1930 beauty huddles at the foot of Fort Street Mall, enclosing its charms in a walled garden. Note the sugarcane motif in the lobby grillwork, recalling the agricultural heritage of C. Brewer, which remains the oldest U.S. company west of the Rockies.

Continue to the end of the block and turn right onto Merchant Street, where most of Honolulu's early trading houses set up shop. Just around the corner, look for the ornate facing of the 1905 *Stangenwald Building,* Honolulu's first skyscraper. This New York–style brownstone edifice housed a notorious furniture store whose owner had connections with city hall. Word seeped out that madams in the area had to buy their brothel beds here to stay open.

At the next corner, stop to take in the architectural splendor of the *Alexander & Baldwin Building.* Originally based on Maui, A&B hired two of Honolulu's leading architects to build this lavish 1929 headquarters as a memorial to its founders. The tile work of the Bishop Street portico depicts Hawaiian fish in a Chinese motif. These and other historic buildings blend seamlessly among the many mirrored-glass high-rises nearby. Thanks to downtown's strict zoning laws regulating urban density and greenery, these modern office blocks retain a tropical charm with miniparks, sculpture gardens, and artificial waterfalls. One such park at the corner of King Street and Fort has a noteworthy statue of Robert Wilcox, Hawaii's first congressional delegate. You can also check out the *Contemporary Museum*'s (526–0232; www.tcmhi.org) satellite

Geography of O'ahu

The third-largest island, O'ahu has a 112-mile coastline with the most swimming beaches of any Hawaiian island, as well as some of the world's most famous surfing breaks. Formed from two overlapping volcanoes, the island's population center, Honolulu, hugs the southern shore. The peaks of the younger and larger Ko'olau range rise more than 3,000 feet, with nearly vertical cliffs along their windward edges. The older Waianae Mountains harbor the island's summit, Mount Ka'ala, at 4,020 feet.

gallery in the First Hawaiian building (the tall one that looks like a giant play-ing deck with a tilted middle card). The gallery within is open Monday through Friday 8:30 A.M. to 4:00 P.M. and Friday to 6:00 P.M. Free. Notice that many men working downtown wear reverse-print aloha shirts instead of suits, especially on "Aloha Friday." Welcome to Wall Street in paradise.

Once haole business became entrenched in Honolulu, Hawaiian govern-ment had to follow, if only to keep an eye on foreign troublemakers. The early Hawaiian monarchs resented the time they were obliged to spend here, pre-ferring the old capitals of Lahaina (Maui) and Kailua (Kona) or even the beach at Waikiki; but finally, by 1850, Kamehameha III yielded to the inevitable and made Honolulu the capital. Government took up its positions to the east of business. Merchant Street appropriately slants into King Street, where most of Honolulu's monarchy-era buildings cluster.

On the ocean side of King, Hawaii's founding monarch, **King Kamehameha,** presides in statue form. The heroic image of the king poses with outstretched arm, clad in the traditional yellow feather cloak and helmet of a Hawaiian chieftain. The money for the statue was originally appropriated to commemorate the one hundredth anniversary of Captain Cook's landing, but most Hawaiians found little to celebrate in that milestone. The committee in charge deemed Kamehameha a better choice to rekindle the people's pride in their own history, leaving Cook's discovery of the islands relegated to a plaque on the pedestal. The statue here is actually a duplicate. The first casting made in Italy was lost at sea, and this one was paid for with the insurance money. (The original was later recovered and is currently displayed on the Big Island, Kamehameha's birthplace.) During Aloha Week and Kamehameha Day, the statue is draped with 18-foot-long leis.

Behind the statue stands **Aliiolani Hale** (House of Heavenly Kings), com-missioned in 1869 as a palace for Kamehameha V. The designs were modified for government use. Its attractive Renaissance Revival chambers housed the cab-inet and legislature under Kalakaua. Unfortunately, around this time, relations between business interests and the government began to sour, culminating in the 1893 overthrow of the monarchy. Some argue that the paramount interest of sugar plantation owners in protecting their access to U.S. markets made the rev-olution and subsequent annexation to the Union inevitable. Aliiolani is where the fateful events began. Haole businessmen occupied the building as the open-ing move in their bloodless takeover. The U.S. ambassador ordered American troops to land from a warship, ostensibly to protect American lives; many saw the act as a sign of U.S. backing for the coup. (In 1993 President Clinton issued a formal apology for the U.S. involvement.) Once in power, the new regime shifted the executive and legislative organs of government across the street to

Aliiolani Hale

Iolani Palace and renamed Aliiolani the Judiciary Building. It remains home today to the Hawaii Supreme Court. Step inside to admire the skylit octagonal rotunda. If you arrive Monday through Friday between 9:00 A.M. and 4:00 P.M., you can visit the *Judiciary History Center* (539–4999) here. Displays trace the evolution of Hawaiian justice from the days of the *kahuna* (priests) and *kapu* (taboos) through the bumpy transition to Western law under the monarchy. Free guided tours are available by reservation.

Facing Aliiolani Hale across the street stands *Iolani Palace* (538–1471), the only seat of royalty in the United States. A palace has stood here ever since Kamehameha III moved his court to Honolulu. Built in so-called American Florentine style, the present two-story palace was occupied by only two monarchs, King Kalakaua and his sister, Queen Lili`uokalani, before the 1893 revolution. Then Iolani served as the "executive building" under the republican, territorial, and state governments that followed, not to mention its stint as the nerve center for television's *Hawaii Five-0*. With the completion of the new state capitol next door in 1968, the Friends of Iolani Palace began a $7 million restoration of the palace. They now conduct forty-five-minute guided tours every thirty minutes Tuesday through Saturday 9:00 A.M. to 2:00 P.M., for $20, which includes a self-guided visit to the basement gallery housing the crown jewels and other royal regalia, plus a short video. If you would prefer to visit only the basement, tickets can be purchased separately for $6.00. Book at least a half hour in advance at the Royal Barracks office (522–0832) between 8:00 A.M. and 3:30 P.M. Children under five are not allowed.

The admission ticket is made up as an invitation to King Kalakaua's ball. You make the magical leap in time after donning protective shoe covers. A guide welcomes you in the name of His Majesty and ushers you through the staterooms of the palace, chatting about royal banquets and distinguished visitors—all in the present tense. Much of the palace's original contents "wandered" during the coup. The

trivia

Electric lights illuminated Iolani Palace four years before the White House wired up.

kingdom's crown jewels were literally gambled away by a looter ignorant of their true value. The Friends are gradually recovering the original furnishings or commissioning exact replicas. One piece was even found in a local thrift shop! A regal staircase handcrafted entirely from koa wood leads upstairs to the living quarters. The indulgent guides reserve a single original pillar for visitors to stroke. Upstairs, you visit his-and-hers bedrooms in opposite corners of the palace. Kalakaua grew to resent the separate rooms and moved to a private bungalow outside the palace where he could sleep with his queen.

The king's office is dominated by a huge desk cluttered with papers of state written in Hawaiian. Kalakaua was quite the renaissance man: He became the first monarch to sail around the world; he teamed up with bandmaster Henry Berger to compose the islands' anthem, "Hawaii Ponoi"; he mounted a campaign to revive the hula and other aspects of the old culture that the missionaries had suppressed; and he personally recorded many of the legends of his people. The king also took an active interest in the progress of science, and he corresponded with Thomas Edison regularly.

Iolani Palace was one of the most technologically advanced buildings of its age. All the bathrooms had flush toilets. A dumbwaiter outside the dining room connected to the basement kitchen. Electric lights illuminated Iolani four years before the White House wired up. Kalakaua even installed Honolulu's first telephone so that he could call to the royal boathouse. The "Merrie Monarch" had his vices, however, and spending money was one of them. His profligacy helped provoke the overthrow of the monarchy.

The tour culminates in the grand throne room, which spreads across half the ground floor. Decorated in crimson and gold, it has crystal chandeliers hanging from the ceiling and a floral carpet print designed by Kalakaua himself. Bishop Museum has recently returned the original thrones and crowns, which are displayed within, along with a royal *kapu* stick crafted from the tusk of a narwhal. At night, an entire wall of French windows opened onto the garden, admitting perfumed breezes to festive balls that ran into the wee hours of the morning. In less happy times, the wall portraits of past monarchs in this room looked on as Queen Lili`uokalani stood trial for treason after an attempt by her supporters failed to win back her throne. The deposed queen spent nine months confined to the guest room upstairs.

While waiting for your tour to begin, explore the grounds outside. You'll find many exotic trees, such as the banyan "forest" that grew out of two trees planted by Queen Kapiolani. Moving counterclockwise from the banyans, the next building is the Royal Barracks, a medieval-looking bastion that was moved brick by brick to make way for the new state capitol. Nearby stands the Royal Bandstand, site of King Kalakaua's coronation, staged nine years into his rule. (His original investiture had been unchivalrously rushed due to rioting by the losing side in the election.) Hawaii's governors today conduct their own inaugural rites at this same pavilion. The Royal Hawaiian Band gives free concerts here every Friday at noon, weather permitting, except for the month of August. Farther around the palace is the former Royal Crypt, where Gerrit Judd carried on a literal "underground government" at night during the British occupation of Honolulu.

From the crypt, you will see a small rock platform in the far corner of the palace grounds. This *ahu*, or offering stand, was built from stones hand-carried from each Hawaiian island in 1993 during ceremonies marking the centennial of the overthrow of the Hawaiian monarchy. The structure remains a focus for activists demonstrating for a return of sovereignty to the Hawaiian people. Continuing your circle from the crypt, find your way to the plaque on an upright boulder commemorating Captain Cook. Lying horizontally beneath the monument, an unlabeled stone slab has a far more interesting history. King Kalakaua brought this stone, a kapu barrier from the fifteenth-century temple of Liloa on the Big Island, to remind his subjects of the legend of Umi. Born an illegitimate son of the High Chief Liloa, Umi was raised as a commoner. To claim his patrimony, he boldly stepped over this stone to reach a father he had never met. As an illegitimate child, Umi could have been killed instantly for violating the kapu of royalty if Liloa had chosen not to acknowledge him. Instead, Umi lived and went on to unify the Big Island.

trivia

Built in 1843, Our Lady of Peace in Honolulu is the oldest Catholic cathedral in the United States

Turning from the secular to the religious, walk east down King Street from Aliiolani Hale to **Kawaiahao Church** (522–1333), built on the site of a former spring. (The name means "the waters of Hao.") Known as Hawaii's Westminister Abbey, this was Honolulu's largest building until Iolani Palace was built. Hiram Bingham, the leader of the early missionaries, drew the plans from memories of his native New England. Almost 14,000 half-ton coral blocks were cut from underwater reefs to build it. Trees from northern O'ahu were floated to Kaneohe and carried over the mountains. Bingham did not remain to witness the church's dedication in 1842; his wife's ill health forced a return to Massachusetts.

From the very beginning, Kawaiahao became an institution of the Hawaiian monarchy. The church provided the setting for royal marriages, funerals, successions, and other courtly ceremonies. Feather *kahilis* (flags) above the velvet pews at the rear of the church signify royalty; the pews are reserved for royal descendants today. Portraits of the entire royal family adorn the walls, with plaques commemorating various historical events. The public is welcome to attend services, conducted in Hawaiian and English, beginning at 9:00 and 11:00 A.M., respectively. Signposts designate other interesting features around the churchyard. The Gothic-looking crypt near the church entrance figures in a real-life Hawaiian ghost story. Its occupant, King Lunalilo, Hawaii's first elected monarch, had died within a year in office. Instead of burial in the Royal Mausoleum, the king's final wish was to be "entombed among my people" in Kawaiahao Cemetery. His successor, King Kalakaua, had lost to Lunalilo in the original election and remained bitter. He refused to order a royal salute from the Punchbowl cannons, saying that if Lunalilo wanted to be buried with the people, he could be buried like a commoner. Instead, eyewitness accounts of the ceremony reported that just as the body was being interred, exactly twenty-one bursts of thunder sounded a supernatural salute to the fallen king.

Surrounded by a wrought-iron fence, the smaller cemetery behind the church belongs to the **Mission Houses Museum** (531–0481) across the road. The names on the tombstones reflect the almost incestuous interbreeding between descendants of the various mission companies. Cross Mission Lane to visit the museum's restored mission buildings and learn about the missionaries' lifestyles.

The first missionaries arrived here in 1820, establishing their headquarters on the outskirts of Honolulu before dispersing to mission stations throughout the islands. In 1821 precut lumber arrived from Boston to erect the Frame House, the oldest Western-style structure surviving in Hawaii. As many as four mission families lived in this house at one time. Cramped bedrooms with trundle beds reflect the lack of space.

The deep cellar caused suspicion among Hawaiians when it was dug. They thought the missionaries might be hiding weapons. The cellar now houses a diorama of 1820 Honolulu. Note that the ocean came within 300 feet of the Mission Homes before landfills pushed back the shoreline. In 1831 Levi Chamberlain, the mission's secular agent, built a larger building from coral blocks and scrap lumber. Most of the space was taken up by stockpiled supplies waiting to be transferred to the seventeen other mission stations around the islands.

In these crowded conditions, babies were born and Hawaiian orphans taken in. The women were kept busy running the home, teaching school in the parlor, sewing dresses to clothe the congregation, and cooking for the endless succession of Hawaiian visitors that had to be entertained. They had to learn how to prepare native foods in a tropical climate without refrigeration, cooking mostly in a large wall oven. Murky water from the local wells had to be drip-strained through porous coral stone. Through all of this, Hawaiians crowded at the windows, fascinated by the chance to watch Western women at work. (In old Hawaii the men did the cooking.)

Meanwhile, the missionary men busied themselves translating the Bible into Hawaiian, writing sermons, and conducting church business. The printing house next door churned out some thirty million pages of Hawaiian-language Bibles and other educational materials by hand. The pages were hung like laundry to dry and then bound with poi. In 1853 almost 75 percent of the

Heading to Market

For a taste of local color and the chance to pick up some unique souvenirs, visit the *Aloha Flea Market* (486–1529). Known locally as the "swap meet," the event is held each Wednesday, Saturday, and Sunday in the parking lot of the Aloha Stadium (except when the stadium is otherwise in use), close to Pearl Harbor. Admission is less than a dollar, and the place is packed with booths selling everything from garage-sale items to exotic foods to custom-designed clothing. The market runs 6:00 A.M. to 3:00 P.M. Come early to catch the best finds and beat the heat.

Also popular with visitors is the *People's Open Market,* a farmers' market held Monday through Saturday at different sites rotating around the island. Call 527–5167 for recorded information giving market times and locations. Other open-air markets in Honolulu include O'ahu Market in Chinatown, for exotic victuals and the weekend art mart outside the zoo in Waikiki.

Hawaiian population was literate, an achievement exceeded at that time only by New England and Scotland—this from a people who didn't even have a written alphabet half a century earlier. The missionaries became victims of their own success when in 1863 their governing body in New England withdrew its support, forcing the missionaries to seek employment to feed their families. Many left Hawaii, some to continue mission work in the South Pacific. Those who stayed founded the commercial dynasties that came to rule the islands.

The Mission Houses are open Tuesday through Saturday 9:00 A.M. to 4:00 P.M. Tours are offered daily at 11:00 A.M., 1:00 P.M., and 2:45 P.M. for $10. Although separate from the museum, the old mission schoolhouse can be seen nearby on Mission Lane. *Likeke Hale,* Hawaii's only surviving adobe building, now serves as a day-care center.

Return to Kawaiahao Church and cross King Street to *Honolulu Hale,* at the corner of Punchbowl, aka city hall. Its Spanish Mission architecture became a signature of C. W. Dickey's much-copied Hawaiian Mediterranean style. Take a stroll through the lofty central atrium that often houses art displays. For functional city bureaucracy, such as county camping permits (523–4525), head a block farther to 650 South King Street, the Municipal Building. Or look in the phone book for the nearest satellite city hall. Except for Kualoa, O'ahu county campgrounds carry a security risk. For state camping permits (587–0300), go inland to 1151 Punchbowl Street at the corner of Beretania ("Britain") Street.

Moving away from downtown on Beretania brings you to Honolulu Police Department headquarters at 801 South Beretania, which harbors its own *Law Enforcement Museum* (529–3351) within. You can learn how Honolulu's finest, including Hawaii's original supercop, Chang Apana, kept the peace from Kamehameha's day onward. Armed with his trademark whip in lieu of a firearm, Chang went undercover through back-alley Chinatown, where he once arrested seventy suspects simultaneously in a gambling bust. Vacationing author Earl Biggers heard of Chang's exploits and fictionalized them in his Charlie Chan novels. Open Monday through Friday 9:00 A.M. to 3:00 P.M. Free guided tours of the museum and police station are available; book online at www.honolulupd.org. On your way out, you might visit the two nearby *Robyn Buntin galleries* (523–5913), which have an impressive collection of contemporary and traditional Asian and Pacific Island art and antiques. Open Monday through Saturday from 10:00 A.M. to 5:00 P.M.

Continue on Beretania Street to *Thomas Square,* a wooded park commemorating British admiral Thomas's restoration of Hawaiian sovereignty after his countryman Captain Paulet seized power in 1843. Across Beretania Street on the inland side of the park, the *Honolulu Academy of Arts* (532–8701) occupies a rambling Mediterranean villa located on land donated in 1927 by its founder, Mrs. Charles M. Cooke. The thirty-two galleries surround six garden courts and include a creditable collection of works by European masters. But the real draw is the academy's top-notch collection of Asian art, from samurai armor to T'ang horses plus a collection of Hiroshige *ukiyo-e* prints amassed by James Michener. Guided tours are offered Tuesday through Saturday at 10:15 A.M., 11:30 A.M., and 1:30 P.M. and Sunday at 1:15 P.M. Admission is $7.00. The academy has also acquired a sizable trove of Islamic art from the estate of tobacco heiress Doris Duke. Much of it is on view in the museum. To see the rest, take a tour of Shangri-La (see Waikiki and Thereabouts), which you can reserve through the academy. Academy volunteers serve lunch Tuesday through Saturday from 11:30 A.M. to 2:00 P.M. in the **Garden Cafe** for a moderate price. The academy is open Tuesday through Saturday 10:00 A.M. to 4:30 P.M. and Sunday 1:00 to 5:00 P.M. Admission is $7.00.

On the other side of King Street stands the concert hall of the Blaisdell Center and, farther down to the left, the grand entrance of McKinley High School. Note the Asian architecture of the **First Chinese Christian Church** across the street and the **Makiki Christian Church** around the corner on Pensacola Avenue. The latter has five stories of dreamlike pagoda roofs modeled on Tamon Castle, the first Christian church in Japan. For excellent Thai food, visit **Pae Thai Restaurant** on King Street near Piikoi. You know you're getting the "real deal" when Buddhist monks frequent the restaurant. Open Monday through Saturday from 11:00 A.M. to 2:00 P.M. and from 5:00 to 9:30 P.M. Inexpensive to moderate.

Returning toward downtown on Beretania Street across Punchbowl brings you to the modern **State Capitol Building,** which stands behind and dwarfs its adjacent predecessor, Iolani Palace. The capitol's innovative design draws on elements symbolic of Hawaii: Its two legislative chambers taper vertically like the volcanoes on which the islands rest; its pillars represent palm trees; and the reflecting pools surrounding the capitol symbolize the ocean. You can pick up a brochure covering the capitol district from the governor's office on the fifth floor. Be sure to peek into the legislative chambers. The house has warm earth tones and a chandelier called Sun. The senate has blue shades of sky and sea and a chandelier called Moon. Both chambers feature enormous hanging tapestries by Ruthadell Anderson. Other artwork on the grounds includes *Aquarius,* a mosaic by Tadashi Sato; a statue of Queen Lili`uokalani, invariably clutching a fresh flower; and a controversial statue of Father Damien by Marisol Escobar. Damien was a Catholic priest who contracted leprosy while ministering to victims of the disease on the island of Moloka`i. Escobar portrays Damien as a frail old man, deformed but radiating inner peace.

More art awaits across Richards Street in the *Hawaii State Art Museum* (586–0900), on the second floor of the Number One Capitol District Building. By law, 1 percent of all state construction money goes to fund the state's "art in public places" program; this museum showcases some of the resulting collection. The artwork—360 pieces in a wide range of media and styles—is arranged thematically, with different rooms highlighting aspects of the state's diverse heritage. Tours are offered by reservation. Call 586–9958. Open Tuesday through Saturday 10:00 A.M. to 4:00 P.M. Free.

Farther down Richards, opposite Iolani Palace, stands the 1927 *YWCA Building,* designed in Mediterranean style by Berkeley Arts and Crafts architect Julia Morgan. Popular with the ladies who lunch, *Café Laniakea* (538–7061), inside the courtyard, features fresh local produce on its seafood, salad, and sandwich menu. Open daily 11:00 A.M. to 2:00 P.M. Moderate. Businesspeople congregate in *Cafe VIII 1/2* (524–4064), an Italian eatery 1 block over at 1067 Alakea Street. Open Monday through Friday 11:30 A.M. to 2:00 P.M.

On the other side of the Capitol Building, across Beretania Street, next to the war memorial, stands *Washington Place* (586–0248), until recently the governor's home. John Dominis died at sea soon after building this home for his family. The building's name arose when his widow rented rooms to the U.S. commissioner. Her son inherited the house and lived there with his wife, Lydia Kapaakea, until she ascended to the throne as Queen Lili`uokalani. Later the deposed and widowed queen moved back across the street from Iolani Palace and lived there until she died in 1917. The current governor, Linda Lingle, has moved into a house next door, and Hawaii's "White House" has been converted to a state museum; open by reservation Monday through Friday.

Walk next door from Washington Place to Episcopalian *St. Andrew's Cathedral,* founded by Kamehameha IV and Queen Emma, both ardent Anglophiles. Continue along Beretania to reach the last of Honolulu's Big Three churches. Completed in 1843, *Our Lady of Peace* is the oldest Catholic cathedral in the United States. It doesn't look like much from the outside, but the interior has beautiful gilded ceiling panels, statuary, and stained glass. Our Lady stands in front of the top end of Fort Street Mall; ethnic eateries of all stripes line this pedestrian arcade and surrounding alleyways along Bishop Street. Try *Ba-Le* (521–4117) for freshly made Eurasian sandwiches or green papaya salad; the name of this Vietnamese chain means "Paris."

One block past Fort Street you'll find Bethel Street, home to two historic theater venues. The *Hawaii Theatre* (528–5535; www.hawaiitheatre.com), on the corner of Pauahi, has been renovated to its original 1922 splendor, lavish with murals and gilding. Ask about the Hawaiian Friday Night concert series.

Tours are offered at 11:00 A.M. on Tuesday for $5.00. Farther down, on the corner of Merchant Street, the ***Kumu Kahua Theatre*** (536–4441) performs in more modest digs in the old Kamehameha V Post Office Building. The theater is known for staging contemporary works dealing with local themes. While here, take a peek inside the ***Walter Murray Gibson Building*** diagonally opposite. One of the most colorful personalities in Hawaiian history, Gibson came to the islands as a Mormon pioneer on Lana`i. Excommunicated, he entered politics as a Hawaiian populist, rising to power as Kalakaua's "minister for everything" before losing out to the opposing missionary-sugar-growers' faction. This building is the only reminder of his brief but dazzling career. Its patterned tile interior looks more like a hotel lobby than the former police station it was.

Moving from the dramatic to the visual arts, the next two streets harbor the galleries of a pair of noteworthy Honolulu artists. ***Pegge Hopper*** (524–1160) has made a name for herself with stylized paintings of giant lounging Polynesian women. Her gallery is located at 1164 Nuuanu Avenue. Open Tuesday through Friday 11:00 A.M. to 4:00 P.M. and Saturday 11:00 A.M. to 3:00 P.M. On the way there, you might stop in at ***Lai Fong*** (781–8140), at 1118 Nuuanu. It's a kind of Chinese department store full of imported fabrics, Chinese antiques, and crafts. Lai Fong came to Hawaii as a picture bride and got her start as a seamstress. You can still order tailor-made clothing here. The office is open Monday, Wednesday, and Friday 11:30 A.M. to 4:30 P.M. and Saturday 7:30 A.M. to 3:30 P.M.

One block farther, ***Ramsay Museum*** (537–2787), at 1128 Smith Street, bears another locally prominent name. Ramsay's beautifully rendered pen-and-ink drawings are no longer for sale here except as limited-edition reproductions, although an extensive collection awaits viewing upstairs. It makes something of a statement for historic preservation to realize that many of the subjects of her drawings no longer exist. The museum is housed in the historic 1926 Tan Sing building. Hours are Monday through Friday 10:00 A.M. to 5:00 P.M. and Saturday 10:00 A.M. to 4:00 P.M. Basement space is occupied by Ramsay's dermatologist husband (read: "bankroll"). You might poke your head inside to view the Hawaiiana woodblock prints by Dietrich Varez in the stairwell. The doctor's office is open Monday and Friday 7:30 A.M. to 4:30 P.M. and Saturday 7:30 A.M. to noon.

Ramsay's and Pegge's success has inspired a new crop of galleries to open downtown. ***Mark's Garage*** (521–2903), at 1159 Nuuanu Avenue, is a cooperative effort run by local artist organizations. Open Tuesday through Saturday 11:00 A.M. to 6:00 P.M. The gallery publishes a free walking tour brochure that will guide you to other downtown galleries. Most of these galleries stay open late on the first Friday of each month, as local art mavens gather for evening receptions, refreshments, and live street entertainment from 5:00 to 9:00 P.M.

For those who like a beer with their art, **Hank's Cafe** (526–1410) beckons at 1038 Nuuanu Avenue. Owner Hank Taufaasau hangs his own paintings, as well as those of others, on the walls of this cozy tavern. Most people come here for the live music nightly. Open daily 1:30 P.M. to closing. And if you want food with your beer, **Indigo's** (521–2900), at Nuuanu, boasts an intriguing Eurasian menu and decor. Moderate prices. Pegge Hopper paintings inside portray the five Chinese elements. There's even nicer seating in the garden out back. The best bets on the menu are the starters. Open Tuesday through Friday 11:30 A.M. to 2:00 P.M. and Tuesday through Saturday 6:00 to 9:30 P.M. The bar is also a popular gathering spot, open until 2:00 A.M. Tuesday through Saturday, with free happy-hour hors d'oeuvres on weekdays.

If you're here for lunch, pop inside **Krung Thai** (599–4803), at 1028 Nuuanu, and choose from a selection of spicy Thai entrees; then carry your goodies out to the back to dine in the garden court. Open Monday through Friday 10:30 A.M. to 2:30 P.M. Or for gourmet renditions of classic diner comfort food, visit **Grand Café & Bakery** (531–0001) at 31 North Pauahi. Open Tuesday through Friday 7:00 A.M. to 1:30 P.M., and Saturday and Sunday 8:00 A.M. to 1:00 P.M.

To see a different kind of artistry, pause to smell the flowers at the lei stands on Beretania Street between Smith and Maunakea Streets, with others on Maunakea itself. The stringers work right in the store, and the variety of colors and textures is staggering. Some have strong fragrances such as *pikake* (jasmine). Others, such as woven *haku lei* (worn on the head), retain their beauty after drying. Choose one for yourself to enjoy all day. Prices range from about $3.00 into the hundreds.

By now you've reached the border of **Chinatown.** This part of downtown developed later than the other two. Sugar plantations began to import Chinese laborers in 1852, but as soon as their contracts expired, the Chinese fled the fields to open shops and small businesses in town. Chinatown soon became a hotbed of gambling, opium dens, and brothels. The Chinatown underground literally ran underground. As developers remodel the buildings here, they keep finding tunnels. Old-timers even whisper of secret trapdoors used to shanghai unwary sailors. The Honolulu detective Chang Apana prowled this turf, inspiring his fictionalized alter ego, Charlie Chan.

This crowded enclave of wooden shops and homes burned to the ground twice. The second blaze in 1900 started when the Board of Health torched homes contaminated with the bubonic plague, and the fire spread. The Chinese suspected a haole conspiracy to drive them out. During World War II the rebuilt district became a GI vice center. Chinatown today thrives as a magnet for immigrants from everywhere throughout Asia. Its mysteries unfold like layers of a fortune cookie.

The Chinese Chamber of Commerce (533–3181) and Hawaii Heritage Center (521–2749) both offer morning walking tours of Chinatown; the chamber on Monday and Tuesday, and the center on Wednesday and Friday; both cost $10. Call ahead for reservations.

For a gastronomic take on the same territory, Tony Chang, a former state senator, leads culinary tours of Chinatown. Learn where to go for the plumpest duck, the tastiest noodle, or the most authentic dim sum, as you soak in local history and gossip. The tour meets every Monday at 9:30 A.M. at the Chinese Chamber of Commerce, 42 North King Street (upstairs). Cost is $10 per person. Call 533–3181 for information.

It can be just as much fun to poke around on your own. Walk down Maunakea to the corner of Hotel Street. This is the center of Chinatown, where the lion dancers prance during the Chinese New Year. Hotel Street is also Honolulu's principal red-light strip, flush with peep shows and porn shops on adjacent blocks. With its ornate pagoda roof, **Wo Fat,** Hawaii's oldest restaurant, keeps a benevolent watch over the comings and goings at the corner from its second-story perch. A pan-Asian galaxy of eating possibilities lurk within the food court of **Maunakea Marketplace** on the opposite corner. A statue of Confucius presides over the courtyard. Farther up Maunakea Street on the corner of Pauahi, a neo-Thai restaurant, **Sweet Basil,** has both lunch and evening buffets. Open for lunch Monday through Saturday 10:30 A.M. to 2:00 P.M. and for dinner Friday and Saturday 5:00 to 9:00 P.M. Inexpensive. **Duc's Bistro** (531–6325), an elegant French-Vietnamese restaurant, is a few doors down. Duc's is open for lunch Monday through Friday 11:30 A.M. to 2:00 P.M. and for dinner Monday through Saturday 5:00 to 10:00 P.M. Live music on Tuesday, Thursday, Friday, and Saturday evenings. Expensive. If it's *pho* you're looking for, follow the faithful to **To Chau** (533–4549), 2 blocks down King Street at the corner of River Street. The lunchtime lines out the door testify to the superiority of the steaming Vietnamese noodle-broth ladled out in this bare-bones diner. Open 8:30 A.M. to 2:30 P.M.

For those in a Chinese frame of mind, **Won Kee** (524–6877) and **Legend Seafood Restaurant** (532–1868), in the Chinatown Cultural Plaza farther up River Street, each have their following. Both are open daily for lunch and dinner. (Legend also has a vegetarian twin next door—a gesture of filial piety for the owner's Buddhist mom.) For the best dim sum in Chinatown, hit **Mei Sum** (531–3268), at 65 North Pauahi Street (at the corner of Smith), where you can devour these Hong Kong–style delicacies by the cartload. Open daily 7:00 A.M.

to 9:00 P.M. Across Nuuanu Street from Mei Sum, *Hasr Wine Company* (535–WINE; www.hasrwineco.com) reflects Honolulu's dual East-West personalities, combining fine California wines from one-of-a-kind case lots with an extensive sake collection. Wine tastings are offered Tuesday and Friday from 5:00 to 7:00 P.M. Strolling slightly farther down on Nuuanu toward downtown is *Island Keepsakes* (550–0996), a Hawaiian specialty shop that features many local-artist creations. Open Monday through Friday from 10:00 A.M. to 4:00 P.M. and on Saturday from 10:00 A.M. to 2:00 P.M. Delicious Chinese food can be found at *Little Village Noodle House* (545–3008), on Smith Street. This inexpensive to moderately priced restaurant is tastefully decorated with bamboo fences and flying butterflies.

A potpourri of vintage Chinatown shops lines the rest of Maunakea Street. The buildings here mostly date from the two decades following the 1900 fire. You'll find acupuncture clinics, martial arts studios, Asian groceries and importers, watch repair shops, and tattoo parlors. Much of the action is out in the streets themselves. People of all ages scurry about on dubious missions. You'll hear bantering in a dozen Asian dialects.

Stop inside *Shung Chong Yuein* (531–1983), a cheery Chinese bakery at 1027 Maunakea, to munch on almond cookies or *manapua,* a local version of dim sum. Around the corner on King Street, you can balance your yin and yang with an herbal prescription from *Fook Sau Tong* (531–6680). The rows of shelved jars and wooden drawers bear mysterious labels in Chinese characters and emit intriguing smells.

Lower Maunakea has a string of antiques shops that offer a dragon's lair of hoarded treasure, including Niihau shells, samurai swords, Tibetan bronze, vintage aloha shirts, and much more.

Continuing your exploring on King Street, heading away from the capitol, you'll pass the open-air *O`ahu Market,* where vendors display food products such as pig snouts, quail eggs, and lotus roots. You can sample all sorts of exotic fruits you may not have seen before. Open daily until 2:30 P.M.

A block farther on King Street brings you to Nuuano Stream, flanked by River Street. Farther up River Street, across Beretania, a statue of Chinese nationalist leader Sun Yat-sen greets you. Sun got his education here in Honolulu and helped launch his revolution with funds raised from Hawaii's Chinese community. The Filipino community has placed a statue of its own hero, Jose Rizal, across the bridge. Listen to the click-clack of mah-jongg played by old men at the pavilion tables.

Behind Sun stands the Chinese Cultural Plaza, a charmless concrete complex. Inside, you can buy Chinese-language magazines from *Dragon Gate Bookstore.* A smattering of English-language works on Chinese folklore are also on sale. The Asian Mall and upstairs Sun Yat-sen Hall display vintage photos, including some "class portraits" of Sun and his émigré cohorts plotting their revolution. Here you will also find the **Hawaiian Chinese Multicultural Museum**. It's a one-man show run as a retirement project by Owner James G.Y. Ho, a self-taught historian who regales visitors with steady stream of anecdotes about the old plantation days. The museum is more of an interpretive space to learn about the Chinese immigrant experience and other aspects of Hawaiian history than a location to view artifacts. Ninety minute guided walking tours of Chinatown are available upon request for the price of admission. Open Monday through Saturday 10:00 A.M. to 2:00 P.M.; $3.00.

The **Lum Sai Ho Tong** has its headquarters at the corner of River and Kukui Streets. The many tongs in Chinatown served as cultural societies for immigrant clans. If the gate to the stairway is unlocked, you can visit the elaborate Taoist shrine on the second floor. Across the river, the **Izumo Taisha Shrine** houses the *kami*, Okuninushi-No-Mikoto, a universal god of love and happiness. The shrine property was seized during World War II and only returned by court order in 1962. Shinto services usually are held on the tenth day of each month, and members also visit at significant milestones in their lives, such as reaching the ages of three, five, seven, sixty-one, and eighty-eight.

Continue up River Street across Vineyard Boulevard to visit a temple for yet another Eastern religion, Buddhism. The **Kuan Yin Temple** (533–6361) has Western-style walls joined to a traditional Chinese ceramic tile roof. Inside, enormous statues stand behind the altars, the largest of which represents the bodhisattva, Kuan Yin, goddess of mercy. Wei Tor (faith) and Kuan Tai (truth) guard her flanks. You can burn a stick of incense to add to the fumes already present. Some worshipers even burn money. Temple priests and priestesses rattle joss sticks to tell fortunes. Open to visitors daily from 8:30 A.M. to 2:00 P.M.

After all this urban exploration, you can seek refuge in the shady confines of **Foster Botanical Garden** (522–7060), Hawaii's oldest botanical garden. William Hillebrand, physician to the royal court, started the gardens in 1853 with specimens he gathered during his travels in India. Many of the tallest trees date from these first plantings, such as the massive kapok tree that soars more than 160 feet overhead, with a trunk over 20 feet wide. You may recognize kapok floss, which comes from the tree's seed pods, as the filler in life preservers. Other names you've heard but may never have seen in the wood, including allspice, chocolate, cinnamon, nutmeg, vanilla, and chicle, grow in the economic section—extra points if you recognized the last one as the main ingredient of chewing gum.

The park also has some truly bizarre specimens named for fruit resembling cannonballs, sausages, and "dead rats" (the baobab). Some of the rarest plants, such as a Hawaiian *loulu* palm taken from upper Nuuanu Valley, are believed to be extinct in the wild. Tours of the garden are available Monday through Saturday at 1:00 P.M. Call 522–7066 to inquire about weekend events. Foster Botanical Garden is open daily 9:00 A.M. to 4:00 P.M. Admission is $5.00.

If you need a waterfall in your garden to meditate properly, the little-known ***Lili`uokalani Gardens*** lies close at hand. Take Nuuanu Street across the freeway and turn left onto School Street. The second right, a small side street, leads to the banks of Nuuanu Stream. Queen Lili`uokalani used to picnic here, and so can you. Most of the plants here are native species. The garden is open daily from sunrise to sunset.

Ridges and Valleys

Above the city, the ridges of the Ko`olau Mountains reach like fingers toward the sea, with a series of valleys spaced in between. As Honolulu grew, the city pushed inland from the harbor, first into Nuuanu ("cool height") Valley. Hawaiians preferred the mild climate and lush beauty, and the many churches and consulates here seem to echo this view today. As you enter the valley, Asian temples predominate along upper Nuuanu Avenue. Most of these also function as cultural centers. Ironically, some of the only civilian casualties of the Pearl Harbor attack happened when a stray artillery shell exploded in one such Japanese-language school.

First up as you cross the freeway on Nuuanu Avenue is the ***Chinese Buddhist Society*** building on your left. The large meeting hall has a lovely altar in back. A couple of doors farther along is the ***Soto Mission.*** The stylized geometry of this Japanese Zen Buddhist temple reflects the Soto sect's homage to Buddhism's Indian origins.

The ***Myohoji Temple*** comes next on the right, 2 blocks farther at 2003 Nuuanu. It's set back from the street along the banks of Nuuanu Stream, sheltered beneath high-rise condos. As you continue on Nuuanu up a short hill, take a peek left down Judd Street at the traffic light to see what seems to be another Asian temple. In fact, you're looking at ***St. Luke's Episcopal Church.*** Just ahead, turn right onto Craigside Drive to visit ***Honolulu Memorial Park.*** Sloping down the gulley of Nuuanu Stream, this Japanese cemetery enjoys a picturesque setting highlighted by detailed replicas of two famous buildings in Japan. The Sanju Pagoda is an enlarged model of the one in Nara's Minami Hokke-ji Temple. A winding garden path leads to a replica of the Kyoto

1. Thomas Square
2. Academy of Arts
3. Foster Botanical Garden
4. Queen Emma's Summer Palace
5. National Memorial Cemetery
   of the Pacific
6. Tennent Gallery
7. Hawaii Nature Center
8. Contemporary Museum
9. Puu Ualakaa State Park
10. Lyon Arboretum
11. Waioli Tea Room
12. Manoa Valley Inn
13. Manoa (AYH) Hostel
14. Dae Won Sa Temple
15. Fish Auction
16. Ala Moana Beach Park
17. Royal Hawaiian Hotel
18. Army Museum
19. Sheraton Moana Surfrider
20. Waikiki Aquarium
21. Hale Aloha Hostel
22. Damien Museum
23. Diamond Head lookouts and beach
24. Bailey's Antique & Aloha Shirts
25. Shangri-La

See also Downtown Honolulu
map detail on pages 54–55

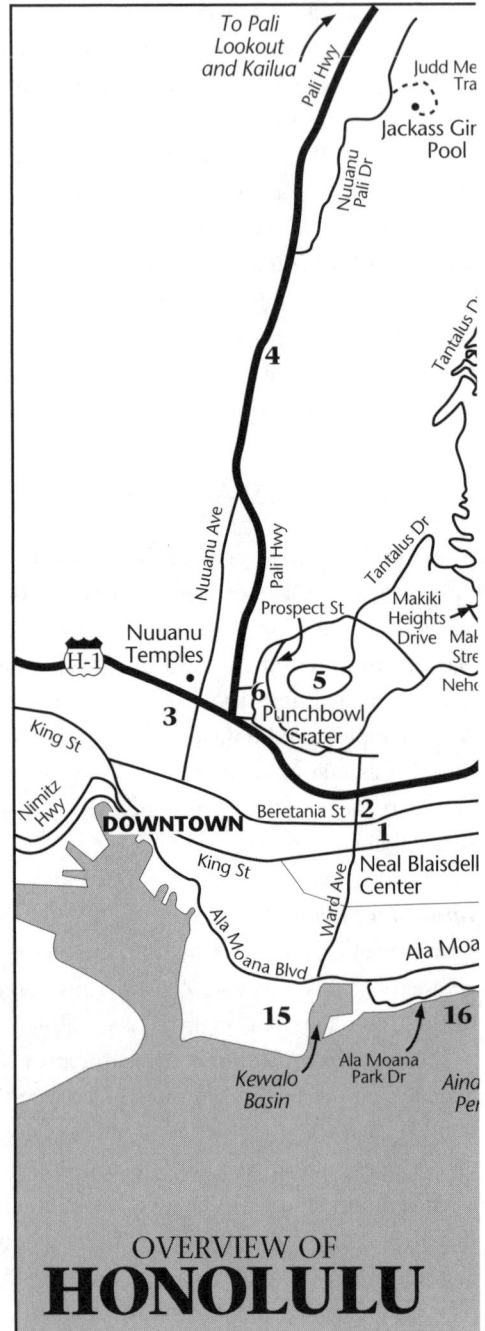

OVERVIEW OF
HONOLULU

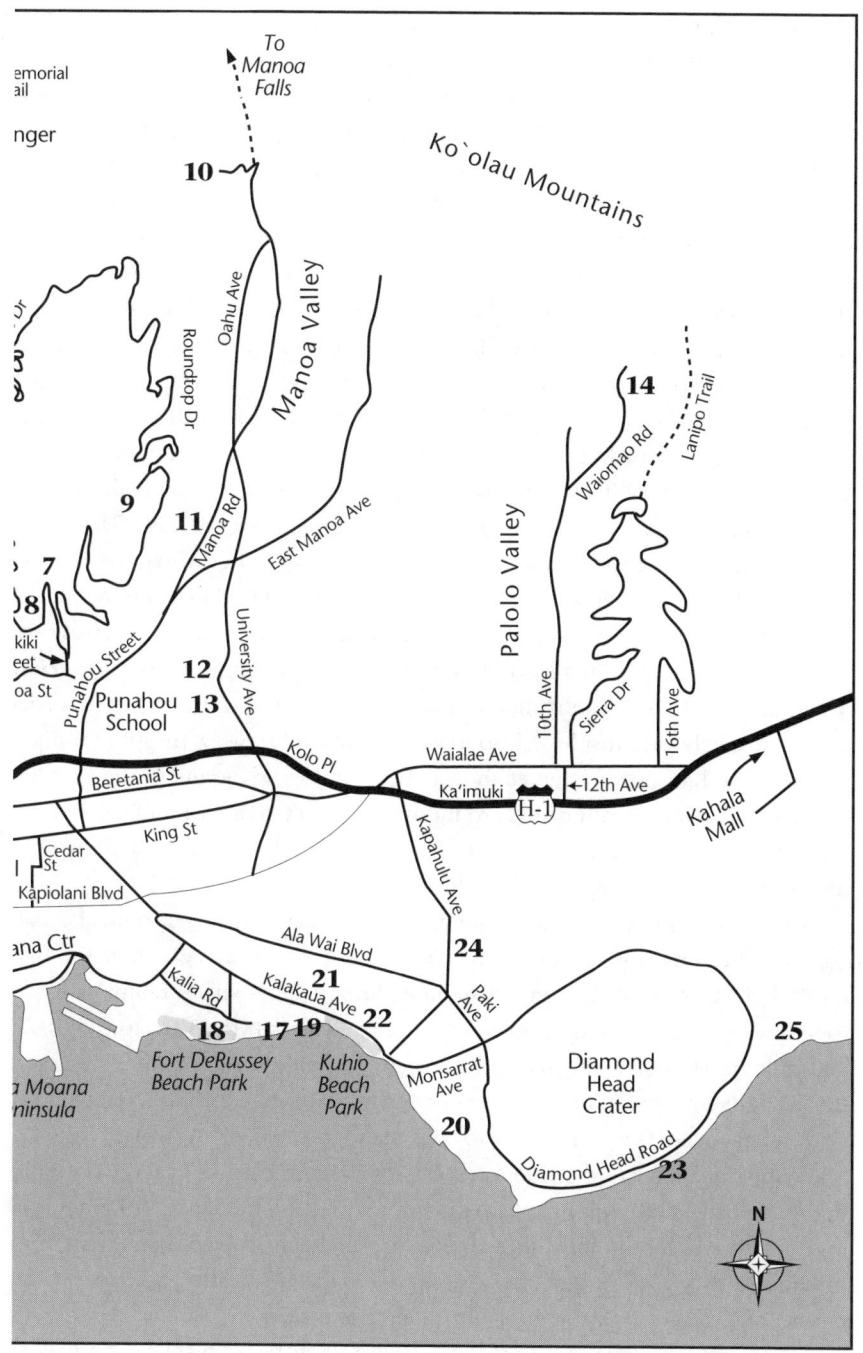

Kinkaku-ji ("golden pavilion"). Note the phoenix on the roof, a symbol of immortality. Both buildings serve as columbariums for cremated remains.

Just uphill on the left side, the Ten Ri Kyo faith (an offshoot of Buddhism) maintains a small shrine within a charming Japanese garden. On the right-hand side, turn through wrought-iron gates into the **Royal Mausoleum** (587–0300). Completed in 1865 as the burial ground for Hawaii's royalty, the mausoleum chapel takes the shape of a Greek cross. Remains from earlier royal graves were transferred here, except for those of Kamehameha I, whose burial place remains a secret as was the old Hawaiian custom. The chapel did not hold all the caskets, and they were moved into underground crypts. Three trusted haole advisers also occupy places of honor here. John Young helped train Kamehameha I's army; Robert Wylie served as Kamehameha III's foreign minister; and Charles Bishop founded Bishop Estate, which remains the state's largest landowner. William Maioho, the curator, is a descendant of the chiefly line that has guarded the Kamehameha family bones since antiquity. He is usually on hand during the week to show visitors around, but it may be a good idea to call first. The mausoleum is open Monday through Friday and Memorial Day, 8:00 A.M. to 4:00 P.M. Guided tours are available with advance reservations.

Turn left onto Kawananako Place to see the final temple of the strip, **Hsu Yun Temple.** This one is Chinese Buddhist and has bolder colors than its Japanese neighbors. Inside, its double-sided altar glistens with gold-trimmed grillwork, and incense perfumes the air. You can follow the life of the Buddha through illustrated serial posters around the room. Two other buildings behind the temple house cremation urns stacked in crowded rows of bleachers. Full-time monks live next door, praying for earthly peace.

From the end of Nuuanu Avenue, take the overpass to get onto the Pali Highway heading toward Kailua. About a mile along, turn right after the first traffic light to **Queen Emma's Summer Palace** (595–3167). Emma's uncle, John Young II, erected the house, which arrived prefab from Boston in 1847, and called it Hanaiakamalama ("adopted child of moonlight"). Emma inherited the property and spent a lot of time here with her husband, King Kamehameha IV. Feather *kahilis,* emblematic of royalty, stand in every room. Woven *lauhala* (pandanus) mats cover the floors, except for Western carpets in the Edinburgh Room, an extension built in anticipation of a visit from the Duke of Edinburgh. The building lacks the imposing appearance of Iolani Palace, but a visit here provides a much more personal experience. Docents guide you around the palace, and almost every item of furnishing has a story.

A rare feather cape that Kamehameha I won in battle displays the yellow feathers of the now-extinct `o`o `a`a bird. A tiger-claw necklace from an Indian maharaja and a lithograph of Napoleon III number among the many gifts from monarchs around the world. Notice the tiny red jacket that belonged to Prince Albert. Like many little boys, the royal heir wanted to be a fireman when he grew up, so Honolulu firefighters made him a miniature uniform.

Despite these tokens of happy times, a sense of tragedy pervades the house. Prince Albert, the only child ever born to Hawaiian royalty after Kamehamaha I, took sick and died at the age of four in 1862. A silver christening cup and holy water sent by Britain's Queen Victoria, who had agreed to be the child's godmother, arrived only hours after his death. Albert's father, the king, blamed himself for his son's death and shut himself in the Summer Palace for almost fifteen months of mourning before dying of what the community called a broken heart.

Faced with a double bereavement and a house full of painful memories, Emma took to traveling and social work. She auctioned off much of the home's furniture to help fund the Queen's Hospital, which she and her husband had founded. Later the house itself was scheduled to be torn down and the grounds converted into a ballpark, but the Daughters of Hawaii intervened. They restored the palace and recovered much of the original contents, and now operate it as a museum. The palace welcomes visitors daily 9:00 A.M. to 4:00 P.M.; $6.00 admission fee.

A trio of Asian temples flanks the Summer Palace. The most interesting of the three, the Shinto shrine of **Daijingu,** sits behind the palace on Paiwa Road. Stone lions guard the entrance, and offerings of hundred-pound rice bags and three-gallon jugs of soy sauce rest before the altar.

About a half mile from the Summer Palace, turn right onto Nuuanu Pali Drive for a scenic detour. The road winds through 2 miles of lush rain forest and bamboo thickets. Halfway along, following a sharp bend in the road, look for a turnoff into a small forest clearing. (You'll recognize it by the litter.) The **Judd Memorial Trail** begins here, an easy 1.3-mile loop that leads to a grove of Norfolk pines named for an early forest ranger. Locals come here to mudslide down the hill slopes on plastic bags, large pieces of cardboard, or ti leaves (the old Hawaiian way); you can wash off in Jackass Ginger, a naturally formed pool reached by taking the right fork of the trail immediately across Nuuanu Stream. Nuuanu Pali Drive continues past a grassy embankment, where kids fish for crayfish in the stream pools, before rejoining the Pali Highway.

As you continue through rain forest on the highway, glance up at the steep walls of the valley above you. Waterfall paths scar the green cliff faces; if it has been raining, the walls sparkle with rivulets. A mile farther, take the turnoff to the **Pali Lookout** for a magnificent view of O'ahu's windward coast. From this cliff-top perch you see at once the dramatic contrast between the two sides of the Ko'olau Range. The gentle ridges and valleys that slope upward from the "town" side terminate here in an unbroken wall of *pali* (cliffs). Rising vertically as high as 3,000 feet, these Ko`olau cliffs tower above the bowl-shaped coastal plains below. Their wind-eroded faces are cloaked in greenery, moistened by a misty crown of rain clouds that the trade winds deposit on their peaks. At just less than 1,200 feet, the Nuuanu Pali represents a low point in the chain; jagged spires on either side of the pass rise 1,000 feet above. Winds funneling through the pass often reach gale force, so hold onto your hat and tether small children securely (just kidding).

The view below encompasses the sweep of Kaneohe Bay, the largest in the state. Below the lookout, the Pali Highway emerges from tunnels to descend to Kailua, the next bay off to the right. Part of the original Pali Highway follows an ancient Hawaiian pathway from the lookout itself. You can walk along this abandoned road to enjoy the view in solitude.

Kamehameha's conquest of the islands reached its terrifying conclusion in 1795 at this very spot. His army had routed a combined opposition of O`ahu and Maui chieftains and driven them up Nuuanu Valley. Many of the defeated warriors leaped over the cliffs to avoid capture. More than 800 skulls have been found at the bottom.

The windward coast is described in a later section; for now, let's stay in town. To the right (east) of Nuuanu Valley, the green volcanic form of Punchbowl Crater rising above downtown Honolulu makes a striking land-mark, whose English name makes obvious visual sense. Hardened ash ejected during violent steam explosions formed this tuff cone in less than a day. *Puu o Waina,* its original Hawaiian name, translates to "hill of sacrifice," an ironi-cally appropriate epithet for the **National Memorial Cemetery of the Pacific** (532–3720) inside. Ernie Pyle, the famous World War II correspondent who covered one battle too many, and Ellison Onizuka, a Hawaiian-born astronaut who died in the *Challenger* crash, lie entombed here along with countless oth-ers. You enter from the mountain side on Puowaina Drive. Volunteers from the American Legion sometimes offer walking tours of the cemetery on weekdays. Call 946–6383 to inquire. Open daily from 8:00 A.M. to 6:30 P.M., closing an hour earlier from September 30 through March 1.

Art lovers may want to stop on the way to the cemetery at the **Tennent Gallery** (531–1987), at 203 Prospect Street. Take Ward Avenue to Prospect, bear right as it curves around Punchbowl, and look for the warrior marker. Madge Tennent was a child prodigy born in England, trained at a French acad-emy, and appointed director of a government art school in South Africa at age sixteen. A self-portrait at age twenty-one exhibited in the gallery reveals aston-ishing depth of character. En route from Samoa to England in 1923, she and her Kiwi husband stopped in Honolulu and decided to stay. Madge fell in love with the Polynesian people and began to paint them in a style influenced by Gauguin, but she found her own idiom in her colorful portraits of large-bodied Hawaiian women. The gallery is housed in a 1954 building designed by noted island architect Vlad Ossipoff. Open Tuesday through Saturday 10:00 A.M. to noon and Sunday 2:00 to 4:00 P.M. Donation. Tennent originals can be found for sale at the **Cedar Street Gallery** (589–1580; www.cedarstreetgalleries.com), at 817 Cedar. It features artwork by an impressive roster of more than one hundred island artists in a midtown location off King Street. Open Tuesday, Wednesday, and Saturday 10:00 A.M. to 4:00 P.M. and Monday, Thursday, and Friday to 5:30 P.M.

The various ridges above Honolulu have dense housing tracts whose twinkling lights at night reflect the star-filled sky. Most have scenic drives, the oldest and nicest of which is the Tantalus/Roundtop loop, inland and east of Punchbowl. Take Punahou Street off King past the cactus-covered walls of missionary-founded Punahou School. Turn left onto Nehoa Street at the light and then right 2 blocks up Makiki Street, which takes you to the start of the loop. Bear left onto Makiki Heights Drive. Just ahead at the hairpin bend, outdoors enthusiasts can stop in at the **Hawaii Nature Center** (955–0100; www.hawaiinaturecenter.org) to get island trail maps as well as advice on the network of trails that crisscross the ridges. Two of the trails begin right behind the center. Open daily 8:30 A.M. to 4:30 P.M. The center also conducts hikes and interpretive activities around the island on weekends for a small fee. Call to reserve a spot.

For more civilized pleasures, continue up the road to the **Contemporary Museum** (526–1322; www.tcmhi.org). The museum occupies the elegant 1925 designer home of the three-acre Cook-Spalding Estate. Creative remodeling allows the museum to display its rotating art exhibits in unique multilevel galleries. The museum also has a small permanent collection that includes a colorfully robust environmental installation by David Hockney that re-creates his opera design for Ravel's *L'Enfant et les Sortilèges*. Guided tours are offered at 1:30 P.M. The soothing, Japanese-inspired gardens outside are adorned by sculpture. The museum also has a pleasant outdoor cafe serving moderately priced lunches from 11:30 A.M. to 2:30 P.M. Open Tuesday through Saturday 10:00 A.M. to 4:00 P.M. and Sunday noon to 2:30 P.M. Admission $5.00.

Makiki Heights Drive runs into Tantalus Drive, which takes you to the top of the loop. The road passes more elegant homes (one of which was the residence-in-exile for Ferdinand and Imelda Marcos) spaced between amazing rain-forest growths of bamboo, ferns, and philodendron creepers. Roll down your window to inhale the smell of ginger and *pikake* (jasmine) flowers. With every bend in the road, you get treated to another breathtaking view of Honolulu.

Tantalus Drive climbs to 2,000 feet and then loops back as Roundtop Drive on the other side of the ridge, providing new viewing angles to contemplate. Halfway down, take the turnoff to *Pu`u Ualakaa State Park* and walk out onto the lookout platform at the lower parking lot. Be sure to bring your wide-angle camera lens because all of Honolulu spreads out below your feet.

Next up comes Manoa ("vast") Valley, an enormous clearing famous for its "Manoa mist," whereby the sun shines through a veil of mistlike rain and forms intense rainbows. This time take Punahou Street to its end and bear left onto Manoa Road.

Follow this tree-lined drive just less than a mile into the valley, and on your left you'll see the entrance to the *Waioli Tea Room* (988–5800), at 2950 Manoa Road. The restaurant here dates from the 1920s; photos from the tea-room's past hang alongside portraits of Hawaiian royalty. Grab a table in the open-air lanai and enjoy light cafe fare while admiring the lushly tropical garden. High tea is also served daily for those who reserve ahead. The service features house-baked breads in tropical flavors such as mango, lilikoi, and taro. Inexpensive to moderate. Another attraction on the property is the *Robert Louis Stevenson Grass Shack,* brought here from Waikiki, in which the author penned some of his famous works.

Continue on Manoa to *Lyon Arboretum* (988–0456) at the back of Manoa Valley. Harold Lyon was a sugar botanist in the 1920s. He belonged to an elite team of roving naturalists who traveled the world, paddling upriver through Malaysian jungle and scaling South American peaks in a never-ending search for specimens of interest or value to the Hawaiian sugar industry. He introduced several thousand new plant species to the islands, many of which you can see today growing in a seminatural state on the 194-acre grounds of the arboretum.

A Hawaiian garden displays the trees and plants used in ancient times. They are grouped according to usage: Foods include mountain apples and breadfruit; clothing came from *wauke* (a mulberry) bark; musical instruments could be a gourd or bamboo rattle; building materials ranged from vines to trees; medicines came from almost anything. You can see how limited the original flora of the islands was, but the Hawaiians found ingenious uses for almost everything. Open Monday through Friday 9:00 A.M. to 4:00 P.M. Donation. The arboretum also offers regular tours as well as other interpretive activities and classes. Call for a schedule.

Just ahead, the road ends at the trailhead to *Manoa Falls.* Although often muddy, this popular trail offers a delightful stroll through rain-forest jungle, some of which was planted by the arboretum. Look for mountain apples and guava along the way and expect mosquitoes. The veil-like ribbon of the 100-

foot waterfall spills into a shallow pool less than a mile up the canyon. It takes about forty-five minutes going up. Just before you reach the falls, the Aihualama Trail branches off to the left to connect with the Tantalus trail system. The first part of the trail offers a good view across Manoa Valley.

Inside the Manoa Shopping Center is ***Hanaki's Japanese Buffet*** (988–1551). This buffet features sushi and tempura stations as well as unusual Japanese fare that changes nightly. Reservations are recommended. Open daily 11:00 A.M. to 2:00 P.M. and 5:00 to 9:00 P.M. Expensive.

On your way out of the valley, take the left fork onto O'ahu Avenue, which turns into University Avenue and bends sharply left as it approaches the University of Hawaii's Manoa campus; a trio of art galleries here is worth noting. The Art Department displays rotating exhibits in its two ***art galleries*** (956–6888). Open Monday through Friday 10:30 A.M. to 4:00 P.M. and Sunday noon to 4:00 P.M. from late August to mid-May. Nearby Kraus Hall harbors the ***John Young Museum*** (956–7198), a collection of Asian-Pacific works, mostly donated by noted island painter John Young. Open weekdays from 11:00 A.M. to 2:00 P.M. and Sunday from 1:00 to 4:00 P.M. Built in 1931, Kraus Hall holds historical interest as the former site of the Pineapple Institute, which did much to establish this iconic crop in the islands. Finally, the ***East-West Center*** (944–7177) has its own rotating Pacific Rim exhibits at the corner of Dole Street and East-West Drive. Open Monday through Friday 8:00 A.M. to 5:00 P.M. and Sunday noon to 4:00 P.M. All three are free. The main East-West Center building farther up the drive (on the right just after the guard post) has a pleasant Japanese garden and koi pond in back; a colorful Korean building waits just up the road. Kennedy Theater (956–7655), the concrete cube across the street, stages some culturally adventurous performances worth checking out.

Just off University Avenue heading away from campus, O'ahu's most intimate luxury accommodation, the ***Manoa Valley Inn*** (947–6019; www .manoavalleyinn.com), awaits on Vancouver Drive. This three-story mansion bristles with gables and buttressed eaves. Built in 1919 by businessman John Guild and now on the National Register of Historic

Manoa Valley Inn

Buildings, the home was refurbished by Crazy Shirts owner Rick Ralston with nostalgic touches, from patterned wallpaper to brass fixtures. Many of the antique furnishings come from Ralston's personal collection. All the necessary ingredients for gentle living are supplied in this self-styled country inn: croquet and billiards, a veranda facing a shady yard, wine, daily newspapers, and fresh-cut flowers. Rooms range from $99 to $190, continental breakfast included. A block seaward of the inn on Seaview Avenue, you can obtain far more modest lodging at Hosteling International's *Manoa Hostel* (946–0591; www.hostels aloha.com). $16 per night.

Waialae Avenue, the continuation of King Street, leads past other ridges and valleys of interest. Palolo Valley hides a startling sight in its rear canyon, the *Dae Won Sa Temple.* Take Tenth Avenue deep into the valley and bear right onto Waiomao Road. You'll see the gaudy colors of the temple's pagoda rooftops before you get there. Hawaii's first Korean Buddhist temple is a massive complex. Fierce larger-than-life statues of "Buddha's guards" secure the entrance to the three temple buildings. The oldest one, on the right, displays the most authentic architecture. Inside, bleacher rows of golden miniature Buddhas surround a central altarpiece. The entire building swims with colors and textures that make the mind boggle. Flower children might appreciate the equally colorful *Kawamoto Orchid Nursery* (732–5808), just around the bend at 2630 Waiomao Road; open Monday through Saturday from 8:00 A.M. to 3:30 P.M.

The next ridge is Maunalani Heights. Take Wilhemina Rise to Maunalani Circle to reach the trailhead for *Lanipo.* This is the best of the many ridge hikes leading up to a Ko`olau *pali* overlook. You pass through a variety of vegetation, including seasonal strawberry guavas, and are afforded great views into the surrounding valleys; the thin ribbon of civilization along the coast recedes with every mile into virgin forest. Three miles along you reach a staggering panorama of the windward coast, 2,500 feet below. The hike is strenuous and takes at least three hours going up. Make sure it's clear up top before setting out; otherwise, your only view will be of your hands groping through the mist.

Waikiki and Thereabouts

Waikiki is like a concrete castle guarded by a less-than-shimmering moat. It's a giant tourist mill, cut off from reality and quarantined lest it contaminate the rest of Honolulu. Yet Waikiki has its own perverse charm in spite of its monumental tackiness and congestion. Long before the first tourists arrived, Hawaii's royalty luxuriated on the golden crescent of Waikiki Beach and surfed its endlessly rolling breakers, with the regal profile of Diamond Head Crater rising in the distance. As the birthplace of Hawaiian tourism, Waikiki has an added nostalgia lacking in other island resorts. While today's clamorous crowds may detract from the beach's beauty and the high-rise hotels block each other's views, Waikiki remains a world-class resort destination that has recently undergone a multimillion-dollar makeover. You may not like it, but you owe yourself a look.

In days gone by, most of Waikiki inland of the beach was a productive wetland with fifty-one acres of fishponds surrounded by taro and rice paddies. The word *waikiki* means "spouting waters." Beachgoers increasingly complained about the swarming mosquitoes bred in "the swamp," and in 1922 the Ala Wai Canal drained the land, allowing Hawaii's first destination resort to be born. Emerging from the primordial slime, greedy developers soon raised a bumper crop of architectural hideousness. The main one-way thoroughfares are Kalakaua Avenue, heading toward Diamond Head past the beach hotels, and Ala Wai Boulevard, running toward Ala Moana along the canal, where outrigger canoe teams practice.

When local people go to the beach in town, they usually head for Ala Moana Beach Park, just west of Waikiki. *Aina Moana* (better known as Magic Island), an artificial peninsula at the Waikiki end of the park, offers great views and protected swimming. Come here at sundown to watch Friday evening sailboat races at the adjacent Ala Wai Yacht Club. On the other side of the beach park lies Kewalo Basin, home port for many of the island's commercial fishermen. You can check out their catch (and bid on it) at the morning fish auction that takes place Monday through Saturday at 117 Ahui Street, on the downtown side of the basin docks. The ocean's colorful bounty—from half-pound snappers to 500-pound swordfish—is laid out on ice-packed pallets for dealers to inspect, and it's then auctioned off fish by fish from 5:30 A.M. onward. Wear closed shoes.

Crossing the bridge over the Ala Wai Canal and harbor, Ala Moana Boulevard enters Waikiki itself. The road curves as it passes the Hilton Hawaiian Village, which now hosts a satellite branch of the ***Bishop Museum*** (947-2458) in the ground floor of the Kalia Tower. Turn right onto Kalia Road to enter. Displays of cultural artifacts and exhibits focus on village life in Waikiki of old and recount the history of the Hawaiian pineapple. Native plants grow in the gardens outside, with descriptions of their traditional uses. Open daily from 10:00 A.M. to 5:00 P.M.; $7.00 admission fee.

Make a right on Kalia Road after the road curves past the Hilton Hawaiian Village and stop at ***Fort Derussey Beach Park,*** one of the two public areas bordering Waikiki Beach. Southern Californians at heart can find pickup games of two-person beach volleyball here. Actor Tom Selleck used to play almost every Sunday while filming the TV series *Magnum P.I.* The ***U.S. Army***

Museum (438–2821) next to the park bristles with weaponry of varying ages and has some realistic Vietnam-style dioramas for Rambo types wanting to experience ersatz jungle combat. Open Tuesday through Sunday 10:00 A.M. to 4:15 P.M. Free.

Saratoga Road leads from the museum back inland to Kalakaua Avenue. On Wednesday and Friday between 10:00 A.M. and noon, you can visit the *Urasenke Foundation* (923–3059), at 245 Saratoga Road, to watch a ritual performance of the *cha-no-yu,* the ancient Japanese tea ceremony. $3.00 donation. Reservations required. Around the bend from Urasenke on Kalakaua sprawls the massive *Royal Hawaiian Shopping Center* (922–0588), which offers free lessons in hula and Hawaiian crafts on weekday mornings. If you shop here, visit the *Little Hawaiian Craft Shop* (926–2662), on the third floor of Building B. Unlike other Waikiki souvenir shops that sell plastic, made-in-the-Philippines tchotchkes, this one has the real stuff, from Niihau shell leis to handmade feather work. The shop thrived for years in Pearl Ridge Shopping Center before moving to Waikiki, so you know they don't sell only to tourists. Prices aren't low, but the selection can't be beat. Open daily 9:30 A.M. to 10:00 P.M. Another place to cast an eye is the *Ukulele House* (923–8587), in Building A. You'll find everything you need to learn to strum sweet sounds from these "jumping fleas" of island music. Open daily 10:00 A.M. to 10:00 P.M.

Threaded between the A and B buildings of the shopping center, Royal Hawaiian Avenue ushers the faithful to the vintage hotel of the same name. It's worth making the pilgrimage to the *Royal Hawaiian Hotel* (923–7311; 866–500–8313; 2259 Kalakaua Avenue) to bask in the lingering romance of old Waikiki. Built in 1927 as the glamour destination Matson needed to attract passengers on its luxury liners, the "Pink Palace" welcomed an endless stream of Hollywood stars. Its Valentino-era Moorish architecture and quiet, grassy courtyard remain an island of grace amid an ocean of vulgarity. Rooms in the historic wing feature four-poster beds, floral wallpaper, and Queen Anne furnishings. The hotel offers free one-hour historical tours Monday, Wednesday, and Friday at 2:00 P.M. Rates begin at $380. Farther down Kalakaua, the *Sheraton Moana Surfrider* (922–3111) claims its own share of nostalgia. Step through the elaborate Colonial porte cochere that fronts the lobby to travel back in time. Built in 1901, the Moana was Waikiki's first hotel. Live music plays throughout the day in the beachfront banyan tree court, where Robert Louis Stevenson once composed and the Prince of Wales caroused. The historical room above the lobby chronicles this glamorous past with photos, video, and memorabilia, and the hotel offers free historical tours lasting more than an hour on Monday, Wednesday, and Friday at 11:00 A.M. and 5:00 P.M. Guest rooms have been refurbished with period touches, such as

Hawaiian quilts on the beds and old-fashioned fixtures for the plumbing. Rates begin at $270.

Across the street from the Moana, the ***Sheraton Princess Kaiʻulani Hotel*** (922–5811) conducts its own historical tour—this one focused less on the hotel than on its namesake, Princess Kaiʻulani, who grew up on these grounds. Historical exhibits on display include a poem Robert Louis Stevenson wrote to the princess in an autograph book. Sent to London for her education, Kaiʻulani was recalled to Washington, charged by her aunt, the deposed Queen Liliʻuokalani, to intercede with President Cleveland for the queen's restoration. Her mission proved unsuccessful, and the princess tragically perished at the age of twenty-three, a death that Western medicine attributed to pneumonia, but Hawaiians knew was from a broken heart. The half-hour tours are offered Monday, Wednesday, and Friday at 4:00 P.M. Free.

Beyond the Moana the shoreline reverts to public beach park, attractively landscaped with garden statuary and lots of waterfall thingies burbling out of nowhere. There are several features of interest (not counting the ones in swimsuits on the beach). Right next to the police substation, four large boulders lounge incognito in the sand. A plaque explains how these ***kahuna stones*** came to contain the healing powers of four powerful kahunas ("one who knows the secrets") visiting from Tahiti in the thirteenth century. Not far from the stones stands a bronzed statue of Duke Kahanumoku, Olympic medalist, a Waikiki "beach boy," and international surfing hero. Raised in a family of eight boys, Duke was taught to swim the old-fashioned way: tossed off a canoe to sink or swim. He learned well enough to garner six medals (three gold) in four Olympics from 1912 to 1932. (He could have competed in six had it not been for World War I's cancellation of the 1916 games and his own illness in 1928.) Named for the Duke of Edinburgh, who had visited the islands the day he was born, Hawaii's Duke rode his Olympic fame to a series of Hollywood roles and traveled the world to hobnob with royalty as the island's unofficial ambassador. He brought his surfboard with him on his travels and did much to spread the sport internationally by demonstrating his prowess. Elected sheriff of Honolulu, Kahanamoku continued his ambassadorial role, taking visiting celebrities, including the Prince of Wales, to surf at Waikiki. Local surfers bemoan the fact that the statue has its back to the ocean, something the experienced waterman would never have done while living. A torch-lighting ceremony and free hula performance are staged on the beach here nightly at sunset. Modern-day ***beach boys*** ply their trade from a concession stand nearby. For $5.00 you can help paddle an outrigger canoe out to sea and ride the waves in. For $25 you can get an hour's surfing lesson with individual instruction. The waves here offer long, gentle rides, making Waikiki one of the best places on the island to learn to surf. If you rent a board on your own, you'll want to get one with a leash so that the board stays with you.

Another unique way to learn to surf is by enrolling in the **Hawaiian Fire Surf School** (737–FIRE or 737–3473; 888–955–7873), run by off-duty firefighters. Lessons are taught at Barber's Point in West O`ahu (transport from Waikiki provided). If you choke on a mouthful of seawater, you can be certain your instructor knows CPR. Prices for a two-hour lesson range from $97 for a three-person class to $139 for a private lesson. Children under eleven are required to have a private lesson for $119.

Continue down the street to watch old-timers face off on the checkered tables of the Kuhio chess pavilions. Across the street, look for the blue V-shaped roof of St. Augustine Church. Take a moment to pop inside the **Damien Museum** (923–2690) in back to see memorabilia of the "Martyr of Moloka`i." Open Monday through Friday 9:00 A.M. to 3:00 P.M. and Saturday 9:00 A.M. to noon. Free.

The main hotel strip ends at Kapahulu Avenue opposite the entrance to the Honolulu Zoo. Look for a schedule of nearby bandstand events and read some park history at the corner visitor kiosk. Those interested in learning more Waikiki history can find self-guiding tour information at www.waikikihistoric trail.com. Next to the kiosk sits a controversial burial mound, Na Iwi Kupuna Waikiki, which translates roughly as "the bones of our ancestors in Waikiki," and it houses just that (said bones having been unearthed during recent work on a water main).

Behind the burial mound is the entrance to the Honolulu Zoo. You can shop for sidewalk art along the fence outside the zoo on Monsarrat Avenue on weekends, purchasing direct from the artists. The zoo itself is fairly standard, but visitors (especially prospective snorkelers) definitely should visit the **Waikiki Aquarium** (923–9741) farther along Kalakaua Avenue. It isn't a big facility, but the exhibits illustrate the colorful diversity of marine life surrounding these islands. You can see some of the world's first chambered nautiluses hatched in captivity, see Hawaiian monk seals at play, and handle marine life in the Edge of the Reef exhibit. Ask about reef walks and other aquarium excursions and events. Open daily 9:00 A.M. to 5:00 P.M. Admission $9.00.

Next to the aquarium, note the elaborate facade of the oceanside **War Memorial Natatorium.** An enclosed, saltwater bathing pool built in honor of World War I vets, the natatorium has been the subject of a decade-long debate: What do you do with an aging war monument no one wants to use anymore? The city recently restored the facade, but the state health department still can't bring itself to sign off on reopening the pool due to sanitation concerns about inadequate water circulation.

Kapiolani Park sprawls along the opposite side of the street. A staging ground for community activities on weekends, it is also a top-rated kite-flying venue. Farther down Kalakaua stands the **New Otani Kaimana Beach Hotel** (923–1555; 800–356–8264; 2863 Kalakaua Avenue; www.kaimana.com). This small "boutique" hotel enjoys a less frenetic, off-Waikiki location on Sans-Souci Beach, another Robert Louis Stevenson hangout. Rooms start at $150. The hotel's **Hau Tree Lana`i** restaurant sits right on the beach. For lodging in Waikiki proper, hostelers can hole up in Hosteling International's **Hale Aloba** (926–8313; 2417 Prince Edward Street). For a bed-and-breakfast alternative, artist Joanne Trotter rents two suites with private baths and a private apartment in her gracious estate on the slopes of Diamond Head, overlooking Waikiki. The rooms and apartment rent for $130 and are full of original artwork and heritage koa furnishings, including a one-hundred-plus-year-old bed that belonged to Princess Ruth. Two-day minimum stay. Call **Diamond Head B&B** (923–3360; diamondheadbnb.com@lava.net).

trivia

O'ahu boasts more miles of swimming beaches than any other island.

Kalakaua Avenue ends near the foot of **Diamond Head Crater.** The largest of the tuff cones on the island, Diamond Head received its English name when British sailors caught the glint of what they thought were diamonds reflecting from its slopes. King Kamehameha I promptly slapped a kapu on the entire mountain, only to discover the "gems" were calcite crystals. You can enter the crater interior via a military tunnel through the inland walls. To do so, turn left onto Paki Avenue, then right at the traffic lights onto Monsarrat. A paved road less than a mile long leads through the tunnel. The military installations inside share space with a state park that the public can visit from 6:00 A.M. to 6:00 P.M. From the parking lot a well-graded trail ascends the 760-foot summit, emerging through the inside of a World War II bunker. The panoramic view from the top extends across half the island. The hike up takes about a half hour. Bring water and a flashlight.

If you'd rather sun by the shore than hike in the hills, turn right from the end of Kalakaua onto Diamond Head Road, which skirts the seaward edge of the crater around the southern tip of the island. The road climbs high onto the slopes past Diamond Head Lighthouse. Just ahead, a paved pathway leads down the steep cliffside to **Diamond Head Beach,** a secluded gem. A fringing reef extends close to shore, making swimming difficult at this spot. Surfers and sailboarders who come here launch through a reef channel a few hundred yards to the left. If you keep walking that way toward Black Point, you'll find some nicer swimming holes and maybe a stretch of sand to call your own.

You can also watch the action from up top at the two lookout points farther along. During summer, the surf off Diamond Head reaches as high as 8 feet, providing exciting conditions for expert wave riders. The first lookout also offers a view east of distant Koko Head and Koko Crater and has a plaque commemorating Amelia Earhart's solo flight across the Pacific.

Some of Honolulu's finest homes are here, with none finer than *Shangri-La* (734–1941), the Islamic pleasure palace that on Diamond Head did Doris Duke decree. In 1935 Duke, a newlywed tobacco heiress, embarked on a round-the-world honeymoon that sparked a lifelong passion—not with her husband (that marriage ended in divorce), but rather with Islamic art. Hawaii was the last stop on Duke's voyage, and, equally captivated by the relaxed island lifestyle, she would return here to build a unique hideaway that combined her two loves. Duke's virtually limitless resources enabled her to amass an amazing trove of art, antiques, tapestries, textiles, metalwork, lusterware, ceramic tiles, and mosaics from Morocco to Molucca, and everywhere in between, in what gradually became a monument to pan-Islamic architecture and decor. She often disassembled entire rooms from historic buildings and had them transported to Hawaii. If she couldn't buy an object, she would commission an exact replica of it or order a custom-made design. The result is a dazzling mélange of architectural styles that blends textures and forms with a daring aesthetic that beguiles without overwhelming. The five-acre property enjoys a dramatic oceanfront perch, providing an almost surreal contrast to the exotic splendor within. Two-and-a-half-hour tours of Shangri-La are offered Wednesday through Saturday by reservation; they begin at the Academy of Art and cost $25. Call (866) 385–3849 to reserve well in advance or go online at www.honoluluacademy.org.

If instead of continuing on Kalakaua past the zoo, you turn left up Kapahulu Avenue, you'll come to some interesting antiques stores. Step inside *Bailey's Antiques & Aloha Shirts* (734–7628), at 517 Kapahulu, and you enter a three-ring bazaar. The eclectic inventory creates a carnival atmosphere rich in color and texture. Most of the items fit the category of Hawaiiana kitsch and collectibles, such as the dancing hula-girl lamps popular in the 1950s. Bailey's specializes in classic aloha shirts, including original 1940s "silkies," whose wild floral patterns became a symbol of the islands. Some of the shirts have celebrity connections and fetch upward of $1,000. You can also find contemporary reproductions for about $50 and used shirts starting at $3.99. Owner David Bailey scours thrift shops in California to find these forgotten treasures and has been known to buy the shirt off a stranger's back. Open daily 10:00 A.M. to 6:00 P.M.

Other antiques shops space themselves along Kapahulu, with the biggest cluster at the far end near the freeway. The five antiques shops in back of the **Kilohana Square** shopping complex, at 1016 Kapahulu, mostly specialize in decorative art and furniture from Asia. On the way down, you might also stop in at Aunty Mary Lou's **Na Lima Mili Huli No'eau** (732–0865), at 762 Kapahulu, a craft shop devoted to the traditional Hawaiian art of feather working. (The name means "skilled hands touch the feathers.") Students take lessons here and then sell their completed projects by consignment. Open Monday through Friday by appointment 9:00 A.M. to 9:00 P.M. and Saturday 9:00 A.M. to 5:00 P.M.

Kapahulu also has a variety of good restaurants. At the high end of the spectrum, **Sam Choy's Diamond Head** (732–8645), at 449 Kapahulu, caters to a local crowd, serving gourmet versions of island food in giant portions. Open Sunday through Thursday 5:30 to 10:00 P.M. and Friday and Saturday 5:00 to 11:00 P.M. Sunday brunch from 9:30 A.M. to 2:00 P.M. Investment-caliber prices. **Hee Hing** (735–5544), downstairs, specializes in seafood and has decent Chinese fare. Open daily from 10:30 A.M. to 9:30 P.M. Inexpensive to moderate. **Irifune** (737–1141), at 563 Kapahulu, serves slightly offbeat, garlicky Japanese dishes in a funky venue for inexpensive to moderate prices. Open Tuesday through Saturday 11:30 A.M. to 1:30 P.M. and 5:30 to 9:30 P.M.

A couple of blocks farther, **Ono Hawaiian Food** (737–2275), at 726 Kapahulu, has the real product. The lines outside the door are both a deterrent and a recommendation. Open Monday through Saturday 11:00 A.M. to 7:45 P.M. Inexpensive to moderate. To experience trendy "revolving sushi service," try **Genki Sushi** (735–7700), at 885 Kapahulu. A conveyer belt trundles rotating menu samples around the restaurant; after you make selections, your order is prepared fresh. Open daily 11:00 A.M. to 9:00 P.M., and until 10:00 P.M. on Friday and Saturday. Inexpensive. Or stop by **India Café** (737–4600), at 1016 Kapahulu, to sample *dosai,* a spicy South Asian take on the crepe made from rice and lentil flour, as well as other specialties. Open for lunch Friday through Sunday 11:00 A.M. to 2:30 P.M. and dinner nightly 5:00 to 9:00 P.M.

The Kapahulu area used to be heavily settled by Honolulu's Portuguese community. Near the inland end of Kapahulu, **Leonard's Bakery** (737–5591) keeps tradition alive with fresh-baked Portuguese *pao doce* (sweetbread) and hot *malasadas* (doughy, holeless doughnuts). Stop by for a gustatory treat. Open daily 6:00 A.M. to 9:00 P.M. and until 10:00 P.M. on Friday and Saturday.

A quick right turn up Waialae Avenue at the freeway end of Kapahulu brings you to the **Kaimuki district,** a newly trendy enclave where locals gather to sip lattes and dine at an eclectic array of restaurants. Most of the action centers around 12th Avenue, near the top of the hill. The **12th Avenue**

Grill (732–9469), at 1145C 12th Avenue, draws raves from the foodie crowd with retro diner fare such as kim chee steak, baked macaroni and cheese, and strawberry shortcake. Expensive. Open Monday through Thursday 5:30 to 9:00 P.M. and Friday and Saturday until 10:00 P.M.; no reservations taken, so come early or late. On the way there, you might stop at *Pzazz consignment shop* (732–5900), which offers designer handbags, shoes, clothing, and jewelry, with doting help and honest critique offered by mother-daughter partners Judy and Susan. It's located at 3057 Waialae, next to Midas Muffler between First and Second Avenues. Open Monday through Saturday 10:00 A.M. to 5:00 P.M.

Just Up the Freeway

Believe it or not, although stuck in the middle of the Pacific Ocean, Hawaii has its own "interstate" highways. The main route through town is the H–1 Freeway. Take any on-ramp and head west to see some more of Honolulu. If you really want to experience the soul of Hawaii, visit the *Bishop Museum* (847–3511), a repository of Hawaiiana from A to Z. Princess Bernice Pauahi, the last heir of the Kamehameha dynasty, left her immense landholdings to educate Hawaiian students at nearby Kamehameha Schools. Her private possessions, however, were left to benefit all of us as the beginnings of the museum established by her American banker husband, Charles Bishop. Today, a century later, the museum's exhibits have swollen to include 76,000 Hawaiian artifacts alone, not to mention 13.5 million insect specimens. Bishop Museum has become the world's leading research institution on Pacific cultures. To reach it, take the Houghtailing Street turnoff from the H–1 Freeway and take the second left.

Budget plenty of time for your visit, as there's lots to see. The bulk of the exhibits fill the massive Hawaiian Hall inside the castlelike main building. The three levels focus on different periods, beginning with precontact Hawaii and continuing through the turbulent changes of the nineteenth century to today's multiethnic society. From the ceiling hangs the 50-foot skeleton of a sperm whale. You'll find most of the old Hawaii exhibits on the ground floor. Here you can meet the gods: those fiercely scowling *akua* (idols) that survived the 1819 abolition of the old religion. In the entrance room, look for Kukailimoku, the personal war god of Kamehameha I. The great conqueror carried this flaming orange-feathered apparition into battle, and its wide staring eyes were witness to the years of carnage. You might also see Kamehameha's full-length yellow feather cloak. Specially trained "bird men" had full-time jobs trapping the more than 100,000 *mamo* birds needed to gather the plumage for the cloak. Each bird yielded only a few yellow feathers plucked from among the black. Upstairs you will find relics of missionaries and mariners, costumes of kings, and immigrant heirlooms all jumbled together much like the history of Hawaii. *Unfortunately, Hawaiian Hall closed for renovation for two years beginning July 2006. Some of its contents are displayed elsewhere in the museum.*

You can compare the Hawaiian exhibits with the displays from other Polynesian islands in the hall next door. Adjacent rooms house artifacts from the related Micronesian and Melanesian peoples. If you're not clear which islands fit where, just consult the color-coded maps.

Open daily, the planetarium introduces you to the world of stars. Shows—which are held Monday through Friday at noon, 2:30 P.M. (including a solar viewing), and 3:30 P.M. and on weekends at 11:00 A.M.—highlight topics of astronomical interest. You can also watch demonstrations of Hawaiian crafts such as feather work, quilting, or lei making. Hula is performed daily at 11:00 A.M. and 2:00 P.M. Museum groupies and crafty types might consider taking one of the museum's specialty tours, such as the "Taste of the Islands"—a half-day program that includes a guided tour and lessons in Hawaiian lei making and hula dancing. Reservations required. At 1:00 P.M. daily a "living stories" tour is available in the Polynesian Hall. The Bishop Museum is open daily from 9:00 A.M. to 5:00 P.M.; $14.95 admission.

Past the museum, the freeway splits temporarily, with H–1 bending seaward to the airport. Continue straight on what's now Route 78 for another mile. Take the Puuloa Road/Tripler Hospital turnoff and make a quick right into **Moanalua Gardens** (833–1944). Prince Lot, who later became Kamehameha V, kept a summer home here, where he encouraged a partial revival of the hula art forms. The annual Prince Lot Festival commemorates his efforts with a weekend of Hawaiian dance during July. The prince's elaborate cottage still stands beside koi and taro ponds. The garden is open from 8:00 A.M. to 5:00 P.M.; free.

You can soak up additional historic scenery by hiking the nearby **Kamananui Valley Trail,** which passes petroglyphs and other historic sites deep into the valley. Kamehameha I (Lot's grandfather) capped his conquest of O'ahu by sacrificing rival chief Kalanikupule on an altar here. Stop by the Moanalua Gardens Foundation (839–5334), just behind the gardens at 1352 Pineapple Place, to purchase an interpretive trail guide keyed to numbered posts along the way ($5.00). Open Monday through Friday 8:00 A.M. to 4:00 P.M.

The best signs to follow to the Pearl Harbor and *Arizona* Memorial are along H–1. If you're already on Route 78, follow signs to the Aiea exit, about 4 miles farther, and turn left over the bridge. This section of Kamehameha Highway runs past the stadium along the East Loch of Pearl Harbor. The

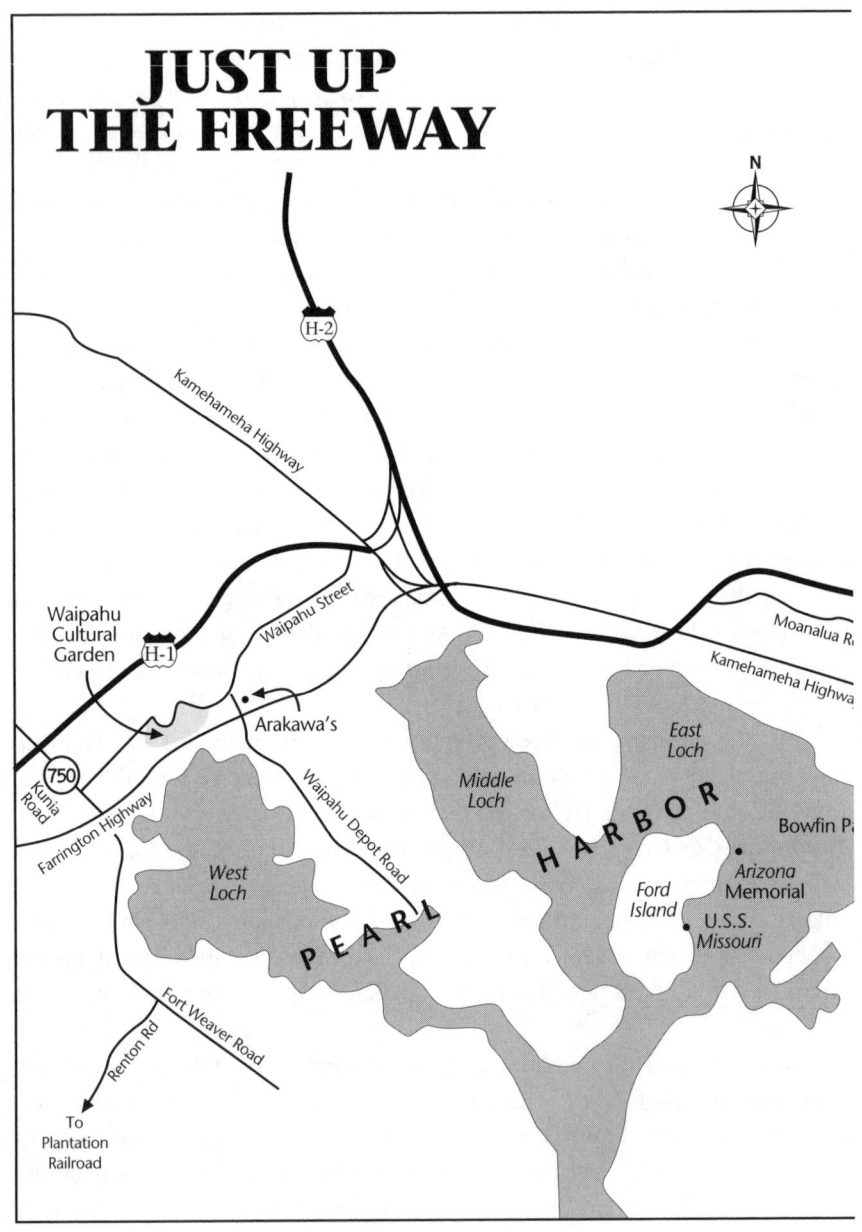

JUST UP THE FREEWAY

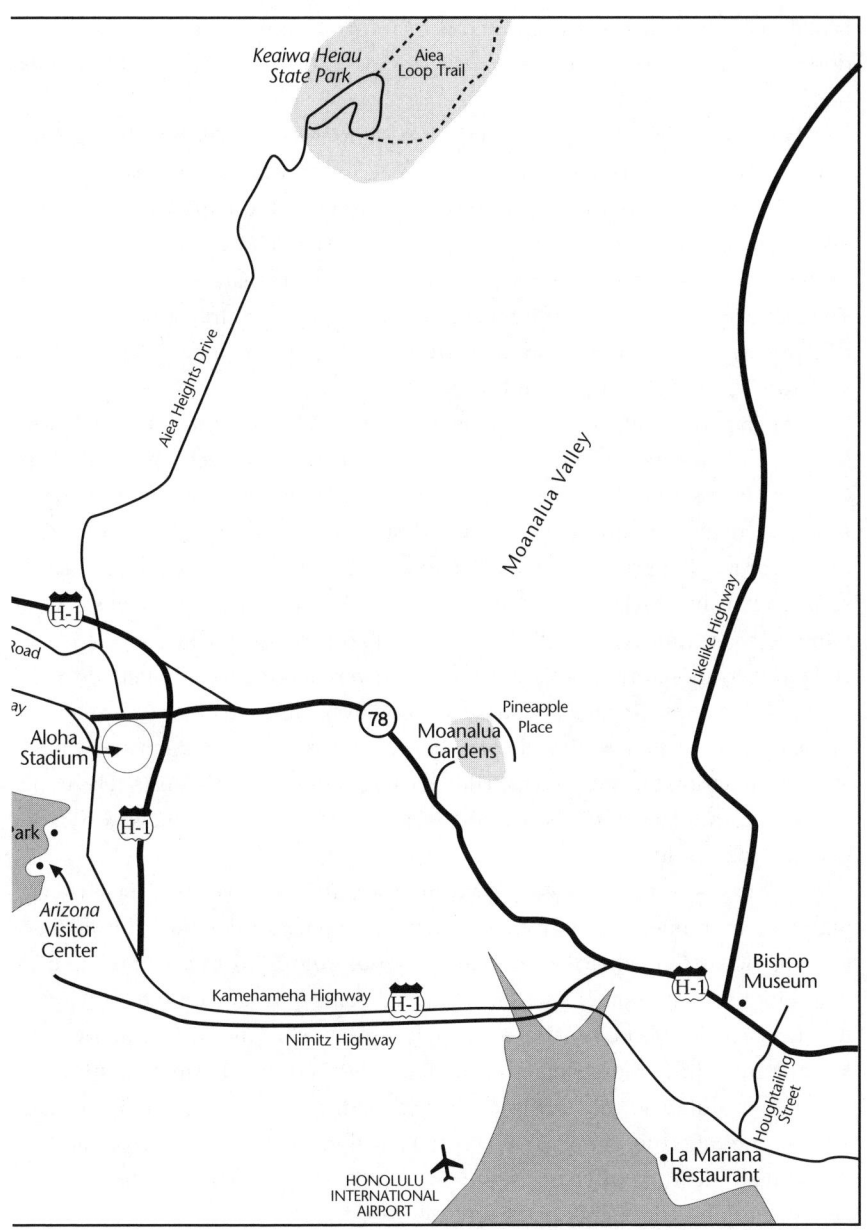

cauliflower-like lakes of this enormous inland lagoon were cut by river valleys during a time of lower sea levels. Oyster beds thrived in the shallow flats, hence the name Pearl.

The American military acquired base rights to Pearl Harbor during King Kalakaua's reign in exchange for tariff-free access to U.S. markets for Hawaiian sugar, but the military didn't get around to dredging the harbor opening until 1902. Hawaiians were perturbed when the U.S. Navy chose to dig its dry dock on the very island where the shark goddess, Kaahupahau, supposedly lived. Their dire warnings came true when, four years into construction, a structural collapse wiped out all the work that had been done to that point. A giant shark skeleton was found amid the rubble.

The Japanese attack on December 7, 1941, brought Pearl Harbor before the eyes of the world and catapulted the United States into World War II. Contrary to popular belief, the attack did not come entirely without warning. A Japanese mini-sub had been found and sunk near the mouth of the harbor hours earlier. Experimental radar stations even tracked the incoming attack squadrons (until their commander told them to turn off their screens). More intriguing yet, American intelligence forces had recently cracked the Japanese code and by monitoring cable transmissions were alerted to the likelihood that Japan was planning a military strike. Some have suggested that top American officials secretly planned to absorb the damage so as to commit the United States to entering the war against Hitler. These "conspiracy theorists" claim that the fortuitous absence of the carrier fleet at the time of the attack was more than a stroke of luck.

You can grapple with your own interpretation as you come face-to-face with the monuments left from that day's violence. Take the turnoff from Kamehameha Highway to the **Arizona *Memorial*** (422–0561). The white concave hull of the monument sits like a shroud across the sunken hull of the battleship *Arizona,* whose number-three gun turret pierces the surface at low tide. More than a thousand sailors and marines perished in this single battleship's destruction—almost half the total deaths in the attack. Most of the victims remain entombed in the ship, which sank within minutes of the explosion in the forward-deck powder magazine. More than sixty years later the *Arizona* continues to bleed, oozing gallons of oil every week.

Free boat trips to the memorial depart from the National Park Service visitor center on a first-come, first-served basis. Browse the open-air museum exhibits while you wait your turn. One display tells the story of Hawaii's Americans of Japanese descent. At a time when mainland cities were incarcerating their Japanese populations, Hawaii's Japanese Americans refused to allow their patriotism to be doubted. Their patient resolve won them the chance to prove themselves in combat in Italy, where they became one of the most decorated battalions in U.S. military history. Equally compelling is the story of Admiral Yamamoto, a Harvard-educated military genius who masterminded the Pearl Harbor strike despite a personal opposition to the war. The museum is open daily 7:30 A.M. to 5:00 P.M.; tours run 8:00 A.M. to 3:00 P.M.

During busy months the wait for the tour can last for hours, and some tours sell out entirely. Come early to reserve a space, then amble over to nearby **Bowfin Park** (423–1341). You can take in the exhibits of the Pacific Submarine Museum and then enter an actual World War II submarine, the USS *Bowfin,* moored nearby. Dubbed the "Pearl Harbor Avenger," the *Bowfin* was launched exactly a year after the Japanese attack and went on to claim forty-four kills (twenty-three confirmed) in Japanese craft sunk. Open daily 8:00 A.M. to 5:00 P.M. Admission is $10, which includes an audiotour in English and Japanese of both the submarine and the museum. The last tour starts at 4:30 P.M. On Wednesday and weekends, check out the massive "swap meet" flea market at nearby Aloha Stadium from 6:00 A.M. to 3:00 P.M.

At Bowfin Park you can also purchase tickets for Pearl Harbor's newest visitor attraction, the **USS Missouri** (423–2263; 877–644–4896). One of the most formidable battleships ever built, the *Missouri* saw duty in three wars, from World War II to the Persian Gulf. It earned its spot in the history books, however, not for its role in the fighting, but rather as the place where World War II ended with Japan signing instruments of surrender on its aft deck. Anchored only 1,000 yards from another World War II battleship, the sunken USS *Arizona,* the two form perfect bookends to America's involvement in the war, from defeat to victory.

Much of the ship is still undergoing restoration, but you can hit the highlights, including the main bridge, armory, wardroom, the panoramic views from the "flying bridge," the retrofitted Tomahawk missile launchers, and, of course, the "surrender deck." Exhibits recount the details of daily life on board ship, and war stories abound, including a heart-stopping moment when a Japanese kamikaze pilot slammed his fighter plane into the starboard side of the ship. Part of the experience is merely appreciating the size of this floating behemoth. Launched in 1944, the *Missouri* was the last battleship the U.S. Navy ever built and one of the largest. Its entire 887-foot-long hull is encased in steel armor plating more than a foot thick. Its massive 16-inch guns, each weighing 116 tons and measuring 65 feet in length, are capable of launching a shell as heavy as a Volkswagen Beetle more than 20 miles—with pinpoint accuracy. Just designing the *Missouri* took 175 *tons* of blueprint paper. Built in three years, the ship required more than three million man-days to complete (and, more recently, 25,000 volunteer-hours to renovate). The USS *Missouri* is open daily ,

9:00 A.M. to 5:00 P.M. Tickets must be purchased by 4:00 P.M. and cost $16 for self-guided visits or $22 for a guided tour, with "premium tours" costing up to $49.

Going straight from the same Aiea freeway exit puts you on Moanalua Road (moving parallel to and inland of Kamehameha Highway, past the stadium). Turn right at the mall just ahead and take Aiea Heights Drive up the hill to **Keaiwa Heiau State Park.** You get some good views of Pearl Harbor and Central O`ahu on the way up. The heiau sits at the park entrance, one of the few healing temples of ancient Hawaii that remain. Here the *kahuna lapaau* (medicine men) mixed herbs and prayers to cure a variety of ailments. Many of the medicinal plants they used still grow around the heiau grounds. The rest of the park consists of groves of ironwoods and eucalyptus and cool fresh air. At the top of the road, the **Aiea Loop Trail** offers an easy 4.5-mile hike through a variety of forest cover and occasional views. You can see the wreckage of a C-47 cargo plane about 3 miles along on your right. The round-trip trek takes about three hours.

Eating Off the Beaten Path in Honolulu

Honolulu's restaurants are every bit as international as its populace. The variety of restaurants here is probably unequaled in a city of its size. Cross-pollination between these diverse culinary traditions has led to some unusual hybrids. Amid the creative energies unleashed by such culinary fusion, a new school of Hawaii regional cuisine (HRC) has emerged. Its leading proponents are scattered among the islands, but common threads link the restaurants. Following the trend of New American regional cuisine, the menus revolve around island-grown produce and fresh seafood, served crusted in, say, a coating of macadamia nuts, then seared, blackened, or wok-charred, and sauced with Pacific Rim flavorings enhanced through classic French reductions. Presentations dazzle with vertiginously layered towers erected in the center of an oversize plate and a multicolored wasabe/sesame/miso/ginger-something drizzled around the edges. Decor is deliberately understated, often with an open kitchen as the centerpiece, and the service is casual, albeit attentive.

Many of today's top HRC performers got their start in hotel restaurants on the neighbor islands. But almost all of them have opened restaurants in Honolulu of late, and the competition has gotten fierce. The current pack of eponymous eateries includes **Roy's** (396–7697), in Hawaii Kai; **Onjin's Cafe** (589–1666), in Ward Center; and **Sam Choy's Diamond Head** (732–8645), in Kapahulu (see Waikiki and Thereabouts). The top dog in town, by most counts, remains **Alan Wong's** (949–2526), at 1857 South King Street, although some complain of overcrowding and inattentive service. Wong's ever-changing menu brilliantly combines an innovative use of ingredients with classical cooking techniques. The Chinese pork-hash-crusted *opakapaka* (pink snapper) is but one example of improbable combinations that you have to taste to believe. Investment-caliber prices. Open nightly from 5:00 to 9:00 P.M. Other standouts include Russel Siu's *3660 On the Rise* (737–1177), at 3660 Waialae Avenue in Kaimuki, which is slightly less expensive than the rest; open Tuesday through Sunday 5:30 to 9:00 P.M. *Chef Mavro's* (944–4714), at 1969 South King Street at the corner of McCully, specializes in food and wine pairings served in a space that is both elegant and intimate. Open Tuesday through Sunday 6:00 to 9:30 P.M. Investment-caliber. *L'Uraku* (955-0552), at 1341 Kapiolani Boulevard, serves upscale Euro-Japanese food. Your best bet is the three-course luncheon served on weekends. Open daily from 11:00 A.M. to 2:00 P.M. and 5:30 to 10:00 P.M. Local people favor Sam Choy's other restaurant, *Breakfast, Lunch and Crab* (545–7979), at 580 North Nimitz Highway, just north of downtown, which serves less pretentious dishes in hearty portions. The centerpiece of this cavernous brewpub is an old fishing sampan with tables in the cabin. Moderate. Open Monday through Friday 7:00 A.M. to 9:30 P.M., Saturday 7:00 A.M. to 10:00 P.M., and Sunday 7:00 to 9:30 P.M.

If Hawaii regional cuisine represents the future of Hawaii's restaurants, *La Mariana Restaurant* (848–2800), located in the sailing club of the same name, retains something of its past. To get there, take Sand Island Access Road from Nimitz Highway north of downtown and look for the sailing masts on the right after the first traffic light. Having survived at least one tidal wave and several lease foreclosures, this rustic beach shack has been around ever since Keehi Lagoon was opened as a "poor man's yacht club." The Polynesian kitsch decor harks back to the classic South Seas restaurants of the 1920s and 1930s— and with good reason: Owner Annette Nahinu bought much of it from her more illustrious but less long-lived predecessors such as Trader Vic's and Don the Beachcomber. A circus sideshow of multicolored bulbs illuminates your choice of lamps made from shells, bamboo, puffer fish, and Japanese fishing floats. Thronelike rattan chairs encircle wooden tables; carved tikis serve as pillars; and, of course, the ubiquitous fishing nets drape both ceiling and walls. No fewer than two trees grow within the restaurant, while a row of coconut palms frames the harbor views. The local American fare and daily fresh fish on the menu are passable, but you might just come here for drinks. Open daily 11:00 A.M. to 9:00 P.M. with live music and dancing every night. Expensive.

Something of the same atmosphere (minus the kitsch) can be found at the *Willows* (952–9200), at 901 Hausman Street, near the university. Pavilions front a small lagoon, and you can load your plate with a generous Hawaiian buffet served Monday through Friday 11:00 A.M. to 2:00 P.M. and 5:30 to 9:00 P.M. and weekends 10:00 A.M. to 2:30 P.M. and 5:00 to 9:00 P.M. A Sunday brunch is also available. Live music plays on Friday nights, and strolling musicians roam tables at lunch. Investment-caliber.

For ordinary good food, try these midtown ethnic restaurants the average tourist might not find:

Russel Siu of 3660 On the Rise also owns the far more modest **Kaka`ako Kitchen** (596–7488), at the Ward Centre plaza off Ala Moana Boulevard, between Ala Moana and Ward. It serves gourmet versions of the classic island plate lunch, as well as fresh fish specials and a zesty sweet chili chicken. Open 7:00 A.M. to 9:00 P.M. Monday through Thursday, to 10:00 P.M. on Friday and Saturday, and to 5:00 P.M. on Sunday. Inexpensive. You'll find a similar menu at the **Side Street Inn** (591–0253), at 1225 Hopaka Street, near the northwest corner of Ala Moana Shopping Center, 1 block in from Kapiolani Boulevard. Some of Honolulu's top chefs gather after hours in this bare-bones diner, lured by gourmet comfort food, including a famous pork chop. Open Monday through Friday 10:30 A.M. to 1:30 P.M. and daily 4:00 P.M. to 2:00 A.M. Moderate. Those on a Tanpopo-like quest for the perfect *udon* will find no less than sixteen variants of this steaming noodle broth at **Jimbo's** (947–2211), at 1936 South King Street, next to the King's Cafe, just before McCully; there's an equal number of udon dishes sans broth, as well as other Japanese fare. Open Monday through Thursday 11:00 A.M. to 2:50 P.M. and 5:00 to 9:50 P.M. and Friday through Saturday to 10:30 P.M. Moderate.

Farther down King, the **Indian Bazaar** (949–4840), at 2320 South King Street, between McCully and Isenberg Streets, dwells in a minimall Monday through Saturday from 11:00 A.M. to 5:00 P.M. You get three tongue-tingling tastes of Madras curry for one low price from a mostly vegetarian, cafeteria-style selection. There are a few tables, but it's nicer to take your food to Stadium Park across the street. Inexpensive. Around the corner of the park at 909 Isenberg, **Maple Garden** (941–6641) specializes in northern Chinese dishes for inexpensive prices. Open daily 11:00 A.M. to 2:00 P.M. and 5:30 to 10:00 P.M.

To get your just desserts, head for the homemade ice cream at **Bubbies'** (949–8984), opposite Varsity Theater, a block inland on University Avenue from King Street. Open Monday through Thursday from noon to midnight, Friday and Saturday to 1:00 A.M., and Sunday to 11:30 P.M. Or find your way to **La Gelateria** (591–1133), at 819 Cedar Street (off King Street between Piikoi and Keeaumoku), to sample Maurice Grasso's inventively indulgent flavor infusions, from rose-petal sorbet to lilikoi champagne. Open weekdays 8:00 A.M. to 5:00 P.M.

A Night on the Town (and Daytime Too)

Waikiki is the entertainment capital of Hawaii. It has plenty of nightclubs for owls on the prowl, and almost all the big hotels book prominent local talent to perform at dinner shows. For free outdoor entertainment, pick an evening with clear skies and stroll along Waikiki Beach. At night the beach is empty and you hear the gentle lap of waves against the shore. As you walk, you can hear the sounds of the many hotel shows staged on oceanfront lanais and linger to watch part of the acts.

If you feel like stopping in for a drink, a good candidate is **Duke's Canoe Club** (922–2268) in the Outrigger Waikiki. Top-notch local entertainers perform contemporary island music daily from 4:00 to 6:00 P.M. and from 10:00 P.M. to midnight. In between, the "aunties" serenade individual tables. Moderate to expensive. Although not in Waikiki, another good venue for Hawaiian music is **Chai's Island Bistro** (585–0011), in the Aloha Tower Marketplace downtown.

Night action outside Waikiki centers around two zones of interest: Collegiate crowds gather at a cluster of bars near the intersection of King and University. Young professionals favor downtown's **Restaurant Row** at the ocean end of Punchbowl Street and the harborside **Aloha Tower Marketplace.**

If your night on the town stirs an appetite, the **Wailana Coffee Shop** (955–1764), at 1860 Ala Moana Boulevard, opposite the Hilton Hawaiian Village on the west end of Waikiki, serves good-value grub amid pseudo-Hawaiian decor. Open twenty-four hours.

For an upscale alternative, **Formaggio's** (739–7719), at 2919 Kapiolani Boulevard, 1 block in from the H–1 Freeway, cultivates the cellarlike atmosphere of an Italian *enoteca* (just ignore the strip-mall location). It serves an impressive array of wines by the glass accompanied with various *antipasti,* tapas, and, naturally, cheese. Open Monday through Thursday 5:00 P.M. to midnight and Friday and Saturday until 2:00 A.M., with live entertainment nightly. Inexpensive.

Almost every weekend in the summer, Japanese temples schedule *bon* dances to honor ancestral spirits, and the public is always welcome. Local hula *hulau* also hold fund-raisers at sites around the island—a great way to catch authentic Hawaiian culture. A number of groups schedule **hiking trips** on weekends.

To see the island on foot, consider hikes with the Sierra Club (538–6616) or Hawaiian Trail and Mountain Club (send $2.00 plus a SASE for a schedule to P.O. Box 2238, Honolulu 96804).

Michael Walther's **Oahu Nature Tours** (924–2473; www.oahunature tours.com) offers a daily schedule of interpretive outings to island ecosystems;

tours range in price from $24 to $47. ***Mauka Makai*** (255–2206; www.hawaiian ecotours.net) fills a slightly different niche. Their tours are essentially bus circuits that stop for a series of short nature walks at sites of historical and archaeological interest, from prehistoric petroglyphs to former heiau (ancient temples). Guides provide vivid descriptions of the activities that took place at each site, from ritual sacrifices to military battles. Tours also touch on the natural environment and include demonstrations of traditional cultural activities, from taro farming to throw-net fishing. Full-day tours (eight and a half to nine hours) cost $80, with a shorter half-day (four-hour) variant for $50. A three-quarter-day tour (six hours) is available on Wednesday and Friday afternoons for $65.

Wild Side Tours (306–7273; www.sailhawaii.com) offers marine ecotours along O`ahu's remote, relatively pristine Leeward Coast. Led by a husband-and-wife team of marine biologists with intimate knowledge of the local terrain, the trips take place on a 42-foot catamaran and may involve dolphin or humpback whale watching, reef snorkeling, and visits to a turtle "cleaning station," with the focus of activity varying according to participant interest and marine conditions. The four-hour early-morning sails include continental breakfast and snorkeling equipment for $95; four-person minimum. They also do night sails, including full-moon and new-moon evening cruises, with the latter focusing on stargazing and celestial navigation; these three-hour outings include dinner for the same $95. ***Twogood Kayak*** (262–5656) offers a guided nature tour in Kailua Bay. An all-day package features an excursion to an off-shore island with hiking and exploration of secluded coves for $109, including lunch. A self-guided version of this tour is available for $69.

For those who prefer hiking in an urban setting, Honolulu offers a number of special-interest tours. Anyone with a taste for the macabre should check into the excellent ghost tours offered by ***Honolulu TimeWalks*** (943–0371). Master storyteller and local historian Glenn Grant, now deceased, filled several volumes with the ghost tales he collected throughout the years. Grant's company continues to offer walking tours based on the stories he collected. The Mysteries of Moiliili and the Old Honolulu Walking Tour are $12. TimeWalks also offers a Ghost Hunters Bus Tour of haunted locales around the island on weekends for $45. Call for a current schedule and book well in advance. World War II history buffs will appreciate the unique tour offered by ***Home of the Brave*** (396–8112; www.pearlharborhq.com). Guides dressed in World War II air corps pilot uniforms lead a half-day excursion to military bases and other sites associated with wartime history, bringing them to life via recordings of actual news bulletins, music, and speeches that aired during the war. The tours run weekdays, beginning at 6:00 A.M. and returning by 2:00 P.M.; the cost is $79.

More conventional walking treks covering historic downtown, island temples, petroglyphs, waterfalls, and rain forests can be arranged through the *Hawaii Geographic Society* (538–3952; 800–538–3950). They charge $15 per person, with a minimum of two people for a two- to three-hour tour.

Those of a crafty bent might consider taking a Hawaiiana class. Besides the Royal Hawaiian Shopping Center and Bishop Museum (see Waikiki and Thereabouts), other places offering instruction in Hawaiian crafts and hula include the *Waikiki Community Center* (923–1802) and the *Lyon Arboretum* (988–0456). *Temari Center* (536–4566) specializes in Asian and Pacific art forms, often bringing in guest artists from Japan and elsewhere. Sign up in advance because these classes fill up quickly. The *Japanese Cultural Center* (945–7633) has its own offerings from time to time.

For many visitors, the number one activity is shopping. Most tourists find their way to Ala Moana Shopping Center, the state's biggest mall. Locals increasingly shop at the many outlets that populate Central O'ahu. But Honolulu has plenty of quirky, offbeat shopping venues as well. The gift shops at the major museums here provide fertile ground to hunt for that one-of-a-kind special find. Ward Warehouse and Ward Centre, off Ala Moana Boulevard between Ward Avenue and Ala Moana Center, both have a nice array of boutiques, patronized by visitors and locals alike. *Native Books and Beautiful Things* (596–8885), at the former, has a fine selection of island crafts; it's owned by a consortium of local artisans working in media ranging from woodcarving to Hawaiian quilts. Open Monday through Saturday 9:30 A.M. to 9:00 P.M. and Sunday to 5:00 P.M. Also good is the *Nohea Gallery* (596–0074), with space at both Ward locations. Antiques hunters should visit *Antique Alley* (941–8551), a cluster of shops at 1347 Kapiolani Boulevard near Ala Moana Center. Open Monday through Saturday 11:30 A.M. to 5:00 P.M. or so. Try to get hold of a copy of the free tabloid *Hawaii Antiques,* published quarterly, for the rundown on other venues for antiques/art/collectibles statewide.

East O'ahu and Windward

All right, enough big-city stuff. You came here to see natural beauty, and O'ahu's got plenty—outside Honolulu. To do the main "circle island" tour, driving up the windward coast and back through the center in a single day, is impractical, though. If you're based in Honolulu, take advantage of the scenic trans-Ko'olau highways—the Pali, Likelike, and H–3—to break the trip into smaller loops.

Start the southern circuit on Kalanianaole Highway at the east end of H–1, "heading Koko Head" (which is how locals say "go east" when you're east of

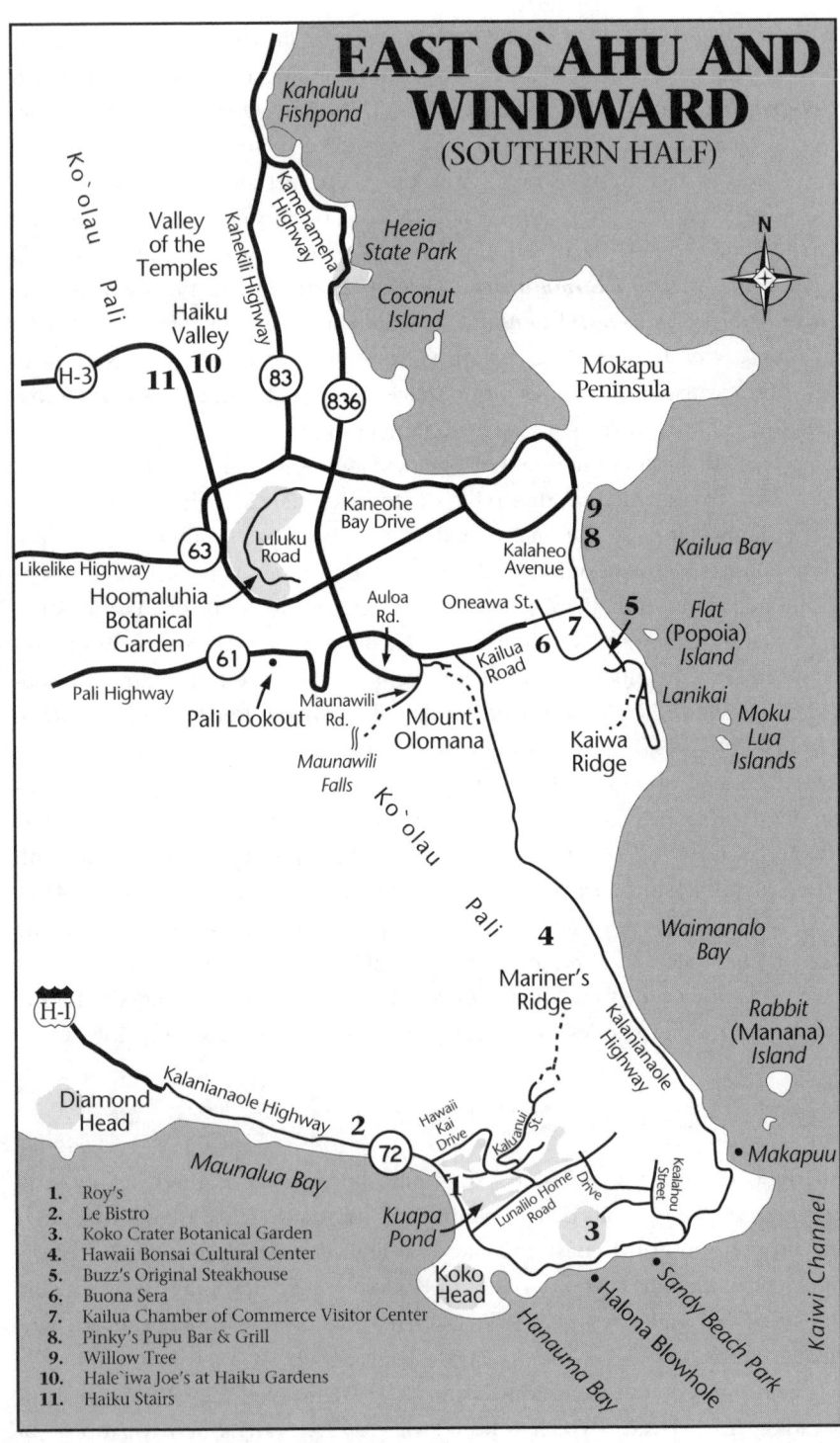

EAST O`AHU AND WINDWARD
(SOUTHERN HALF)

Kahaluu Fishpond

Ko`olau Pali

Valley of the Temples

Kamehameha Highway

Kahekili Highway

Heeia State Park

Coconut Island

Haiku Valley

H-3   **11** **10**   (83)

(836)

Mokapu Peninsula

N

Kaneohe Bay Drive

9
8

Kailua Bay

Likelike Highway   (63)   Luluku Road

Kalaheo Avenue

Hoomaluhia Botanical Garden

Auloa Rd.

Oneawa St.

5

Flat (Popoia) Island

(61)   **6** **7**

Kailua Road

Pali Highway

Maunawili Rd.

Lanikai

Moku Lua Islands

Pali Lookout

Mount Olomana

Kaiwa Ridge

Maunawili Falls

Ko`olau Pali

4

Mariner's Ridge

Waimanalo Bay

H-1

Kalanianaole Highway

Rabbit (Manana) Island

Diamond Head

Kalanianaole Highway   **2**

Hawaii Kai Drive

Kalanianaole Highway

Kealahou Street

Makapuu

Maunalua Bay

(72)

1

Lunalilo Home Drive

Kalanui St.

Kuapa Pond

3

Koko Head

Halona Blowhole

Sandy Beach Park

Kaiwi Channel

Hanauma Bay

1. Roy's
2. Le Bistro
3. Koko Crater Botanical Garden
4. Hawaii Bonsai Cultural Center
5. Buzz's Original Steakhouse
6. Buona Sera
7. Kailua Chamber of Commerce Visitor Center
8. Pinky's Pupu Bar & Grill
9. Willow Tree
10. Hale`iwa Joe's at Haiku Gardens
11. Haiku Stairs

Diamond Head). Four miles along the highway, you reach Hawaii Kai, a large suburb built around a converted fishpond. **Mariner's Ridge** is one of the few built-up hillsides here. If you take Kaluanui Street off Hawaii Kai Drive all the way to the top, there's an excellent one-and-a-half-hour hike to a Ko'olau *pali* overlook. It's similar to Lanipo but not as long or hard, and the view is almost as good.

Surprisingly, out here in the 'burbs you'll find one of the best restaurants on the island. **Roy's** (396–7697) showcases the inventive talents of chef Roy Yamaguchi. Combining Asian instincts with classical training, Roy has helped pioneer the new Hawaii regional cuisine, with dishes such as *opakapaka* with macadamia-nut lobster sauce. His restaurant occupies space in the Hawaii Kai Corporate Plaza, overlooking Maunalua Bay across the highway; turn off at Keahole Street. Open Monday through Friday 5:30 to 9:30 P.M. and Saturday and Sunday 5:00 to 9:30 P.M. Live music on weekends; for a quieter meal, ask for a table outside. Investment-caliber prices.

Another good dinner bet, closer to town, is **Le Bistro** (373–7990), in the Niu Valley Shopping Center off Kalanianaole Highway. Local boy Alan Tagasaki cooked his way across Europe, plus a stint in New Orleans. The menu features what he learned along the way. Open nightly except Tuesday 5:30 to 9:00 P.M. Expensive to investment-caliber.

After Koko Marina, the divided highway ends. Continue up the hill between Koko Head and Koko Crater, two large tuff cones formed during O'ahu's most recent eruption. (Not to worry, it happened about 100,000 years ago.) At the top of the hill, turn right into **Hanauma Bay Beach Park** (396–4229; www.hanaumabayhawaii.org). Peering over the rim into this unique indentation on Koko Head's east flank from the parking lot, you won't need a geology degree to recognize that the bay was once a volcanic crater, part of a chain of craters along the east coast. Hanauma's seaward wall has yielded to the assault of the ocean. You'll find a unique, sheltered bay with large coral deposits and a white-sand beach.

As a state underwater park off-limits to fishing, Hanauma has blossomed into a natural aquarium with fish of every shape, stripe, and color. You'll see giant rainbow parrotfish, banded convict tangs, exotic Moorish idols, and maybe even reed-thin trumpetfish. The different schools glitter like so many points of light. If the water inshore is murky, try the outer reef (but not in big surf). Newcomers have to watch a short video before they walk or ride a trolley down the steep path to the beach. A concession rents snorkeling equipment, and if you want to make yourself really popular with the fish, buy some food packets. There is a $3.00 entry fee ($1.00 parking). Open 6:00 A.M. to 6:00 P.M. (till 7:00 P.M. in summer months). Due to overcrowding, the park is closed on Tuesday and exercises capacity controls on parking. On the second

Saturday of the month (plus the fourth Saturday in summer), the park stays open until 10:00 P.M. for night snorkeling.

Before you leave Hanauma, there are a few more options for the adventurous to explore. Look for the **Toilet Bowl,** a unique rock formation in a hidden inlet just outside the mouth of the bay. Incoming waves are channeled into an exposed lava tube; as they ebb and flow, they "flush" a small pool at the end in a vigorous imitation of your household porcelain pot. The rocks around the edge are slippery, so be careful getting in. Once inside, it's safe so long as you stay in the center of the pool, and it's loads of fun. To get here, you used to be able to walk from the beach along the left side of the bay and around the outer rim. Access has been closed of late due to fear of falling rocks. Instead, you will need to find your way down from the parking lot following the top of the crater rim through an arid scrubland toward the mouth of the bay and then descending into the narrow canyon that opens into the back of the inlet. (There is no marked trail.) For those who prefer the high road, an alternative to visiting the Toilet Bowl is to ascend the spine of the crater by taking the blocked-off road that splits off near the park entrance from the highway. Your reward is a sweeping view of the island's southeastern coastline.

Past Hanauma Bay the highway swoops around another sunken crater (used as a firing range), then clings to the striated slopes of **Koko Crater,** which overlooks the deep blue of the Kaiwi Channel. This is the sort of drive you see featured in sports-car commercials. You wind in and out of the volcano's ridges and grooves, while beneath the highway the ocean crashes against the coast in a fury of foam and spray. Across the channel, Moloka`i darkens the horizon. If conditions are clear, you can make out Maui and Lana`i as well.

Less than a mile along the road, look for a small stone monument on your right, a hundred yards *before* the **Halona Blowhole** parking lot where the tour buses disgorge their loads. Pull over here instead and walk up the steps to this fishing shrine built by the Honolulu Japanese Casting Club. Carved into the upright rock, O Jisan, a guardian spirit, keeps a watchful eye on anglers casting from the wave-swept lava shelf below. The view from the monument extends along the coast in both directions. Below to your left, the tiny picturesque cove you see earned a cameo in the "kiss in the sand" scene in *From Here to Eternity.* Beware of currents beyond the rim if you swim here. Just around the cove, the Halona Blowhole sprays a fine mist through a hole in the lava shelf, driven by incoming waves that fill a sea cave underneath.

Past the blowhole, the highway straightens as it descends to the flat coastline of **Sandy Beach.** The bodysurfing here is famous, but for experts only. Because of the steep slope of the beach, waves crash with spine-snapping force directly onto the shore, and the undertow from the backwash is fierce. Red flags mean stick to the sand. In the summer, when trade-wind swells build up, the surfing circuit migrates here for bodyboarding contests. Youngsters favor "Sandy's" year-round as the hangout of choice for sand, sun, and scoping. The windswept field next to the beach is popular for stunt kites.

Just ahead you might turn up Kealahou Street and take another left to visit the **botanical gardens** inside steep-walled Koko Crater. Known as Kohelepelepe ("the fringed vagina") to the ancient Hawaiians, the crater's resemblance to that portion of the female anatomy is explained by legend. It seems that the swinish pig-god Kamapuaa had been in amorous pursuit of Pele. To distract him, Kapo, Pele's sister, threw her magically detachable vagina to O'ahu; its imprint remains on this spot. Notice that, as with Diamond Head, the higher southwestern walls reflect the direction of the trade winds when the crater formed. The garden inside mostly features xerophytic plants appropriate to the dry climate. Open daily 9:00 A.M. to 4:00 P.M.

After Kealahou Street, Kalanianaole Highway turns inland and climbs through a funnel-shaped valley between the edge of the Ko'olau Mountains and Makapuu Point. On your right, halfway up, look for a turnoff to a paved road with a locked gate. You can park here and hike 1.4 miles to the road's end at the scenic **Makapuu Lighthouse** at the eastern tip of the island. It's a great place to watch whales in winter.

You get a lesser version of the same view from the lookout farther ahead on the highway. Take a deep breath as you approach the top. More than half the windward coast unfolds before you, bordered by the bluest of ocean. From this side-on perspective, it's easy to trace the boundaries of the original 5,000-foot volcano that formed this half of the island. Instead of ending at the vertical wall of the windward cliffs, picture the Ko'olau ridges continuing to rise to a summit peak hovering somewhere above the present coastline and then descending roughly symmetrically on the other side. The line of islands dot-

Makapuu Point

The Case of the Missing (Half) Island

One of the most striking features of O'ahu is its Ko'olau Mountain pali, a wall of sheer cliffs that extend along half the island from Waimanalo to Waikane. Rising more than 3,000 feet at their highest point, the pali dominate the landscape of the southern windward coast. Their characteristic fluted indentations add an element of delicate beauty to the drama of their near-vertical slope.

This sheer cliff face stands in marked contrast to the gently sloping ridges of the Ko'olau Mountains' leeward slopes, which reach like so many fingers toward the coastal settlements of Honolulu, with deep valleys etched in between. Trails leading up these ridges to a pali overlook offer some of the island's most dramatic vistas. But what accounts for this very different topography on either side of the same mountain mass? Originally, the Ko'olau—along with most of the island—formed as a single volcano with roughly symmetrical edges. The summit of this ancestral volcano, which once reached perhaps 5,000 feet in elevation, was centered above the windward coast, roughly where Kailua and Kaneohe are today. Somehow, a huge chunk of this island mass disappeared along its southern windward edge, leaving only the leeward slopes, whose abrupt end at the pali bears witness to a now-vanished mountain.

That much of the geologic evidence is clear. The chain of islands dotting the windward coast offshore mark the outer edges of where the Ko'olau volcano once stood. Geologists tried to account for this disappearing mountain by citing the normal forces of erosion—the constant trade winds that weather the windward side and the ocean waves that tear against the coast.

ting the coast offshore formed as rift eruptions along the outer flank of this now-vanished mountain.

Anchored in the blue waters closest to the lookout, Rabbit and Turtle Islands are the southernmost members of this chain of offshore islands. The larger of the two, Rabbit Island got its name from a rabbit farm that once flourished on its scrub-covered slopes. Appropriately, the island's shape resembles the profile of a giant rabbit's head swimming offshore. Walk a little ways onto Makapuu Head for a better view along the coast. Notice the many rounded boulders here, garlanded by tiny orange blossoms of *ilima* scrub. These are river stones. The hanging valley you just drove up was gouged by an ancient river that drained the slopes of the mountain that was.

The highway descends from the lookout to picturesque ***Makapuu Beach.*** The waves here outdo even Sandy's and funnel into the cliff-ringed bay year-round. Surfers of all kinds come here, but inexperienced swimmers should stay out of the water. Look up to the sky to see the black *iwalani* ("bird of heaven") frigates that circle effortlessly above, watching for fish. These winged pirates

The problem was that O'ahu is simply not old enough (geologically speaking) for these slow-moving forces to have carved away that much rock in such a short time. It was a mystery.

A decade ago, however, an unmanned navy submarine made a remarkable discovery. Operating in very deep waters many miles off the coast of O'ahu, the sub was searching for the "black box" flight recorder from a downed airplane. The sub's sonar revealed a strange accumulation of debris—giant boulders, rubble, and so on—piled along the ocean floor. Subsequent investigation revealed that this debris had the same geologic composition as the Ko'olau Mountains. The stuff down there had come from up above.

Scientists calculated that for so many tons of rock to have traveled so far and so deep offshore, it had to have been moving very, very fast. This discovery led to a new explanation for the formation of the pali. Geologists now believe that somehow half of the island all at once took a cataclysmic plunge into the sea.

It turns out the Ko'olau pali are not the only example of such massive island-wide landslides. The sea cliffs along the north shore of Kaua'i and Moloka'i also appear to have formed in a similarly abrupt fashion. The lava flows that built these islands hardened into unstable layers like a pile of bricks without mortar. The impact of so much rock crashing into the ocean all at once gave rise to some amazing splash waves. Scientists have traced a massive prehistoric tsunami that flooded the island of Kaho'olawe up to the 500-foot level to one such monster landslide along the Big Island's Kona Coast.

This process is continuing still. A new peninsula formed off Moloka'i's North Shore from a recent collapse. For young islands, Hawaii's geologic history has been anything but dull.

often steal the catch from other birds. Trade winds running into the 1,000-foot wall of the Ko'olau cliffs create a constant updraft that hang gliders also can enjoy. Launching from the cliff-top, these daring flyers have set endurance records at this spot.

Across the road from the beach park, Sea Life Park (259–7933) operates a popular Sea World–type attraction. Open daily 9:30 A.M. to 5:00 P.M. $31 general admission. Snorkeling can be good to the left of the pier just ahead.

A couple of miles farther on Kalanianaole Highway, you reach **Waimanalo Beach,** a magnificent strand that stretches more than 3 miles around the gentle curve of Waimanalo Bay. The city and state beach parks here are lined with ironwood trees, and both are popular with weekend picnickers. Waimanalo Beach does get waves, but an offshore reef provides some protection. Its shallow waters offer an ideal learning ground for bodysurfing and boogie boarding.

As you move north, the Ko'olau cliffs grow taller and more lush as they recede from the shoreline. The interior plains area of Waimanalo is mostly farms run by Hawaiian homesteaders. Signs advertising accommodations here are for horses. Turn up any country road, and you'll see pig farms, equestrian stables, and fruit and vegetable gardens galore.

If you call ahead, you can arrange to visit the ***Hawaii Bonsai Culture Center*** (259–6886), open by appointment only. Home to almost 300 "elite bonsai" housed in exquisite ceramic pots with another 400 candidates in the making and 5,000 "pre-bonsai" under cultivation, the sixteen-acre landscaped property is a retirement project of master grower Walter Liew and his wife, Ann. The art of bonsai began more than 2,000 years ago in China, when Chinese physicians tired of constantly traveling to collect the healing herbs they needed from the mountain forests. What began as a practical method to cultivate a living pharmacy-in-miniature soon evolved into a sculptural art form. A wide variety of trees can be used, including elm, juniper, ficus, myrtle, and bougainvillea. Wires and other artifacts are used to curve the tree into the desired shape. It takes about five years to make a true bonsai, but the process can continue for decades, if not centuries. Walter's former career was as an antiques dealer, and the furnishings in his warehouse office reflect this; they include a wooden one-panel carving that came from the back of a settee used by the emperor of China and his two wives in their summer palace. The back ended up with General MacArthur in Japan. (The other half of the settee became a coffee table used by William Randolph Hearst in Hearst Castle.)

Farther on, ***Honolulu Polo Club*** takes to the field on the inland side of the road every Sunday at 2:30 P.M. from June to October. As the highway continues, it skirts the green peaks of ***Mount Olomana*** ("forked mountain"). Rising 1,643 feet from flat surroundings, this daggerlike spire often splits the clouds.

On the other side of Olomana, Kalanianaole Highway runs into Kailua Road opposite Castle Hospital. A right turn takes you past ***Kawainui Marsh,*** a waterfowl sanctuary, into Kailua Town. Kailua Road bends right at the town's main intersection, with Kuulei Road continuing straight ahead and Oneawa Street to the left.

Nature lovers should turn left onto Oneawa and continue about a mile before turning left onto Kaha Street (two streets before the canal). Park in the park at the end and follow the path that leads around to the right, across the canal and onto the elevated ***Dike Trail*** that borders Kaiwainui Marsh. Tame mallard and Muscovy ducks beg for handouts as you leave the park. Once you reach the dike, you have an ideal perch from which to observe the rich birdlife that the marsh sustains. In the distance, a breathtaking panorama of green hills and ridges rises above the marshland, silhouetted in ascending tiers that climax with the towering wall of the Ko`olau *pali.* You can walk on the dike the full mile to Kailua Road, emerging just before the entrance to town.

Finally, back at the main intersection, bearing right on Kailua Road brings you to the Kailua Chamber of Commerce's *visitor center* (261–2727), just ahead on the left in a remote section of the Kailua Shopping Center. There you can get information on other windward coast attractions. The center is staffed by volunteers Monday through Friday 10:00 A.M. to 4:00 P.M., Saturday till noon.

Those who just want to hit the beach should continue straight on Kuulei Road until you dead-end into Kalaheo Road, which runs along the coast. Turn right to get to *Kailua Beach Park.* Curving around from Mokapu Peninsula, Kailua Bay shelters its turquoise waters behind an outlying reef, where turtles are common. Flat (Popoia) Island floats offshore, but it's a long swim out. Sun worshipers delight in the fine white sand of Kailua Beach, and the onshore winds and calm seas make ideal learning conditions for windsurfing. But when the wind kicks up, the same onshore breezes turn the beach into a desert sand-blast and whip the bay into a frothy mass of whitened chop. That's when Robby Naish, Kailua resident and eight-time world-champion windsurfer, rigs up. You can rent equipment or arrange lessons at *Naish Hawaii* (262–6068), the Naish family shop on Hamakua Drive (the first cross street as you enter town on Kailua Road), or at *Kailua Sailboards* (262–2555), near the intersection of Kailua Road and Kalaheo; both also do kite surfing and kayaks. When the wind is down, the windward coast is ideal for kayaking, as both Kailua and Kaneohe Bays have numerous islands and sandbars to paddle to. The view from the water looking back at the Ko'olau Mountains is unsurpassed. You can also rent equipment for kayaking from *Twogood Kayak* (262–5656), at 345 Hahani Street. See page 100 for information on kayak tours.

If you continue east from Kailua Beach around the tip of Puu Halo Ridge, you enter Lanikai, a secluded residential area ringed by mountains and blessed with azure waters that beckon toward a distant pair of island peaks, the Moku Luas. Park and walk up any beach access path. If you come here at night during summer, you might see glow-in-the-dark plankton wash ashore, miniature phosphorescent specks that sparkle in the sand like fairy dust.

You can scale Kaiwi Ridge behind Lanikai for breathtaking coastal vistas. Turn up Kaelepulu Drive and pass the turnoff to the country club. The trail begins just before the entrance to the Bluestone Estates, starting from a driveway off to the left and running outside the wire fence of the estates. After the first 100 feet, you get on top of the ridge, and the views get better and better. You'll pass some military bunkers higher up. The ultimate panorama arrives with the second bunker about a half mile along.

If you linger to catch the sunset, you might end your day with a steak dinner or fresh grilled fish at *Buzz's Original Steakhouse* (261–4661). Resembling an oversized tree house, with a *hau* tree growing through the roof,

Buzz's sits directly across the street from Kailua Beach Park. Ask for the table where Bill and Hillary dined. Open daily 11:00 A.M. to 10:00 P.M., with a limited menu between 3:00 and 5:00 P.M. Moderate.

Other Kailua eateries cluster in town, near the main commercial intersection between Kailua and Kuulei Roads and Oneawa Street. Tucked away on a small side street just inland of the Kailua Shopping Center, **Buona Sera** (263–7696), at 131 Hekili Street (around the block from Naish), serves up zesty Italian seafood nightly 5:30 to 9:00 P.M. On the other side of the Kailua–Kuulei Road divider, **Casablanca** (262–8196), at 19 Hoolai, the second left as you enter town, belies its name with a cheerful blue exterior. Inside you'll find exotic Moroccan cuisine served Tuesday through Saturday 6:00 to 8:30 P.M. If you're in town before 6:00 P.M., be sure to stop at **Agnes Portuguese Shop** (262–5367), at 46 Hoolai, to sample ethnic specialties, including bean soup, sweetbread, and hot *malasadas* (a kind of doughnut). The malasadas are made fresh to order—yum! Open Tuesday through Saturday 6:00 A.M. to 6:00 P.M. and Sunday to 2:00 P.M. Closed Monday.

Two more eateries await at the Kaneohe edge of Kailua Bay. **Pinky's Pupu Bar & Grill** (254–6255), at 970 North Kalaheo Avenue, is a festive plantation ranch house overlooking a canal. Colorful giant fish, some carved from surfboards, swim among the rafters, among other nautical trappings. The menu roams island ethnic specialties with a few hip twists, but you might just stick to the broad range of pupus. Tuesday nights are kids' nights, and award-winning balloon sculptors create amazing objects. Open Monday through Saturday 3:00 to 10:00 P.M.; Sunday brunch served 8:00 A.M. to 2:00 P.M. Inexpensive to moderate.

To spend the night in Kailua, you can't beat the value offered by **Kailua Beachside Cottages** (262–4128; www.patskailua.com). Several units abut Kailua Beach Park (three have ocean views). The rentals range in price from $80 to $500 for an oceanfront unit right on the water. Three-night minimum stay. Over in Kaneohe, **Alii Bluffs B&B** (235–1124; 800–235–1151; www.hawaii scene.com/aliibluffs) offers two rooms overlooking the bay for $65 to $75 in a home full of Old World antiques and original oil paintings. Three-night minimum stay. Otherwise, **Hawaiian Islands Bed & Breakfast** (261–7895; 800–258–7895; www.lanikaibeachrentals.com) has the local bed-and-breakfast market pretty much cornered with almost a hundred listings in the area. Rooms with private baths start at $85.

Backtrack on Kailua Road past Castle Hospital. Kailua Road turns into the Pali Highway as a mass of green mountains surround you. Mount Olomana juts out on the left, with the Oneawa Hills to the right. Straight ahead, the corrugated cliff line of the Ko`olau pali marches forward with Puu Konahuanui, the highest peak at 3,150 feet. To the right, the deeply notched V of Nuuanu Pass stands out.

Those undeterred by Olomana's jagged profile can attempt the ascent from this side. The climb takes about one and a half hours. The view is fabulous. To reach the start of the **Olomana Trail** from the highway, take the first left after the hospital (Auloa Road), then turn left again immediately and bear right after the bridge.

For an equally scenic, but less taxing trek to Maunawili Falls, continue a block farther on Auloa, bear left at the fork onto Maunawili Road, and continue until it ends at Kelewina Street. The trail meanders through 1.5 miles of lush tropical jungle that alternates between mango, kukui, banana, ginger, heliconia, (abandoned) coffee trees, and even some nice ridge views. You'll cross Maunawili Stream four times before ending at the swimming hole beneath the falls a short distance up the left fork of the stream. It takes less than an hour each way.

To call it a day, return to the Pali Highway and continue straight to climb over the mountain pass into town. Otherwise, to continue circling the island, turn right onto Kamehameha Highway, a mile farther up (at the opposite end of Auloa Road). This road cuts behind the Oneawa Hills to reach Kailua's next-door neighbor, Kaneohe.

Two miles off Kamehameha Highway, turn left at Luluku Road for a restful visit to **Ho'omaluhia** ("peaceful place") **Botanical Garden** (233–7323). The road climbs into the lush Ko'olau foothills through banana farms at the edge of the park. Encompassing 400 acres of former farmland, the county's newest botanical park remains more of a forest reserve than a landscaped garden. The towering curtain of pali overhead creates a magnificent natural setting, while the thirty-two-acre artificially created lake provides the flood protection buffer that led to the park's creation.

Stop at the visitor center a mile from the park entrance to pick up information on the park's offerings and take in some exhibits on Hawaiian ethnobotany. From here you can drive the 2 miles of winding road past endlessly varied vegetation, with views of Kaneohe Bay and the hypnotic presence of the pali above. For those willing to walk, a number of trails meander through the gardens. Various sections have been planted with specimens from Africa, India, tropical America, Polynesia, and Hawaii. Ask the staff at the visitor center for free self-guiding pamphlets. The garden schedules a variety of walking tours, usually on weekends, as well as evening moon walks. Camping is allowed by advance permit Friday through Monday. Open daily 9:00 A.M. to 4:00 P.M.

After relaxing in Hoomaluhia, those continuing onward have to make a difficult choice. Two different routes will take you north. If you like ocean views, stick with Kamehameha Highway. You'll wind through residential gardens past stunning ocean vistas. You can stop at **Heeia State Park** (247–3156) at the beginning of the coastal stretch to learn some of the history of the area. Friends of Heeia staff the visitor center Monday through Friday 8:00 A.M. to 4:00 P.M. The park itself juts onto Kealohi Point in the middle of Kaneohe Bay, the largest in the state. Coconut Island, the biggest of many offshore islands in view, appeared on television as Gilligan's Island. To the right of the point, you can see Heeia Fishpond, one of dozens of former aquaculture ponds the Hawaiians of old cultivated along Kaneohe Bay. The Friends of Heeia also offer educational kayaking tours at a cost of $40 per half day.

If you prefer the majesty of mountains, turn left at the main intersection at the end of the mall. From here, Likelike Highway and H–3 tunnel back to Honolulu. The latter, a recently opened and highly controversial trans-Ko`olan route, is something of an eyesore, rising on stilts above the misty depths of Haiku Valley. To stay on the windward side, take the next right onto Kahekili Highway to continue north in the shadow of the Ko`olau pali. A left turn onto Haiku Road, at the fourth traffic light, leads you to Haiku Gardens, where **Hale`iwa Joe's** (247–6671) serves pleasant, open-air dinners for moderate prices from 4:30 P.M. nightly. Not far from here are the **Haiku Stairs,** a heart-stopping, near-vertical ascent up the face of the pali to a 2,800-foot summit. The stairs were originally built by the U.S. Coast Guard to maintain a ridgetop radio antenna. Unfortunately, legal problems have kept the city from opening them to the public. Call 523–2489 to see if the situation has changed.

Farther along Kahekili Highway, you'll pass the **Valley of the Temples,** an interdenominational mortuary park and the late Ferdinand Marcos's temporary resting place. The Byodo-In Temple at the back is particularly picturesque. Token admission charge.

The two highways reunite at Kahaluu Fishpond. To visit the secluded **Gallery & Gardens** (239–8146), at a nearby mountain retreat, take the second left onto Wailehua Road, then bear right onto Lama`ula Road and head up the hill. More than fifteen years of botanical plantings enhance the already beautiful natural setting, with exotic flowers to smell and seasonal fruits to taste. Try the "magic fruit" (sepotia berry), which turns sour tastes to sweet. A garden map and labeled markers help tell you what's what. Birdsongs from the aviary and wind chimes provide soothing melodies. The architecturally intriguing, Japanese-style gallery blends well with the beautiful artwork it contains. Hours vary; call for appointment.

Around the next ridge are the Waiahole and Waikane Valleys, havens for rural Hawaiians, with backyard taro and sweet-potato patches. The demise of O`ahu's sugar industry has freed up irrigation water for these traditional crops, which used to be diverted to the leeward side of the island. The highway leaves

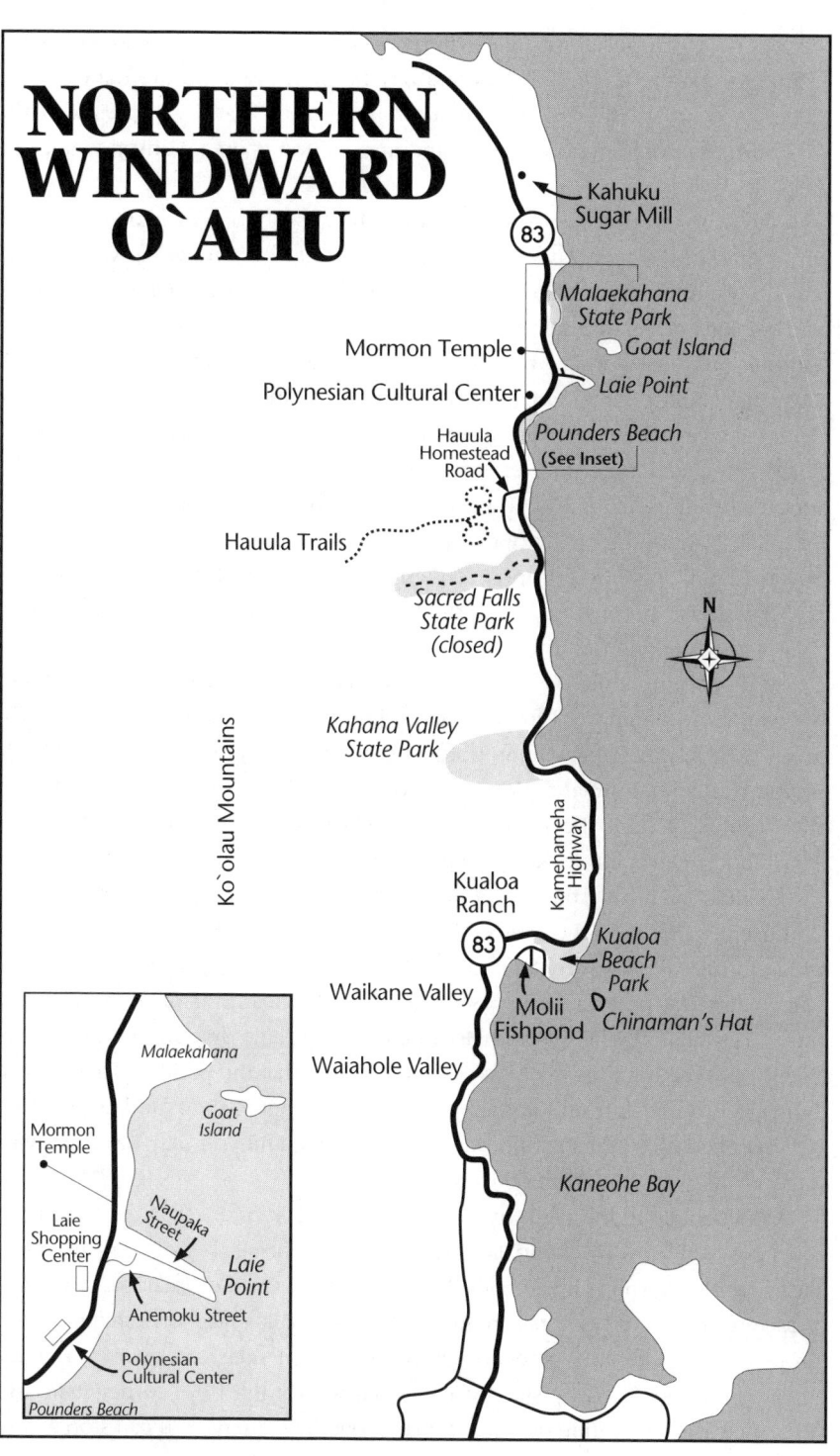

NORTHERN WINDWARD O`AHU

Kahuku Sugar Mill

83

Malaekahana State Park

Goat Island

Mormon Temple

Polynesian Cultural Center

Laie Point

Hauula Homestead Road

Pounders Beach (See Inset)

Hauula Trails

Sacred Falls State Park (closed)

Kahana Valley State Park

Ko`olau Mountains

Kamehameha Highway

Kualoa Ranch

83

Kualoa Beach Park

Waikane Valley

Molii Fishpond

Chinaman's Hat

Waiahole Valley

Kaneohe Bay

Malaekahana

Goat Island

Mormon Temple

Naupaka Street

Laie Shopping Center

Laie Point

Anemoku Street

Polynesian Cultural Center

Pounders Beach

the valleys to slope along hills where cattle graze. As you begin to curve around the northern edge of Kaneohe Bay beneath the imposing Kanehoalani Ridge, look through the forest on the right-hand side to catch glimpses of **Molii Fishpond,** the only pond on the island in continuous operation since ancient times. Its harvest includes mullet, moi, and tilapia.

The fishpond belongs to **Kualoa Ranch** (237–8515), which also owns the land inland of the highway. The ranch's history dates from the early Hawaiian monarchy, and it has remained under the original family ownership. The crumbled remains of a stone smokestack visible from the highway mark the site of a former mill built during owner Gerrit Judd's short-lived attempt at running a sugar plantation prior to ranching. The ranch has since diversified into several ventures, of which aquaculture is only one. It runs a range of tourism activities aimed at the adventure traveler, from ATV rides to a shooting range (as well as horseback riding, naturally). The ranch also conducts a Tropical Garden and Hawaiian Fishpond tour that includes a short boat ride to the ranch's offshore "secret island." It's offered upon request on weekdays 11:00 A.M. to 3:00 P.M.; $15. If you ask permission, you might be able to visit the fishpond on your own, without taking the tour.

At the far rim of the bay, pause for a scenic break at **Kualoa Beach Park.** *Wiliwili* trees, flaming red in late winter, line the entry road. A narrow sandy beach with adequate swimming borders the long grassy park. The views back around the bay and inland along the Ko`olau wall are breathtaking. Note the turtle profile of Kaneohe Peninsula—the other side of the bay—now well in the distance. Gates are locked at night here for secure camping.

Kualoa has a long history as one of the most sacred spots on the island. O`ahu chieftains brought their children here to learn the necessary arts with which to rule. Passing canoes had to lower their sails out of respect. Offshore, Chinaman's Hat bears a close resemblance to the headgear of Chinese immigrants. Hawaiians call the island Mokolii, meaning "little dragon," because their legend says the island is really the tail of a dragon that the goddess Hiiaka slew during her trip back from Kaua`i. People do wade out to the island at low tide, but you need footwear to walk on the sharp coral, and you may have to swim some of the way. It's about 500 yards out.

Continue along the highway past the smokestack of an 1864 sugar mill. As you round the tip of Kanehoalani Ridge, brace yourself, because in the miles ahead your eyes will struggle with divided loyalties. On the ocean side, a series of picturesque bays beckons. In sunlight, these shallow lagoons shimmer like turquoise, sapphire, and emerald. On the mountain side, you peer into virgin green valleys bordered by steep cliffs. You'll want a third eye to negotiate the bends in the road! A string of hamlets spaces out the scenery. You can stop at any of the beach parks along the way for a dip. During the week, your only company may be a few fishermen casting bamboo poles or throw-nets from the reef.

About 3 miles along, the road curves around the deep indentation of Kahana Bay. Pass some overgrown fishponds and turn left into **Kahana Valley State Park** (237–7766). Extending inland the length of the valley, this is the only publicly owned *ahupua`a* in the state. Ahupua`a were the old wedge-shaped land sections that ran from the top of the mountains down to the sea, making each community self-contained in the raw materials needed for every-day life. Wetland taro and a working fishpond help do so today. Kahana Valley still contains about thirty-one families, whom the state has incorporated into a "living history" program to teach schoolchildren about the valley's heritage and demonstrate traditional crafts. You can turn up the road to the park orientation office and chat with the staff, if anyone is in. If not, obtain a trail map for a val-ley hike from a rack outside, or take a swim in the stream mouth or ocean. The many tall trees with red-tinged leaves around here are known as false *kamani*, or tropical almonds.

Past Kahana Bay in Kaaawa, look for the 1921 federal flatbed truck parked in front of **Ahi's Restaurant** (237–8474), a funky green bamboo cantina. The menu at this eatery is standard local American, with tasty shrimp specials. Grab a table out back to enjoy the mountain views. Open Monday through Saturday 11:00 A.M. to 8:30 P.M. and Sunday 11:00 A.M. to 7:30 P.M. Enjoy live Hawaiian music on the weekend, with the bar open until 2:00 A.M.

About 5 miles up the road, next to the 21-mile marker, you'll see the ruins of Lanakila Church next to its replacement. If you turn up Hauula Homestead Road and continue a few hundred yards straight ahead on the unpaved Maakua Road, you'll reach the heads of two alternative trails. You can choose from a scenic 2.5-mile loop up the ridges on either side of the valley on the Hauula and Papali Trails.

Past the 20-mile point, **Pounders Beach** has a lovely setting and body-surfing waves that live up to its name. Next comes the overwhelmingly Mormon town of Laie. You'll see the thatched roofs of the **Polynesian Cultural Center** (293–3333) run by the church on your left. Authentically re-created villages from the major Polynesian islands are "populated" by Polynesian students attending the nearby Hawaii campus of Brigham Young University. Various traditional crafts are demonstrated, from coconut husking to *lauhala* weaving. It's fairly educational but definitely geared to tourists. Admission is $30. Open Monday through Saturday 11:00 A.M. to 6:30 P.M. If you visit the center, consider returning at 7:30 P.M. for the Polynesian revue, which has a cast of more than one hundred performers. The Ali`i Luau package, which includes admission to the center, *luau* dinner, and show, is $79.

Past the cultural center, opposite Laie Shopping Center, turn right onto Anemoku Street and then right again onto Naupaka Street to the tip of *Laie Point.* A magnificent view awaits at the end of this narrow peninsula. You can see the green mass of the Ko`olau Mountains stretching as far back as Kaneohe. Waves crash against the many islets offshore, one of which has a natural *puka* (hole) gouged through its middle. Anglers cast their lines into the teal-colored sea. As you continue north on the highway, gaze back along the stately drive that leads to the *Mormon Temple,* the self-styled "Taj Mahal of the Pacific."

Malaekahana State Park, a mile farther, enjoys a truly idyllic location. Deep deposits of white sand are piled along this mile-wide bay. The steep hills backing the beach offer shade from beautifully diverse forest. If you wade a few hundred yards through the shallow waters, you'll reach *Goat Island,* a seabird sanctuary. You can explore the island perimeter with views along the coast, but don't disturb the nesting sites in the center.

The Kahuku section of the beach, accessed by a separate entrance, has rustic "cabins" available for rent, maintained by friends of Malaekahana. Most are two- or three-bedroom cottages, with a bath, that sleep six to eight people. They rent for $66 to $250. Campsites cost $5.20 per person. There's only one hot shower on-site. Gates lock at 7:00 P.M. Call 293–1736 for information.

Beyond Malaekahana you enter Kahuku, a former plantation town largely settled by Samoans. The *Kahuku Sugar Mill,* which closed in 1971, still stands in the center of town. You can ogle its innards in a free self-guided tour. The flywheels, crushers, clarifiers, and myriad connecting pipes are all color coded in bright paint. When operational, the mill could churn through fifty tons of fresh cane an hour, burning the leftover bagasse for power. Gift shops and restaurants crowd the machinery in the factory center, taking the edge off the heavy industrial atmosphere.

Just ahead, the Tanaka Plantation Store complex is home to *The Only Show in Town* (293–1295)—for antiques, that is. The tiny store is crammed with antique bottles, vintage campaign buttons, classic aloha shirts, and much more. Open daily 11:00 A.M. to 5:00 P.M. The highway continues around the northern tip of the island, but it runs inland and you hardly notice the bend. Windmills on the ridge above the highway make up an experimental energy project.

North Shore and Central O`ahu

Surfing was born in the Hawaiian Islands, and the North Shore of O`ahu remains the supreme venue for the sport. Winter surf hits the north and west shores of all the islands, but Nature and her handmaiden, Geology, have con-

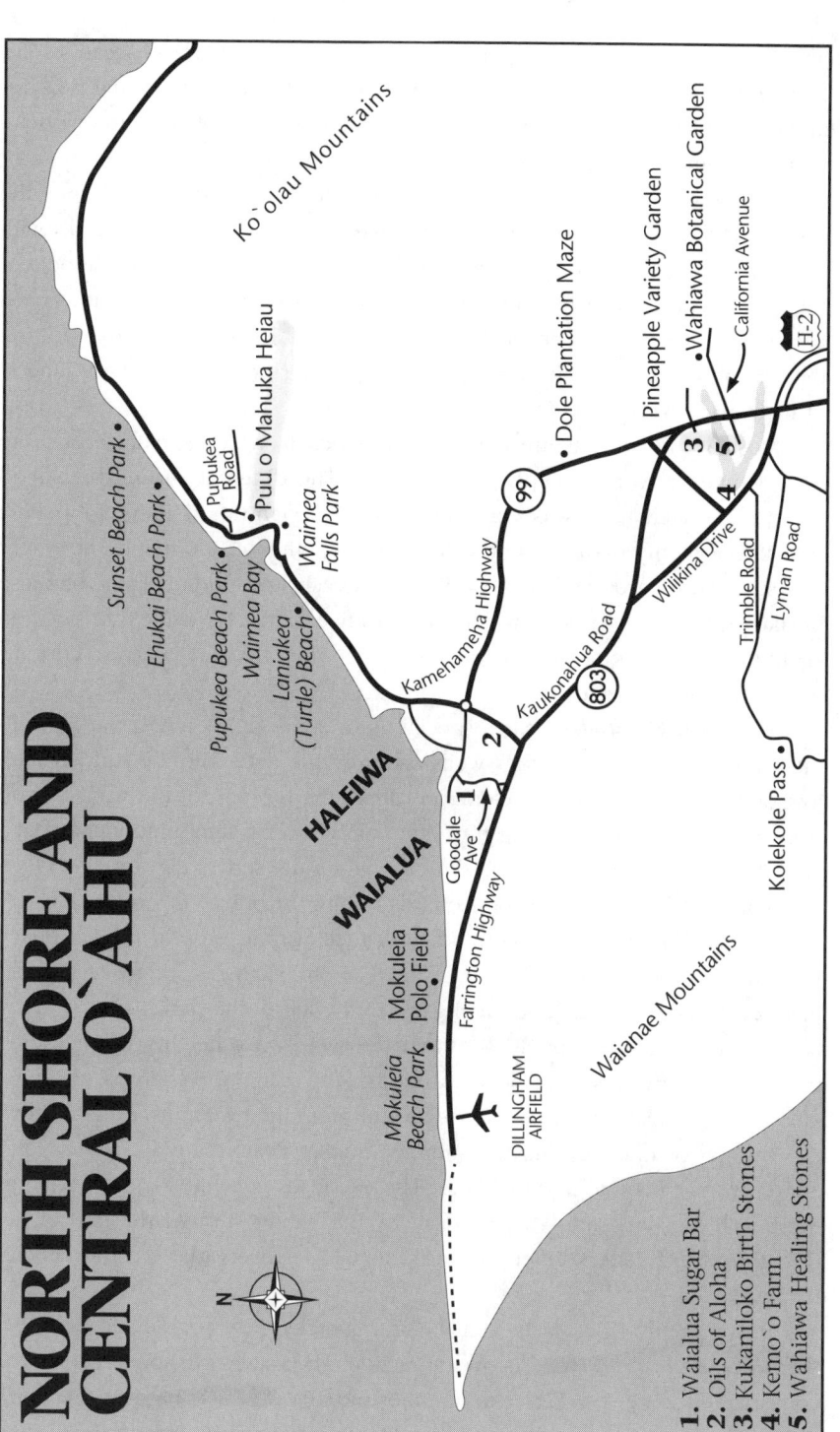

spired to make O`ahu stand apart. All along this coast, incoming ocean swells, having traveled thousands of miles from storms off Alaska, reach the beaches and rise to form the most perfect tubes and the biggest breakers in the world—and the ultimate surfing challenge.

Winter surf typically lasts from November to April, during which time the professional surfing circuit descends in force. If your visit should overlap with a major competition, the spectacle is worth taking in. The hype and hoopla of big-time surfing—with its corporate sponsors, rock music, and bikini beach contests—electrify these normally sedate beaches. Competitors are judged on the size of the waves they catch, the length of their ride, and the "radicalness" of their maneuvers.

Most of the contests are held at Sunset Beach, which stretches for more than 2 miles of wide, steeply sloping sand. The different surfing breaks all along have such names as Gas Chambers, Velzyland, and Banzai Pipeline. WARNING: At any place along the North Shore, when it's pumping, the waves can snap surfboards and spines. The backwash and undercurrent of these breakers can hold you underwater for up to five minutes. Needless to say, you shouldn't even walk near the shoreline. Even when the surf is down, currents pose a danger all winter.

The **Banzai Pipeline** has a special notoriety as the home of the "world's most dangerous wave." As big swells rise from the deep into the sudden shallow of a coral shelf, their acceleration causes the top part of the wave to curl over into a tunnel of breaking fury that combs over waters only inches deep and filled with razor-sharp coral. On days when the surf swells above 15 feet, you will find but a handful of diehards willing to brave the "tube ride" off Banzai reef. To watch them cut and slash their way in, stop at Ehukai Beach Park, the second beach park along Kamehameha Highway, opposite the elementary school. The Pipeline breaks just to the left of the park.

By the way, you should know that Hawaiian wave heights are measured from behind. Because the water in front of a rising wave drops an equal amount, the waves will appear twice as high from the beach. It's quite a show.

In total contrast, during the summer, Sunset Beach, like all of the North Shore, transforms into a glassy lake. The expanses of white sand broaden as the beach reclaims sand carved away by the winter surf. At the end of the day, the placid waters reflect the unforgettable sunsets that are the beach's namesake.

Beyond Sunset Beach the coastline turns rocky. Few people surf here, but **Pupukea Beach Park** has its own attraction. The waters offshore are a marine conservation zone. During calm summer months, Shark's Cove, at the north end of the park, offers especially breathtaking underwater terrain, flush with fish, seaweed, coral, and lava cave formations. Don't worry: "Shark's" is a misnomer.

To the left of the cove is the site of a former rock quarry. An ancient coral reef has been excavated, leaving a horseshoe-shaped outer wall enclosing a shallow lagoon. During winter, huge waves flood the walls; as the water level inside rises, a swift current draining out to the cove can sweep the unwary off their feet. The sound and spray can be mesmerizing, but stay out of the water at these times.

Turn left up Pupukea Road at the Foodland supermarket, just past the quarry. Climb a half mile uphill and take the turnoff on the right for *Pu'u o Mahuka Heiau.* Several speed bumps later, you reach O'ahu's largest ancient temple. The low, terraced walls slope in sections down a grassy field overlooking the angled coastline. In 1793 three British sailors from one of Capt. George Vancouver's ships ended up as sacrifices here. Walk to the far side of the heiau to peer down into lush Waimea Valley and Waimea Bay. On the other side of the valley, cane fields cover the ridge plateaus.

Across the highway from "three tables" reef at the southern edge of Pupukea Beach Park is *Backpackers Vacation Inn & Hostel* (638–7838; www.backpackers-hawaii.com). It was started by the late Mark Foo, a local boy turned surfing legend. When Mark left to paddle his surfboard around the world, his sister Sharlynn took over operations and has expanded them considerably. In addition to a hostel bunk, you can rent private rooms, cottages, and apartments in the area—some are actually beachfront. For a unique experience, ask to stay in "plantation village," a lane of tiny clapboard homes formerly used by immigrant cane workers. The colorfully painted cottages offer a range of lodging options, from dorm beds for $22 to $27 to private bedrooms in a shared cabin with kitchens for $58 to $67. Oceanfront studio apartments rent for $80 to $200. Even funkier lodging can be found up the hill at *Ulu Wehi B&B* (638–8161; www.uluwehi.com), on the site of a working fruit and flower farm. Guest quarters that can accommodate three people are in a rustic one-room shack that has a full kitchen, laundry facilities, and a separate bathroom outhouse with an outdoor shower. It rents for $120, which includes a daily breakfast basket filled with fruit from the garden. The one-acre property is nicely landscaped and includes an 85-foot lap pool. No smoking.

South of Pupukea, *Saints Peter & Paul Mission* has a tall tower and an unusual origin. The church building was erected as a rock-crushing plant during the construction of the highway and only later was converted to a mill of a more spiritual nature. After passing the mission, the highway curves around the mouth of world-famous *Waimea Bay.* The island's highest ridable surf breaks on the bay's outer bowl, with monster combers that sometimes tower more than 30 feet and can flood the highway. Expert bodysurfers tackle an equally daunting shore break. In the summer, calm returns as crystalline waters mirror the beauty of Waimea's picture-postcard setting. Then you can join locals in diving off "the rock" on the left side of the bay.

Inland from the bay, **Waimea Valley Audubon Center** (638–9199) spreads across the entire valley. If you want to get an idea what Puu o Mahuka might have looked like in ancient times, you can inspect the restored **Hale o Lono Heiau** near the parking lot free of charge. While nowhere as big as its neighbor up on the ridge, the structure includes a reconstructed oracle tower, offering stand, and drum house that are considerably more photogenic. If you pay admission to the park, you can explore other archaeological sites, including a reconstructed Hawaiian village. You can also try your hand at Hawaiian crafts and games, watch and learn hula, and explore the gardens, whose thirty-six sections include more than 6,000 species of plant life from around the world, including the only known specimen of *Kokia cookei,* a flowering tree of the hibiscus family. At the back of the valley, cliff divers plunge 60 feet from the top of Waimea Falls in acrobatic displays, and visitors are welcome to swim in the natural pool below at other times. Open daily from 9:30 A.M. to 5:00 P.M. Admission $8.00; $2.00 parking. Free ethnobotany tours on Thursday and Sunday at 2:00 P.M.; historical tour of Native Hawaiian living site Tuesday and Saturday at 1:00 P.M.

Past Waimea Bay, Kamehameha Highway continues through dairy pastures past hidden surfing beaches. About 2 miles along, just after the highway's second junction with the Pohakuloa beach loop, you'll reach an unobstructed view of the shoreline at **Laniakea Beach,** a tiny surfing cove that is also one of the best places in the islands to see *honu* (green sea turtles). Weighing up to 400 pounds, these gentle giants feed on seaweed offshore, and usually one or two of them can be found basking on the sand, to the delight of visitors. (Look— but don't touch.) Honu can live up to seventy years, reaching sexual maturity only in their mid-twenties or later. Their green color comes from the fat tissue stored inside their bodies. These turtles migrate throughout the Hawaiian Islands, nesting primarily at the remote French Frigate Shoals, 560 miles northwest of O'ahu. Nesting females deposit a hundred or more ping-pong-ball-size eggs in a sand pit that they dig and then cover with their flippers. The temperature of the eggs during incubation determines the gender of the hatchlings, with lower temperatures producing males. You can distinguish mature males from females by their much longer, wider tails.

A few miles farther down the highway, Haleiwa sits at the crook in the angle formed by the coastline. The highway now bypasses the town, but it's worth a stop. Haleiwa took its name from an early mission outpost here. It grew into a popular seaside resort when the Haleiwa Hotel opened at the end of the railroad line in 1899. Things quieted down after the war, but hippies and surfers brought the town back to life in the 1960s, and artists have made up the most recent wave of invaders. Many of the original plantation shops remain along the highway, nestled in between modern plazas full of boutiques. The town's commercial district stretches almost a mile.

If you didn't get to see surfing on the beaches, you might stop before the bridge at **Surf and Sea** (637–9887), the biggest of the many surf shops in town. Continuous surfing videos inside offer a vicarious substitute. All the top brands of boards and designer beachwear are here, blazing with neon color. You can buy or rent all types of water-sport equipment, as well as intriguing accessories such as Dr. Zogg's Sex Wax (for your surfboard). Open daily from 9:00 A.M. to 7:00 P.M.

For more conventional surfing exhibits, continue into town to the **North Shore Surfing Museum** (637–8888), in the North Shore Marketplace. A variety of displays and memorabilia recount the story of how "Hawaii's gift to the world" became an international craze and icon of free-spirited youth. Open Wednesday through Monday from 11:00 A.M. to 6:00 P.M. To get there, cross the arching concrete bridge over the Anahulu River. The attractive **Lili'uokalani Church,** on your left at the second cross street, was founded in 1832 and rebuilt in 1961. Queen Lili'uokalani attended services here during her frequent vacations in Haleiwa. In 1892 she presented the church with an elaborate seven-dial clock that Queen Victoria had given her. Instead of numerals, the hour hand points to the twelve letters in Lili'uokalani's name. You can still see it ticking today.

Across the street, **Matsumoto's** perpetuates another longtime Haleiwa tradition. This forty-plus-year-old plantation store cranks out the most famous shave ice on the island, packed into paper cones. Choose from a range of tropical fruit–flavored cane syrups to sweeten your ice or ask for a "rainbow" of any three. Local connoisseurs eat theirs with sweet azuki beans or ice cream on the bottom.

For a more substantive repast, visit **Cafe Haleiwa** (637–5516) near the south edge of town, owned by Duncan Campbell, a noted surfboard designer. The surfing posters on the wall reflect the clientele who come by for an early-morning feed before hitting the waves. The food's great, but the catch is that they close daily at 1:45 P.M. Farther down, **Kua Aina Sandwich** (637–6067) serves a hefty grilled mahimahi sandwich and great burgers. Open daily 11:00 A.M. to 8:00 P.M. Or, if it's a caffeine fix you crave, visit **Coffee Gallery** (637–5355), in the North Shore Marketplace. Order from an impressive collection of coffees grown on four different Hawaiian islands, and sip your java in a *très* funky painted/mosaic lanai. Open daily from 7:00 A.M. to 8:00 P.M. If you want a sunset dinner to remember, double back to **Jameson's by the Sea** (637–4336) or **Hale`iwa Joe's** (637–8005), across from the harbor near the entrance to town. The menu at both features fresh seafood as well as other items. But the real feast is the view as the sun drops behind Kaena Point, bathing the water and harbor sailboats in a rosy glow. Jameson's upstairs has the better view, but Joe's has a more varied and tastier menu and nicer ambience. Jameson's is open Monday through Friday 10:30 A.M. to 9:00 P.M. and weekends 9:00 A.M. to 9:00 P.M.; expensive. Joe's is open Monday through Friday 11:30 A.M. to 9:30 P.M. and weekends to 10:30 P.M.; moderate.

Haleiwa has no shortage of galleries in which to browse. In the center of town, **Wyland's Gallery** (637–7498) has the biggest name, though the artist's most famous works don't fit in his gallery. Robert Wyland paints giant murals of humpback whales to promote marine conservation (and himself). Open Monday through Saturday from 9:00 A.M. to 9:00 P.M. and Sunday to 7:00 P.M. Inside, you'll find works in various media by a range of artists revolving around a basic ocean theme. For women's clothing check out **Oogenesis Boutique** (637–4580), which features the work of Inge Himmelmann, a German fashion designer who's been working in Haleiwa since the hippie days. Open daily from 10:00 A.M. to 6:00 P.M.

After disporting yourself in Haleiwa, continue straight on Kaukonahua Road, past the rotary, following the sign to Mokuleia. About a half mile farther, on your right, you'll pass the **Oils of Aloha** (637–5620), set up in a former movie house. The company is most notable for producing a unique line of cosmetics made from *kukui* nuts. The kukui, a relative of the castor bean, is Hawaii's state tree, whose versatile nuts had many uses in ancient times. The word *kukui* literally means "light"; the oil-rich nuts are known in English as candlenuts and were used as just that. The meat from the kukui nut also served as a potent laxative, and the shells were polished for jewelry. Kukui oil has useful skin care properties, and the company concentrates on this angle. A kukui tree grows right outside the company building, which unfortunately is not open to visitors.

Continue on Kaukonahua Road until it runs into Farrington Highway. Turn right, and then, a half mile along, exit right from the rotary onto Goodale Avenue to enter Waialua. Waialua is Haleiwa's less glamorous twin across the bay. While Haleiwa basked in the limelight as a resort/recreation center, Waialua schlepped along as a working sugar town. Now that sugar has ended, its fortunes are uncertain, although a portion of former sugar land has been replanted with coffee. Because Waialua lies off the highway, few people come here. You'll see some vintage clapboard homes and the red-dirt-stained remains of the former mill.

Return to Farrington Highway and continue west through the cane fields. *Mokuleia Beach Park* arrives a few miles farther along, but the wide sandy beach stretches for miles on either side, and unmarked turnoffs from the highway allow you to find secluded spots. Swimming can be hazardous, especially during winter surf. If you're here on a Sunday afternoon from late April to June or October to early December, stop by the polo grounds to watch a chukker or two. Matches start at 2:00 P.M. If you think beaches and polo are too down-to-earth, continue on to Dillingham Airfield, where *glider rides* (677–3404) take off daily from 10:00 A.M. to 5:30 P.M. Rides ranging from ten to sixty minutes are available; prices range from $59 to $129 per person. Call for more details and for reservations.

Mokuleia has a couple of accommodation options for those who want to spend more time on the North Shore. Spartan quarters can be had at *Camp Mokuleia* (637–6241), which offers lodging on a beachfront lot for $65 to $80 per couple and tent camping for $10 per person. No tent camping is available on Wednesday. *Camp Erdman* (637–4615; www.camperdman.net) has cabins for $75 to $150, which includes a full meal plan. Linens can be provided if requested two weeks in advance.

The road ends at the start of *Kaena Point Nature Preserve,* a unique coastal habitat of endangered wildlife and plants. Kaena Point lies 2 miles farther, but the walk from the Waianae side is more scenic. Backtrack on Farrington Highway and continue on as the highway begins to climb onto the Leilehua Plateau between O'ahu's two mountain ranges. At a certain elevation you emerge from some trees, and voilà, something's changed. Instead of tall cane grass walling you in, you find that your gaze stretches unobstructed across miles of spiky pineapple rows. James Dole introduced Hawaii's first commercial pineapples in nearby Wahiawa. Unlike sugarcane, the plants are not native, but thanks to Dole, they soon became an international symbol of the islands. You can still see heavily garbed workers stooped over the fields, planting and harvesting by hand.

Four miles along the highway, take the right fork 2 more miles to Del Monte's *Pineapple Variety Garden* to see all the unique forms these thorny bromeliads take. *Dole Plantation* (621–8408) has its own touristy visitor center, angling 1 mile back on Kamehameha Highway (Route 99). It includes the "world's largest maze," planted from hibiscus and other tropical flower bushes and forming the pattern of guess what fruit? There's also a "pineapple train" ride and a plantation garden tour. Open daily 9:00 A.M. to 5:30 P.M. $5.00 admission charge for the maze.

Continue on a half mile past the garden in the same direction and turn right at the traffic light onto an unpaved plantation road. A few hundred yards

Stone Age Magic

The ancient Hawaiians practiced a religion that was basically animist. They believed that everything in nature had a spiritual dimension that people needed to respect. Canoe builders would say a prayer before cutting down giant koa trees. Fishermen would leave offerings at fishing shrines to thank the ocean gods for the ocean's bounty. So it was with *pohaku,* the Hawaiian word for stone or rock.

Even today in this modern age, stories abound of farmers who clear giant boulders from their fields only to return the next morning and find the stones back in their original positions. Hawaiians explain this by saying that the pohaku "did not want to be moved." Certain pohaku were inhabited by powerful spirits whose influence men and women could elicit through ritual offerings. For example, barren women would seek out fertility stones known to exist on each island. Moloka'i's phallic rock is the most famous example. Travelers crossing dangerous terrain would leave offerings at guardian stones, such as the giant boulder at Kolekole Pass. The sacred birth stones at Wahiawa's Kukaniloko provide yet another well-known example.

Wahiawa is home to another set of somewhat more obscure pohaku, the so-called Wahiawa Healing Stones, which have their own curious history. Although the stones have an ancient lineage, the origins of their healing powers remain shrouded in mystery. The stones came to the public's attention in the 1920s after some well-publicized miracles and for a time attracted mass pilgrimages, which continued until the outbreak of World War II.

Although largely forgotten since then, the stones continue to attract visitors from diverse religious backgrounds. Housed in a makeshift cinder-block shrine of sorts, the stones had a statue of the Virgin Mary placed beside them for many years. More recently, the stones have been adopted by a group of local Hindus, who perceive one of the stones to be a Shiva *lingam* and another to bear the likeness of the elephant god Ganesh. The Hindu community has built a newer marble structure around the stones and visit on the morning of the third Sunday of each month to conduct *pooja,* a ritual ceremony.

If you would like to visit the stones, too, you can find them in Wahiawa town on California Avenue, a half mile west of Kamehameha Highway (the opposite direction from the botanical garden), at the corner of Kaalalo Place just past the elementary school.

into the pineapple fields, you'll reach a tight ring of eucalyptus and palm trees encircling a cluster of largish boulders. Hawaiians called this curious oasis *Kukaniloko,* and women of royal descent came here to give birth so that their children would be born with the necessary *mana* to rule as kings and queens. If you look to the Waianae Mountains in the distance, you can trace a profile of the *wahine hapai* (pregnant woman) to the right of the V-shaped Kolekole Pass. Kamehameha I wanted to send his sacred wife, Keopuolani, to O`ahu to bear his first child at these birth stones, but she took sick and couldn't leave the Big Island. Some say Liholiho's early death at age twenty-six sprang from this inauspicious birth.

Continue on the same road, and you'll cross Lake Wilson, an artificial reservoir used for sugar irrigation, on your way into Wahiawa town. Wahiawa grew up as a plantation town, but its lifeblood today rests in the mammoth Schofield Army Barracks nearby, as the countless fast-food and chain restaurants attest. One restaurant, however, stands out. *Molly's Smokehouse* (621–4858) features real Texas barbecue and homemade goodies. Open daily from 11:00 A.M. to 9:00 P.M. Inexpensive to moderate.

For a quiet picnic spot, turn left up California Avenue, the second cross street, and go about a half mile to the *Wahiawa Botanical Garden.* Sugar planters began the twenty-seven-acre garden as an experimental forest growth in the 1920s. The mature trees now rise majestically from the slopes of a sunken ravine, leavened with ferns, palms, and other tropical plants. Open daily 9:00 A.M. to 4:00 P.M. Free.

South of town you can loop back around the lake to Schofield Barracks. Across the highway from the base, stop at *The Pub at Kemo'o Farm* (621–1835) for a touch of local nostalgia. The farm got its start in 1916. It evolved from a farmer's market to an ice-cream parlor before capitalizing on the first liquor license issued after Prohibition.

Today three different bars on the premises carry on the tradition with thirty kinds of beer on tap and forty-five more bottled. Live music is featured Thursday through Saturday with your choice of rock 'n' roll, island style/reggae, and country music. Open daily from 7:00 A.M. to 2:00 A.M., with the lakeside lounge open from 2:00 P.M. (noon on weekends).

To crown your central O'ahu visit in spectacular fashion, enter the barracks and ask the guard to direct you to *Kolekole Pass.* (Lyman or Trimble Road will put you on the main road up.) You can see the deep notch in the mountains as you drive up. About 5 miles from the entry gate, you reach a parking area at the top. On your right, a tall white cross stands on a nearby hill facing back toward central O'ahu. A short hike in the opposite direction brings you to a spectacular overlook onto the Lualualei Valley on the Waianae Coast. It's less panoramic than the Nuuanu Pali, but at 1,720 feet, the cliff-top perch is just as exhilarating, and you may well have it all to yourself. Watch your footing, though; no handrails here!

On the way to the overlook, you pass *Kolekole Stone,* a massive boulder along the trail. An eroded basin on the top of the stone, drained by curious troughlike ridges, has given rise to some latter-day legends about gruesome human sacrifices. Actually, Hawaiian executioners dispatched their victims without bloodshed; a mangled corpse was not a fitting offering to place before the gods. An older, perhaps more comforting tradition holds that the stone is inhabited by a guardian spirit that keeps watch over travelers crossing this lonely mountain pass. Kolekole Road continues over and down to the other side of the pass, but only military types can drive it.

Departing from the outskirts of Wahiawa and Schofield, the H–2 Freeway whisks you back to Honolulu. As you leave the central plateau, you see mountains on both sides, pineapple fields, steep gulches, and then suddenly the blue lakes of Pearl Harbor stretched out below.

Leeward O`ahu

Having done Honolulu and the "circle island" drives, it's time to "head Ewa," which is the local version of "go west" toward the Ewa District. Honolulu itself is moving this way. Having spread all the way east to Hawaii Kai, Honolulu has shifted course to ooze into the "second city" of Leeward O`ahu. Few tourists make it out here. Few rain clouds blow this way, either. That's what *leeward* means (sheltered from the wind). All this land was originally scrubland, too arid even to support cattle. But underground, where the folds of the island's two volcanoes had overlapped, millions of gallons of freshwater waited to be tapped. In 1877 a canny Scotsman named James Campbell bought 40,000 acres of the "worthless" land and successfully dug a series of artesian springs that made him an instant millionaire. The sugarcane that once covered these lands is being replaced by diversified crops, although the biggest new crop is housing projects.

To the west of the modern Pearl City metropolis, the town of Waipahu grew up as a separate plantation community. To explore, take the Waipahu exit from H–1 and get onto Farrington Highway. About 1.5 miles along, turn up Waipahu Depot Road toward the sugar mill.

At the mill, turn left onto Waipahu Road, and just ahead on your left is *Hawaii's Plantation Village* (677–0110; www.hawaiiplantationvillage.org), surrounded by taro fields. You enter the park through a "time tunnel" to get to an authentically re-created nineteenth-century plantation camp inside. You can then wander through life-size dwellings representative of the many different ethnic groups that worked Hawaii's plantations.

The garden organizers have acquired many unique items, such as an antique *tofu-ya*, used to grind bean curd in Kahuku, and the Inari Shinto Shrine, rescued from destruction in Moiliili. Some of the displays offer hands-on learning; others provide fascinating vignettes. Learn the folklore that guided immigrant women facing childbirth in a foreign land. Master a few phrases of

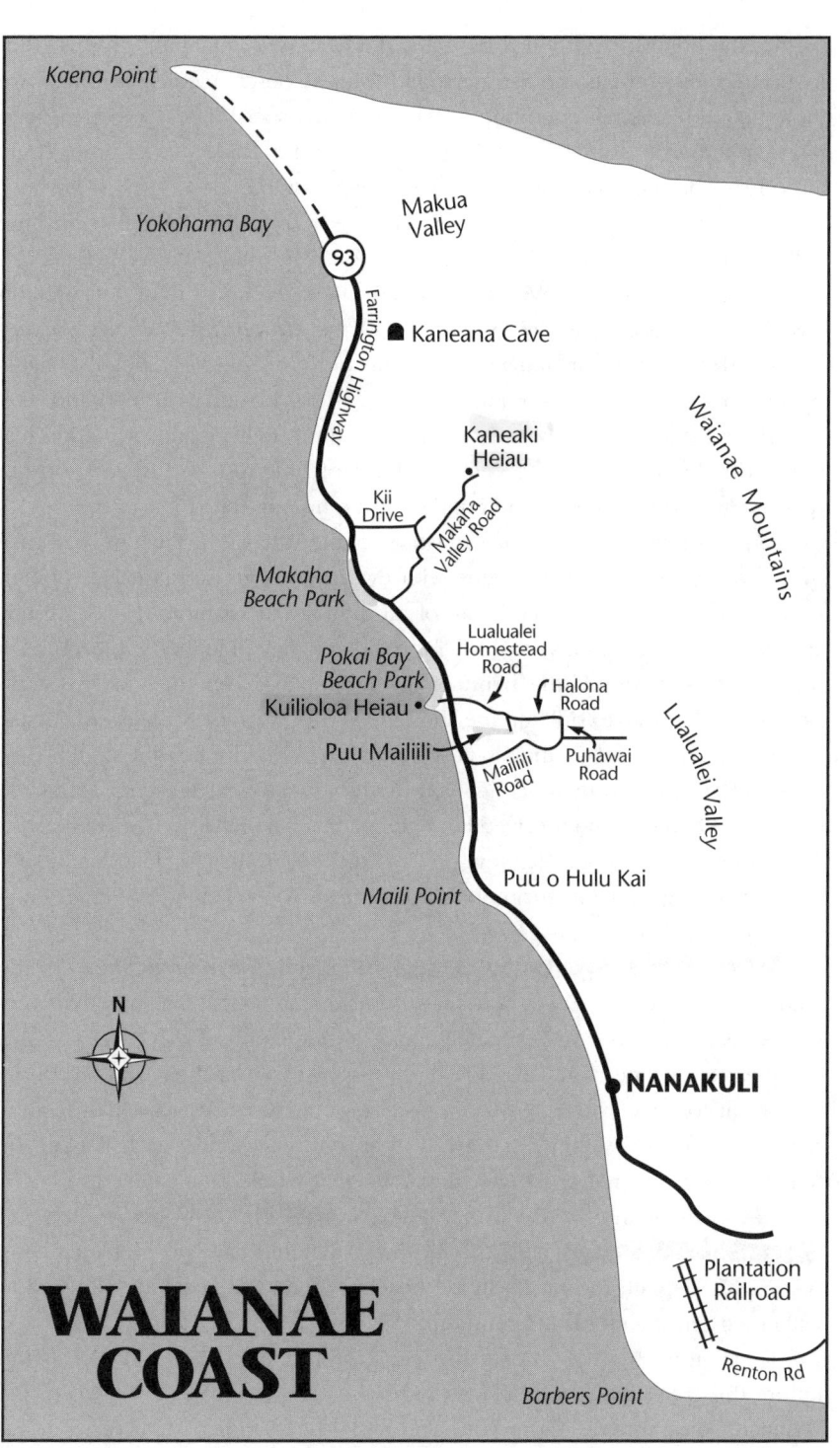

Kaena Point

Yokohama Bay

93 Farrington Highway

Makua Valley

■ Kaneana Cave

Kaneaki Heiau

Kii Drive

Makaha Valley Road

Makaha Beach Park

Pokai Bay Beach Park

Kuilioloa Heiau

Puu Mailiili

Lualualei Homestead Road

Halona Road

Mailiili Road

Puhawai Road

Waianae Mountains

Lualualei Valley

Maili Point

Puu o Hulu Kai

N

NANAKULI

Plantation Railroad

Renton Rd

Barbers Point

WAIANAE COAST

pidgin, the linguistic potpourri by which the different immigrant groups communicated. Inspect Filipino fish traps and Chinese herbal medicines. These are the ethnic threads that contribute to Hawaii's rich social tapestry today. Open Monday through Saturday 10:00 A.M. to 2:00 P.M. for guided tours only. Tours are offered on the hour until 2:00 P.M.; $13 admission.

Continue on Waipahu Street to Kunia Road (Route 750). A right turn here will get you back on H–1. If it's a Sunday, you may want to turn left for a historic train ride. Take Fort Weaver Road 2.5 miles, then turn right onto Renton and drive until it ends at the Ewa station of the **Hawaiian Railway Society** (681–5461; www.hawaiianrailway.com). An old navy diesel locomotive hauls passenger cars on a ninety-minute round-trip every Sunday at 1:00 and 3:00 P.M. Along the way you'll hear the story of O`ahu's railway and plantation history. Adult admission is $10. Reserve ahead of time to travel in style on the "parlor car," offered the second Sunday of the month, for $15.

As you drive along the southern slopes of the Waianae Mountains, you gaze over a vast sunken plain that starts with Ewa cane fields and housing subdivisions and extends across Pearl Harbor all the way to Diamond Head. All this land rests on an enormous coral shelf formed at a time of higher sea levels. H–1 peters out as it rounds the bend of the mountains. Continue northwest on Farrington Highway to sidle up the shoreline of the Waianae (or leeward) Coast.

Sheltered behind O`ahu's tallest mountains, this dry coastal stretch provides refuge to Hawaiians clinging to a traditional rural lifestyle. Many are homestead farmers who received land grants through the Hawaiian Homelands Act. Almost everyone keeps a few pigs or chickens in their backyard, and subsistence fishing remains an important source of food. Extended families still gather for weekends on the beach.

Most tourists are put off by the region's lingering bad reputation. On the whole, you'll find the people here more overflowing with aloha spirit than anywhere else on O`ahu. Unfortunately, some residents (justifiably) feel that this openhearted, giving nature has left them dispossessed of their land, and now they want to keep what's left to themselves. The Waianae Coast has scenery rivaling the most beautiful in Hawaii, with miles of coral beach backed by rugged mountains that open into rural valleys. It would be a shame to miss. If you exercise common sense with valuables, maintain a low-key profile, and stay away from groups of drinking locals, you should have no problems here. WARNING: As with the North Shore, beaches along this coast are exposed to winter surf; swimming is often unsafe.

Farrington Highway meets the coast at the Kahe Point Power Plant. Ignore this monstrosity and instead gaze ahead to the majestic sweep of the Waianae Coast spread before you. The rocky headland of Maili Point dominates the arcing shoreline, with taller mountains silhouetted beyond. The beach park on your left bears the unofficial name Tracks because of the railroad tracks from former sugar trains that parallel the highway. Continue north past other beach parks through the town of Nanakuli, where you can peer into the remote depths of Nanakuli Valley. Near the north edge of town, you pass the **Samoan Assembly of God,** only one of the many picturesque churches along the way.

Beyond Nanakuli, Farrington Highway skirts the Puu o Hulu Kai, the headland at Maili Point, to reach the town of Maili. Here you get a frontal view into the staggering expanse of **Lualualei Valley,** the ancestral fire pit of the Waianae Range. Two tall, red antennae near the mouth of the valley and a whole farm of smaller structures behind it make up the Navcom Radio Transmitting Facility, for which the navy has sequestered most of the valley floor. Puu Mailiili, another headland, walls in Maili's northern limits. Consider turning onto Mailiili Road at the edge of town to circle inland around the hill past some homestead plots. You'll see dairy farms, vegetable plots, and more stunning valley scenery. Two miles in, turn left onto Puhawai Road and left again onto Halona. This will take you past some curious Quonset hut homes and back onto Lualualei Homestead Road to rejoin the coast.

Cross Farrington Road and continue straight onto Kaneilio Point at the southern tip of **Pokai Bay Beach Park.** Walk out on the peninsula through a coconut grove to **Kuilioloa Heiau** at the end. Built on three neatly terraced platforms, the heiau enjoys sweeping views along the coast. Pokai Beach, the beautiful sandy strip curving north behind the breakwater, offers the only safe winter swimming on the Waianae Coast. It serves as a popular canoe-launching site. The harbor here is also home port to the e`ala, a double-hulled Polynesian voyaging canoe, used to educate local Hawaiians about their seafaring heritage. Inland, the rear wall of Waianae Valley rises to Mount Ka`ala, the 4,020-foot pinnacle of O`ahu.

As far as restaurant selection goes, the Waianae Coast features drive-ins galore, a handful of Chinese chop sueys, and not much else. This would be a good place to acquire a taste for a plate lunch, which dominates the menus here. Your best bet is the **Waianae Ice House** (696–6685), at the harbor, which serves fresh, locally caught fish, Hawaiian *lau lau,* and *poke* (a sashimi salad). Open daily 4:00 A.M. to 6:00 P.M. Otherwise, try the **L&L Drive In** (696–7989), near the entrance to the beach park, for a wide selection of multiethnic entrees served with the standard two scoops of rice and macaroni salad. Open 7:30 A.M. to 11:00 P.M. daily.

A worthwhile stop at the Waianae Mall is **Na Hana Lima** (696–5462), an artisans' cooperative owned by Waianae Coast residents whose "working hands" (the store name) excel at a variety of traditional Hawaiian crafts. Open Monday through Saturday 9:00 A.M. to 5:00 P.M. The nearby Makaha Resort also stages weekend craft fairs and other Hawaiian cultural programs. Call 695–9544 for schedule.

Continue north to Makaha, the next town and valley on Farrington Highway. The name Makaha means "savage," referring to a clan of highway robbers who long terrorized passersby. The savage predator today is resort development. At the rear of this steeply grooved valley lies **Kaneaki Heiau,** which has been reconstructed in a similar fashion to the one at Waimea Valley. To get there, take Makaha Valley Road inland, zigzagging left past the Makaha Resort, then right onto a road through the housing estate. Entry is permitted only Tuesday through Sunday 10:00 A.M. to 2:00 P.M.

Loop back along the north side of the Makaha Valley on Kii Drive to **Makaha Beach Park** on the coast, where pro surfing began. Spectators flock to this wide crescent of steeply sloping sand every year for the Buffalo Big Board Surfing Classic in March. Competitors ride vintage "tankers"—long boards up to 12 feet in length and weighing more than 80 pounds—as did the surfers of old.

Two miles farther, look for **Kaneana Cave** on the right side of the highway. The cave opening faces north, so you have to look behind you as you drive. Carved by wave action during a time of raised sea levels, the narrow, high ceiling of the cave slants 450 feet into the mountain flank. The cave's legendary denizen was a shark-man named Nanaue, who used his dual nature to prey on unsuspecting victims in the area.

Just ahead the mountains recede, opening into the amphitheatric bowl of **Makua Valley.** This seemingly pristine valley harbors a deadly secret. The military has long used the area as an artillery range, and unexploded shells litter the valley floor. Across the highway, Makua Beach continues the pearly white lining of the Waianae Coast. Farther up the road, the beach at **Yokohama Bay** marks the end of the highway. You can sift for tiny puka shells in the sand.

From here a rugged jeep trail continues 2 miles to Kaena Point. The Waianae Coast curves majestically into view, stretching back as far as Kepuhi Point. On the way, you pass more caves. Look also for *ilima,* a native ground cover that thrives along the roadside. The tiny, pale-orange blossoms of the plant are O`ahu's official flower. Threaded by the hundreds, they form an unusual crepe-paper lei. Pregnant women used to chew the buds to stimulate their muscles during childbirth. Waves breaking near the point sometimes reach 40 feet during winter, a height unequaled anywhere else on Hawaiian shores. During calmer summer months, the tide pools can be fun to explore.

Kaena Point itself is a narrow, sand-dune peninsula protruding from the tapered ridge of the Waianae mountain range. This westernmost promontory was another legendary "jumping off" place for the souls of O`ahu's fallen warriors. A Coast Guard observation tower stands at the far end of the point. If you climb the swaying ladder to the top, you can get an exquisite view of this desolate, windswept peninsula. Incoming waves, angling from both sides of the point, sweep across a string of rocks offshore. On a clear evening, this is also a great spot to watch for the elusive "green flash" that occurs when the sun sets over a cloudless ocean horizon. Shield your gaze until the instant when the last puddle of molten sun oozes out of view. Instead of orange sun, a brilliant spot of green light will shine for the briefest moment.

Places to Stay in O`ahu

HONOLULU

Manoa Valley Inn
2001 Vancouver Drive
947–6019
This three-story mansion exudes a wonderful historic air. Rates start at $99.

Royal Hawaiian Hotel
2259 Kalakaua Avenue
923–7311
www.royal-hawaiian.com
Although not exactly "off the beaten path," this pink palace is a landmark in Waikiki, and its historical grandeur offers a unique type of luxury. Rooms start at $380.

Sheraton Moana Surfrider
2365 Kalakaua Avenue
922–3111
www.moana-surfrider.com
Expensive and ultra-luxurious but definitely a place you'll

remember. Built in 1901, it has been restored to perfection, and the Old World charm remains intact. Rooms from $270.

KAILUA

Hawaiian Islands B&B
1277 Mokulua Drive
261–7895, (800) 258–7895
A booking agency that offers a variety of budget accommodations, including some beachfront.

Kailua Beachside Cottages
204 South Kalaheo Avenue
262–4128, 261–1653
Offers quiet retreats on the scenic windward side. Rates start at $70.

NORTH SHORE

Backpackers Vacation Inn and Plantation Village
59–788 Kamehameha Highway, Haleiwa
638–7838
www.backpackers-hawaii.com

Places to Eat in O`ahu

HONOLULU

Alan Wong's Restaurant
1857 South King Street
949–2526
www.alanwongs.com
State-of-the-art Hawaii regional cuisine. Investment-caliber.

Hau Tree Lana`i
2863 Kalakaua Avenue
921–7066
Located in the lobby of the Otani Kaimana Beach Hotel, this open-air restaurant features a beachfront location with unsurpassed views. It's situated at the far east end of Waikiki. Moderate.

Maple Garden
909 Isenberg Street
941–6641
Specializes in northern Chinese dishes and Szechuan cuisine. Moderate.

Ono Hawaiian Food
726 Kapahulu Avenue
737–2275
The place on O`ahu to go for
an authentic Hawaiian meal.
Inexpensive.

Roy's Restaurant
6600 Kalanianaole Highway
396–7697
www.roysrestaurant.com
Inventive East-West cooking
in a raucous Hawaii Kai
eatery. Expensive to
investment-caliber.

Sam Choy's Breakfast,
Lunch, Crab & Big Aloha
Brewery
580 North Nimitz Highway
545–7979
www.samchoy.com
A cavernous brewpub with
hearty fare in hefty portions.
Moderate.

KAILUA

Buzz's Original Steakhouse
413 Kawailoa Road
261–4661
Across the street from Kailua
Beach Park. The surf 'n' turf
menu makes a nice end to a
day on the beach. Moderate.

NORTH SHORE

Haleiwa Joe's Seafood Grill
66–011 Kamehameha
Highway, Haleiwa
637–8005
Bring sunset serenity to your
North Shore sojourn.
Moderate to expensive.

Moloka`i

Located midway between the bustle of Honolulu and Lahaina, the island of Moloka`i clings to a seclusion that has long been its birthright. With a legacy of ancient sorcery and the stigma of its leper colony, Moloka`i's image as the "Lonely Island" was until recently reinforced by a declining population. Moloka`i likes to bill itself as the most Hawaiian of the visitable islands; almost half of its inhabitants share native Hawaiian ancestry. From a visitor's viewpoint, Moloka`i also remains one of the least "spoiled" islands. It contains only one resort and a handful of smaller hotels. There are no traffic lights or shopping malls on the island. Instead, Moloka`i offers a laid-back atmosphere, a lingering glimpse of old Hawaii, and a low-key tourist industry conducted with a genuine warmth that has given Moloka`i its new nickname, "the Friendly Isle."

Moloka`i stretches 37 miles from end to end but no more than 10 miles in width. Three main highways partition its interior, making exploration fairly simple. The road east, Route 45, is named for Kamehameha V. Running to the west, Route 46 goes by the name of Maunaloa Highway. Branching north from the Maunaloa Highway, Route 47 provides the only access to the island's North Shore. Moloka`i hides much of its scenery within a remote interior, inaccessible by road and often private

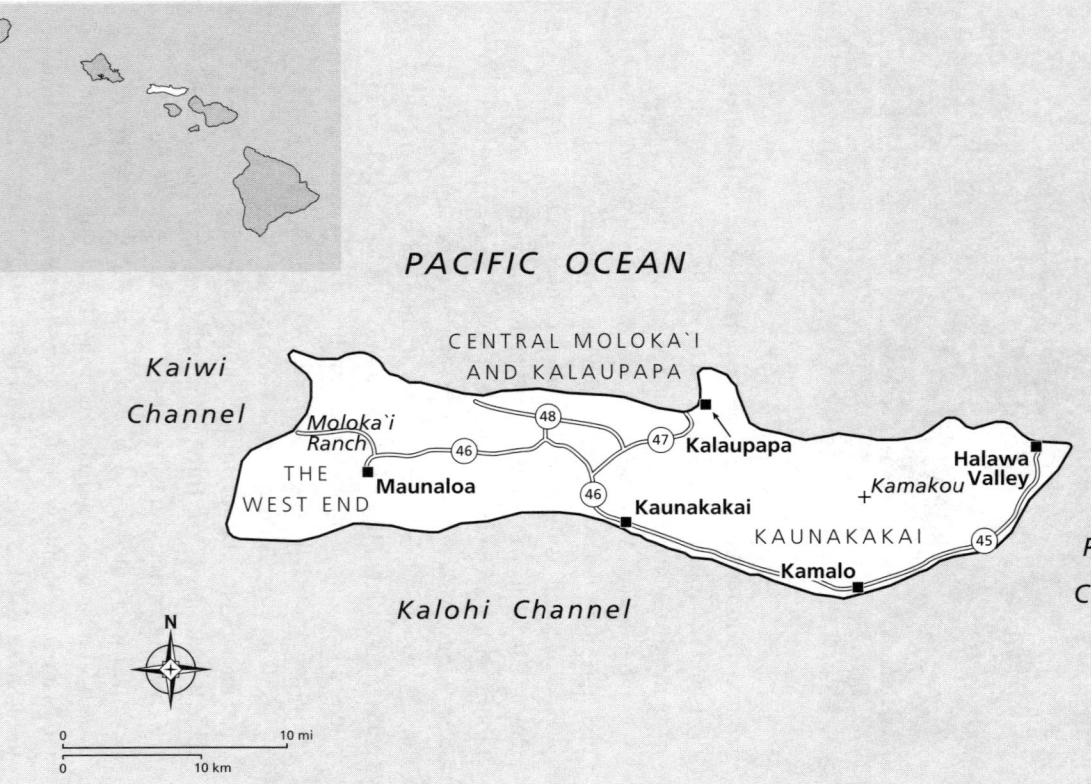

MOLOKA`I

PACIFIC OCEAN

Kaiwi
Channel

CENTRAL MOLOKA`I
AND KALAUPAPA

Moloka`i
Ranch

THE
WEST END

Maunaloa

Kalaupapa

Kaunakakai

+ Kamakou

Halawa
Valley

KAUNAKAKAI

Kamalo

Pailolo
Channel

Kalohi Channel

N

0   10 mi
0   10 km

property to boot. Most visitors will be content to spend a day or so exploring the roadside attractions in each direction. **Budget** (567–6877; 800–527–0700) and **Dollar** (567–6156; 800–800–4000) rent cars at the airport; reserve early for weekends. For a less corporate alternative, **Island Kine Auto Rental** (553–5242; e-mail: info1@molokai-car-rental.com) has a mixed fleet of quality used cars, which they rent out of Kaunakakai town. Free airport pickup and personalized advice are included. Island Kine also rents a limited

moloka`ifacts

Population: 7,404 (2000)
Principal city: Kaunakakai
Flower: White kukui blossom
Color: Green

number of four-wheel-drive vehicles. For those who want to see more, two local residents offer their expertise and access to the action traveler. Alex Puaa's **Moloka`i Off-Road Tours** (553–3369) will take you four-wheeling. Walter Naki's **Ma`a Hawaii** (558–8184) has a number of guiding services, including hiking. His specialty is snorkeling, though: He will guide you through Moloka`i's reef environment, roust an octopus for you to play with, and, if you wish, spear fish for your dinner.

While planning your stay, contact the **Moloka`i Visitor Association** (553–3876; 800–800–6367, or interisland 800–553–0404), a publicity organization for the entire island.

Kaunakakai and Things East

Begin your sightseeing on Moloka`i by heading into town. Located midway along the island's south shore just off Route 45, the single-block business district of Kaunakakai comes as close to urban clutter as Moloka`i gets. Walking the strip along Ala Malama, the main drag, will put the rest of the island in perspective and get you in the right frame of mind.

You will find most of the island's nonhotel restaurants here. All offer downhome local cooking at budget prices. Dining atmosphere not included. **Big Daddy's** (553–5841) offers a selection of authentic Filipino dishes, such as pork adobo, as well as traditional Hawaiian *lau-lau*. Open daily 8:00 A.M. to 5:00 P.M.

Kanemitsu Bakery (553–5855) produces a repertoire of island-flavored breads famous throughout the state. The bakery is open Wednesday through Monday 5:30 A.M. to 6:30 P.M., and breakfast and lunch are served 5:30 A.M. to 1:30 P.M. Nearby, **Outposts Natural Foods** (553–3377) offers a tropical juice bar and plate lunch takeout. Open Monday through Thursday 9:00 A.M. to 6:00 P.M., Friday 9:00 A.M. to 4:00 P.M., and Sunday 10:00 A.M. to 5:00 P.M. Closed on

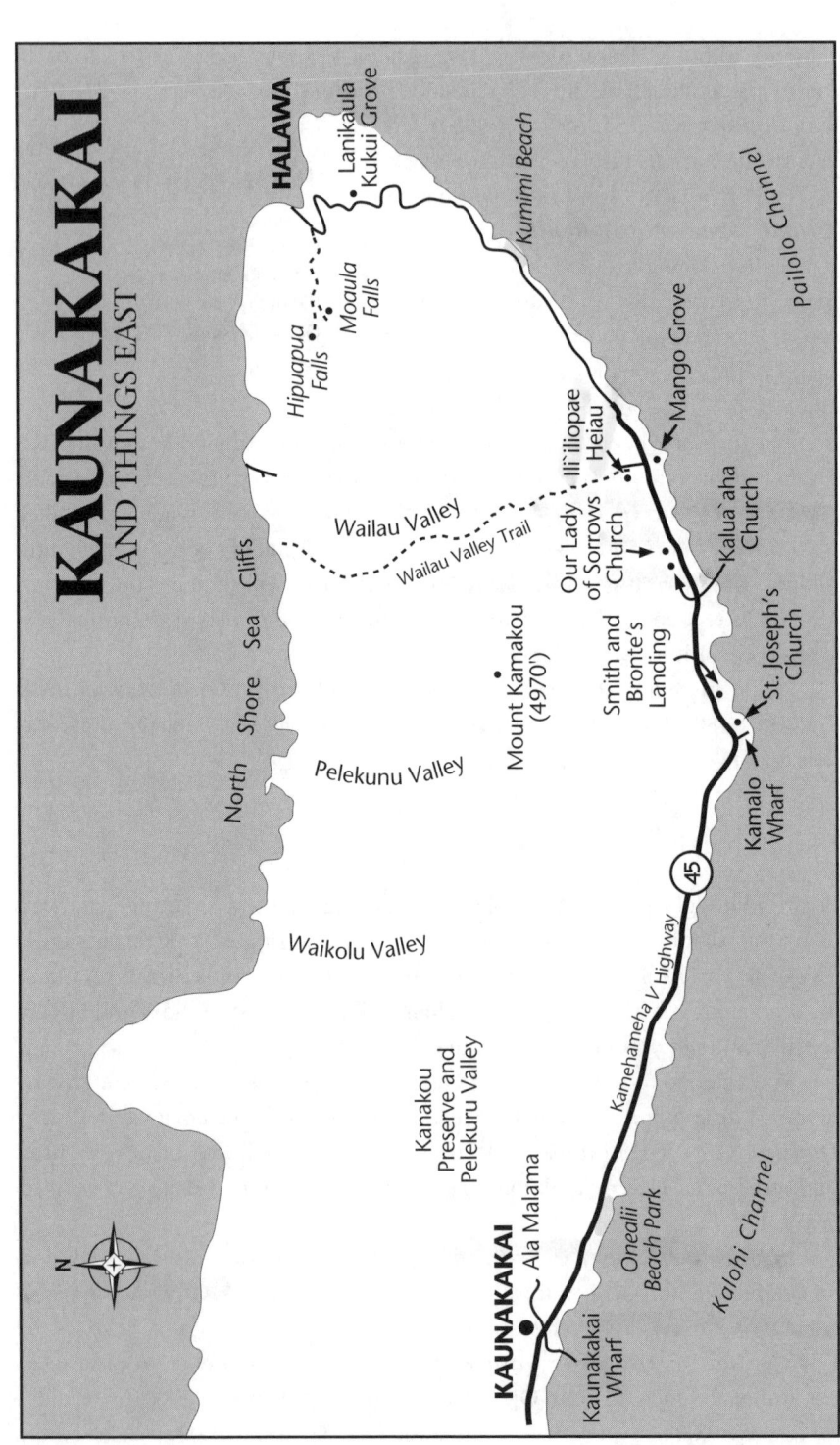

Saturday. *Oviedo's Lunch Counter* (553–5014), another tasty Filipino kitchen hidden in dingy quarters, waits at the end of the strip; open Monday through Friday 10:00 A.M. to 5:30 P.M. and weekends 10:00 A.M. to 4:00 P.M. Meanwhile, across the highway on Wharf Road, *Moloka`i Pizza Cafe* (553–3288) fills another vital niche in the island repertoire; they also serve pasta, fish, and chicken. Open Monday through Thursday 10:00 A.M. to 10:00 P.M., Friday and Saturday 10:00 A.M. to 11:00 P.M., and Sunday 11:00 A.M. to 10:00 P.M. The new restaurant in town is *Paddler's Inn* (553–5256), located at 10 Mohala Street. Featuring standard American fare, the restaurant is open weekdays 7:00 A.M. to 8:30 P.M. and weekends 9:00 A.M. to 8:30 P.M. Live entertainment on the weekends.

While in town, be sure to stop by *Molokai Fine Arts Gallery* (553–8520), at 2 Kamoi Street, Suite 300; it showcases the work of more than a hundred Moloka`i artists, who turn out everything from handmade *pahu* ("drums") to Hawaiian quilts. Open Monday through Friday 9:30 A.M. to 5:30 P.M. and Saturday 8:30 A.M. to 2:30 P.M.

And if you're here on a Saturday, don't miss the early-morning farmers' market for fresh produce, arts and crafts, and plenty of local color. It's held at the corner of Ala Malama Avenue and Kamehameha V Highway.

At the end of Ala Malama, across from the baseball diamond, stands the Mitchell Pauoli Center (553–3204), where you can get camping permits to tent in county parks. For state camping permits for Palaau State Park, contact the Maui office (984–8108) or call the park caretaker directly (567–6923).

It is worth driving to the end of *Kaunakakai Wharf,* where barges unload supplies from O`ahu but no longer head out laden with pineapples. The wharf extends almost a half mile offshore due to the shallow mudflats along this coast. As you savor the view of Moloka`i's southern shoreline and its three neighbors across the Kalohi Channel, you'll see why Mark Twain called

Geography of Moloka`i

The fifth largest of the Hawaiian Islands, Moloka`i has an elongated shape that represents the union of two volcanoes with a third. Reaching a summit of 4,970 feet at Kamakou, the mountains of eastern Moloka`i are much taller and greener than those in arid western Moloka`i, whose highest point barely tops 1,000 feet. The cliffs along Moloka`i's largely inaccessible northern coast, from Kalaupapa east, soar to more than 3,000 feet in elevation, rising directly above the ocean. They are held to be the tallest sea cliffs in the world.

Hawaii "the loveliest fleet of islands anchored in any ocean." From left to right are Maui, Kaho`olawe, and Lana`i. You may also see O`ahu rising in the distance above West Moloka`i. At the base of the wharf, the stone foundation behind the canoe club was the site of King Kamehameha V's summer retreat.

The daily **Molokai Princess** (667–6165; 800–275–6969; www.mauiprincess .com) ferries Moloka`i commuters across Pailolo Channel to work in West Maui hotels in exchange for the tourists who stay in them. The fare between Kaunakakai and Lahaina Harbor is $42 one way; call for a current schedule.

About 1.5 miles east of Kaunakakai, the Polynesian rooftops of the *Hotel Moloka`i* (553–5347; 800–535–0085; www.hotelmolokai.com) appear on a cluster of low-rise bungalows facing the ocean. The simple but recently refurbished rooms here start at $90, with rates rising to $140 for ocean views and $150 for kitchenettes. The real charmer of the property is the hotel restaurant, Hula Shores (553–5347). Decorated in the nostalgic style of old Hawaii, the dining area spreads across a large oceanfront lana`i

moloka`itrivia

The water reservoir in Kualapu`u holds 1.4 billion gallons and is the largest rubber-lined reservoir in the world.

with carved-tiki pillars, rattan paneling, and lava-rock sidewalls. Plop yourself down in an oversized patio chair and gaze out through the palm trees to views across the Pailolo Channel. At night, tiki torches flicker in the ocean breeze as locals gather to hear live music from island performers. Menu choices here embrace an eclectic mix of steak, pastas, and seafood, with lunchtime sandwich choices. Preparations are simple but tasty, and prices moderate. Open daily 6:00 A.M. to 2:00 P.M. and 5:00 to 9:00 P.M., with a limited menu from 2:00 to 5:00 P.M.

Four miles east of town is *Onealii Beach Park.* The beach here is still muddy and flat, but it's a nice spot with coconut trees and the remains of a fishpond. These shallow, protected waters were ideal for such ponds, and more than sixty of them ring the coastline, some dating from as early as the thirteenth century. The Hawaiians were the only Polynesian people to practice aquaculture, building saltwater enclosures as big as football fields from coral and lava rock, with intricate sluice gates. Some of the ponds have been restored, and aquaculture is again becoming an industry on the island, restoring Moloka`i's reputation as the "land of the fat fish." Another thing being restored on the island is its population of native geese. If you call in advance, a visit to nearby *Nene O Moloka`i* (553–5992) will put you face to feather with Hawaii's state bird. This captive propagation site also has a collection of native plants and displays on migratory birds, but the stars of the show are the nene, "the most endangered goose in the world." Open weekday mornings at 9:00 A.M. by appointment; call one week in advance.

For an aerial view, take the next left up to **Kawela Plantation,** a new hillside housing development. As you climb, vistas extend along the south shore, revealing the outlines of several more fishponds fronting the deep cobalt blue of the channel seas.

The road ahead is rich in Hawaiian history in other ways as well. Kamehameha I landed on this coast near Kawela with an invasion force of canoes that was said to stretch more than 4 miles. Slingshot stones from the fierce battle still litter the scrub-covered foothills. The conqueror's prize was a child bride. Keopuolani, one of Maui's highest-born chieftesses, had fled during Kamehameha's invasion of that island. By capturing and later marrying her, Kamehameha assured his heirs of the *mana* necessary to rule.

Just after the 10-mile marker, where the highway veers sharply to the left, take a dirt road turnoff to the right and drive out to the abandoned wharf at Kamalo. Absorb the views of the coast and the islands offshore, then gaze up at the mountains behind you. **Mount Kamakou,** the highest peak directly above, forms the pinnacle of the island at 4,970 feet.

Around the bend from **Kamalo Wharf,** on the ocean side, stands **St. Joseph's Church.** Built in 1876 by Father Damien, the celebrated priest of Kalaupapa, it is the second-oldest church on the island. An often lei-draped statue of Damien greets visitors in front of the chapel. The door is rarely locked, so be sure to take a peek inside.

Brief History of Moloka'i

While ancient Moloka'i's reputation for sorcery protected the island from marauders, the people of Moloka'i were skilled in other arts as well. The island is the legendary birthplace of the hula, and both men and women excel at this traditional dance form. Aquaculture was also practiced here to a greater extent than on other islands. Fishponds all along the south shore of the island ensured a reliable source of sustenance.

Modern history has been less kind to the island. The establishment of a leprosy settlement at Kalaupapa in 1864 made the island a byword for the horrors of that disease. The closing of the pineapple plantations on the island in recent decades has left a legacy of economic hardship. Today almost 20 percent of the island's population remains unemployed, the highest rate in the state. Moloka'i residents remain stoic about their island's future. Having seen the social and economic dislocation caused by development on the neighboring islands, many prefer to keep Moloka'i the way it is.

Continuing east on Kamehameha V Highway, you will pass (in addition to many more fishponds) a wooden sign on the right indicating the site of ***Smith and Bronte's Landing.*** In 1927 these pioneering aviators abruptly ended the first civilian flight from the United States mainland to Honolulu when they ran out of fuel here after twenty-five hours in the air. Both survived the crash. A few miles farther on, a large wooden cross on the left marks the barnlike ruins of ***Kalua`aha Church.*** This first outpost of Christianity on Moloka`i was built by the original missionary congregation in 1844. The mission's location here reflects the original population center around the lusher east and north coasts. Two hundred yards farther, Damien's second church, ***Our Lady of Sorrows,*** built in 1874, stands in much better repair.

Moloka`i's eastern shore remains the population center for island bed-and-breakfasts and vacation rentals. Most of these keep fairly full, so book early. One of the nicest is ***Kamalo Plantation B&B*** (558–8236). Glenn and Akiko Foster rent a private studio cottage for $95; two-night minimum. Their landscaped gardens include fruit orchards as well as a former heiau. They also have an oceanfront two-bedroom cottage, farther east at the 20-mile marker, which rents for $150; three-night minimum. Other rental options on the east end include ***Honomuni House*** (558–8383), ***Dunbar Beachfront Cottages***

Our Lady of Sorrows

(558–8153; 800–673–0520; molokai-beachfront-cottages.com), and ***Molokai Vacation Rentals*** (800–367–2984). The latter two have several properties, some oceanfront. Finally, ***Pu`u o Hoku Ranch*** (558–8109) rents both a two- and a four-bedroom cottage, about 25 miles out, surrounded by acres of open ranch land and forest, both with great hillside views. The simply furnished but fully equipped rentals are a steal at $140. There is an additional charge of $20 per person in the four-bedroom cottage.

Past the 15-mile marker, the highway passes a giant mango grove. Reputedly the world's largest, the patch features thirty-two different varieties of this prolific fruit tree spread across forty-nine acres. It was planted in the 1930s by Hawaiian Sugar as an experimental venture.

On the other side of the highway lies the entrance to ***Ili`iliopae Heiau,*** ● Moloka`i's most impressive ancient temple. Look for the gate immediately after the bridge. Don your safari camouflage (and mosquito repellent) and strike out on the jeep trail into the jungle. At the end of the road, cross the streambed. Hidden in the vegetation on the far side, Ili`iliopae makes a dramatic and mysterious appearance. Legend—backed by geology—holds that the lava-rock used in this heiau originated in Wailau Valley on the island's North Shore and was carried across the mountains by a human chain.

The heiau is much bigger than it appears, extending almost 300 feet across the valley. It was once even larger, but according to legend a flood washed away half the structure. The story goes that a father whose sons had been sacrificed by an evil kahuna as temple offerings had petitioned the shark god for vengeance. The floodwaters carried the evil priest and his attendants out into the ocean, where a gathering of sharks waited. What you see today is just the foundation of a once elaborately designed complex that used to be visible for miles. Unfortunately, it has become quite overgrown in recent years.

Continuing on the highway, you'll pass the ***Manae Food and Grinds*** (558–8498), your last chance to stop for supplies or take-out lunch. The store is open daily 8:00 A.M. to 5:00 P.M.; the food counter is open Monday through Friday 10:00 A.M. to 5:00 P.M. and weekends 8:00 A.M. to 5:00 P.M. As you drive onward, look for the ubiquitous *hala* (pandanus) trees, whose knotted fruits are often called "tourist pineapples." The tuft-tipped "nuts" made serviceable paintbrushes, and the *lauhala,* the long fibrous leaves, were woven into mats. The trees along this shoreline are said to derive from an ancestral tree whose stiltlike roots upset the fire goddess Pele's canoe. The enraged goddess tore the tree to bits, sending splinters flying in every direction. They took root in the fertile soil. Of course, almost every rock in Hawaii has its story to tell, but here on Moloka`i, more people remember.

As you continue east, the highway narrows to a single lane, and the scenery grows more and more dramatic as the road curves around one spectacular cove after another. The tiny beaches nestled along the coast, beginning at the 20-mile marker, are all superb for snorkeling or fishing, but they can get rough, especially in winter. *Kumimi Beach,* at 21 miles, has facilities. From here you get a first glimpse of Moku Honii, an offshore island used for bombing practice in World War II. The West Maui Mountains loom across *Pailolo Channel* as if it were a mere puddle. The highway then makes an abrupt turn inland, winding around—and through—some interesting rock formations before climbing to the lush pastures of *Pu`u o Hoku Ranch* (558–8109). In addition to its bread-and-butter cattle business, the ranch has diversified into niche crops such as `awa (also known as kava), a Polynesian medicinal plant and mild intoxicant used in traditional rituals and now a popular ingredient for alternative medicines.

On top of the hill, just seaward of the ranch headquarters, the sacred *Lanikaula Kukui Grove* grows on the spot where a powerful sixteenth-century *kahuna* ("one who knows the secrets") lies buried. Lanikaula's influence pervaded Hawaii and made Moloka`i, an island dedicated to spiritual pursuits, off-limits to warfare. Lanikaula died as a result of being betrayed by a visiting kahuna from Lana`i. His sons planted these light-green *kukui* (candlenut) trees to conceal their father's final resting place. Moloka`i's isolation continued in the seventeenth century, belligerently enforced by the Kalaipahoa, whose magic poisonwood led other islands to give Moloka`i a wide berth. As these legends testify, Moloka`i's "Lonely Island" reputation long predated leprosy. You can feel some of that loneliness today as you approach the North Shore. Once populous, it is now largely deserted due to lack of road access.

Somehow, after leaving the main ranch, the highway manages to lurch around even wilder turns, and the vistas across lush canyons leading to the ocean become ever more stunning. Just as the scenery reaches its climax, a wide turn allows space to pull over and absorb your first lingering view into *Halawa Valley.* A pair of waterfalls topple over cliffs at the back of the steep-walled valley. Halawa Stream descends from there through a thousand shades of green to emerge at an estuary at the mouth of a horseshoe-shaped bay complete with black-sand beach. As soon as you can tear yourself away from the lookout, maneuver the last hairpin turns to the valley floor, where you can enjoy Halawa up close.

One of the oldest settled valleys in Hawaii, *Halawa* continued to support a thriving community that supplied most of the island's taro long after the more remote North Shore valleys had been deserted. Then tragedy struck, beginning with a 1946 tidal wave that devastated the valley. Today only a handful of diehards remain in this Shangri-la. Some have begun to farm taro again, as well as tropical flowers and fruit. Unfortunately, valley residents are now claiming that the main hiking trail to the waterfalls passes through their private property and are demanding that visitors pay to take a guided tour. For the time being, there appears no alternative. Expect to pay about $75 for a half-day tour. Call 553–5926 to reserve. The trail to the falls begins at the dirt road leading into the valley, past the photogenic green Halawa Church. It takes an hour or two of hiking to reach **Moaula Falls,** the lower of the two falls visible from the lookout. Hawaiians used to drop a ti leaf in the pool below before swimming to see if the *mo`o* lizard for whom the falls are named was prowling underwater. The cautious of mind can continue up the streambed to the larger **Hipuapua Falls** and bathe in its pool, sans mo`o.

There are showers back at the park pavilion to wash off any mud collected on your descent, and the bay itself stays sufficiently sheltered to permit swimming in all but the roughest weather. Camping at the pavilion is not permitted, but Pu`u o Hoku Ranch allows tenters on its land by the south shore of the bay. Campers can obtain a permit at the Pu`u O Hoku Ranch office (558–8109).

Beyond Halawa, inaccessible by land, begins the spectacular Moloka`i North Shore, where a 1,750-foot waterfall (the state's highest) topples from the slopes of the world's highest sea cliffs. The stormy weather and winter surf that pummel this rugged coastline are such that even boat traffic to the North Shore is largely restricted to the summer months.

Central Moloka`i and Kalaupapa

One and a half miles west of Kaunakakai, the hundreds of coconut trees swaying in the ocean breezes make up **Kapuaiwa Grove,** a royal coconut grove planted for Kamehameha V (whose nickname was Kapuaiwa, "mysterious taboo") on the site of seven sacred ponds. It was once much larger, but adjacent construction, an encroaching coastline, and basic neglect have all taken their toll. Still, the grove—one of the few such sites remaining—merits a visit. Just beware of falling coconuts.

Strung like a cordon against temptation, eight different congregations of Moloka`i worshippers gather on Sunday at **Church Row** across the street. Any denomination with Hawaiian members can build here. Some of the services are still conducted in Hawaiian, and visitors are welcome. Locals boast that the only traffic jams on the island occur here on Sunday morning.

After Kapuaiwa, the highway climbs inland past a plumeria flower farm. Just shy of the 4-mile mark (a half mile before the junction between Routes 46 and 47 and immediately preceding the white concrete bridge), an unmarked

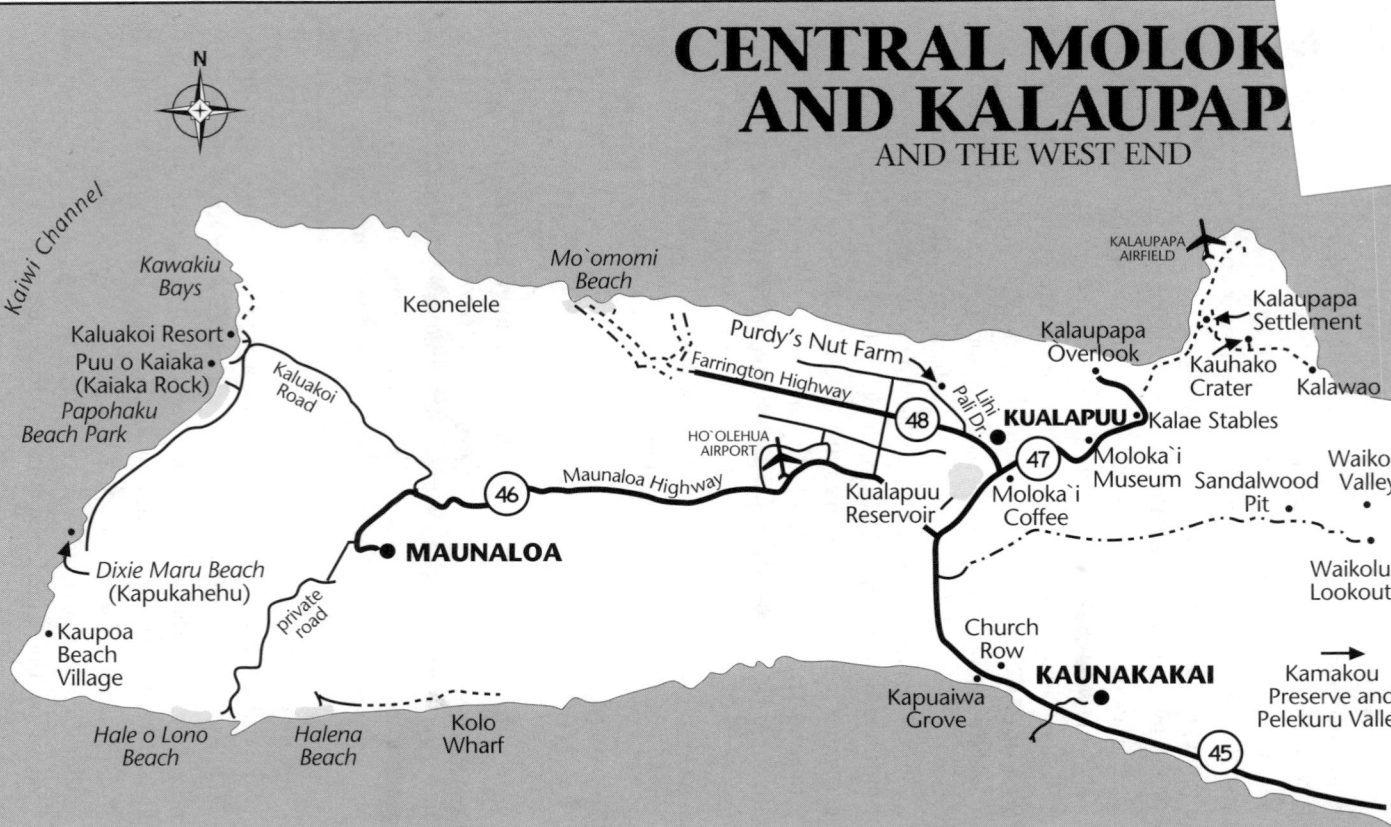

CENTRAL MOLOK
AND KALAUPAP
AND THE WEST END

forest preserve road on the right leads the intrepid explorer 10 miles through the island's lush interior to the **Waikolu Lookout.** The road quickly becomes unpaved and in all but the driest weather will require a four-wheel-drive vehicle. Ignore the many turnoffs to smaller hunting trails.

About 9 miles in you pass a famous **sandalwood pit,** dug in the shape of a ship's hold to measure an exact cargo of the fragrant wood for export to China. Run as an exclusive monopoly of Kamehameha I, the business exchanged a full cargo of sandalwood for the brig that carried it. The king amassed a fair-sized fleet in this fashion. You aren't likely to see any sandalwood near the pit

trivia

The first Hawaiian fossils were discovered on Moloka'i, lodged in sandstone at the Mo'omomi Dunes.

today, or anywhere else in Hawaii, either. After Kamehameha's death, greedy chieftains inherited the franchise and led long forays into the mountains, eventually harvesting Hawaii's sandalwood to virtual extinction. Some credit the tree's demise to commoners who, tired of being forced on these expeditions away from their fields and fishing, deliberately pulled out saplings by the roots.

A mile farther, the road ends at a picture-perfect view of **Waikolu** ("three waters") **Valley,** one of the three major valleys of Moloka'i's virtually inaccessible North Shore. Stretched out 3,000 feet below, furrowed by waterfalls and carpeted in lush vegetation, this valley supplies much of the island's water. Try to arrive in the morning before the clouds move in. Beyond Waikolu lies the entrance to the **Kamakou Preserve,** a fragile parcel of native rain forest managed by the Nature Conservancy of Hawaii. You can hike along a boardwalk trail through Pepeopae Bog to an overlook into Pelekunu Valley, yet another inaccessible North Shore valley. The stunted, rain-drenched native vegetation in this summit "cloud forest" makes the trip one of Moloka'i's most interesting experiences. The only problem is getting there. Be sure to call the **Nature Conservancy** (553–5236) office in Kualapuu before entering the preserve because the area is subject to violent weather changes. If possible, contact them months in advance to reserve a spot on either of their all-day excursions into the preserves at Kamakou and Mo'omomi. These are staged monthly and are offered for the cost of a donation.

To get to **Kualapuu,** take the turnoff north on Route 47 and head uphill 2 miles until the intersection with Farrington Highway (Route 48). The plantation village of Kualapuu stretches to the left, behind the now-derelict pineapple factory on the corner. On the right, across the road from the factory, is the former headquarters building for Del Monte Pineapple, now home to a new island crop, coffee. You can sample a cup of the house brew at the **Friendly**

Isle Coffee Company (567–9490) espresso bar. Open Monday through Friday 7:00 A.M. to 5:00 P.M., Saturday 8:00 A.M. to 4:00 P.M., and Sunday 8:00 A.M. to 2:00 P.M. Java junkies can choose from two tours: a ninety-minute "expresso tour," which explains how the coffee processing takes place, or the two-hour "mule-drawn wagon tour" through the coffee fields. Priced at $25 and $45, respectively. Call ahead to make a reservation. Kualapuu's claim to fame rests in its reservoir, which houses irrigation water piped from the rain-drenched North Shore via a 5-mile tunnel bored through the mountains. You can dine here in the renovated *Kamuela's Cookhouse* (567–9655). The country Hawaiian decor complements the tasty, local American specialties served here at moderate to expensive prices. Open Monday 7:00 A.M. to 2:00 P.M. and Tuesday through Saturday 7:00 A.M. to 8:00 P.M.

Head west on Farrington Highway and enter Ho`olehua, a larger community engaged in diversified agriculture. In 1921, after Congress passed the Hawaiian Homelands Act, the homestead program began here on Moloka`i. At first Hawaiian farmers struggled on the tiny lots they received. Most ended up leasing their land to the pineapple companies. Since pineapple's demise in 1982 and with today's better capital and water allocation, the homestead program is at last reaping some successes.

After passing the island's high school, turn right up Lihi Pali Drive and look for the sign outside *Purdy's Nut Farm* (567–6601). Visit this single-acre orchard on Hawaiian homestead land Tuesday through Friday 9:30 A.M. to 3:30 P.M. and Saturday 10:00 A.M. to 2:00 P.M. One of the Purdys will tell you everything you want to know about macadamia-nut farming and provide hands-on demonstrations. You can also try or buy their home-roasted nuts, which taste much better than the commercially packaged version.

Speaking of nuts, while in Ho`olehua, you might also take advantage of the unique *"post-a-nut"* service offered by the local post office (567–6144). Postmaster Gary Lam keeps a supply of coconuts on hand that await your inscription with a felt marker pen to mail as mementos to friends and family back home. All you have to pay is postage (around $6.05 for a two-pound nut). Gary stocks his basket with unhusked brown nuts. Green coconuts contain water and are thus much heavier. Both are edible if you strip off the outer husk and crack the inner nut. The post office is located at the corner of Farrington Highway and Puu Pele`ula. Open Monday through Friday 8:00 A.M. to noon and 12:30 to 4:00 P.M.

Farrington Highway turns to dirt a couple of miles outside town, but the road is usually in good condition. If you're game, follow it as far west as you can go to beautiful *Mo`omomi Beach.* It's popular with locals for unofficial camping. Turnoffs along the way lead to other nice locales; the whole coastline is studded with tiny strands of deserted beaches hidden between rocky outcrops. The land west of Mo`omomi, Keonelele, "the flying sands," belongs to the Nature Conservancy and consists of windswept sand dunes covered with native vegetation. Entrance by road requires permission, but you can follow a coastal trail on foot from Mo`omomi to take in the rugged isolation of the terrain. The first Hawaiian fossils were found lodged in sandstone here, and the cliffside sea caves harbor ancient burial sites.

Return to Kualapuu and continue north on Route 47. About 2 miles up the road, a wooden signpost announces the **Moloka`i Museum & Cultural Center** (567–6436) on the left. One of the first sugar mills in the islands and the oldest left standing, the **Meyer Sugar Mill,** the museum's principal attraction, has been restored to working order. Rudolf Meyer left his native Hamburg to seek his fortune in the California Gold Rush. His ship detoured in the Pacific, however, and

trivia

Meyer Sugar Mill on Moloka`i was built in 1878; it is the oldest mill still standing in Hawaii.

he ended up taking a surveying position on Moloka`i during the Hawaiian kingdom's land reform of 1848. Meyer married a Hawaiian chieftess and stayed on as an overseer, managing what has become Moloka`i Ranch, while wearing many different hats as a government official. His venture into sugar, beginning in 1878, was never entirely successful.

Almost all the original machinery of the mill—a mule-driven crusher, copper clarifiers, redwood evaporating pans—survives in working condition. The adjacent cultural center focuses on Hawaiian crafts, including *lauhala* weaving, woodcarving, lei stringing, and quilting. While on the premises, take the time to inspect the Meyer family cemetery nearby and unwind in its shade and solitude. Visible on the hill above the parking area is the original Meyer family home. It has a reputation for being haunted and is closed to the public. Meyer Sugar Mill receives visitors Monday through Saturday 10:00 A.M. to 2:00 P.M. Admission charges are nominal.

Farther uphill through green fields of grazing bovines, you reach **Kalae Stables,** home base for the "world-famous Moloka`i mule ride" to **Kalaupapa** ("flat leaf") **Peninsula.** The descent to Kalaupapa begins at the UNAUTHORIZED PERSONS KEEP OUT sign just ahead, where the highway turns left. The trail drops 1,600 feet over a mere 3 miles and has 26 switchbacks. Manuel Farinha, a Portuguese immigrant, carved the trail while hanging from ropes over the cliff; but it's named for Jack London, who descended it in 1907 and wrote of his experience. (There's a lesson here.) The views along the trail are predictably stunning, but you need to make special arrangements to enter the Kalaupapa settlement (keep reading for details).

Continue by car into Palaau State Park around the corner. The road ends at the official ***Kalaupapa Overlook,*** where you can take in the unearthly view of the leaflike peninsula jutting out into the Pacific from beneath the impossibly steep cliffs of Moloka`i's North Shore. From the same parking lot you can take a short hike through ironwood pines to ***Phallic Rock,*** which, when seen, needs no explanation. Barren women spent the night in this forest in order to conceive, and offerings are placed on the rock to this day. Camping in Palaau (at a safe distance from phallic effects) is allowed by state permit. Call 567–6923 or 984–8109.

A visit to ***Kalaupapa National Historic Park*** will almost certainly provide the highlight of any Moloka`i experience. It is essential if you are to comprehend the emotional scars of this onetime "Lonely Island." Leprosy (Hansen's disease) was first observed in Hawaii in 1835 and soon grew to epidemic proportions. The biblical stigma (and physical repulsiveness) of the disease moved missionary doctors to push for drastic quarantine measures. The physical isolation of Makanalua ("the given grave") Peninsula made it a natural place to exile leprosy patients, a process that began in 1866.

View from Kalawao, Kalaupapa Peninsula

Priapic Geology

Precontact Hawaiians believed various stones were inhabited by spirits and held magical powers. Among the more famous of these stones is Moloka'i's Phallic Rock, located in Palaau State Park. The legend is that the male fertility god Nanahoa lived nearby and was caught staring at a beautiful young girl who was admiring her own reflection in a pool. Nanahoa's wife, Kawahuna, saw her husband leering and in a storm of jealousy attacked the young girl by yanking on her hair. Nanahoa became outraged in turn and struck his wife, who rolled over a nearby cliff and turned to stone. Nanahoa also turned to stone, appropriately enough, some might say, in a phallic shape. According to legend, he still sits there today. Barren women make the pilgrimage to this rock, where it's said if they spend the night and pray for fertility, they could be blessed with a child.

There was once a female stone (the wife) that stood next to the male. As the legend suggests, this stone has since fallen down the hillside.

Flows from **Kauhako Crater** created the 2-mile peninsula as a geologic afterthought, long after the rest of Moloka`i had taken shape. As a natural viewing platform from which to marvel at Moloka`i's stunning northern coastline, the peninsula provides a serene counterpoint to the saga of its troubled past. A visit to Kalaupapa, however, does not wallow in the misery caused by man's inhumanity to man as much as it celebrates the redemptive qualities of human compassion and altruism. You will learn of the *kokuas* ("helpers") who volunteered to follow their loved ones into exile and who lived out their lives among the diseased. You will pay homage to the courage of Father Damien, a Catholic priest who came here alone to minister to the afflicted and helped transform their lawless purgatory into a life of newfound dignity.

Damien eventually contracted leprosy and died among those he had come to serve. His work did not lack controversy. During Damien's lifetime, his plight attracted headlines around the world, and soon others came to labor alongside him. The original settlement at rainy Kalawao was moved to more hospitable Kalaupapa, a fishing village on the other side of the peninsula. Bit by bit, the suffering of leprosy patients abated, and the advent of sulfone drugs in the 1940s offered a permanent cure to the progress of the disease. Despite this, the isolation laws governing the settlement were not rescinded until 1969. Children younger than age sixteen remain barred from entry even today.

The classic way to get to Kalaupapa has always been to take the **Moloka`i Mule Ride** (567–6088; 800–567–7550; www.muleride.com) out of Kalae Stables. Bumper stickers on O`ahu advertise "I'd rather be riding a mule on

Moloka`i." The ride and tour cost $165, which includes lunch. The other options are flying and hiking, with direct flights from Ho`olehua ("topside"), Kahului (Maui), or Honolulu available. However you get there, to enter you need a permit, which you can only get by registering for a tour; tours are offered Monday through Friday. Non-mule riders should book directly with **Damien Tours** (567–6171; best times to call are 7:00 to 9:45 A.M. or 2:00 to 4:00 P.M.), which runs the four-hour ground tours of Kalaupapa in a rickety old school bus. If you hike in, your ground tour is only $40. Air packages vary greatly, as a number of small charter airlines compete. **Moloka`i Air Shuttle** (545–4988 in Honolulu; 567–6847 in Moloka`i) has good rates ($100 round-trip). Ask Damien Tours or your travel agent for advice on current service. Children under sixteen are not allowed on the tour. Best to reserve a spot on a tour three to five days in advance. The owner of Damien tours, Richard Marks, moonlights as the sheriff of Kalawao County (distinct from the rest of Moloka`i, which is part of Maui). He is a self-taught authority on leprosy and former patient himself, who has had audiences with the pope and Mother

Land of Powerful Prayer

Ancient Hawaiian name chants record that Moloka`i was known in olden times as Moloka`i pule o`o, "land of powerful prayer." Legends of sorcery on the island abound. Some of this magic was benevolent. The island's most powerful kahuna, Lanikaula, became famous throughout Hawaii for his wisdom and learning. Chiefs from all of the islands would travel to his home on the island's east end to seek his counsel. During Lanikaula's lifetime Moloka`i became a spiritual haven, off-limits to warfare. Unfortunately, Lanikaula was betrayed by a visiting fellow kahuna from Lana`i named Kawelo, who stole a stool sample from the sage and used it to work a magic death-by-constipation on his erstwhile colleague.

The west side of the island became equally famous for a more ferocious style of magic. Discovered in a dream by the chief Kaneiakama, a miraculous stand of trees suddenly appeared on the slopes of Maunaloa, into which the Kalaipahoa, or "poisonwood gods," entered. Birds flying over the trees would drop dead out of the sky, and chips sent flying from an ax blow would poison woodcutters sent to harvest the timber of these magical trees. Under the guidance of Kaneiakama, the Moloka`i priests finally learned how to harness the power of the Kalaipahoa through ritual offerings. From the wood of the trees, they carved fearsome *ki`i* ("god images"), whose magic rendered the island immune to attack from its neighbors. Traveling war canoes gave the western coastline of Moloka`i a wide berth. Also at Maunaloa lived Kapo, an early master of the hula and legendary relative of the volcano goddess Pele. Embittered at her younger sister Laka for her greater fame as a hula dancer, Kapo is reputed to have turned to *ana`ana* ("black magic") in her old age.

Teresa. Although he rarely leads the tours himself anymore, you would be very lucky to have him.

All the tours cover the basic fixtures and monuments of the Kalaupapa settlement, where more than thirty-five of the original patients still reside. You then cross the peninsula to the earlier settlement at Kalawao. Here you visit *St. Philomena Church,* which Damien built. Note the square holes he cut in the wooden floor so that ailing worshippers could spit without feeling self-conscious. Nearby you stop for a picnic lunch at a stunningly beautiful site overlooking the mouth of Waikolu Valley and Mokapu Island. (Those who hike or fly in should bring their own food.) If time permits, ask to take a short hike to the rim of *Kauhako Crater* (400 feet) for an awesome view of the entire peninsula. A "bottomless" lake, the habitat for at least one species of shrimp found nowhere else in the world, fills the crater floor.

The West End

Moloka`i's coastline lacks good swimming beaches. The south coast consists of shallow mudflats, and the North Shore is mostly inaccessible. The tiny beaches and coves on the east coast have their charm, but they are peppered with rocks. It is along the west coast (see map on page 144) that Moloka`i has stationed its major white-sand creations. Not coincidentally, it's also the site of the island's only real tourist resorts.

The Maunaloa Highway (Route 46) heads west past Ho`olehua Airport, where it climbs the gentle slopes of its namesake, the 1,381-foot volcano that formed this half of the island (not to be confused with the vastly bigger Mauna Loa on the Big Island). The slopes of the mountain yielded an ultra-hard basalt prized for making adzes and other tools. The name of the older of the two resorts in this region, Kaluakoi, translates to "the adze pit." The other outstanding feature of West Moloka`i is the red volcanic soil that blows in the constant trade winds and sooner or later daubs everything (tree trunks, houses, cars) with its ruddy palette.

To hit the beaches on the other side of the mountain, take the signposted turnoff on the right to *Kaluakoi Resort.* The road down traverses extremely dry scrubland, whose rolling hills are covered with thorny *kiawe* (mesquite) trees. Kiawe briquettes make great barbecue, as any native of the American Southwest will testify. What's more, the pollen from the tree's flowers makes great honey. Moloka`i at one time led the world in honey production, before disease struck the hives. Island honey is still sold in stores and is a popular gift item.

Kaluakoi Resort, the hotel and two condominiums, and the scattering of surrounding private estates were only part of an ambitious development plan for the West End, whose unrealized boundaries are indicated by the miles of paved roads leading nowhere. Residents of Moloka`i remain skeptical of these plans, and limited water allocation (largely controlled by the Hawaiian Home Lands Commission) has proved an effective obstacle to further development. For now, the focus of West End development has shifted to Maunaloa. Kaluakoi Hotel itself has been closed for several years and was recently purchased by the Molokai Ranch. Plans call for it to reopen in 2007. Call (888) 627–8082 for information.

Kephui Beach fronting the hotel is rocky and often unsuitable for swimming. Instead, walk a few hundred yards north across the golf course, past the tenth hole, to reach *Pohaku Mauliuli,* a patchy sand beach sheltered beneath the eroded face of blackened cinder cone. Known as Make ("dead") Horse to locals after an unfortunate equine fell from the cliffs, the beach's deep waters offer exciting terrain for experienced snorkelers. Almost a mile farther north, tucked inside tiny coves along the rocky shoreline, the determined beachgoer can enjoy the island's finest strands at *Kawakiuniu and Kawakiuiki* ("big and little Kawakiu") *Bays.* To get there, you must choose between hiking along the coast or bumping along the badly eroded jeep road that splits from the road to the Paniolo Hale condos, passing the fourteenth-hole restroom. Stay on the left fork to follow the coastline. The two coves are sheltered from the elements, but in winter the waters may be too rough for swimming.

Immediately south of Kepuhi Beach and Kaluakoi Resort, *Pu`u o Kaiaka,* or *Kaiaka Rock,* a massive basalt outcrop, juts into the ocean. Of spiritual significance to the ancient Hawaiians, Pu`u o Kaiaka was the site of a heiau that was demolished by army bulldozers in the 1960s. If you scramble up the short jeep trail leading from Kaiaka Road to the top, you will, in addition to having breathtaking views of the western coastline, come upon some curious concrete-block structures that resemble a modernistic rendition of the heiau the army destroyed. In fact, the blocks are the forgotten remains of a cable-car winch erected by Libby Pineapple Company to lower its fruit to ships anchored offshore. The pineapple offerings ceased flowing from this sacred spot when Kolo Wharf was built.

On the other side of Kaiaka Rock, the vast windswept sands of Papohaku Beach extend for 2 miles of white powder, accessible through several turnoffs from Kaluakoi Road. Sand from the beach was for years illegally mined to replenish Waikiki's own diminishing strands. *Papohaku Beach Park* offers attractive facilities maintained by Kaluakoi Resort. (WARNING: Offshore currents make the waters unsafe at times, and the wind can generate a fierce sandblast.) Every May, a festival at the beach park commemorates the legendary birth of the hula on Moloka`i. Turnoffs farther along Kaluakoi Road lead to

The Birth of Hula

The graceful movements of this traditional dance have long been synonymous with the romantic image of the Hawaiian Islands around the world. Although the story of the hula's creation varies greatly among sources, many accounts credit an early hula school established at Kaʻana as the progenitor of the art form. The demand for hula soon exceeded the limited capacity of the school. Accordingly, Laka, a *kumu hula* ("dance teacher"), left Kaʻana to travel to the other islands, spreading the art of hula throughout Hawaii. Today Laka is revered as a goddess and patroness of the dance. Every year, Molokaʻi celebrates Ka Hula Piko ("the birth of hula") through offerings at Kaʻana and an islandwide hula festival held at Papohaku Beach Park. The annual celebration takes place on the third Saturday of May. If you plan to attend, book your Molokaʻi stay early, as island accommodations fill up.

additional beaches, most of them unblemished by human footprints. *Kapukabebu,* the last beach before the paved road ends, is known to locals as *Dixie Maru,* after a Japanese fishing boat that shipwrecked offshore. The beach's tiny cove may be more sheltered than those before it.

To escape the coastal heat, follow the Maunaloa Highway for another 2 miles past the turnoff into Maunaloa Town, a tiny former plantation community nestled among cool pine trees. After Dole Pineapple pulled out of the island in 1975, Maunaloa became a virtual ghost town that nobody visited. Jonathan Socher's *Big Wind Kite Factory* (552–2364) almost single-handedly put Maunaloa back on the map. Jonathan's elaborate designs translate the artistic visions of his wife, Daphne, into airborne motion. The tiny front-room shop comes alive with colorful kite fantasies, from dancing hula girls to pineapple windsocks. Tour the factory in back, where the Sochers happily demonstrate the finer points of kite making. Big Wind also imports high-performance stunt kites, for which Jonathan gives free lessons. In an adjacent room, the Sochers operate *Plantation Gallery* to showcase the craftwork of local artists as well as carefully chosen imports from Bali, where the Sochers vacation. Open Monday through Saturday 8:30 A.M. to 5:00 P.M. and Sunday 10:00 A.M. to 2:00 P.M.

In recent years Maunaloa has witnessed a number of great changes. *Molokaʻi Ranch* (552–2741), which owns most of the land on this half of the island, has carefully nurtured its plans for controlled development in a number of complementary ventures. To start with, the ranch literally rebuilt the town of Maunaloa, replacing its worn-out plantation homes with updated models and Molokaʻi's first movie theater (a cineplex no less). A few of the original homes were relocated and will form the basis for a future museum and cultural center.

Big Wind Kite Factory

The ranch has also gone into tourism, transforming portions of its surrounding property into a kind of ecotourist resort/adventure park. Offering an ersatz "camping" experience combined with a smorgasbord of daily activities, the ranch caters to well-heeled travelers who want to experience the great outdoors without roughing it. Overnight guests at ***The Beach Village of Moloka`i Ranch*** (660–2824; centralized reservations 888–627–8082; www .molokairanch.com) lodge in "tentalows," a kind of hybrid tent/bungalow with fabric walls built over wooden platforms. The solar-powered tentalows, equipped with comfortable beds, self-composting toilets, and private outdoor showers, front lovely Kaupoa Beach. Daily all-you-can-eat meals at the Kaupoa Dining Pavilion revolve around a large salad bar and grilled-to-order meats and fish, priced in the expensive range. Evening entertainment is provided, and the whole operation is conducted in refreshingly low-key Moloka`i style. Room rates start at $148 per night, with various meal and activity packages available.

Daily activities operated by ***Moloka`i Fish and Dive*** (553–5926) include hiking, archery, kayaking, mountain biking, lei making, and deep-sea fishing.

Urban cowboys can ride herd (literally) by signing up for the ranch's **Cattle Trail Drive** or hone their skills in rodeo games. All activities are open to visitors staying elsewhere. Sign up at the front desk or with the camp host at the Beach Village. Costs range from $25 to $95. Of special interest is the Sunday-night *kapuna* jam session between 5:00 and 7:00 P.M., featuring local elders who gather to play ukulele and guitar, as well as dance hula. The event draws both tourists and locals, and reservations are a must.

Much of the ranch land around the campsites and elsewhere remains fenced-in cattle pasture. The ranch has preserved public access to Hale o Lono Harbor on the island's southwestern coast. To get there from Maunaloa, turn onto the paved road just above the activity center. The road turns to dirt before passing the rodeo arena. Farther along, take the right fork and follow the bumpy road 2 miles down to the harbor. There is a small swimming beach nearby. In October competitors launch from Hale o Lono for the annual Moloka`i-to-O`ahu canoe races, a 40-mile paddle through monstrous swells and fierce channel currents. Camping is permitted at both Hale o Lono and Kawakiu Bay. The ranch has also built more traditional quarters in Maunaloa town. The twenty-two-room **Moloka`i Lodge** (660–2824; 888–627–8082) cultivates the rustic charm of a gentleman rancher's manor and overlooks sweeping hillside views. Rooms start at $218.

Moloka`i Nightlife

Folks in Honolulu will tell you nothing happens on the island of Moloka`i after dark. But as with most places, the truth is you just have to know where to go. In Kaunakakai the hot place to be (literally) is the alley in back of Kanemitsu Bakery, where locals gather for fresh-baked bread, hot out of the oven starting around 10:15 P.M. every night but Monday. Here's how it works. You enter the alley to the right of the bakery storefront and head for the light at the end. Most nights you'll find a line already formed there. If not, knock on the door under the light. You have to knock hard to be heard. Eventually, footsteps will approach, and the door will open about 8 inches wide, no more. A voice will ask you what kind of bread you want. You counter by asking what they have. You may have a choice of toppings, either butter with cinnamon sugar or cream cheese with guava jelly. Once your order is placed, the door slams shut again and the footsteps disappear. You wait in the alley, inhaling the aroma of fresh-baked bread, impatient with anticipation. Eventually, the door cracks open once more, and a hand extends your order to you. You pay and wait for change, clutching the piping hot bread. The loaves are cut lengthwise down the middle, with the toppings slathered inside. You may just have to take a bite right there.

Places to Stay in Moloka`i

KAUNAKAKAI

Dunbar Beachfront Cottages
HC 01, Box 901, 96748
558–8153, (800) 673–0520
www.molokai-beachfront-cottages.com
The name says it all. $170, three-night minimum.

Hotel Moloka`i
Kamehameha Highway
553–5347
www.hotelmolokai.com
Has rooms by the sea from $90.

Kamalo Plantation B&B
Mile 10 on Kamehameha
V Highway
HC1, Box 300, 96748
558–8236
A lush oasis on the island's east end; private cottages for $95 and $150.

Pu`u o Hoku Ranch
P.O. Box 1889, 96748
558–8109
www.puuohoku.com
Offers two secluded cottages on the far eastern tip of Moloka`i for $140.

MAUNALOA

Molokai Ranch & Lodge
100 Maunaloa Highway
660–2824, (888) 627–8082
www.molokairanch.com
Offers upscale "camping" with a smorgasbord of action adventures to choose from and a traditional twenty-two-room lodge. Rates start at $148.

Molokai Vacation Rentals
P.O. Box 1979, 96748
(800) 367–2984
www.molokai-vacation-rental.com

Places to Eat in Moloka`i

KUALAPUU

Kamuela's Cookhouse
Uwao Street
567–9655
A renovated plantation eatery. Good, casual fare. Moderate to expensive.

KAUNAKAKAI

Hotel Moloka`i
Kamehameha Highway
553–5347
Charming oceanfront dining in a nostalgic old Hawaii setting. Moderate to expensive.

Kanemitsu Bakery
79 Ala Malama Street
553–5855
An impressive selection of breads that is coveted statewide. Inexpensive.

Moloka`i Pizza Cafe
15 Kaunakakai Place
553–3288
A menu full of variety and casual fare. Inexpensive.

MAUNALOA

Maunaloa Dining Room at the Moloka`i Ranch
660–2824
Plantation tavern serves steak and seafood. Expensive.

TO LEARN MORE ABOUT MOLOKA`I VISIT THE FOLLOWING WEB SITES:

www.molokai-hawaii.com   www.visitmolokai.com

Lana`i

For a small island, Lana`i has seen a lot of changes. In a legendary past, Hawaiians shunned the island, believing it to be inhabited by a nasty breed of *akua* ("spirits"). Kaululaau, the mischievous son of a Maui chieftain, was banished here for chopping down his father's breadfruit trees. He defeated the akua and opened Lana`i to human habitation. Mormon settlers came here beginning in 1853, hoping to build a "City of Joseph" as a model of earthly peace. The mission folded when the settlers discovered that their leader, Walter Gibson, had secretly registered title to the land in his own name. The Mormon Church promptly excommunicated him and relocated to Laie on Oah`u. Undeterred, Gibson brought in new settlers and converted the entire island into an open cattle range, which he managed until King Kalakaua appointed him prime minister.

Unrestricted grazing turned the already dry landscape into a barren wasteland. The arrival of New Zealand naturalist George Munro, who was called in to manage the ranch, helped reverse some of the damage. Munro literally replanted a forest with introduced flora, including the Norfolk Island pines that have become a local trademark. While Munro worked to undo the excesses of ranching, Jim Dole introduced a different type of pine as ranching's replacement, purchasing the entire island

Kalohi Channel

Auau
Channel

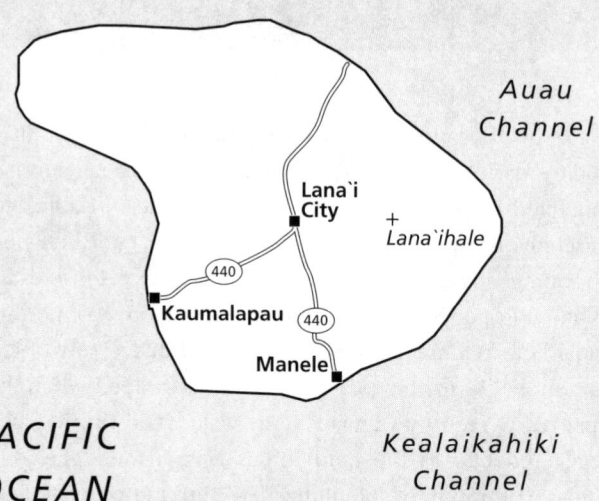

Lana`i
City

+
Lana`ihale

440

Kaumalapau

440

Manele

PACIFIC
OCEAN

Kealaikahiki
Channel

N

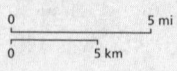

0   5 mi

0   5 km

in 1922 to begin the world's largest pineapple plantation. Castle & Cooke, the current
owner, has phased out pineapple production
in recent years, shifting workers from agriculture to hotel work in two newly opened
resorts. The erstwhile "Pineapple Island" is
now being promoted to well-heeled vaca-
tioners as "Hawaii's Private Island."

These changes mean less than they
might sound. The substitution of tourists for
pineapples might seem like a backward

lana`ifacts

Nickname: Pineapple Isle
Dimensions: 18 x 12 miles
Highest elevation: Lana`ihale
(3,370 feet)
Population: 3,193 (2000)
Principal city: Lana`i City
Flower: Kauna`oa
Color: Orange

step, but less than one-fifth of the island ever grew pineapples to begin with.
Shaped roughly like a kidney, Lana`i measures 18 miles long by 12 miles
across. Adventurous travelers will have no difficulty losing themselves amid
untamed wilderness and hidden locales. As you explore, you cannot help but
stumble upon a variety of wildlife. Axis deer and mouflon sheep mingle with
countless game fowl that flourish here in the absence of the mongoose found
on other islands. You probably will want to rent a jeep to get around. Be prepared for unchivalrous bumps and thick red clouds of dust. Be warned that
landmarks might change as fields are abandoned, and with them the access
roads cleared through the bush. Get good directions and advice on weather
and road conditions before setting out anywhere away from pavement. The
only game in town for car rentals is Dollar Rent-A-Car (800–800–4000), and the
prices reflect it.

Lana`i City

Though a small island, Lana`i has always thought big. Its tiny town has been
optimistically named Lana`i City and is situated in the center of the island with
plenty of room to grow. An elevation of 1,650 feet keeps cool breezes blowing
through Lana`i City even during summer. Most of the houses here date from
the town's origins in 1922. Their brightly colored iron roofs punctuate the green
of the ubiquitous Norfolk Island pines. Almost all of Lana`i's inhabitants live
here in town, the majority of them of Filipino extraction. More by tradition than
function, the plantation horn still sounds every evening, although thankfully
the 4:30 A.M. wake-up calls have ceased. Sunday cockfights, although illegal,
remain a fixture of island social life.

Dole Park, a grassy square shaded by rows of Norfolk Island pines, occupies the town center. Lana`i's few commercial buildings mostly cluster around
the park. Visit the *Lana`i Art Center* (565–7503) to view the work of local

artists and take classes to create your own. Stop by **Pele's Other Garden** (565–9628) to munch New York–style deli grub for breakfast and lunch or Italian fare at dinner. Open Monday through Friday 10:00 A.M. to 2:30 P.M. and Monday through Saturday 5:00 to 8:00 P.M. The **Blue Ginger Café** (565–6363) serves inexpensive local-style meals daily from 6:00 A.M. to 8:00 P.M. It doubles as a bakery. **Canoe's** (565–6537) operates a tasty lunch counter every day but Wednesday from 6:30 A.M. to 1:00 P.M. **Henry Clay's Rotisserie** in the **Hotel Lana`i** (565–7211; 877–665–2624) serves moderately priced dinners featuring spit-roasted meats, an excellent rotisserie chicken, and some Cajun specialties such as seafood gumbo. Open nightly 5:30 to 9:00 P.M. Built in 1925 as a club-house for Dole executives, the hotel has ten rooms and a separate cottage that rent for $115 to $175, less than half the rates charged by its upmarket sisters, the **Manele Bay** and **Koele Lodge** resorts. Call (800) 321–4666 for centralized reservations for the latter. **Dreams Come True** (565–6961; 800–566–6961; www.dreamscometruelanai.com) offers bed-and-breakfast rooms with private sky-lit baths, whirlpool tubs, and some four-poster beds in a restored planta-tion house with kitchen access for $112. You might contact statewide bed-and-breakfast agencies for alternatives (see the Introduction).

Camping at Hulopoe Bay is private, scenic, and peaceful and even offers solar-heated showers. The bay is a marine life conservation area, so while there's no three-prong fishing allowed, you can snorkel to your heart's content. Permits are issued for a three-night maximum stay, and the fee is $5.00 per person per night and a one-time $5.00 registration fee. For more information, contact **Castle and Cooke Resorts** at P.O. Box 630310, Lana`i City 96763, or phone 565–2970.

Branching Out

From Lana`i City, paved roads cut across an inland plateau and drop sharply to the coast on each of Lana`i's three sides; hunting tracks climb the slopes of the central mountain and, together with the former pineapple field roads, partition the island's interior. Begin by heading west on Kaumalapau Highway, the only road truly deserving the designation of highway. As the main access road to the airport and harbor, it is wide, well graded, and smoothly paved. Thus, as you might expect, it has little of interest lying along it. Drive down to the har-bor anyway. The transition from the flat tableland to the steep slope down the coast offers some vistas over the craggy gulches, sheer cliffs, and rocky sea stacks that characterize Lana`i's western shore. The very industrial-looking har-bor squats beneath the rocky cliff from which it was blasted. It may no longer buzz with its previous pineapple-related activity, but it and the airport are still Lana`i's main gateway to the outside world.

Brief History of Lana'i

Pineapple King James Dole, who purchased Lana'i in 1922, combined innovative methods of mass production with mass marketing to make the pineapple synonymous with Hawaii the world over. But in Hawaii, he made pineapple synonymous with Lana'i, transforming the island's population and economy in the process. Lana'i became the world's largest pineapple plantation, although it was not the first place in Hawaii that pineapple (not a native fruit) was grown.

Ironically, Lana'i claims distinction for another "first" regarding a different crop: sugar. The Polynesians grew sugarcane but never produced refined sugar. In 1802 a Chinese man on Lana'i is believed to have been the first to have done so. Sugar would go on to transform Hawaii, becoming the dominant crop in the islands, but not on Lana'i.

A side trip from Kaumalapau to Kaunolu, on the other hand, demonstrates the reverse trade-off and offers a fascinating destination—an ancient village that was Kamehameha I's favorite fishing retreat—at the price of a hellishly difficult access. Definitely get current directions for this one: As empty pineapple fields are converted to pastures, new fences might arise. For one possible route, turn left at the stop sign onto Kaupili Road, just past the airport turnoff as you are coming down the highway. The road deteriorates to gravel and then dirt as it winds through some curves and then follows a fenced border along the former pineapple fields. You soon will see the island of Kahoolawe ahead on the horizon. As you drive, scan the southwestern tip of the island, on your right, for a tiny lighthouse; this is your destination. You should find the road down to Kaunolu 2.1 miles from the highway, where the fencing ends at a runoff ditch. The 3-mile descent is incredibly steep and rocky. Do not attempt this unless you are experienced at handling a four-wheel-drive vehicle.

A bruising half-hour ride down the left side of a gully brings you to **Kaunolu Bay,** whose archaeological treasures constitute a National Historic Landmark. The stone foundations of more than a hundred Hawaiian homes cling to the slopes above this tiny cove. Tufts of *pili* grass used for thatching grow wild in the rocky terrain. If you wet the wispy seeds of the pili, they will rotate—a unique self-planting mechanism adapted to intermittent rainfall. Just to the right of the kiawe tree at the end of the trail, on a bluff overlooking the dry streambed of the gully, you can find the terraced foundation believed to be the site of King Kamehameha's house. Facing Kamehameha's house, on the bluffs across the gully on the right side of the bay, stands **Halulu Heiau;** and on the far side of this bluff, a small gap in the rocky rim marks the entrance to

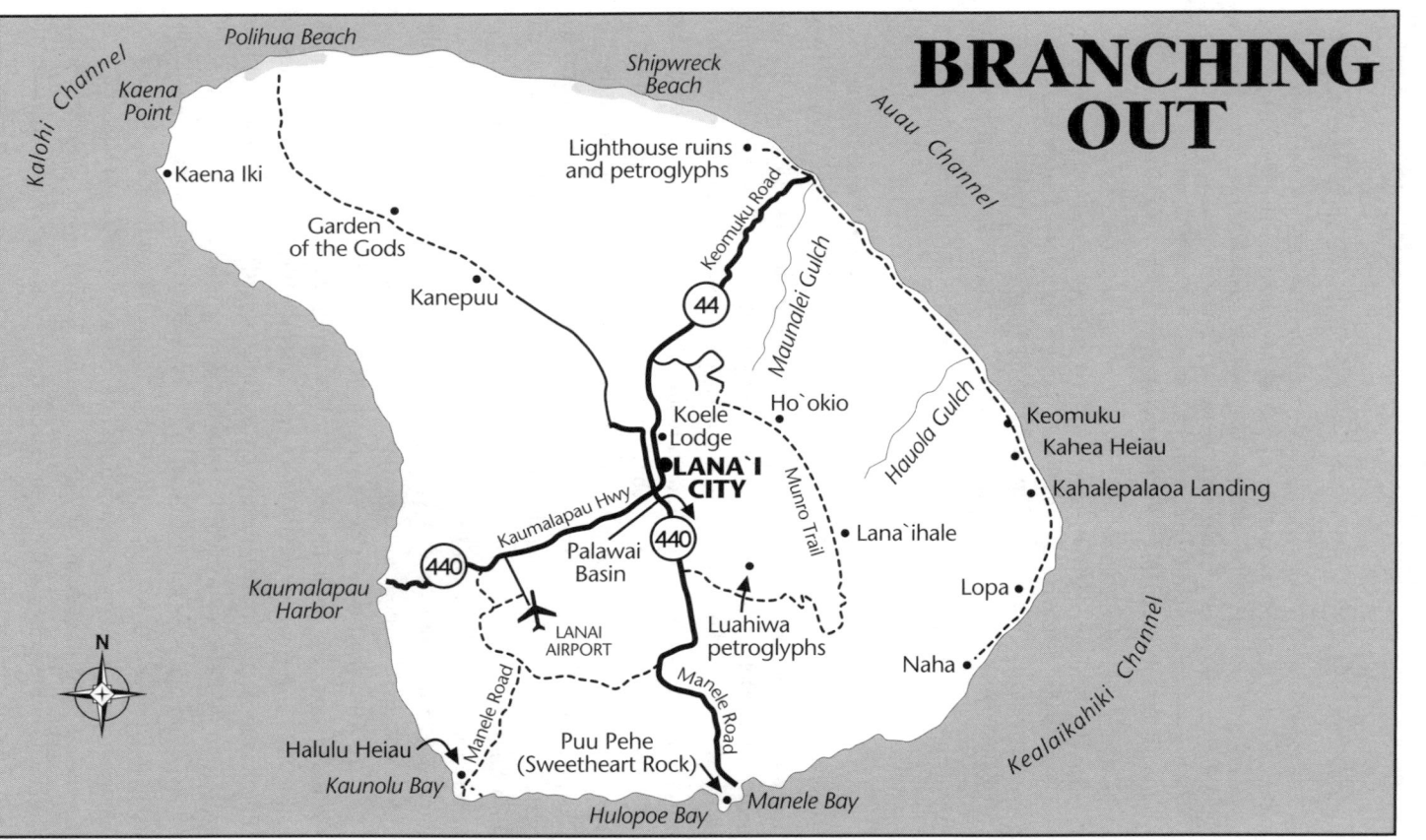

BRANCHING OUT

Polihua Beach

Kalohi Channel

Kaena Point

Kaena Iki

Garden of the Gods

Kanepuu

Shipwreck Beach

Auau Channel

Lighthouse ruins and petroglyphs

Keomuku Road

(44)

Maunalei Gulch

Ho`okio

Hauola Gulch

Keomuku

Kahea Heiau

Kahalepalaoa Landing

Koele Lodge

LANA`I CITY

Kaumalapau Hwy

(440)

Kaumalapau Harbor

Munro Trail

Lana`ihale

Palawai Basin

(440)

LANAI AIRPORT

Luahiwa petroglyphs

Lopa

Naha

Kealaikahiki Channel

N

Manele Road

Manele Road

Halulu Heiau

Kaunolu Bay

Puu Pehe (Sweetheart Rock)

Hulopoe Bay

Manele Bay

Kahekili's Leap, named for Kamehameha's greatest rival, the High Chief of Maui, who excelled at cliff diving.

Climb down the slope to the base of the bay, then walk up the streambed. On your left you will pass a narrow rock wall enclosure that formed part of a shelter for repairing canoes. Above on your right you can now clearly see the terracing of Kamehameha's house site. Climb up the opposite wall of the gully to reach the heiau. Kamehameha rebuilt the temple after he conquered Lana'i, making it one of the last monuments to the old gods. Its carefully fitted

Kahekili's Leap

rock walls stand in excellent repair. (Please take care that they remain so.) Walk over to Kahekili's Leap for a dramatic view of *Pali Kaholo,* Lana'i's tallest sea cliff, which rises 1,000 feet above deep-blue ocean. At the base of the cliff, the pounding surf echoes inside a large sea cave like rolling thunder. Kamehameha's warriors used to dive from the ledge you are standing on to prove their loyalty and courage. Merely imagining the 62-foot plunge into the Pacific—with a 15-foot rock outcrop to clear at the base—should be enough to give most visitors a jolt of vertigo.

Your next excursion takes you south on Manele Road, descending from Lana'i City through the historic Palawai Basin. Once the caldera of the volcano that formed Lana'i, the basin became the site of the short-lived Mormon settlement and later cradled Dole's first pineapple fields. The foothills east of the

Geography of Lana'i

The sixth largest of the Hawaiian Islands, Lana'i is the smallest island open to visitors. Formed from a single central volcano, it has 47 miles of coastline, two resort hotels, few roads, no traffic lights, and only a handful of swimming beaches. The island summit at Lana'ihale reaches 3,370 feet, and the widest point of the island spans 18 miles.

Palawai hold some of the best-preserved *petroglyphs* in the state. To probe their secrets, look for the large water tower on the hillside above the basin. On the right of the water tower is a wide gulch, and to the right of the gulch grows a stand of trees where the petroglyphs lurk. To get there, turn left onto Hoike Road, a former pineapple road marked by a YIELD sign (facing south). Turn left at the second irrigation ditch and follow the water pipe to the third power pole, where a NO TRESPASSING sign marks the beginning of the trail up to the petroglyphs. The petroglyph-laden rocks are located at the far lower edge of the trees amid a clump of exotic-looking sisal plants with spiky leaves and tall central stalks. A jeep trail leads up the hill to the first carved boulder. Proving that on Lana`i nothing comes easily, the better-preserved, more intricate carvings lie on rocks farther up the slope. Patterned images of canoes, warriors, and animals abound. One shows a man on horseback, dating its origin to after the arrival of Western ships, but no one today can explain why these carvings were made or what they signify. Please be respectful of their fragile condition.

lana`itrivia

Luahiwa Petroglyphs are among the best preserved in all the islands.

Continue along Manele Road as it rises out of Palawai Basin and then descends steeply to the coast. You will see Kaho`olawe again across Kealaikahiki ("the way to Tahiti") Channel and maybe the twin towers of the Big Island beyond. Two beautiful bays await you at the end of the road. Both are marine-life conservation zones offering excellent snorkeling. *Manele Bay* arrives first on your left, its former black-sand beach now converted to a small-boat harbor. Guarded by fortresslike cliffs, the cove offers views of Maui's Mount Haleakala rising above the clouds on the horizon. *Expeditions* (661–3756) offers ferry service to and from Lahaina Harbor on Maui five times daily. The fee is $25 one way.

An extension of Manele Road curves west to *Hulopoe Bay* around the point. Hulopoe Beach, often called Manele as well, dazzles visitors with its wide crescent of snowy white sand edging a lovely bay. The shorebreak can be rough in summer, suitable for bodysurfing. A pod of spinner dolphins frequents the waters offshore. (Federal law prohibits harassment of this endangered species.) Pele's Other Garden operates a small sandwich stand. Unfortunately, this idyllic location has not gone unnoticed. Day-trippers from Maui now come daily, and the 250-room Manele Hotel perches on the bluffs above the bay. Note the murals showing Kaululaau's legendary deeds at the hotel's entrance.

For seclusion, walk around the left side of the bay, past some enormous tide pools, to the cove at *Pu`u Pehe.* Also known as *Sweetheart Rock,* it was named for a legendary beauty who drowned in a nearby sea cave, where her jealous husband had confined her, and was buried on this giant sea stack. You can sun yourself on the hidden beach below, although the water is too rocky for good swimming. Walk to the far edge of the bluffs facing Sweetheart Rock for a sweeping view of Lana`i's southern coast, with the mountains of Maui and Kahoolawe, and sometimes even the Big Island, visible across the sea.

Keomuku Road, Lana`i's third paved road, departs north past the Koele Lodge Hotel. *Kalokahi o Ka Malamalama,* the tiny church next to the lodge, survives from the ranch days. You can attend Sunday services in Hawaiian here. The road then climbs past guava trees and curves right toward Lana`i's eastern shore. Just beyond the bend, a small paved road on the right leads to the old Koele cemetery and the start of Lana`i's famous *Munro Trail.* This 9-mile-long jeep path showcases much of the exotic vegetation that Munro introduced to reestablish a viable watershed in the island's upcountry. The trail climbs the summit of 3,370-foot *Lana`ihale* ("house of Lana`i"), which resembles a second-story addition to the island. Rising steeply above the surrounding tableland, the Hale, as locals call it, presents panoramic views of Lana`i and up to five other islands in the chain. Look for guavas and thimbleberries along the trail. Do not attempt the ascent if it has been raining or looks like it will start.

From the cemetery, bear left to avoid the golf course and look for a small sign marking the Munro Trail's entrance into the forest proper. If you are traveling on foot, it might be easier to take the recently created *Koloiki Ridge Trail,* which begins behind Koele Lodge (565–4000) and joins the Munro Trail halfway along. Ask the concierge for a self-guiding pamphlet. (Guided interpretive hikes are also available; $15 for nonguests.) After descending through forest for the first few miles, the trail then climbs to reach a telephone relay station overlooking the steep walls of Maunalei ("mountain lei") Gulch, named for the wreathlike clouds so often draped around the mountain here. In 1778 Kalaniopuu's invasion force from the Big Island laid siege to Lana`i's last defenders in this valley. The trail continues along the ridgeline above the upper valley to overlook a lower middle ridge, Ho`okio, where keen eyes can still discern the *Ho`okio Notches,* carved by the stalwart Lana`i warriors to fortify their stronghold. Kalaniopuu eventually starved them out and then proceeded to massacre and pillage the entire island.

At 4.7 miles, just before the summit, a side trail heads left through eucalyptus trees for a view of *Hauola Gulch,* a 2,000-foot gash in the mountain's side, the deepest on the island. From the windswept, rain-soaked summit, you get the island's best views, provided the Hale breaks free from its cloud cover. The trail then descends steeply down the drier backside of the mountain to link up with Hoike Road, the main jeep access from Palawai Basin.

Keomuku Road continues northeast and begins another bumpy, winding descent to the coast. The stacks of rocks you see along the highway here and elsewhere are not ancient Hawaiian monuments but rather a form of graffiti. While Hawaiians did use such cairns as trail markers, these were built by latter-day visitors to "ward off the ghosts." Game abounds in this area, and if you're not careful, you could violate hunting regulations by running over a few wild turkeys with your car.

The paved road ends at the bottom of the hill. An unpaved extension on the left, fairly easy going, leads north to **Shipwreck** or **Kaiolohia Beach.** Situated equally between the islands of Maui and Moloka`i offshore, this long, desolate beach gets battered by fierce trade winds and ocean swells funneling through the Pailolo Channel. Littered with debris that drifts across its protective outer reef, the beach has witnessed countless shipwrecks and intentional groundings since the days when flotillas of whalers laid anchor in the famous Lahaina waters off Maui. Although swimming is less than ideal, beachcombers will have a field day. As you drive farther, notice the dwellings of "Federation Camp," built from driftwood and salvaged wreckage. Filipino fishermen built these as weekend shelters during the 1930s. At the end of the drivable road, a path leads to the site of a former lighthouse. Offshore, an abandoned World War II Liberty Ship lists just beyond the reef, stubbornly holding out against the punishing waves.

Heading in the other direction from the end of paved Keomuku Road requires a jeep to reach Keomuku itself and points beyond. To navigate the 12-odd miles to Naha on the southeastern coast takes at least an hour. Four miles along you reach the ghost town of **Keomuku,** headquarters of the hapless Maunalei Sugar Company. Gibson's daughter started this short-lived venture at the turn of the century. The plantation was visited by the plague in its first year and was forced to fold after the second year, when the sweet well water mysteriously turned brackish.

Ka Lanakila o Ka Malamalama, a picturesque wooden church nestled in a coconut grove, remains the only intact building in Keomuku. Behind the church, three large whaleboats rot on land that was shoreline in 1935. Soil runoff has added the new land. Less than a mile farther south, you'll pass **Kahea Heiau,** whose stones were pilfered to line the plantation rail bed. Hawaiians believe such desecration led to Maunalei Sugar's demise.

Beyond the heiau lies the old sugar dock, **Kahalepalaoa Landing.** Queen Ka`ahumanu came from Maui near the end of her life to preach to Lana`i's people on this spot and convert them to Christian ways. Today Maui day-trippers follow in her footsteps to indulge in more hedonistic pursuits at Club Lana`i. The road turns inland from here, with the coast hidden behind a forest of kiawe trees, and emerges a few miles farther along at Lopa, where the beach is somewhat more sheltered than the windswept coast farther north. Traveling an additional 2 miles brings you to **Naha** and the end of your jeep trail. Another abandoned fishing village, Naha had one of the island's few fishponds, and its walls can still be traced offshore. According to legend, after outwitting all the *akua* on the island, Kaululaau built a huge bonfire here to signal his victory to the people of Maui. Beyond Naha an ancient paved trail built by the Hawaiians leads over the mountains to Palawai; for now, however, you will do better to backtrack on Keomuku Road.

The last compass direction accessible from Lana`i City by road is northwest. Your route follows what Lana`i maps euphemistically label Kanepuu Highway. In reality, it's a dirt extension of Fraser Avenue from town. Follow this road as it curves to the left, then take the first right. After passing through former pineapple fields for the first few miles, you reach the lowland forest of **Kanepuu.** Munro recognized the value of this pristine habitat of native plants and trees and planted a surrounding rectangle of eucalyptus trees and sisal plants as a windbreak. Today the Nature Conservancy continues to preserve this bastion of native vegetation, which includes rare Lana`i sandalwood and Hawaiian gardenia. Interpretive signposts line a short nature walk.

The edge of the forest brings an abrupt transition to a now-barren landscape, weakened first by overgrazing and then stripped entirely of vegetation by the punishing winds that sweep across the north coast. At about 7 miles in, you come to a series of bizarre rock formations covering a rugged landscape of peaks and canyons. Welcome to the **Garden of the Gods.** The beauty of this bleak terrain lies in the burning mineral colors of its soil and eroded rock. The changing hues at sunset become dramatic. Not far from here is where legend says the treacherous kahuna Kawelo engineered the death-by-constipation of Moloka`i's sage, Lanikaula, by burning his rival's stool in a magic fire.

Beyond the Garden of the Gods, the road deteriorates as it drops steeply to the coast. WARNING: Do NOT continue if it has been raining here or looks likely to start. If you do go all the way, you will reach beautiful **Polihua** ("bosom of eggs") **Beach,** a former haven for green sea turtles coming to deposit their eggs. Lana`i chants tell of Pele's love for turtle meat. Perhaps the goddess has been especially hungry, as the species is now endangered; nest sites should not be disturbed. Offshore currents make swimming risky, but it is a quiet spot to look for whales passing through Kalohi Channel and to watch the clouds blow across Moloka`i.

trivia

The temperature of the sand in which turtle eggs incubate determines the sex of the hatchlings.

Kaena Point to the west served as a penal colony for women between 1837 and 1850; thieves and adulteresses were forced ashore here to fend for themselves. In fact, the concept of adultery did not exist in old Hawaii. Missionaries had to make do with translating the seventh commandment as "Thou shalt not sleep mischievously." Apparently, the exile system was no more successful than the commandment. Male convicts from Kaho`olawe swam ashore to Maui and stole canoes, which they promptly used to liberate the women on Lana`i.

Farther around the point, at Kaena Iki, lies Lana`i's largest heiau. This ancient temple is difficult to find and hard to reach, but as you survey this lonely corner of the island, just knowing it exists adds a touch of mystery.

Places to Stay in Lana`i

LANA`I CITY

Dreams Come True
547 Twelfth Street
565–6961, (800) 566–6961
Three-room bed-and-breakfast for $112 per night.

Hotel Lana`i
828 Lanai Avenue
565–7211, (877) 665-2624
www.hotellanai.com
A quaint ten-room structure that's been accommodating guests since 1925. Rooms from $115.

Lodge at Koele
One Keomoku Highway
565–4000, (800) 450–3704
www.fourseasons.com
An upscale resort that cultivates the aura of an old English hunting lodge. Rooms from $350.

Manele Bay Hotel
One Manele Bay Road
565–7700, (800) 450–3704
www.fourseasons.com
This upscale resort has a Mediterranean feel and sits on bluffs overlooking Lana`i's best beach. Rooms from $400.

Places to Eat in Lana`i

LANA`I CITY

Blue Ginger Café and Bakery
409 Seventh Street
565–6363
Inexpensive local-style meals in Lana`i City.

Henry Clay's Rotisserie
828 Lanai Avenue
565–7211, (877) 665–2624
www.hotellanai.com/rest.html
Located in Hotel Lana`i, Henry Clay's serves American/Cajun cuisine nightly. Moderate.

Lodge at Koele
One Keomoku Highway
565–4000, (800) 450–3704
www.lodgeatkoele.com
Provides a variety of dining options. Moderate to investment-caliber.

Manele Bay Hotel
One Manele Bay Road
321–4666, (800) 450–3704
www.manelebayhotel.com
Provides a variety of dining options. Moderate to investment-caliber.

Pele's Other Garden
811 Houston Street
Lana`i City 96763
565–9628
Serves New York–style deli and Italian food.

Maui

Sailboarders come from around the world to frolic at the beaches of Maui's windy central isthmus. Humpback whales also make Maui their winter destination of choice. Although they visit all the Hawaiian Islands, the biggest groups gather in sight of Maui's coastline. The island has much to recommend to other visitors as well. Within an area not much bigger than O`ahu, Maui boasts a 10,000-foot volcano, a historic whaling town, a rain forest laced with countless waterfalls, and miles of beach colored with white, red, and black sands.

The island of Maui takes its name from a demigod, Maui of a Thousand Tricks, whose exploits form legends across Polynesia. Maui's magic fishhook pulled up the first islands from the Pacific floor, so that man could have a place to live. Maui pushed up the sky so that man could stand erect. Maui stole fire to warm man's hearth. It was on the island of Maui that the demigod performed his most celebrated feat: slowing the passage of the sun. Some say that the shape of the island resembles the trickster's body. The West Maui Mountains are the demigod's head, with Haleakala's girth a limbless torso to the east. A narrow isthmus forms the neck between these mighty mountains, fetching Maui its nickname of the Valley Isle.

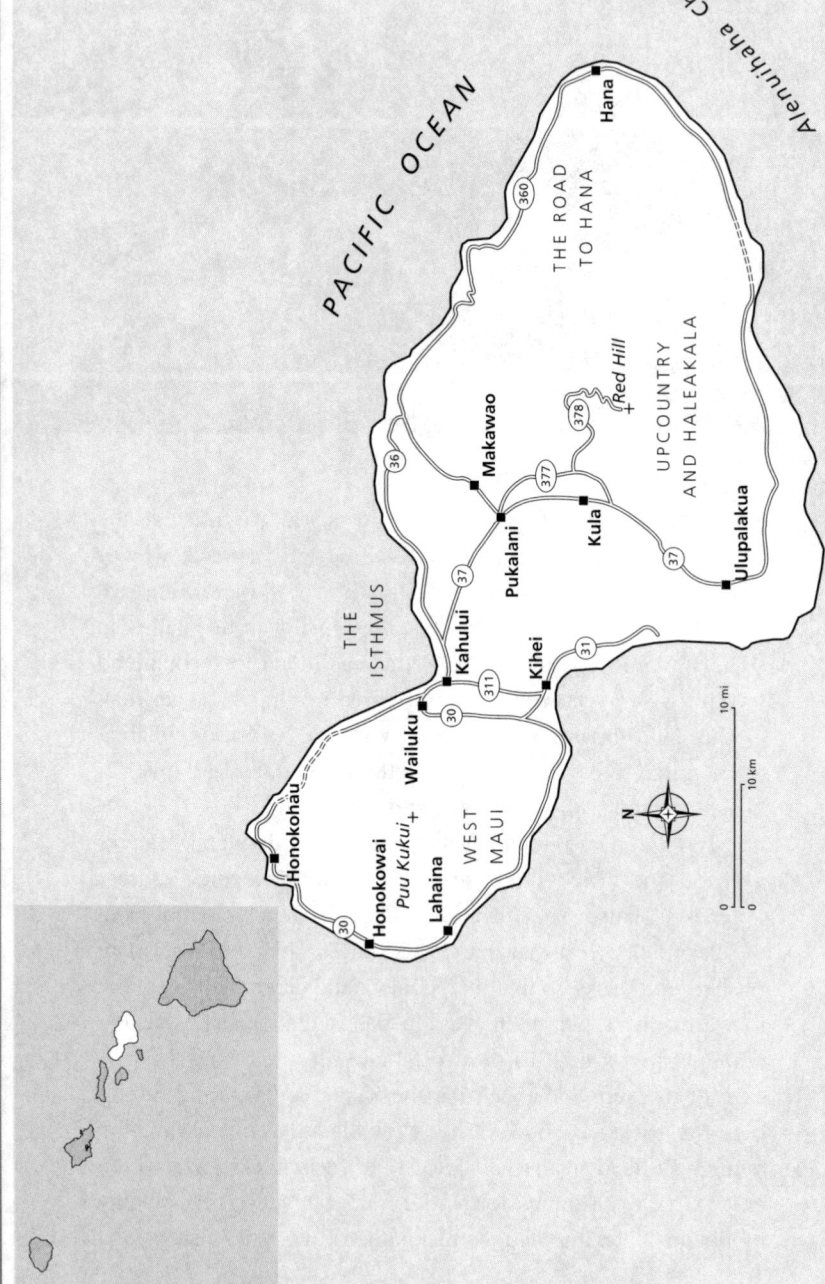

Those seeking a guided hiking experience on Maui have several choices. Ken Schmidt earned his naturalist spurs living off the land for three years in the Maui jungle. He has recruited a team of kindred spirits to serve as *Hike Maui* (879–5270; www.hike maui.com) guides. Prices start at $70 for a three-hour trip. They also do a unique kayak, snorkel, and waterfall hike in West Maui for $149; four-person minimum. Randy Warner leads his own *Maui Hiking Safaris* (573–0168; 888–445–3963; www .mauihikingsafaris.com) and has similar prices with a maximum group size of eight. *Maui Eco-Adventures* (877–661–7720; www.ecomaui.com) offers the biggest range (including kayak trips) and enjoys exclusive access to private land for some of its trips. It charges a little more.

mauifacts

Nickname: The Valley Isle
Dimensions: 48 x 26 miles
Highest elevation: Haleakala (10,023 feet)
Population: 134,007 (2002)
Largest city: Kahului
County Seat: Wailuku
Flower: Lokelani (a rose)
Color: Pink

The Isthmus and Points South

Maui's population centers on the northern edge of the central isthmus, the nape of Maui's neck. Modern Kahului has the main airport and harbor. In the foothills to the west, its older brother, Wailuku, retains prominence as the seat of Maui County and has the historical flavor Kahului lacks. As Ka`ahumanu Avenue (Route 32) heads west from Kahului, it slopes uphill to become Main Street in Wailuku. At the top of Main Street, begin your tour at the *Bailey House Museum* (244–3326). This restored mission station portrays both the lifestyle of the early missionaries and the Hawaiian culture that preceded them. The Wailuku mission began in 1837 under the Reverend Jonathan Green, who established a young women's seminary on the property. The main goal was to instruct them in "employments suited to their sex," primarily to produce suitable companions for the graduates of the boys' school across the mountains in Lahaina.

Reverend and Mrs. Green were joined and eventually replaced by the Baileys, who converted the adobe building to coral stone in 1841. Young women in the seminary donated their hair as the binding agent for the plaster. Edward Bailey was a multitalented man who later founded a sugar plantation when the seminary closed in 1849. An accomplished artist, he gifted posterity with oil paintings of nineteenth-century Maui, many of which are displayed in the museum gallery.

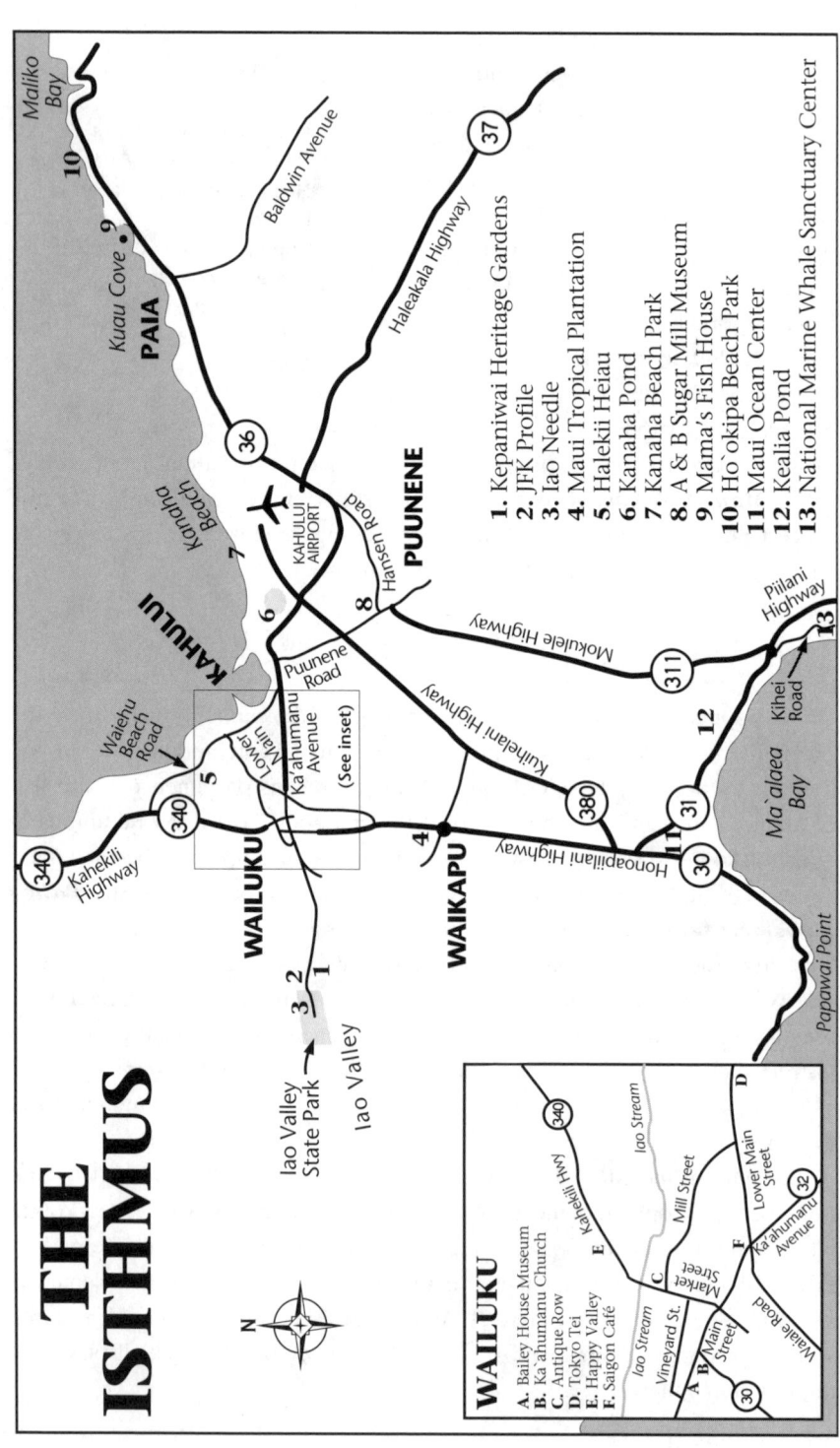

The upstairs rooms of the Bailey home feature missionary-period furnishings, including some beautifully patterned Hawaiian quilts in the bedroom. You'll also find hand-operated spinning wheels and looms, sewing having been one of the principal employments taught at the seminary. The rooms below are devoted to Hawaiiana. Jewelry junkies will marvel at the variety of materials Hawaiians used for necklaces. Instead of perishable flower leis, the well-dressed Hawaiian might wear a strand of shells, *kukui* nuts, feathers, teeth, or even human hair. The museum also offers rare examples of Hawaiian *kapa,* some of the most beautiful bark cloth produced in Polynesia. Another room displays the enormous *ipu,* or Hawaiian gourds, decorated to be used as containers, musical instruments, or lamps. Open Monday through Saturday 10:00 A.M. to 4:00 P.M.; modest admission charge. The garden in front displays plants found during the missionary era, with the back garden devoted to precontact botany. Ask about the self-guided ***walking tour*** if you wish to explore other historic buildings in Wailuku.

Brief History of Maui

As they lived on the second-largest island in Hawaii, Maui chieftains long rivaled those of the Big Island in the bid for preeminence. In the mid-eighteenth century, a Maui warrior by the name of Kahekili embarked on a bold mission of conquest, uniting O'ahu, Moloka'i, and Lana'i under his rule. Had his conquests continued, we might today know the archipelago as the Maui Islands instead of Hawaii. Instead, Kahekili was eclipsed by a younger warrior from the Big Island named Kamehameha, who eventually succeeded in unifying the entire island chain under his rule.

Maui's most enduring legacy in the newly unified kingdom of Hawaii was wrought by two women. Keopuolani, a Maui princess of the highest rank, became Kamehameha's "sacred" wife. Her royal lineage (superior to his own) ensured that his heirs would have the *mana* to rule and became the foundation for the Kamehameha dynasty.

But Kamehameha's favorite wife, Ka'ahumanu, played an even greater role in Hawaiian history. Also Maui born, Ka'ahumanu had a stormy relationship with Kamehameha during their marriage. After his death, Ka'ahumanu served as regent, sharing power with Liholiho, Kamehameha's heir. To consolidate her position, Ka'ahumanu maneuvered Liholiho into overthrowing the *kapu* ("taboo") system that repressed women; she later encouraged the advent of Christian missionaries. Ka'ahumanu also succeeded where even Kamehameha I had failed in "conquering" the northernmost island, Kaua'i. She accomplished this by the novel stratagem of abducting and then simultaneously marrying both Kaua'i's former king, Kamuali'i, and his eldest son.

Geography of Maui

Maui is the second largest of the Hawaiian Islands. Built from the overlapping flows of two volcanoes that meet along a narrow isthmus, this natural wind tunnel makes the "Valley Isle" a mecca for windsurfers. Of the two landmasses, the western Maui mountains are older and more heavily eroded. Their summit at Puu Kukui reaches 5,788 feet. Haleakala, the volcano that forms eastern Maui, rises gently to a 10,023-foot summit and harbors an enormous erosive crater within.

Walk a block downhill to High Street, where **Ka`ahumanu Church** sits in Honolii Park. Its weighty steeple points heavenward in classic New England style, while the white walls and green roof invert the colors of the cloud-draped West Maui Mountains behind. Named for Queen Ka`ahumanu, an early convert to Christianity, the present structure dates from 1876, but its predecessors go back to the earliest missionaries. Wailuku's government buildings huddle under shady trees nearby. The State Building at 54 South High Street issues state camping permits, dispenses free hiking guides, and books cabins; call well in advance for the latter (984–8109). Open Monday through Friday 8:00 A.M. to 3:30 P.M. Camping in the county's Kanaha Beach Park is not recommended.

So much for religion and power. Now for shopping. Stroll north on Market Street, 2 blocks below High Street, to explore the stores and galleries along **Antique Row.** You never know what treasures you might discover as you sift through Asian and Pacific artifacts, genuine antiques, and various arts and crafts. For classic aloha wear, check out **Sig Zane** at 53 Market Street (249–8997). Open Monday through Friday 10:00 A.M. to 5:00 P.M. and Saturday 10:00 A.M. to 3:00 P.M.

Locals all over Maui rave about the Vietnamese cuisine at the **Saigon Cafe** (243–9560), at 1792 Main Street. (The steaks on the menu are holdovers from the venue's former incarnation as Naokee Steak House.) The sign for the cafe is not visible from Main Street itself. You'll find it near the bridge where Ka`ahumanu Avenue crosses over Lower Main, at the corner of Kaniela and Main Streets. Open Monday through Saturday 10:00 A.M. to 9:30 P.M. and Sunday 10:00 A.M. to 8:30 P.M.

Saeng's (244–1567), at 2119 Vineyard Street, serves tasty food, with a pleasant garden lanai in back. Open weekdays 11:00 A.M. to 2:30 P.M. and weekends 5:00 to 9:30 P.M. Inexpensive.

For boxed lunch to go, try **Bentos & Banquet** (244–1124), around the corner on Church Street, for local ethnic fare (open weekdays 10:00 A.M. to 2:00 P.M.) or **Maui Bake Shop & Deli** (242–0064), nearby on Vineyard, for haole food (open Tuesday through Friday 6:30 A.M. to 2:30 P.M. and Saturday 7:00 A.M. to 1:00 P.M.). Both also have in-store seating.

Heading north (downhill) on Market across the Iao Stream bridge leads you into Happy Valley for more dining options. You won't find the "action" this former red-light district once attracted, though all eleven of Maui's hostess bars hover nearby. Just before the bridge, Mill Street leads east off Market Street into Wailuku's industrial sector along Lower Main Street. **Tokyo Tei** (242–9630), 1063 Lower Main Street, ensconced in an ugly two-story office complex, has served tasty Japanese fare since 1935. Open Monday through Saturday 11:00 A.M. to 1:30 P.M. and 5:00 to 8:30 P.M. and Sunday 5:00 to 8:00 P.M. Another longtime local diner is **Sam Sato's** (244–7124), at 1750 Wili Pa Loop, famous for its *manju* (rice flour pastry filled with sweetened adzuki beans) and tropical fruit turnovers. To find it, turn left off Lower Main, opposite the school. Open Monday through Saturday 7:00 A.M. to 2:00 P.M. (with take-out service until 4:00 P.M.).

mauitrivia

Haleakala is the world's largest dormant volcano.

Built in 1801 the Brick Palace in Lahaina is Hawaii's first Western-style building.

Piilani Heiau, Hawaii's largest temple, was built in A.D. 1400 near Hana.

Mosquitoes first arrived in the islands in 1872, as stowaways aboard the *Wellington*, a merchant ship.

For late-night dining, you have to go to Kahului. Visit **Kobo's** (877–5588) in Kahului's Ka`ahumanu Shopping Center for local diner fare. Open daily 7:00 A.M. to 10:00 P.M. Worth a visit any time of day, **Mañana Garage** (873–0220), at Ka`ahumanu and Lono Avenue, across the road from the Chevron station, serves hip Latin fare prepared with an island flair in a sleek, industrial setting. Open Monday through Saturday 11:00 A.M. to 10:00 P.M., Sunday 5:00 to 10:00 P.M. Live music on Friday nights, with a late menu of light foods served until 10:30 P.M. on Saturday and Sunday nights.

Wailuku sleeps as cheaply as it eats, with a number of flophouses catering to transients and workers. The influx of sailboarders to Maui's North Shore has led some to upgrade. The best of the bunch is the **Banana Bungalow** (244–5090; 800–846–7835; www.mauihostel.com), at 310 North Market Street. It offers doubles for $60 and dorm beds for $25, as well as daily tours and activities, many of which are free to guests.

Wailuku does offer one luxury accommodation option in **The Old Wailuku Inn at Ulupono** (244–5897; 800–305–4899; www.mauiinn.com; 2199 Kaho`okele Street). Built in 1924 by a wealthy island banker as a wedding gift for his daughter-in-law, the inn has been lovingly restored to evoke the grandeur of that earlier era. Woven *lauhala* mats rest on hardwood floors, while full-size Hawaiian quilts drape the beds. A variety of Hawaiian heirlooms and antique furniture from Asia enhance the period look. The inn also pays tribute to Hawaii's poet laureate, Don Blanding, and contains several features inspired by his poems. Views from the breakfast room encompass Haleakala, while the front porch faces Iao Valley. The ten rooms range in price from $140 to $190 and include a full breakfast; two-night minimum.

To visit a far older shrine than Ka`ahumanu Church, continue down the hill on Lower Main and turn left onto Waiehu Beach Road. Cross Iao Stream and turn left at Kuhio Place, then left again up Hea Place to *Halekii Heiau*. Built atop a massive sand dune overlooking Kahului Bay, the temple was partially reconstructed in 1958, but the carved wooden images *(kii)* that presumably stood there to deter invaders no longer exist.

While in Wailuku, every Maui visitor must undertake the pilgrimage into *Iao Valley,* by far the largest, steepest, and deepest cleft in the West Maui Mountains. The head of the valley opens onto the ancient crater that formed this half of the island. Its rear wall rises 5,788 feet to *Pu`u Kukui,* West Maui's highest peak. Because of this western mountain screen, darkness comes early to the valley. Mornings can be memorable as the sunlight descends the ridgetops probing through the mist. Equally dramatic are late afternoons, when the clouds that crowd into the narrow valley opening reflect ethereal bolts of sunlight that backlight the stage.

To get there, take Main Street west past the Bailey House and bear left onto Iao Valley Road. Drive into the steep-walled canyon entrance and watch the scenery unfold. The valley gradually widens as its walls grow taller, serrated by narrow side canyons and hanging valleys. Waterfalls concealed in these dark crevasses often spray mist that the sun's probing rays transmute into rainbows.

Kepaniwai, a clearing halfway up the valley, literally means "damming of the waters." The name has its gruesome origins in a battle in which Kamehameha's Western cannons massacred Maui defenders in a carnage that left Iao Stream literally dammed by piles of corpses. Today, *Kepaniwai Heritage Gardens* on the bank of Iao Stream celebrate Hawaii's diverse ethnic heritage. As you roam the grounds, try to puzzle out the different motifs, from a Japanese sculpture of cane workers to a traditional Filipino bamboo house. Local kids of all ethnic groups come here to splash in the stream and fish for tadpoles in the ponds. Free. The *Hawaii Nature Center* (244–6500) next door showcases a different facet of Hawaii's diversity, with hands-on, interactive exhibits focused on Iao Valley's ecology. You'll meet such Hawaii originals as the world's only carnivorous caterpillar, and the *o`opu,* Hawaii's "sucker fish," with the unique ability to climb its way upstream. The center also offers rain-forest hikes and other interpretive activities. Open daily 10:00 A.M. to 4:00 P.M. Admission $6.00.

The road continues deeper into the valley through a winding gorge. Pause to squint at the **JFK Profile**, a natural rock formation noticed only after President Kennedy's death. Ahead is **Iao Valley State Park.** Various paved paths crisscross the valley floor, and hiking trails lead up the different tributary branches of Iao Stream as well as up a central ridge to the tableland above the upper valley floor. Wherever you roam in the park, your eyes are drawn toward **Iao Needle,** a basalt spire jutting 1,320 feet above the valley floor. A narrow ridge actually connects the Needle to the valley wall, but its freestanding illusion is maintained until you walk behind it.

South of Wailuku, the Honoapiilani Highway (Route 30) continues out of High Street to reach the small pineapple plantation town of Waikapu, home of **Maui Tropical Plantation** (244–7643). This 112-acre "working farm" showcases Hawaii's agricultural history and diversity. It's worth visiting but would seem less of a tourist trap if the gift shop did not sit firmly athwart the entrance. If you skip the narrated ride, admission is free. Open daily 9:00 A.M. to 5:00 P.M.

Iao Needle

Don't let the sedate pineapple fields around Waikapu fool you; the rest of the isthmus "raises cane." Surrounded by tall, waving cane fields, the tiny town of Puunene sits southeast of Kahului at the intersection of Puunene Avenue (Route 350) and Hansen Road. Puunene centers around its sugar mill, a monster of hissing pipes and ducts and throbbing machinery, one of the few working mills left in Hawaii; visitors are barred for safety reasons. Instead, the curious can learn the sugar story—and even see a working scale model of a mill—by visiting the *Alexander & Baldwin Sugar Mill Museum* (871–8058) right across the street.

Housed in a 1902 plantation superintendent's residence, the museum brings to life the people and events that created Hawaii's once dominant industry. Begin by mastering Arithmetic Lesson Number 1: Constant Sunshine Plus a Ton of Water Equals a Pound of Sugar. Maui's isthmus gets plenty of sunshine, but the water comes from irrigation. In 1878 Samuel Alexander and Henry Baldwin, children of Lahaina missionaries, began the Hamakua Ditch, a 50-mile engineering miracle that tunneled and bridged its way across Haleakala's rainy windward gulches to tap millions of gallons of water. You can see remnants of it on the drive to Hana. In addition to its inherent difficulties, the project became a race against time. If they didn't finish in a year, the water rights and all their work would go to their rival, Claus Spreckels, who held financial strings on King Kalakaua. They made it—barely.

With the increase in irrigated lands under production, a labor shortage arose. Different immigrant groups were brought in to work the fields and were housed in separate camps with names like Ah Fong for the Chinese and Codfish for the Portuguese. Such segregation helped new arrivals adjust to the culture shock of relocation and also prevented a united labor front from forming. Photo murals illustrate the different pastimes these plantation workers indulged in: sumo wrestling for the Japanese, cockfights for the Filipinos, with baseball serving as the one "melting pot" sport. The museum is open Monday through Saturday (also open Sunday seasonally) 9:30 A.M. to 4:30 P.M.; $5.00 admission.

South of Waikapu, Route 30 leads to Ma`alaea Bay on the isthmus's southern shore. The *Maui Ocean Center* (270–7000) here presents a fascinating introduction to Hawaii's underwater environment. Grasp a squishy sea cucumber in the "touch pool." Test your knowledge of cetacean trivia by playing the Humpback Dating Game. Stroll through a glass tunnel that leads into a 750,000-gallon "open-ocean" tank, with sharks and other colorful fish swimming overhead. Naturalist talks/feedings are scheduled at different tanks throughout the day. Open daily 9:00 A.M. to 5:00 P.M.; $22 admission.

If your ocean center visit has inspired you to do some marine explorations of your own, stop by the nearby *Pacific Whale Foundation*'s (249–8811) marine resource center for free reef and whale-watching guides and helpful advice. Open daily 6:00 A.M. to 9:00 P.M. (They have another location in Lahaina, at 612 Front Street.) The foundation also operates a coral reef information station at Ulua Beach in Wailea (with a second station in Ka`anapali during summer), which offers free reef tours; call for schedule. They also run educational whale- and dolphin-watching boat trips, with all profits donated to conservation research. If you'd rather do your whale-watching from dry land, the foundation mans a free information station at McGregor Point (on the road to West Maui) during winter months.

Humpback Heaven

Like many species, humpbacks head south for the winter as Arctic ice packs encroach on their summer feeding grounds off Alaska. Fashionable humpbacks gather in Hawaii; roughly 3,000 whales, more than two-thirds of the North Pacific population, winter in island waters. The whales begin arriving in November, reaching peak numbers by February, and stick around until about May. They do not eat while in Hawaiian waters, as their preferred food, krill (a tiny shrimp), is not found in tropical oceans. Instead, the humpbacks live off stores of blubber accumulated during the summer and devote their time to other pursuits.

Topping their list of vacation activities is reproduction. Whales breed and then give birth a year later in the warm, sheltered waters offshore from all the major Hawaiian islands, with the largest numbers gathering around Maui. Female humpbacks calve every two to three years, with a ten- to twelve-month gestation period. Their newborns measure 12 to 14 feet and weigh two tons. Drinking fifty to one hundred gallons of milk, the newborns will grow as much as one hundred pounds per day, reaching up to forty tons and 50 feet long by maturity.

Humpbacks communicate through unusually complex whale songs, haunting rhythmic melodies that extend from the subsonic range to high-pitched whistles and can travel hundreds of miles of open ocean. Only male humpback whales sing complete songs; the tunes they use vary by region in the Pacific and evolve over time.

Humpbacks are also known for their playful acrobatics, often leaping from the water or splashing with their flukes and fins. The purpose of this behavior is not well understood, but it makes for fascinating whale watching. Any number of whale-watching tours operate during the season from Lahaina or Malaia harbors.

To learn more about humpbacks on dry land, visit the National Marine Sanctuary in Kihei or the Pacific Whale Foundation's Ma`alaea, Lahaina, or McGregor Point locations.

Further information on whales and marine life generally can be found at the *National Marine Sanctuary* (879–2818; 800–831–4888) headquarters, just around the bay at 1726 South Kihei Road. Scientists monitor Hawaii's whale population from here. Visitors can use free telescopes to do a little monitoring of their own as well as peruse exhibits on marine ecology and its importance to native Hawaiian culture. Open Monday through Friday 9:00 A.M. to 3:00 P.M.

If looking at so many fish has made you hungry to eat some, wander over from the ocean center to nearby *Blue Marlin* (244–8844), a good seafood choice. Bedecked in fishing memorabilia (including the inevitable mounted marlin), the restaurant has harbor views and a pleasant open-air ambience. Open daily 11:00 A.M. to 9:00 P.M. Expensive.

Moving from fishes to birds, you pass *Kealia Pond* (875–1582), a wetland bird sanctuary, heading southeast around the bay toward Kihei. Ornithology enthusiasts can stop at the visitor office located on the inland side of the pond at mile marker six along the Mokulele Highway (Route 311) for a free brochure. Open Monday through Friday 7:30 A.M. to 4:00 P.M.

The rest of Kihei is cluttered with condos and holds little of interest to the off-the-beaten-path traveler. Instead, take advantage of the Piilani Highway to bypass them and fast-forward to the less-traveled territory that begins farther south at Makena. Turn left (south) from Wailea Alanui Drive and then right (seaward) at the second juncture with Old Makena Road to swing past historic *Keawalai Congregational Church* (879–5557). Sunday services, at 7:30 and 10:00 A.M., are conducted half in English, half in Hawaiian. Churchgoers might also appreciate open-air services farther north in Kihei, held (weather permitting) in the ruins of a church built by David Malo, Hawaii's first native ordained minister. Look for *Trinity-by-the-Sea Church* (879–0161) off South Kihei Road on Kulanihako`i Street, 1 block south of Kalepolepo Beach Park.

On the horizon you can see all the islands of Maui County floating in an inland sea. From left to right they are Kaho`olawe, Lana`i, and Moloka`i. During the Ice Age, a drop in the sea level welded these lands together into a single mass. Molokini Islet, in the middle of Alalakeiki Channel, formed during this period as a tuff cone on a once-larger Haleakala.

Continue about a mile past the Maui Prince Hotel to the parking lot for *Oneloa* ("long sands") *Beach.* The last undeveloped beach on the coast, Oneloa glories in a half mile of wide, white sand bordering azure waters. Rising from the northern edge of the beach, *Pu`u Olai,* a 360-foot cinder cone, resembles a pimple on the slope of Haleakala. Climb over its seaward edge to reach *Little Beach,* a popular (and illegal) nudist enclave. Dangerous conditions arise during high surf at both beaches.

As you move south from Oneloa, you enter the **Ahihi-Kinau Natural Area Reserve.** A glance up the slope of Haleakala reveals a dark scar on the volcano's green flank. This black, congealed mass of lava came from the unexpected 1790 **Paea Flow,** the last eruption on Maui. Scientists ascribe the flow to an isolated pocket of lava trapped underground after its source had dried up. Hawaiian legend interprets it as the wrath of Pele consuming Paea, a young man who had spurned her affections. The eruption formed the massive Cape Kinau south of Ahihi Bay and has left the entire coastline rocky and barren. If you're feeling adventurous, a little more than a half mile across the lava-covered cape you can follow the paint splotches on the trail that starts between telephone poles 17 and 18; it crosses the lava for about a mile to reach **Fishbowl,** a sandy snorkeling spot.

Another mile south across the flow brings you to **La Perouse Bay,** named for an early French explorer who claimed it for his country, sailed off, and was

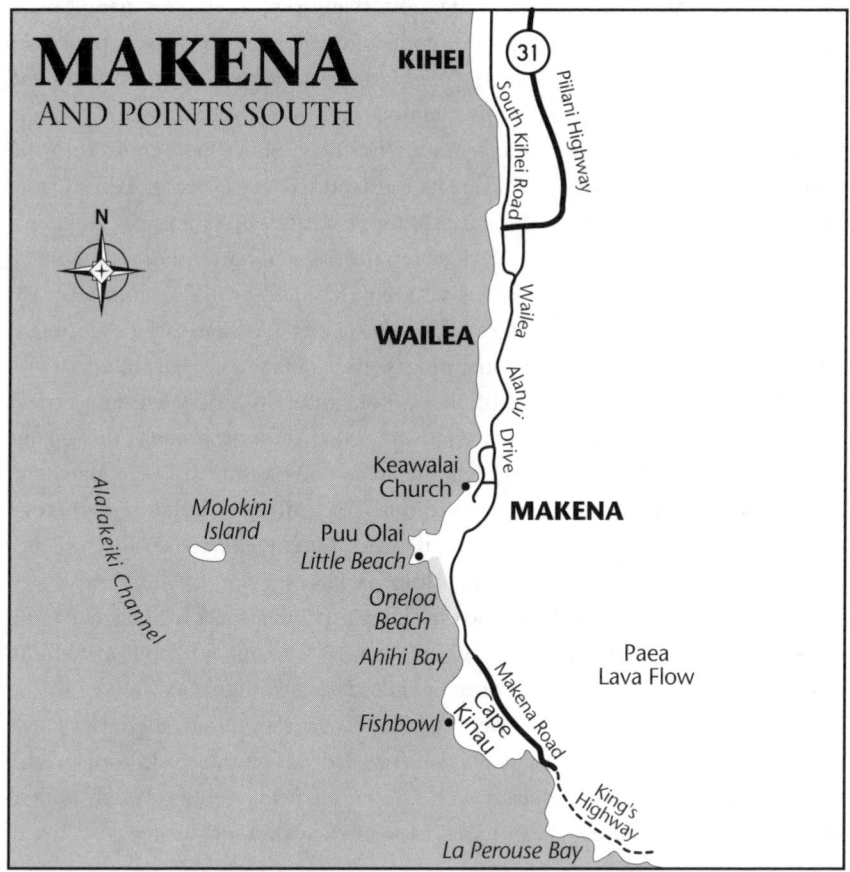

never heard from again. Drivable road ends here, but remnants of the ancient **King's Highway** continue closer to the shore. Oral histories testify that this stone-paved pathway, built in the fifteenth century by the great chief Piilani, once girded the island. Part of the conservation zone, the waters here are a snorkeler's paradise, although the center of the bay can be murky. Make your way to the rocky coves to the right (north). Dolphins often frequent La Perouse Bay in the morning. To the south, rock foundations and walls from Hawaiian houses are readily discernible, haunting the desolate lava with vestiges of a once-flourishing settlement.

For those wanting to explore more of this desolate coast, **Blue Water Rafting** (879–7238) weaves its way in and out of sea caves, with snorkeling stops and historical narratives. The daily four-hour Kanaio Coast trip costs $90.

Finally, to explore some more of the isthmus's north shore, head east from Kahului along the Hana Highway (Route 36). As you leave Kahului, you pass **Kanaha Pond Waterfowl Refuge,** once a freshwater fishpond sacred to royalty and now the nesting site for migratory waterfowl as well as native birds such as the Hawaiian heron, stilt, and coot. Birdwatchers can walk a perimeter trail accessed from the airport road. The highway continues through sugarcane and passes some of the world's most famous sailboarding beaches.

Trade winds sweeping across Maui's northern shoreline funnel into the central valley isthmus. As the sun heats the land, cooler air is sucked in from the ocean, and by afternoon the winds whip to a fury. Incoming swells generate constant surf, creating the perfect terrain for acrobatic jumps and rides. When the wind is blowing, beaches all along Maui's North Shore glisten with the butterfly wings of neon-colored sails. The latest fad here is kite surfing, a new variant that is basically windsurfing with a detachable sail tethered to a pair of ropes. **Kanaha Beach,** by the airport, offers the best learning conditions for windsurfing. Most of the windsurf shops offering rentals and lessons cluster nearby on Dairy Road (straight ahead as you exit the airport). Many can also arrange beachfront accommodations. Try **Maui Vacation Advisors** (808–871–7766; 800–736–6284; www.mauivacationadvisors.com) for "off-the-beaten-path" accommodations and custom packages.

Five miles east, Paia once had the largest population on Maui clustered around its now-closed sugar mill. When the new "dream city" built in Kahului lured workers around the bay, Paia dwindled to a virtual ghost town. In the sixties, the town acquired a hippie tinge that it has not entirely shed, but Paia's revival dates from the advent of windsurfing. Hordes of mostly European sailboard fanatics have descended upon the town environs, renting beach bungalows and filling the streets with rental cars laden with windsurfing gear.

Paia's ramshackle plantation buildings spread along the T formed by the Hana Highway and Baldwin Avenue. They house an incongruous mix of surf shops, old-style markets, and clothing boutiques ranging from aloha wear kitsch to hemp chic. Near the western entrance to town, the *Maui Crafts Guild* (579–9697) offers a sampling of Maui artistry in media from *raku* pottery to handpainted silks. A cooperative society of artists stocks and staffs the green two-story home, allowing you to meet creator and creations under the same roof. Open daily 10:00 A.M. to 6:00 P.M. You'll find a different kind of artistry at *Natural Impressions* (579–9066), at 40 Baldwin Avenue, which showcases the ancient Japanese art of *gyotaku* (fish printing). Owner Kalani Lickle promotes the art as an alternative to taxidermy in commemorating the trophy catches of sport fishermen. Instead of being mounted on a wall, the fish can leave behind a colorful imprint before making their way to a supper plate. Some of the fish Lickle prints end up at his fish taco stand outside the store. Open daily 10:00 A.M. to 4:00 P.M. For art-as-exercise, you could try *Maui Yoga Shala*'s (579–9767) hula and Tahitian dance workouts, part of a global menu of classes at 618 Hana Highway; call for schedule.

Paia boasts a number of funky restaurants. The sailboarder crowds gather at *Jacques* (579–8844), at 120 Hana Highway, a boisterous French bistro. The menu features classic bistro standards such as duck confit gone tropical with island fruit glazes, as well as nightly fresh-catch specials. Moderate. Open daily 5:00 to 10:00 P.M., with late-night service till 2:00 A.M. on weekends and live music on Monday and Thursday nights. If you're feeling more Mexican than French, *Milagros* (579–8755), at the foot of Baldwin, takes seafood south of the border from ono enchiladas to ahi/spinach chimichangas. Open daily 8:00 A.M. to 10:00 P.M. Expensive. Another good bet is *Moana Bakery & Cafe* (579–9999), a few doors over at 71 Baldwin Avenue, which offers an eclectic menu centered on fresh island produce and seafood as well as classic French pastries. Dinners run in the expensive range. Open Monday 8:00 A.M. to 2:30 P.M. and Tuesday through Sunday 8:00 A.M. to 8:00 P.M. Even more eclectic is the crepe and curry combo across the street at *Cafe des Amis* (579–6323). *Charly's* (579–9453), next to Jacques, is famous for its breakfasts. Be sure to read the story printed on the menu. Open daily 7:00 A.M. to 10:00 P.M. Daytrippers bound for Upcountry or Hana can get gourmet box lunches from *Café Mambo* (579–8021).

A mile and a half east of town, in a romantic beach shack just off the highway in Kuau Cove, *Mama's Fish House* (579–8488) serves seafood as fresh as its oceanside views. Mama buys only from local fishers; the menu tells who caught each fish where and how. It's up to you whether the end product comes grilled, seared, sautéed, or baked. Open daily 11:00 A.M. to 2:00 P.M. and 4:30 to 9:00 P.M., with happy-hour *pupus* served in between. Investment-caliber prices. Reservations recommended.

Mama's also rents well-equipped, albeit pricey, cottages, clustered on the same lot, from $175 to $475. Call 579–9764; (800) 860–4852.

As you head east of town, take a look at *Mantokuji Buddhist Temple.* The huge gong sounds daily at dawn and dusk. The windsurfing faithful worship 2 miles farther at *Ho`okipa* ("hospitality") *Beach Park.* Their mecca, a small rocky beach with less-than-hospitable currents and surf, offers experts unbeatable windsurfing terrain. When conditions are right, you can watch the world's top talents launch themselves into aerial loops off the face of mountainous waves, then jibe to surf the next breaker in.

The Road to Hana

The road to Hana is perhaps the most famous off-the-beaten-path adventure in Hawaii. A constant stream of rental cars embarks on this 52-mile odyssey, negotiating fifty-six single-lane bridges and more than 600 curves. You should, too—but if at all possible, break up the trip by stopping overnight; it'll take the pressure off your drive. The road to Hana is like life: It's not the destination that counts but what you do along the way.

The Hana Highway (Route 360) traverses Maui's shoulders, the rainy northeast slopes of Haleakala. You pass isolated valleys, hidden (and not-so-hidden) waterfalls, and stunning seascapes. Along the way grow tropical plants of every description. Roll down your windows and smell the flowers—there's always something in bloom. Do, however, check the weather before leaving (877–5111). Heavy rains along this windward coast can cause landslides and close the highway entirely. Beyond Hana, the southern route to Ulupalakua Ranch (Route 31) is poorly maintained and sometimes impassable.

Stock up before you leave Paia because it's a long, empty road ahead. East of Hookipa Beach Park, Route 36 winds around *Maliko Gulch.* This was the last obstacle in building the Hamakua Ditch, an early irrigation channel bringing water to the isthmus sugar fields, and weary workers balked when they saw its steep walls. To rally his troops, Henry Baldwin—who had lost an arm in a mill accident only months before—grabbed a rope and lowered himself into the ravine using his one good hand. He repeated this feat every day until the gulch was spanned.

After leaving Maliko, the highway climbs inland past pineapple fields and smaller gulches before reaching Haiku, a semirural community once anchored by a pair of pineapple canneries. The canneries closed long ago and have

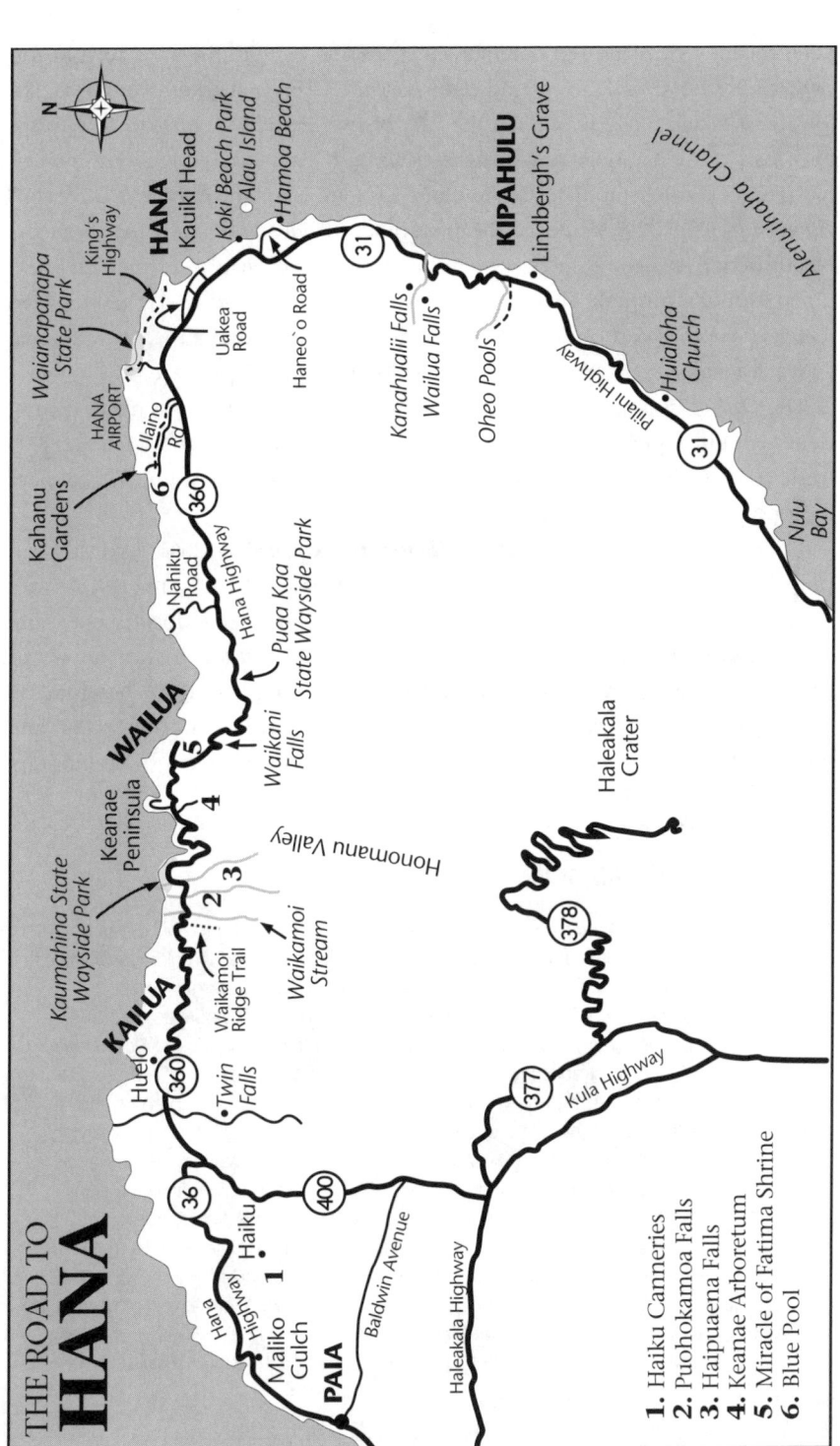

been recently converted to commercial space. To explore the area, turn inland onto Haiku Road; it's the second right past the 11-mile marker. Stay on Haiku for about a mile until you reach the first cannery building. Instead of pineapples, part of the cannery now processes *noni,* a traditional Polynesian medicinal plant used to stimulate the immune system. Stop by ***Hawaiian Herbal Blessing*** (575–7829), opposite the post office, where you can learn about the health benefits of noni, inspect its bulbous fruit, and taste its fermented juice. Open Monday through Thursday 8:00 A.M. to 4:00 P.M. and Friday 8:00 A.M. to 3:00 P.M. Another part of the erstwhile cannery is devoted to taro, the traditional Hawaiian staple crop. You'll find the taro burgers produced here on the menu at ***Veg Out*** (575–5320), a cafe across the street that also bakes a mean peanut butter cookie. Open daily 10:30 A.M. to 7:30 P.M. Non-veggies could grab a $3.00 fresh fish, chicken, or steak taco from the ***Island Taco*** stand in the cannery lot; open daily 11:00 A.M. to 4:00 P.M.

For a more substantial meal, try ***Hana Hou Cafe*** (575–2661), which occupies the former cannery cookhouse on the far side of the cannery lot, with open-air seating perched above a jungle gulch. The eclectic local menu samples island ethnic staples from traditional Hawaiian *lau lau* to Korean *kal bi* ribs, as well as daily fresh-catch specials. It's a popular local hangout on Mondays, with traditional Hawaiian music, serenading troubadours, and impromptu hula by customers when the spirit moves them. Contemporary

Cave Legends

Near Hana, a well-marked trail in Waianapanapa State Park leads to two caves formed from ancient lava tubes and now partially filled with water. An old Hawaiian legend tells of a beautiful princess, Popoalaea, who ran away from her cruel husband, Kakae, and hid with her handmaiden in the first of these caves on a dry inner ledge not visible from the opening. Kakae came after her, furious at Popoalaea's betrayal. Although her tracks led to the cave, Kakae could not at first tell where she had vanished and started to move away. Unfortunately, just then the torchlight he carried revealed the bright colors of the princess's feather *kahili* (a standard of royalty) mirrored on the clear water of the cave. Venting his anger with savage strokes of his dagger, Kakae slew the women there on the spot, their blood spilling into the pool. The tiny opaekaa shrimp that live in this pool annually recall this act of cruelty. In spawning every spring, they turn the water red, supposedly in deference to the slain princess. Adventurous travelers today can swim to the inner ledge where Popoalaea hid, equipped with a flashlight wrapped in a Ziploc bag. Those interested in more extended spelunking should contact Maui Cave Adventures (248–7308; www.mauicave.com), for self-guided tours through the much larger Ka'eleku Caverns nearby.

Hawaiian music performed on Saturday nights. Open daily 11:00 A.M. to 9:30 P.M. Moderate to expensive.

If you continue to follow Haiku Road (turning left at the cannery) as it wends its meandering bucolic path, you'll rejoin the Hana Highway a couple of miles farther east. Or turn left onto West Kuiaha Road a half mile along Haiku Road, and you'll arrive at Cannery Number 2, now used by surfboard manufacturers. Perhaps unsurprisingly, *Pauwela Cafe* (575–9242), also housed in the cannery building, is a popular surfer hangout. Many of the elite surfers who come here are drawn to Haiku by the chance to tackle "Jaws," Haiku's infamous winter surf spot that breaks on a distant offshore reef only during the biggest winter surf. The Hawaiian name for the break is *pe`ahi* ("beckon"), but only the bravest (or most foolhardy) surfers heed the call. Towering up to 50 feet high, the waves are so big that to catch them surfers have to be towed by Jet Skis to reach launch speed. Grab a table at the cafe when the surf is up and listen to the war stories of the "men who ride mountains." Even without the surfers, the wholesome cafe fare could justify a visit. Open Monday through Saturday 7:00 A.M. to 2:30 P.M. and Sunday 7:00 A.M. to 1:00 P.M. Inexpensive.

Hawaiian Fish Prints (575–2734) next door is both a gyotaku gallery and a studio. Carrie Brady is a painter who married a fisherman, so fish printing was perhaps inevitable. If you're lucky, you can watch her work. Open Monday through Thursday 9:00 A.M. to 3:00 P.M. or by appointment.

Get the jump on the drive to Hana by lodging at one of these Haiku hostelries: *Haikuleana B&B* (575–7500; www.haikuleana.com) offers three suites in an elegantly restored 1870 plantation home; all have private baths and rent for $130 to $160, full breakfast included. Ann DeWeese's *Tea House Cottage B&B* (572–5610; www.mauiteahouse.com; P.O. Box 335, Haiku 96708) awaits a few miles down the highway. Set in a tropical jungle setting with ocean views, this rustic cottage relies on solar power for electricity. It is comfortably furnished with most modern conveniences, except that the bathroom is separate. It rents for $125 per night, with a two-night minimum.

The Hana Highway officially begins after the 16-mile marker at the intersection with Route 400. Route 36 changes to Route 360, for whatever reason, and the mileage markers begin at zero. As if to justify this symbolism, the road immediately launches into wild turns through lush jungle. Continue to the first bridge (Ho`olawanui Stream) past mile marker two. A trail leads from a gate on the near side of the bridge a quarter mile inland to *Twin Falls,* the first of many to come. You can swing from a rope into the swimming hole below the falls. A larger falls waits a half mile upstream; bear left along the irrigation ditch. Daredevils leap from the top of this one as well. WARNING: As with all streams on the Hana Coast, beware of flash flooding. Heavy rain on the mountainside and swollen, mud-gorged water are warning signs.

A mile farther, roughly one-third of the way to Hana, **Huelo Point** boasts a couple of old churches and some very new, splashy vacation rentals in a tropical jungle setting. The most extravagant of these, **Pali Uli Estate** (573–0693; 800–861–9566; www.maui.net/~paliuli) offers all the opulence and privacy of a sultan's pleasure palace. Its perch on the edge of a 300-foot cliff affords a dramatic view of a waterfall toppling into an oceanfront gorge, with the Hana coastline and Haleakala Crater framed in the background, a view you can admire from the Jacuzzi decks. The sumptuous decor includes private, landscaped gardens, Balinese statuary, Javanese textiles, a marble kitchen, and a private pool for each rental. The one-and-a-half-bedroom Waterfall House consists of six glass-sided, skylit octagons, with a marble fireplace and a baby grand piano. It rents for $445 ($495 from December to February 15); two-person maximum occupancy. The one-bedroom Cliffhouse has its own marvels, such as the garden shower that pours from inside an urn held by a 10-foot Balinese stone maiden. It rents for $350/$395. Both rentals have a three-day minimum stay and require a security deposit.

On the other side of the point, the **Cliff's Edge** (572–4530; 866–262–6284; www.cliffsedge.com) offers simpler quarters but an equally stunning view of Waipio Bay. The three bed-and-breakfast rooms along with a saltwater pool and hot tub go for $145 to $195, with separate studio and two-bedroom cottage rentals for $325. Three-night minimum stay. WARNING: Whales splashing offshore at night might disturb your slumber. Other distinctive rentals are offered by **Huelo Point Flower Farm** (572–1850; www.mauiflowerfarm.com) and **Huelo Point Lookout** (573–0914; 800–871–8645; www.maui-vacation rentals.com).

Kailua Village, at 5.5 miles, is the headquarters of the East Maui Irrigation Company, Alexander & Baldwin's irrigation arm. All along the Hana Highway, you will see E.M.I. CO. signs, and portions of the original nineteenth-century stone aqueducts shadow the road, funneling water to the island's dry side. Rainbow and robusta eucalyptus trees planted for lumber at the turn of the last century predominate for the next few miles.

At 9.6 miles, a wide pullout space marks the start of the short **Waikamoi Ridge Trail,** a half-mile nature walk with scenic overlooks with picnic tables at beginning and end. Exotic plants along the trail, including mahogany, paperback, and tree ferns, are labeled. The trail also passes through a "musical" forest of bamboo; the slightest wind sets these hollow trees creaking and sighing cacophonously. A sign at the trailhead reads QUIET, TREES AT WORK.

Waikamoi Stream, at the next bridge, has a small pool for swimming, but most people stop here for the springwater that runs from a metal pipe in the rock wall just past the bridge. For splashier aquatic antics, continue to **Puohokamoa,** the next stream at mile marker eleven. There are three waterfalls here, involving hikes of graduated difficulty. A leisurely stroll on a paved pathway leads past picnic tables to the nearest falls and swimming hole below. *Laua`e,* a multilobed, spore-studded fern that was a symbol of romantic love in old Hawaii, grows here. For a bit more seclusion, cross the stream and hike up the steep (often slippery) left bank to a larger pool and falls upstream. The really adventurous hiker can rock-hop a half mile downstream (there is no trail) and peer over the edge of a 200-foot cascade that tumbles into a narrow gorge below. A tamer alternative is to walk back 100 yards on the highway to glimpse the lower falls peeking through the rain-forest canopy. A trail from behind the telephone pole at the bend descends to even better views.

The next stream after Puohokamoa, **Haipuaena,** has two less well-known falls with swimming pools to enjoy. A white cross painted on a rock marks the start of the trail upstream along the left bank past coconuts, ti leaves, and heliconia flowers. The first pool and falls are pleasant, but they are really only a false front for the true beauty upstream. Getting there requires a short but treacherous climb.

Past the 12-mile marker, **Kaumahina State Wayside Park** has restrooms and a picnic area that serves up coastal views stretching to Keanae Peninsula and beyond. African tulip trees flame with frilly orange blossoms. The heart-stopping scenery continues as the highway winds along a narrow ledge above the ocean to descend into **Honomanu Valley,** one of the few ancient valleys not flattened by subsequent flows from Haleakala. A side road just past the bridge follows the stream down to a gravel-sanded bay, with views up valley.

Just past mile marker fifteen, the YMCA's **Camp Keanae** (248–8355; www.mauiymca.org) perches on an isolated headland in a lush garden setting with spectacular coastal views. Run as a sanctioned American Youth Hostel, the camp offers both dorm berths and camping at $17 per person. Bring your own bedding. A pair of two-bedroom cottages can be rented for $125. Just around the bend on the inland side, **Keanae Arboretum** spreads across six acres of labeled botanical specimens, although it's not always well maintained. Amble up Piinaau Stream past ginger and banana to enter the arboretum grounds. There are three main sections. In the first, you encounter native trees, huge sheaths of bamboo, and all manner of palms. The second showcases taro and other Hawaiian crops. A tougher trail forges through the last section, a mile of rain forest. Free.

Beyond the arboretum, a turnoff on the left provides a bumpy but scenic detour onto **Keanae Peninsula.** Lava from Haleakala's last crater eruption funneled through the Ko`olau Gap, filling Keanae Valley to form this flat, crusted appendage. Horses roam the grassy pastures, and an old stone church poses impassively. As you circle the perimeter road, savoring the coastal views in either direction, please respect the privacy of residents who cling to the rustic lifestyle here. The road dead-ends short of a full loop in front of extensive taro fields. Oral histories tell of the transformation of this barren peninsula into rich farmland by a thousand loads of topsoil hand-carried from the hills.

The highway, meanwhile, climbs above the peninsula and offers a lookout point near the 17-mile marker. Keanae marks the halfway point to Hana; a series of roadside food vendors lies ahead.

At 18 miles, a left turn onto Wailua Village Road takes you into this isolated taro-farming community. **St. Gabriel's Catholic Church** and the **Miracle of Fatima Shrine** stand on the ocean side of the road. The church features an attractive altar draped in *kapa* cloth, but the story behind the shrine is what merits a visit here. In 1860, when the Catholic community set out to construct this tiny chapel (the original St. Gabriel's church), they lacked adequate building materials. Harvesting underwater coral blocks required enormous time and effort until, answering their prayers, an ocean storm miraculously washed abundant chunks of coral onto the shore. When the grateful Catholics had taken all they needed, a second storm washed the remainder back to sea—or so the story goes.

The highway climbs on above the village. The **Wailua Wayside Lookout,** a half mile up on the right, should not be missed. Steps tunneled through a thicket of *hau* lead to a panoramic view of the patchwork taro paddies below, and inland up the broad slopes Wailua Valley rises to Haleakala Crater. A half mile farther, the spectacular **Waikani Falls** plunges forcefully from cliffs above the highway.

Near 22 miles you pass the smaller **Kopiliula Falls,** and a half mile farther, you can pause for a breather at **Puaa Kaa** ("rolling pigs") **State Wayside Park.** Spread along the banks of a stream, the park has picnic tables in a pleasant setting overlooking a small waterfall.

The next 3 miles of highway break into stretches of open country in between overgrown streams and waterfalls. Roadside ginger grows along this section of the road; be sure to inhale the natural perfume. Rainfall in the hills above the highway here averages an inch a day. For a coastal detour, take Nahiku Road, near the 25-mile marker, which descends through 2 miles of lush greenery to the sea. Nahiku was the site of an early-1900s rubber plantation;

you'll pass rubber trees along the way. Coastal views at the shoreline extend back to Keanae. A trail to the left leads to a small, freshwater pool.

The road breaks clear again into pastureland at the 27-mile point, with ocean and crater views. Notice the cluster of giant travelers' palms by the upcoming ranch house on the left. These fantastic fan-shaped specimens can store up to a quart of water at the base of their leaves for thirsty travelers to access. ***Nahiku Ti Gallery & Coffee Shop*** (248–8800), just ahead, is the largest of the many roadside stands spaced along the Hana Coast. The smoked fish tacos sold here, eaten with steamed breadfruit, a starchy Hawaiian staple (add lots of salt), make for a tasty picnic lunch. The fish can be dry so ask for plenty of lemon juice or eat it with your favorite tropical fruit. Inexpensive. Other island products sold here include `awa tea and noni fruit, two traditional Polynesian medicinals. The gallery is open daily 10:00 A.M. to 5:00 P.M., although the food stand is closed on Thursday.

Around 30 miles, the road descends to the flat expanses of the Hana Coast. Past the 31-mile point, turn left and bump your way seaward on Ulaino Road. About 1.5 miles in, a sign points to ***Kahanu Gardens*** (248–8912). You drive in past dense groves of coconut, *hala, kukui, hau,* and breadfruit trees, all of which played key roles in the ethnobotany of ancient Hawaii. Even plant haters should come here, if only to gaze in awe at ***Piilanihale Heiau,*** the largest such temple in the state. Built by the Piilani chiefs in the fifteenth century, this massive stone complex rises 40 feet above the ground and spreads across more than an acre. Unfortunately, the gardens are open only by appointment; self-guided tours are available Monday through Friday between 10:00 A.M. and 2:00 P.M. Admission is $5.00, guided tours $10.00.

If Kahanu's schedule does not match yours, you might stop at ***Hana Maui Botanical Gardens B&B Vacation Rentals*** (248–7725, www.ecoclub.com/hanamaui), 1 mile back up Ulaino Road. This twenty-seven-acre fruit and flower farm owned by a native Hawaiian family offers its own self-guided "botanical walk" for $3.00. It's fairly primitive, but owner JoLoyce Kaia is a pleasant lady to chat with. (Ask her how she got her first name.) Open daily 9:00 A.M. to 5:00 P.M. The ranch also rents simply furnished studios for $100 for two or more nights.

If it has not rained recently, and the road is passable, you can follow Ulaino Road as it curves around left past Kahauu Gardens, ending up near the ocean; continue walking across the stream straight ahead to reach the waterfall-fed ***Blue Pool,*** a tropical vision, at the ocean's edge.

Back on the highway, the next crossroad leads to Hana's tiny airport, currently served only by Pacific Wings (873–0877; 888–575–4546) and Dollar Rent a Car (248–8237; 800–800–4000). Continue past the 32-mile point before turning seaward to ***Waianapanapa*** ("glistening water") ***State Park*** (984–8109).

Notice the many breadfruit trees on the way in. The bowling ball–size fruit provided a starchy Hawaiian staple, and the sticky tree sap was used to trap birds. Pass the housekeeping cabins at the park office (book at least six months in advance for these) and drive on to the second parking lot to explore the park's caves and beach.

A lovely nature trail loops around the lava-tube caves. Begin on the left fork and descend to the first water-filled cavern, where according to legend, a Hawaiian princess hid from a jealous husband. With a flashlight in a plastic bag, you can swim a short distance to the ledge of a dry inner chamber where she hid. The trail continues past other caves, then returns through a tunnel-like thicket of hau trees.

Another short trail descends to the black "sand" beach, actually composed of fine lava gravel. A rugged sea arch juts from the mouth of the bay, and seabirds nest in the rock islands offshore. Swimming becomes dangerous during periods of high surf. Coastal footpaths follow remnants of the ancient

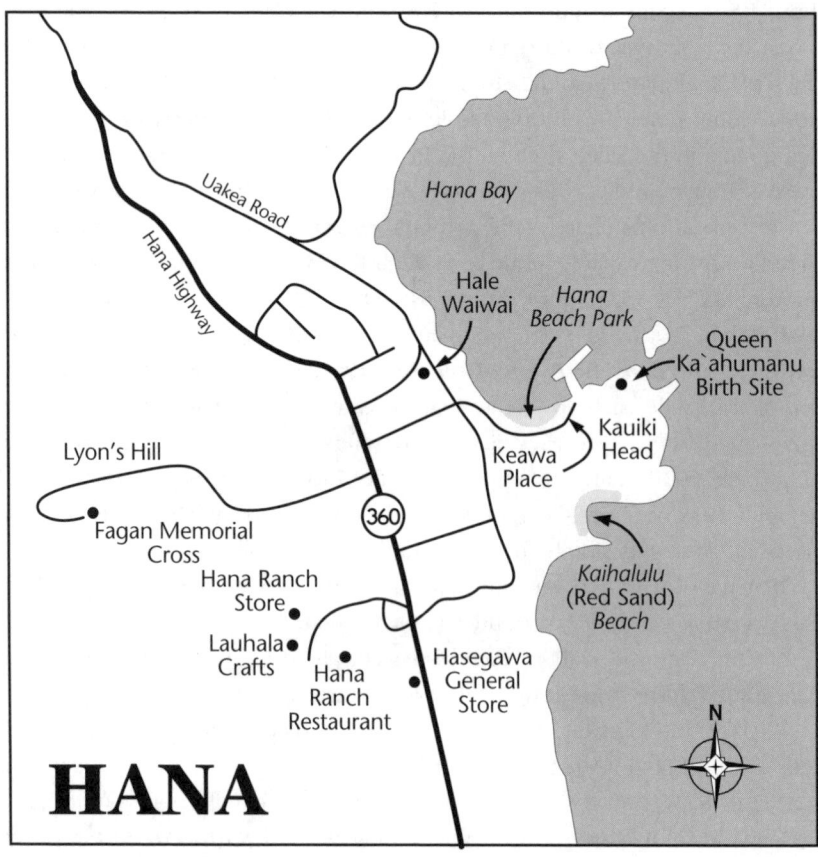

King's Highway for miles in either direction past burial mounds and heiau. The stark vegetation, composed predominantly of beach naupaka and hala trees, evokes images of a much older Hawaii.

Just ahead, a fork in the road marks the entrance to Hana proper. Forty-eight percent of the almost 2,000 inhabitants here claim native ancestry. To explore this cultural heritage, veer left from the highway onto Uakea Road and continue a half mile to the ***Hana Cultural Center*** (248–8622). Begin at the museum building, Hale Waiwai. The treasures here resemble family heirlooms, which many of them are. Coila Eade started the museum as a retirement project, and it blossomed with community support. She carved the beautiful koa doors at the entrance as well as the busts inside of prominent Hana residents. Hawaiian artifacts on display include a century-old *olona* fishnet, coconut-frond brooms, and all manner of specialized stones used by a Stone Age people. The center also includes a restored 1871 courthouse, which still sees occasional use, and a replica of a traditional Hawaiian village, complete with ethnobotanical gardens and authentic thatched *hale*. Museum open daily 10:00 A.M. to 4:00 P.M. Donation.

Past the museum, turn left onto Keawa Place to unwind at peaceful ***Hana Beach Park,*** a pleasant, dark-sand swimming beach on the right side of Hana Bay. Rising above the beach, tree-covered ***Kauiki Head*** blushes with oxidized iron. Kauiki dominates its surroundings, as it does Hana history. The extinct cinder cone served as a natural fortress guarding Hana during invasions to and from the Big Island. In 1773 two decades of clashes between Maui's Kahekili and Big Island invaders led by Kalaniopuu culminated in a dramatic siege in which the Maui forces surrounded the hill and, by cutting off his water supply, forced Kalaniopuu to withdraw. Polished sling stones thrown in the battle litter Kauiki's slopes.

From the wharf at the mouth of the bay, you can follow the narrow trail around Kauiki's red flank. A five-minute walk brings you to the tip of the headland, where a small copper plaque marks the cave in which Queen Ka`ahumanu was born to exiled *alii* and hid during Kalaniopuu's first invasion. She was almost lost as an infant when, unbeknownst to her parents, she fell off a canoe. While Hana remained under Big Island rule, Ka`ahumanu met and married the up-and-coming Kamehameha, and her fortune began to shift. She became his favorite wife, but although he placed a kapu ("taboo") on her body, she tormented him by sleeping with other men. Visiting British Captain Vancouver helped reconcile the couple, and upon Kamehameha's death she became queen regent. To reinforce her position, Ka`ahumanu led the way in breaking the old taboos restricting women and later became the most important convert of the missionaries.

Just inland of the bay, a traditional *hale akule* stands on a rise at the edge of Kauiki, built from ironwood beams joined by traditional rope lashings (no nails), with a thatched roof of *loulu* palm leaves. Old-timers frequent this fish spotting station, keeping an eye on the bay below to alert local fishermen when the akule is running, but always happy to talk with visitors in the meantime. You may have noticed other such hale on the highway leading into Hana, opposite the high school and elsewhere around town. They were built by local Hawaiians as an expression of their cultural heritage, under the guidance of Hana resident Francis Senensee, a world expert on native architecture.

Continue on Uakea Road until it ends at the beach cottages of Hotel Hana-Maui. From here, another trail winds around the opposite flank of Kauiki to **Kaihalulu** or **Red Sand Beach.** Erosive cinders along the path make the footing treacherous, and the hotel keeps the trailhead deliberately obscure to discourage its use. The reward for the fleet of foot is a gorgeous pocket of red cinder sand enveloped in a secluded cove. The crystalline waters are a vision of blue on red. A protective wall of jagged lava rock just offshore keeps swimming conditions safe. The near side of the beach is less rocky. Clothing optional.

Backtrack a block on Uakea Road and turn left onto Hauoli Street. At the corner of the Hana Highway is **Wananalua Church,** dating from 1842. Hana's first missionaries deliberately built this coral block temple over the site of a pagan heiau. A white cross atop nearby **Lyon's Hill** honors the memory of Paul Fagan, who introduced ranching to Hana after sugar died out. Fagan opened the **Hotel Hana-Maui** (248–8211; 800–321–4262; www.hotelhana-maui.com) in 1946 as a guesthouse for his millionaire friends.

Newly restored, the hotel today consists of sixty-nine guest rooms housed in single-story bungalows spread across sixty-seven acres of bayfront property, right in the center of town. The humble exterior of the plantation-style cottages in which guests are housed sets the tone for the understated elegance within. Cross-ventilating windows let you savor the island breeze and the sound of the surf. The main hotel building, also low-rise, has a similarly relaxed, open-air ambience. (Be sure to look at the "Hawaiian weather stone" at the lobby entrance.) Cows grazing in a paddock across the street show that the resort has not strayed too far from its ranching roots. Most employees are descendants of former ranch or plantation workers, and almost all are local. They welcome guests in an easygoing manner that is both warm and professional. Rooms here start at $425.

Non-millionaires who wish to stay overnight in Hana have several choices. The **Heavenly Hana Inn** (248–8442; www.heavenlyhanainn.com), 2 miles north of town, cultivates the atmosphere of a *ryokan,* the traditional country inn of Japan; its four suites rent from $200 to $300. For those who prefer lodging with a Balinese motif, *Hamoa Bay House & Bungalow* (248–7884; www.hamoabay.com) sits on four acres of tropical splendor complete with its own herb garden and a myriad of tropical fruit trees, all within walking distance of Hamoa Beach. Decorated with a mix of Balinese charm and old Hawaii nostalgia, a (decorative) mosquito net above the beds, the studio cottage also includes a Jacuzzi tub and outdoor shower and rents for $195; three-night minimum. The two-bedroom main house features an outdoor shower and indoor *furo* (steeping tub). It goes for $285, with a three-night minimum. Both have full kitchens. If you'd rather be above it all, *Ekena* (248–7047; www.ekena maui.com) offers more conventional comforts in a spacious, modern, hilltop pole home, with sweeping coastal views. It has two levels but rents to only a single party at a time, as anything from a one- to four-bedroom unit with full kitchen; price starts at $195, with a three-day minimum stay.

Back in town, *Hana Kai Maui Resort* (248–8426; 800–346–2772; www.hanakaimaui.com) offers far more modest studio and one-bedroom condos with functional, motel-style amenities (including a kitchen) in a pair of drab, two-story buildings. Why bother? Location, location, location. The bayfront perch is even better than the hotel's, and some units have fabulous ocean views. Studio rates range from $125 to $135, with one-bedroom units from $145 to $195. *Hana Accommodations* (248–7868; 800–228–4262; www.hana-maui.com) rents studios and two- and three-bedroom units in plantation-style bungalows with communal spa, in a pleasant garden setting within walking distance of Waioka Pond (see page 196) for $80 to $175.

Simpler quarters in town can be found at *Aloha Cottages* (248–8420; P.O. Box 205, Hana 96713) at 83 Keawa Place. Fusae Nakamura, the owner, offers her guests fresh fruit from her garden. Almost all of the cottages have full kitchens and rent for $65 to $100. Bargain-basement rooms await at *Joe's Place* (248–7033; P.O. Box 746, Hana 96713), around the block at 4870 Uakea Road. Rooms with communal bathrooms and kitchens go for $45. A private bath costs $10 more.

Kitchen facilities may come in handy because dinner options are limited to the hotel and *Hana Ranch Restaurant* (248–8255), uphill from Hana Highway on Mill Road. The restaurant offers moderately priced take-out breakfasts (6:30 to 10:00 A.M.) and lunches (11:30 A.M. to 4:00 P.M.). Take-out food is available until 7:00 P.M., and moderately priced sit-down dinners are served on Wednesday, Friday, and Saturday from 6:00 to 8:00 P.M. Hotel Hana-Maui's main dining room serves decent, if pricey, renditions of Pacific Rim cuisine using primarily local ingredients, with a buffet hula show on Friday night. Veranda tables overlook the bay, while the ceiling inside is draped with colorful fabric screens that form a silhouetted canoe floating atop the ocean waves. Open daily 7:30 to 10:30 A.M., 11:30 A.M. to 2:30 P.M., and 6:00 to 8:30 P.M. Investment-caliber prices at dinner. Reservations recommended. The adjacent **Paniolo Lounge** offers cocktails starting at 10:30 A.M. and pupus from 2:30 to 9:00 P.M., with live music Thursday through Sunday at 6:30 P.M. **Tutu's** (248–8224), a concession stand in the community center across the street, serves inexpensive plate lunch, sandwiches, and fresh Hana fish when available. Open daily 8:00 A.M. to 4:00 P.M. Otherwise, for do-it-yourself options, the **Hana Ranch Store** (248–8261) sells groceries and fresh seafood. Open daily 7:00 A.M. to 7:30 P.M. Hana's most famous retail establishment—celebrated in bumper stickers and in song—is nearby **Hasegawa General Store** (248–8231). Occupying the former Hana theater building, it stocks an amazing hodgepodge of goods crammed under one roof. Open Monday through Saturday 7:00 A.M. to 7:00 P.M. and Sunday 8:00 A.M. to 6:00 P.M. The **Hana Coast Gallery** (248–8636; 800–637–0188) at the hotel also has an excellent collection of higher-end pieces. Open daily 9:00 A.M. to 5:00 P.M.

One and a half miles south of town on what has now become Route 31, a county road, you reach another prominent cinder hill, **Ka Iwi o Pele** ("the bones of Pele"). According to the legend, "the bones" are an anatomical monument from the fire goddess's defeat by her older sister, the ocean. Turn onto Haneo`o Road to loop around the coast. The multicolored sands of **Koki Beach Park**, to the left of Ka Iwi, face Alau Island offshore. To the right of the beach park are some ancient fishponds. On the far side of the loop, Haneo`o Road passes **Hamoa Beach,** a pearly strand in a semicircular cove encased by tall cliffs and shaded by tropical almond (false Kamani) trees. Body surfing is excellent here; stick to the middle of the beach, as currents sweep outward to the sides. Hotel Hana-Maui guests get shuttled in, between 10:00 A.M. and 4:00 P.M., but the beach belongs to everyone to enjoy.

trivia

In Ulupalakua, Upcountry Maui, the Ranch Store has the distinction of maintaining the oldest Levi Strauss account in the world.

The highway continues through pastureland, and white-faced Herefords return your stares as you drive past. Just past the 48-mile marker, follow the trail on the near side of the bridge toward the ocean. A five-minute walk brings you to **Waioka Pond,** commonly called Venus Pool, an enormous pool of azure freshwater surrounded by black lava rock, with a waterfall at one end and the ocean at the other. The beauty of the spot is almost surreal. Another name for this gulch is Waihonu ("turtle water"); algae flourish in the brackish water offshore, and guess what feeds on them? The road narrows and begins to wind as the pavement deteriorates and lush jungle returns. About 7 miles from Hana, you will see **Helio's Cross** marking his grave on a hill just ahead. Helio Koa`eloa left this valley of his birth to learn the forbidden faith of Catholicism and returned to win converts by the thousands. He died in 1848.

Around the bend comes **Kanahualii Falls,** followed shortly by **Wailua Falls.** You can descend a half-mile trail opposite the former to the valley floor and take a dip in the secluded pools where the river meets the rocky shoreline. Around you lie the ruins of an abandoned village. The road winds on past the **Virgin by the Roadside** shrine, cut into the cliffside. Ocean vistas alternate with stream-fed jungle. Near the 10-mile point, you enter Haleakala National Park's **Kipahulu District** at Oheo Gulch. Tourist crowds come here to see the "seven sacred pools," formed as Pipiwai Stream spills down a watery staircase of hollowed-out lava basins. The pools actually number more than twenty and never were sacred. You have a choice of trekking a few hundred yards down to the lower pools or hiking a half mile uphill to **Makahiku Falls** and an optional 2 miles farther to **Waimoku Falls.** The descent to the lowest pools takes you near the ocean past some archaeological remains of Hawaiian house sites. You can see the Big Island offshore on a clear day. Sharks and currents make ocean swimming a bad idea. Instead, try a dip in one or all of the pools, working your way upstream where the crowds thin out. Currents are gentle, but heed warning signs of flash flooding. Look for the reddish conical flowers of the *awapuhi* (ginger) plants that grow here. The Hawaiians crushed these bulbous hand grenades to extract a natural shampoo. Lather up and rinse in a waterfall!

If you choose the hike, you get a great overlook of Makahiku Falls cascading 200 feet below. From here, an old irrigation ditch allows you to detour to more secluded pools above the falls. The main trail continues through pastures studded with guava trees and then meanders through darkened thickets of dense bamboo that creak and rattle in the wind. The trail gets muddy at stages, but the Park Service has placed boardwalk planks across the worst spots. The trail ends beneath 400-foot cliffs, from which the threadlike fingers of Waimoku Falls descend in shimmering rivulets.

Park rangers lead regular hikes and conduct other interpretive activities. The Park Service has also formed a partnership with Kipahulu `Ohana, a local Hawaiian group, to offer cultural demonstrations, exhibits, and other activities, from canoe carving to taro farming. Call 248–7375 to check the current schedule. See the box, pages 222–23, for additional information. Primitive camping facilities are also available. There is a $10 parking fee for visitors.

A mile past Oheo, aviation buffs and old-timers make the pilgrimage to **Lindbergh's Grave** at Ho`omau Church, on the ocean side of the road. Here "the Lone Eagle" chose to die, enveloped in the remote beauty of the land. His epitaph reads from Psalm 139: "If I take the wings of the morning and dwell in the uttermost parts of the sea."

As you continue onward, you enter Haleakala's rain shadows; *wili wili* trees give way to patchy scrub, opening up stunning coastal views. The next 6 miles of road reach an axle-grinding low and may constitute forbidden territory for rental cars. The worst patches have been paved, but the road is still occasionally washed out in stormy weather. The reward for those who persevere is a rugged coastline whose desolate beauty forms a striking contrast with the lush rain forest on the road to Hana. Call the Hana Public Works Office at 248–8254 to check road conditions before you chance it. As you wind your way along the coast, you'll see the 1857 **Huialoha Church** on a barren windswept point. To reach it, angle back on the side road, marked by mailboxes 192 and 193. It's a tranquil spot enveloped in the beauty of the sea and land around it. From here peer uphill into Kaupo Gap, through which ancient lava flows once poured from Haleakala Crater; today hikers follow the same route via an overnight trail.

The variably open **Kaupo Store** (248–8054), founded in 1925 by Chinese immigrants, waits just up the highway. It is now run by Linda and Manuel Domen. Many of the shelves display artifacts decades old, from Brownie cameras to antique radios, culled from surplus stock found in storage. Next door is the new **Koali Café** (248–8011), featuring smoothies, pizza, and sandwiches. Open daily 11:00 A.M. until dark. Three miles farther, the road edges back toward the shoreline at **Nuu Bay,** the best swimming beach on the coast. It's the first of the two bays here, reached by a short walk down from the highway. The road then begins to climb slowly inland through the barren landscape along Maui's hairless underbelly. Remains of ancient villages haunt the lava, and the endless miles of parched terrain overlook wide horizons of ocean. Above it all, the Haleakala Crater dominates the landscape, its steep slopes etched by erosive gullies. The road crosses a few steep ravines and dips a final time before climbing high above Popowai sea arch. Kaho`olawe appears on the horizon, and the slopes below are pockmarked by cinder cones and scarred by lava. Twenty-one miles after leaving the Kaupo Store, the cool eucalyptus forest surrounding Tedeschi Winery signals your arrival in Upcountry.

West Maui

The West Maui Mountains are older, lusher, and more scenically eroded than Haleakala. Good highway rings the entire landmass. Departing southwest from the isthmus, the Hanoapiilani Highway climbs high bluffs overlooking the

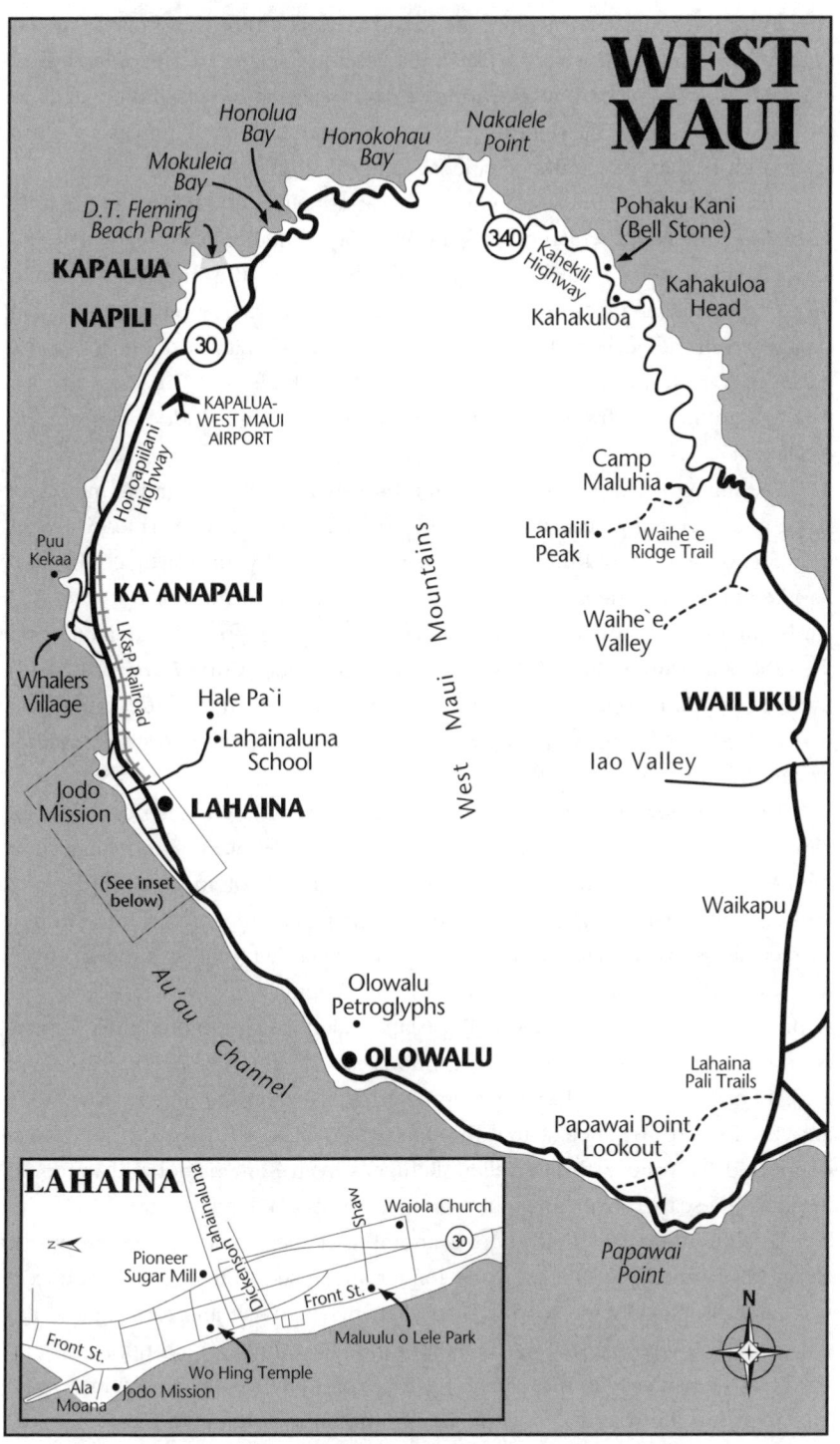

WEST MAUI

Honolua Bay
Mokuleia Bay
D.T. Fleming Beach Park
Honokohau Bay
Nakalele Point

KAPALUA

NAPILI

Pohaku Kani (Bell Stone)

340 Kahekili Highway

Kahakuloa Head

Kahakuloa

30

KAPALUA-WEST MAUI AIRPORT

Honoapiilani Highway

Camp Maluhia

Puu Kekaa

KA`ANAPALI

Lanalili Peak

Waihe`e Ridge Trail

Waihe`e Valley

West Maui Mountains

Whalers Village

LK&P Railroad

Hale Pa`i

Lahainaluna School

WAILUKU

Iao Valley

Jodo Mission

LAHAINA

(See inset below)

Olowalu Petroglyphs

Waikapu

Au'au Channel

OLOWALU

Lahaina Pali Trails

Papawai Point Lookout

Papawai Point

N

LAHAINA

z

Lahainaluna

Shaw

Waiola Church

30

Pioneer Sugar Mill

Dickenson

Front St.

Maluulu o Lele Park

Front St.

Wo Hing Temple

Ala Moana

Jodo Mission

ocean. As you round Maui's chin, the island of Lana`i joins Kaho`olawe on the horizon, rising from the ocean like a giant humpback whale. People stop at the marked lookout here at **Papawai Point** to watch for real humpbacks in the Au`au Channel. The sight of a forty-ton leviathan breaching offshore has caused more than one traffic accident along this highway.

You can admire these same views (and better) by hiking the 5-mile **Lahaina Pali Trail,** which crosses the West Maui Mountains to reach a 1,600-foot elevation before emerging south of Olowalu at the highway's 11-mile marker. Numbered posts along the way are keyed to a free hiking guide you can get from the state parks office in Wailuku, which narrates features of the area's history and ecology. The trail starts at the highway's 5-mile point. It's best to start the hike from this side and if possible arrange a ride back from the other end.

The highway continues to carve and burrow its way through the mountain slope and eventually descends through cane fields on the other side. A row of monkeypod trees and a drop in the speed limit signal your arrival at Olowalu. Snorkeling is good here at the 14-mile marker; head to the offshore reef 100 yards out. Olowalu town consists of two establishments—one is a general store, the other's a gourmet French restaurant. Many consider **Chez Paul** (661–3843) the best on the island. You will want to reserve a table well in advance. Open nightly 5:30 to 8:30 P.M. and weekends 11:00 A.M. to 2:30 P.M. Investment-caliber prices.

The **Olowalu** region is steeped in history. In 1790 an American captain, Simon Metcalf, opened fire on native canoes he lured into range, killing more than eighty Hawaiians to avenge the theft of his longboat and the murder of a Western sailor. The Hawaiians retaliated by seizing a companion ship captained by Metcalf's son and slaughtering most of the crew. Two English survivors from this bloodshed, Isaac Davis and John Young, became prisoners of Kamehameha, then an ambitious Big Island chieftain. Combining their expertise with the firepower of the cannons also acquired in the incident, Kamehameha won his bloody victory later that year in the alluvial Iao Valley above Olowalu. An ancient trail through a now-blocked mountain pass once connected Olowalu with Iao Valley. Refugees from Kamehameha's triumph at Kepaniwai escaped over this trail, bringing events full circle.

Hidden in the cane fields here is an impressive collection of **petroglyphs.** Because of vandalism, the site is no longer advertised to the general public. If you take the paved cane road that parallels the highway and turn right at the water tower a few hundred yards west of the Olowalu Store, an unpaved cane road leads a half mile to these markings. The petroglyphs are carved into a cliff face just after the road forks. Look for the former viewing platform.

Five miles northwest of Olowalu, a flotilla of yachts anchored offshore signals your arrival at the town of **Lahaina.** More than any other place in the islands, Lahaina embodies a feeling of old and new superimposed. The town has gone through many incarnations over the years: a center of royalty, then a raucous whaling port, then a sleepy sugar settlement. Although thriving today as a tourist center, Lahaina has retained its sense of romance and history. The Lahaina Restoration Foundation (661–3262) moved early to preserve many of the historic sites, and building codes keep new developments in line with the old. The foundation also provides volunteer docent tours at many of Lahaina's historic sites and publishes a free self-guiding map, available at the Baldwin Home and other sites. Also good is the *Lahaina Historical Guide,* which you can pick up for free at any of the commercial centers in town to read more about the town's many landmarks. Plan on spending some time; there's lots to see.

Front Street serves as the town's main drag, with a boardwalk strip running partway along the ocean. At the corner of Front and Dickenson stands the **Baldwin Home** (661–3262), Lahaina's oldest building, now run as a museum. In 1838 newlywed missionaries Edwin and Charlotte Baldwin moved into this home after a 161-day honeymoon trip around stormy Cape Horn. The museum displays some of their possessions, among them Charlotte's sewing kit and china brought from Connecticut. Mosquito nets over the four-poster beds reflect the arrival in 1872 of the winged parasites, carried unwittingly aboard the *Wellington,* a merchant ship docked at Lahaina.

The Reverend Edwin Baldwin ran a medical clinic in an adjacent room and serviced three islands in addition to his pastoral duties. His medical instruments fill the shelves of his study. Notice the hilarious English translation of his official posted rates. Licensed native doctors in 1865 could levy charges ranging from $50.00 for "very great sickness" to $3.00 for "incantation to find out disease" and could even assess a $10.00 fee for "refusal by patient to pay." The museum is open daily 10:00 A.M. to 4:30 P.M.; token admission.

Lahaina's first missionaries, the Richardses, used to live in a house next door. In 1827 these stubborn crusaders had to crouch in their cellar while cannonballs whistled overhead, fired by a sea captain furious at the edicts of Christian morality that the Richardses had persuaded local chiefs to impose. Whalers had begun arriving in large numbers about the same time as the missionaries, setting the stage for epic battles between the two groups. Rallying to the motto "No God West of the Horn," the lusty sailors rioted to win back their grog and women, but as whaling gradually died as an industry, the missionaries won by default.

Walk a block seaward to the waterfront, where you'll see the stone foundations from Kamehameha I's 1802 **Brick Palace,** the first Western building in the islands. Kamehameha never lived here because his wife, Ka`ahumanu, refused to move in. Kamehameha III later tended a wetland taro patch nearby to demonstrate "the dignity of labor." He also built the harbor lighthouse in 1840, reputedly the oldest of its kind in the Pacific. Walk to the seawall at the edge of the lot. The **Hauola Stone,** just below, is shaped like a reclining chair. You're supposed to sit here with legs dangling in the surf to activate the stone's curative powers.

Inland from the harbor entrance stands the historic **Pioneer Inn** (661–3636; 800–457–5457; www.pioneerinnmaui.com; 658 Wharf Street, Lahaina 96761). George Freeland, a Canadian Mountie, tracked a notorious criminal to Lahaina and stayed to open in 1901 what for many years was the only hotel in town. Now a Best Western, its raucous atmosphere has tamed considerably. To get a sense of the inn's former clientele, ask for a copy of the inn's original house rules, written in comical pidgin English. Rooms start at $155.

Next to the Pioneer Inn, Lahaina's massive **Banyan Tree** shades almost an acre of the central courthouse square. Planted in 1873, the tree has aerial roots that have grown into twelve major trunks, giving it the appearance of a small forest. The **Courthouse** next to the tree, built in 1859, served as a center of Maui government. Inside, the **Lahaina Art Society** (661–0111) exhibits its members' works. Check out the Old Jail Gallery in the basement, where iron-barred cells now imprison painted canvas. You will find works from some of the island's top talents in mediums ranging from *sfumato* (smoke painting) to basket weaving. On weekends, member artists gather to display additional works under the Banyan Tree outside. Open daily 9:00 A.M. to 5:00 P.M. In the corner of the square, you will notice "ruins" of the original waterfront fort built

Fright Night

If you frighten easily, stay away from Front Street on October 31. Monsters, witches, and an assortment of scary creatures will be on the prowl during the annual Halloween festivities. No one is really sure how the tradition started, but Halloween in Lahaina has grown into an event of mythic proportion. Lahaina hotels now charge special Halloween rates. No costume is too bizarre, far-out, or ghoulish. In fact, the weirder the better.

Festivities begin with the children's parade at 5:00 P.M. down Front Street, followed by dancing in the streets, as hundreds of weird-looking people vie for thousands of dollars worth of prizes in a costume contest.

in the 1830s to intimidate rowdy sailors. The fort was actually torn down completely in 1854. Rather than damage the Banyan Tree, the Restoration Society settled on this partial reconstruction.

Farther south on Front Street, take a peek inside the **Episcopal Church** to see the painting by DeLos Blackmar of a Hawaiian Madonna.

The area around here overflowed with sites of royalty. **Maluulu o Lele Park** once held a seventeen-acre fishpond called Mokuhinia, home of Kihawahine, a legendary *mo`o* (lizard-woman). Maui's royal *alii* lived on Moku`ula, an island in this sacred pond, protected by the mo`o, and Kamehameha's heirs enjoyed its seclusion while growing up. The island even housed a royal mausoleum for a time. In 1918 the pond was filled in and the ground leveled. Today all you see is an ordinary ball field. The legacy of Moku`ula has not been forgotten, however. In 1995 the erstwhile royal residence was entered on the National Historic Registry. Teams from Oahu's Bishop Museum have twice surveyed the site to locate buried features. Plans to excavate and restore the complex are under way, and a new cultural/historical tour company has formed to help raise funds (see sidebar on pages 222–23). For tours, call 661–9494.

Turn inland up Shaw Street to the corner of Wainee Street and **Waiola Church.** Formerly named Wainee Church, the original 1832 edifice here could seat 3,000 people and was the first stone church in the islands. In 1858 a whirlwind funneled out of Kaua`ula Valley and tore off the roof, and in 1894 royalists protesting Hawaii's annexation burned the church to the ground. Rebuilt, it burned down again in 1947 and was restored, only to be demolished by another Kaua`ula windstorm. Reoriented with its front door facing Kaua`ula Valley and renamed Waiola, the church has remained standing . . . so far. In the old cemetery next door, elaborate tombstones designate the likes of Queens Ka`ahumanu and Keopuolani and Maui governor Hoapili. Next to Ka`ahumanu lies Kamualii, the husband she kidnapped from Kaua`i, thus consolidating the united Hawaiian kingdom.

Return north on Wainee Street past the Indian-style **Hongwanji Mission.** A block farther, **Hale Paahao** ("stuck in irons house") is surrounded by a high wall built from coral blocks from the old fort. The wall and wooden jailhouse inside were built by the prisoners themselves, most of whom were jailed for disorderly conduct. You can peer inside one of the cells where prisoners were locked up at night and listen to a recorded account of prison life. Notice the list of crime statistics from the period. It seems that 1857 was a big year for "giving birth to bastard children," "violating fish taboos," and "felonious branding." You enter Hale Paahao appropriately on Prison Street.

Other historical sites lie north of the Bailey House on Front Street. Don't miss **Wo Hing Temple,** a colorfully restored two-story building affiliated with the Chee Kung Tong fraternal society. Exhibits chronicle the history of Chinese immigrants, the first Asian group to arrive in Hawaii. Commercial sugar production on the islands was started by Chinese entrepreneurs, although most of the Chinese came later as field workers for plantations run by white owners. In the Taoist temple upstairs, incense burns alongside offerings on a richly decorated altar honoring Kuan Ti, the god of wealth. The cookhouse outside shows footage from Thomas Edison's movies of Hawaii shot in 1898 and 1903.

The **U.S. Seamen's Hospital,** farther north, was originally built as a bachelor pad by Kamehameha III. Here he could escape his missionary advisers' watchful eyes to drink, gamble, and even meet for clandestine trysts with his sister, Princess Nahienaena. Such incestuous unions between high-ranking alii had been a sacred duty in the old days, to assure offspring of the purest bloodlines. The new Christian morality of the missionaries condemned incest. Distraught by the strain of these conflicting moralities, Nahienaena suffered an early death. A special path was cleared through the breadfruit trees of Lahaina for her body to be carried to Maluulu o Lele; the path today exists as Luakini Street. The word *luakini* describes temples where human sacrifices were performed. To the grieving Hawaiians, Nahienaena was a sacrifice to the new

Heavenly Maui

For an off-the-beaten-path experience that's literally out of this world, try stargazing from the top of 10,000-foot Mount Haleakala. The elevation and isolation ensure some of the clearest night skies on earth. Even without a telescope, you'll see more stars than you've ever dreamed of. Jim Lindsay's *Stargazers Maui* (281–9158) stages summit astronomy viewings after dark. Lindsay provides the telescope, warm clothing, a picnic meal, and the celestial know-how to narrate a tour of the evening sky. He points out heavenly highlights such as planets, nebulae, galaxies, and star clusters—the content varies with the changing sky. He charges about $75 for the experience, which lasts at least an hour and a half, depending on interest and weather permitting.

If you'd rather do your stargazing from the comfort of a luxury hotel, Stargazers also does regular, one-hour astronomy shows at the Grand Wailea Resort (875–1234) and the Ka'anapali Embassy Suites (661–2000), open to nonguests for $20; call for schedule. The sky isn't as clear, and weather's more iffy, but it's a whole lot warmer than a windy mountaintop. The Hyatt Regency (661–1234) in Ka'anapali holds its own nightly shows for $30 and offers a "champagne special" for couples on Friday and Saturday at 11:00 P.M.

Lahaina Jodo Mission

morality of the missionaries. The United States later leased the building as a home for destitute and disabled American sailors. Consular officials in charge of the hospital ran a profitable racket, charging the U.S. government inflated prices and even billing for "patients" interred in the nearby seamen's cemetery.

Continue north along Front Street to meditate beneath the giant Buddha of **Lahaina Jodo Mission.** To find it, look for the helpful JESUS IS COMING SOON sign and turn seaward onto Ala Moana Street. The majestic Buddha sits lotus-style atop an outdoor platform against a backdrop of green hills. The mission compound also includes a three-story pagoda housing cremated ashes and a large bell whose "voice of Buddha" speaks nightly at 8:00 P.M.

Lahaina means "merciless sun." If you're ready to holler uncle, take to the cooler hills. Lahainaluna Road leads uphill past the Pioneer Sugar Mill to **Lahainaluna** ("above Lahaina") **School.** Founded by missionaries in 1831, it's the oldest school west of the Rockies. Boarding students from as far away as California once enrolled here. On the campus you will find **Hale Pa`i** (667–7040), the old mission printing house. The printery's hand press cranked out Hawaiian translations of the Bible as well as an early newspaper, paper money, and even drafts of the Hawaiian constitution. Hale Pa`i is open from 10:00 A.M. to 4:00 P.M. weekdays. Call to confirm they are open when you're planning to visit.

Among Lahainaluna's first students was David Malo, a brilliant scholar whose book *Hawaiian Antiquities* forms the basis for much of our knowledge of precontact Hawaiian culture. A Christian minister himself, Malo respected the missionaries for their spiritual exertions. At the same time, he saw clearly the devastating impact of Western contact on Hawaiian society. He died a bitter man, asking to be buried "above the tide of foreign invasion." His grave rests on top of Mount Ball, near the giant L cut into the forest above the school.

To many people, Lahaina doesn't mean history but shopping. Rows of Western-style arcades lining Front Street create a carnival atmosphere. Art is a major commodity here. Notice how many galleries carry works showing dual underwater/surface landscapes in the "two worlds" style pioneered by Robert Lyn Nelson. Every Friday evening, local galleries host special Art Night receptions. For those who like their art aged, *Lahaina Printsellers* (667–5815) has amassed an amazing collection of antique maps and prints. They specialize in drawings made by early Pacific explorers, with a selection from Captain Cook's voyages second only to that in the British Museum. Their Lahaina store, located at 505 Front Street, is open daily 9:00 A.M. to 10:00 P.M. A larger store, located at Whalers Village in the Ka`anapali shopping complex, is open 9:00 A.M. to 10:00 P.M.

For gift items, browse *Totally Hawaiian Gift Gallery* (667–2558), in the Cannery Mall at the north end of town. Open daily 9:00 A.M. to 9:00 P.M. This being Lahaina, you should also stop in at *Lahaina Scrimshaw* (669–0018), at 845A Front Street. Sailors of old started the tradition of engraving ivory teeth from sperm whales to while away the hours at sea. Upon returning to their home port, they would present the completed work to their sweethearts as a testament to their undying ardor and constancy. In fact, stores like Lahaina Scrimshaw were cottage industries even in those days. Lazy sailors could purchase mass-produced art from these early precursors of the airport gift shop. The *Crazy Shirts* outlet (661–4775), two doors down from Lahaina Scrimshaw, has a wall devoted to whaling memorabilia.

Restaurants rival shops in Lahaina in variety, number, and mutability. Popular standbys overlooking the waterfront on the 800 block of Front Street include *Kimo's* (661–4811) for seafood and *Longhi's* (667–2288) for hip Italian; both expensive.

Farther south at 505 Front Street, *Pacific `O* (667–4341) features trendy Pacific Rim creations, such as prawn and basil wontons and shiso spicy tuna, served right on the beach, with live jazz on weekend nights. Open daily 11:30 A.M. to 4:00 P.M. and 5:30 to 9:00 P.M. Investment-caliber prices. If you head a few blocks north, you'll find the most budget-friendly meals on the Lahaina waterfront at *Aloha Mixed Plate* (661–3322), located at 1285 Front. The Hawaiian/island-ethnic fare won't win any culinary awards, and it's served on paper plates, but you can savor the same great views, along with passable mai tais, seated on a tiki-torch-lit deck, all for a low price. Open daily 10:30 A.M. to 10:00 P.M.

The lack of a waterfront location has hardly hindered **David Paul's Lahaina Grill** (667–5117), located at the corner of Front Street and Lahainaluna Road. His top-rated new American kitchen creates a rotating menu with southwestern touches such as Tequila Shrimp and Firecracker Rice, served in a chic black-and-white-tile salon with molded tin ceilings. Opens daily at 6:00 P.M. Investment-caliber prices.

If all you want is a quick bite for lunch, **Lahaina Bakery** (667–9062), hidden behind the train station at 991C Limahana Place, prepares made-to-order sandwiches and scrumptious pastries. Open Monday through Friday 5:30 A.M. to 1:00 P.M., Saturday until 12:30 P.M., and Sunday until 11:00 A.M. If you prefer your sandwiches with a Eurasian twist, make your way to **Ba-Le** (661–5566), in the Lahaina Cannery on the north edge of town. They also have fresh Vietnamese salads and summer rolls. Open daily 10:00 A.M. to 9:00 P.M.

But for West Maui's best meal deal, you have to go all the way north to Honokowai, past Ka`anapali. Turn left off the highway at Star Market and descend Lower Honoapi`ilani Road until you see the 5-A Rent-A-Space shopping plaza at 3608. The somewhat redundantly named **Honokowai Okazu & Deli** (665–0512) (*okazu yas* are the Japanese equivalent of delis) may be a bare-bones hole-in-the-wall serving local ethnic staples, but the food, prepared by former chefs of Mama's Fish House, is first rate. Their *ono* (wahoo—a fish) dinner special is usually fresh-caught and costs less than $13. They do a mostly take-out trade, but there is limited table and counter space. Open Monday through Saturday 10:00 A.M. to 2:30 P.M. and 4:30 to 9:00 P.M.

Moving on to accommodations next door to (and above) David Paul's, the **Lahaina Inn** (661–0577; 800–669–3444; www.lahainainn.com), at 127 Lahainaluna Road, bears the hand of Crazy Shirts founder Rick Ralston, whose extensive renovations have outfitted each of the twelve rooms with a period look from the late 1890s, in many cases using antiques from Ralston's personal collection. Under new ownership, the inn has kept the antique touches, such as leaded-glass lamps and needlepoint handwork on pillowcases. Rooms start at $140, with harbor views from $160.

Just down the road from the Lahaina Inn, the **Plantation Inn** (667–9225; 800–433–6815; www.theplantationinn.com), at 174 Lahainaluna Road, has its own faux-Victorian look going; it was built that way. A white balustrade surrounds the two-story building. The interior features lavish use of natural woods, stained-glass windows, and polished brass. Floral wallpaper, lace curtains, and Persian rugs add to the indulgent feel. The rooms have authentic period furniture, from pull-chain toilets to four-poster beds; a few have ceilings with faux paintings; and suites include whirlpool baths and kitchenettes. Modern conveniences are discreetly concealed. Rates range from $157 to $245 and include a full breakfast.

A block north of Lahainaluna Road on the highway is the Lahaina terminal of the **Lahaina-Kaanapali Railroad,** also known as the Sugar Cane Train (667–6851). The islands' only remaining steam locomotives now haul tourists instead of sugarcane along the 6-mile track. The narrated journey takes thirty-five minutes each way and costs $19.95 round-trip. Rides feature a singing conductor.

Ka`anapali, north of Lahaina, was the first planned resort in the Hawaiian Islands. In the middle of 3-mile-long Ka`anapali Beach, **Pu`u Kekaa,** commonly called Black Rock, is an eroded black cinder cone that rises from the ocean. Hawaiians believed that spirits of the dead leaped from this rocky bluff to enter the world beyond. Maui's powerful eighteenth-century ruler, Kahekili, inspired his men by diving into the ocean alongside the invisible spirits. Today the Sheraton-Maui sprawls across Black Rock, and during its nightly torch-lighting ceremony this leap is dramatically reenacted.

trivia

Early whalers didn't go after humpbacks because they sink upon death.

To explore more Ka'anapali history and legends, reserve in advance for the **Ka'anapali Resort Association**'s (661–3271) free ninety-minute walking tour on Tuesday and Friday mornings at 9:00 A.M. It starts at the Royal Lahaina Resort's activity area parking lot.

If Lahaina has piqued your interest in whaling, be sure to visit the **Whalers Village Museum** (661–5992), in the Ka`anapali shopping complex of the same name. James Campbell, who founded Pioneer Sugar Mill, began his career as a carpenter on a whaling ship. The museum is funded by his estate in his memory and does a good job of conveying the story of whaling in Hawaii. Relive the drama of the chase as tiny whaleboats row stealthily into battle with "the enemy." Learn how the economic factors governing whaling's rise and fall included women's fashions in hoopskirts and the discovery of petroleum in Pennsylvania. You can even see a life-size model of a forecastle where common sailors slept.

A separate gallery focuses on the whales themselves. Extensive interactive displays include videos of humpbacks at play accompanied by recorded whale songs. In fact, Lahaina's whalers of old didn't hunt humpbacks. Lahaina merely served as a central staging ground for the North Pacific fleet's pursuit of sperm whales off Japan and Alaska. With modern technology, humpbacks were indeed hunted to near extinction, but this happened long after the last whale ships left Hawaiian waters. Open daily 9:00 A.M. to 10:00 P.M. Free.

Newer resort developments, alternating with abandoned cane fields, have sprouted north of Ka`anapali. Now that King Cane has shut down, the scent of

"West Maui incense" from burning cane (the most efficient method of harvesting) no longer wafts through the luxury hotels. After Napili, the fields switch to pineapple cultivation, which holds better long-term prospects, as pineapple is a higher-value crop. To learn more about these spiky icons of the Hawaiian Islands, sign up for Maui Pineapple Company's tour (see sidebar on page 210). Other islands fade from view as East Moloka`i looms across the channel. Kapalua, the last tourist enclave on this coast, ends at the 30-mile marker. The demons of development have left three beautiful beaches beyond. WARNING: These northern strands can become dangerous for swimming, especially during winter.

At 31 miles, a side road leads to **D. T. Fleming Beach Park** in Honokahua Bay. The facilities here are the last you will find before Wailuku. To the left of the beach park, the northern edge of Makaluapuna Point has some curious lava formations whose unusually light color and vertical, thrusting shape have earned them the nickname "dragon's teeth." You can get to them most easily by turning off the highway onto Office Road just before the beach park, following it to its end, then walking across the edge of the golf course.

A half mile past the 32-mile marker, the road winds above **Mokuleia Bay.** Beachgoers descend very steep trails from either side to the secluded beach below; locals call this Slaughterhouse because such a facility once stood on the cliffs above. The bay belongs to a marine-life conservation zone. **Honolua Bay,** the northern limit of the conservation zone, awaits a half mile farther at the mouth of a lushly tropical valley. The beach here, accessed by several trails down from the highway, suffers seasonal depletions of its sand and can be quite rocky during winter. The right side of the bay receives the best winter surf on the island, rivaling O`ahu's North Shore. In calmer months snorkelers take advantage of the abundance of marine life in the conservation zone. The inner bay can be murky, but excellent coral formations farther out await exploration.

The road continues through pineapple fields and open forest. Near the 36-mile point, it rounds a sharp corner and begins a dramatic descent into Honokohau Bay. The Honoapiilani Highway ends here at the last of six bays *(bono)* claimed by the fifteenth-century chief Piilani. As you curve around the bend, glimpses of the rugged coastline beyond beckon. Route 340, a narrow county road, continues up the other side of the bay, with mile markers enumerated in the reverse direction descending from twenty-two. Don't miss this road. It wriggles through the mountains, passing remote farms and villages. The tiny town of Kahakuloa is the epitome of small-town Hawaii, where lazy dogs sleep in the middle of the road, the air is fragrant with sweet ginger, the cobalt blue ocean laps at the shoreline, and the neighbors are welcoming.

Tours and Tales

Pineapples appear on many a Maui restaurant menu, and although not endemic to the islands, the fruit is a symbol of Hawaii known around the world. But very few visitors actually know how these spiky bromeliads grow. Mischievous tour guides have been known to prey on this ignorance by pointing to similar-looking fruit on hala (pandanus) trees, which they call "tourist pineapples." Maui Pineapple Company's two-hour plantation tours remedy this gap by bringing visitors up close and personal with Hawaii's famous fruit. You'll learn the history behind Hawaiian pineapples, see how they are cultivated today, and visit fields currently being harvested to pick your own edible souvenir. Tours are offered weekdays 9:30 A.M. to noon and 12:30 to 3:00 P.M.; cost is $29. Book through the Kapalua Resort activity desk: 669–8088.

Also at Kapalua, during the warm summer nights between April and August, be on the lookout for the Ritz-Carlton's monthly Moonlight Mo'olelo sessions. Held on a beach house lawn under the full moon, these gatherings celebrate the age-old tradition of island storytelling, inviting *kupuna* (elders) from throughout the state to swap stories on a designated topic during an evening of music and pupus. Call 669–6200 for the schedule of these free events.

Yet another Kapalua event happens only once a year and is far from being free. The Kapalua Nature Society manages much of the West Maui Mountains, including the summit of 5,877-foot Puu Kukui. Usually inaccessible, the summit area is opened to twelve visitors once a year, ferried by helicopter for a tour of this unique, cloud-forest habitat of native birds and plant life. A boardwalk enables visitors to move across the boglike terrain, whose rain-soaked soil reduces vegetation to stunted growth. A lottery is held to choose the lucky twelve; to enter call (808) 669–2440. The only catch is the cost: $1,200, which helps to fund native forest conservation.

About a mile along Route 340, a white Coast Guard beacon marks *Nakalele Point.* Bizarre rock formations spewed from a volcanic spatter cone close to the shoreline give this region its nickname of Hobbitland, after author J. R. R. Tolkien's fantasy world. To the right of Nakalele Point, a blowhole powered by this coast's constant surf sends ocean sprays wafting through the air. To explore this unearthly terrain, take the newly constructed *Ohai Trail,* which starts between the 40- and 41-mile markers and continues about half a mile along the seashore. The trail is named for the silver-leaved native shrubs with red flowers that you pass on the way in.

As you continue along the highway, signs warn of falling rocks. Hidden hands have stacked many of these rocks into cairns that line the road like sentinels. Clinging to the edge of cliffs, the road winds through knobby green hills and past remote valleys with abandoned settlements. The tree cover fades as the scenery grows more and more dramatic, and almost every turn begs you to pull over. Below the highway, the blue vastness of the Pacific Ocean hisses and seethes, crashing in fury and then retreating in restless agitation.

Just shy of the 16-mile point, near the top of a hill, **Pohaku Kani,** an enormous solitary boulder, squats above the highway on the inland side. Now marred by graffiti, the rock once served as a bell stone, struck by ancient Hawaiians to produce a resonant, bell-like tone. Immediately after the bell stone, the road crosses a cement culvert. On the right, a gate blocks a road inland. To explore a section of this coast that you can't see from the highway, turn onto the dirt road opposite the gate, heading toward the ocean and parking when the going gets rough. From here you can scramble down a short, rocky headland slope to reach a spectacular cliffside ledge roughly 100 feet up, with the ocean almost directly below, coastal views in both directions, and Moloka`i on the horizon. Below you lies a patchwork of small pools on a low lava shelf. After watching to be sure that the biggest breaking waves do not engulf this shelf, you can clamber down to swim in the pools' brackish, partly spring-fed water.

A mile and a half farther, the road narrows to a single lane as it climbs around the twin valleys of Kahakuloa Bay. **Kahakuloa** ("the tall lord") **Head** towers above the far edge of the bay. Visible for miles along this coast, this green volcanic knoll shelters a tiny Hawaiian settlement in the valley floor below. Residents of Kahakuloa Village tend taro fields and fish in the traditional manner. As you begin to head up the far side of the valley, there's a roadside stand that sells very yummy banana bread. Notice the irrigation channel bringing water under the highway to the taro fields below. This water comes from centuries-old irrigation works built upvalley by Hawaiians of yore and managed communally by the village. For those curious to learn more about Kahakuloa and its residents, Ekahi Tours (877–9775; 888–292–2422) and Maui Eco-Adventures (877–661–7720) both offer half-day tours of the valley that access private land otherwise closed to visitors, each for $80.

From here, the road turns uphill through mountain pastures past the Honolua Ranch headquarters. The contortions of this single-lane road reach a climax as it winds in and out of deserted valleys high above the coast. By the 10-mile point, the road begins a slow descent with views along the coast and across the isthmus to East Maui. The **Turnbull Studios & Sculpture Garden** (244–9838) is worth a stop. Bruce Turnbull's imaginatively shaped wood and bronze creations have an uplifting, almost mythical quality. Open Tuesday through Friday 10:00 A.M. to 5:00 P.M. or by appointment. Just beyond the 7-mile marker, a side road leads to Maluhia Boy Scout Camp. A mile up this road, just before it curves into the camp, is the start of the **Waihe`e Ridge Trail.** Hardy hikers can climb 1,563 feet (a little less than 3 miles) to reach scenic

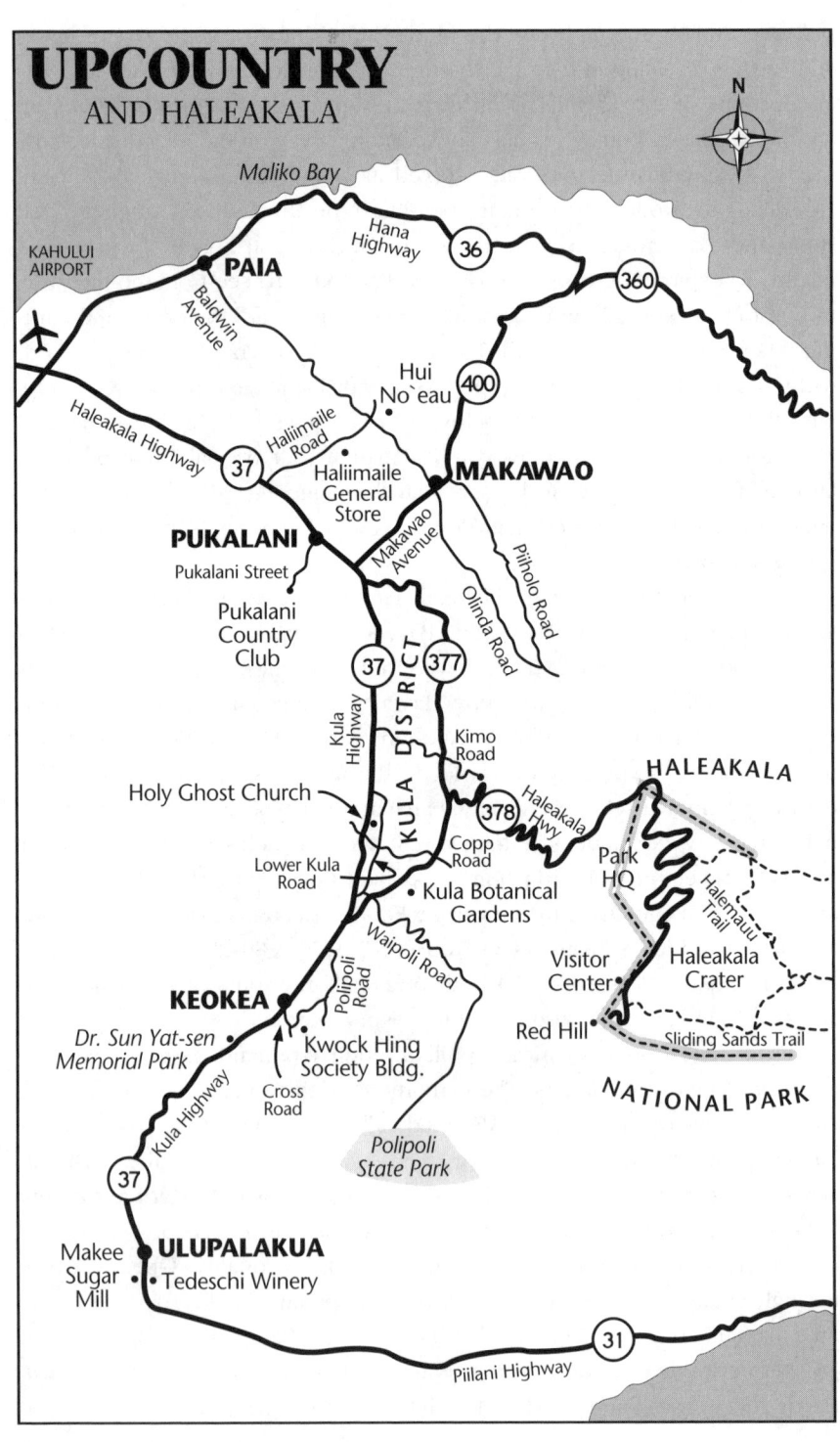

UPCOUNTRY
AND HALEAKALA

N

Maliko Bay

KAHULUI AIRPORT

PAIA

Hana Highway

36

360

Baldwin Avenue

Hui No`eau

400

Haleakala Highway

37

Haliimaile Road

Haliimaile General Store

MAKAWAO

Piiholo Road

PUKALANI

Pukalani Street

Makawao Avenue

Olinda Road

Pukalani Country Club

37

377

Kula Highway

KULA DISTRICT

Kimo Road

HALEAKALA

Holy Ghost Church

378

Haleakala Hwy

Copp Road

Park HQ

Halemauu Trail

Lower Kula Road

Kula Botanical Gardens

Visitor Center

Haleakala Crater

Waipoli Road

Polipoli Road

KEOKEA

Red Hill

Sliding Sands Trail

Dr. Sun Yat-sen Memorial Park

Kwock Hing Society Bldg.

Cross Road

NATIONAL PARK

Kula Highway

Polipoli State Park

37

Makee Sugar Mill

ULUPALAKUA

Tedeschi Winery

31

Piilani Highway

Lanilili Peak. For a less strenuous hiking option, continue 1.5 miles to Waihe`e Valley Road, across the bridge on the far side of the valley. Follow the road past taro patches until the pavement ends at a T-junction with a former cane road. Take this road to the right for a stroll up the valley, past streamside taro patches, across a hanging footbridge, to reach a natural pool 2 miles in. Enjoy the pristine beauty while you can. The road soon improves, and before you know it you're on a two-lane highway, speeding back to civilization.

Upcountry and Haleakala

Unlike Vesuvius, St. Helens, Fuji-san, and Kilimanjaro, **Haleakala** ("the house of the sun") lacks the classic upsloping shape and explosive pedigree of its volcanic peers. Hawaiian volcanoes form through comparatively gentle eruptions that spread layer upon layer of viscous lava over a broad area. The flattened appearance of the "shield volcanoes" that result can be deceiving. Haleakala does not look 10,000 feet tall because it is so wide—it spreads across most of the island. In mass, its concave dome packs more solid rock than a dozen of the world's more visually impressive "tall" volcanoes put together.

Wrapped around Haleakala's gentle western slopes, a loosely defined agricultural zone known as Upcountry takes advantage of the temperate climate and fertile volcanic soil. Truck farmers grow a variety of vegetable crops, floral nurseries cover hillsides with exotic blooms, and two of Hawaii's largest ranches herd cattle along Haleakala's upper slopes. Upcountry residents are an easygoing lot. Comforted by cool breezes and chilly nights, they boast that their sunset views across West Maui can't be beat.

The many different routes to Upcountry all climb through pineapple-covered foothills planted in countered rows like the whorl of a fingerprint. The Haleakala Highway from Kahului passes through Pukalani, the largest settlement. Two "back door" routes lead first through Makawao, an Upcountry outpost with far more character. These roads, Baldwin Avenue, which climbs from Paia, and Route 400, which starts farther along the Hana Highway and turns into Makawao Avenue, intersect each other at right angles in the center of Makawao town.

If you take Baldwin Avenue up, stop at the **Holy Rosary Church** on the right past the sugar mill to see Maurice Felbier's rendition of Father Damien comforting a leper. Three miles farther, look for the sign to **Hui No`eau** (572–6560), at 2841 Baldwin Avenue. A beautiful lawn drive lined with trees leads to a tile-roofed Mediterranean mansion, built by noted architect C. W. Dickey for Harry and Ethel Baldwin in 1917. Ethel helped found Hui No`eau, the oldest art society on Maui, and today the *hui* maintains the home as a workshop center for the benefit of its membership and visiting artists. Although it is not set up as a commercial gallery, various artists exhibit their works here and frequent shows and art classes are held. Wander around the garden courtyard and peek into the stables where potters manipulate their wheels. Open daily 10:00 A.M. to 4:00 P.M.

Two miles farther, Makawao, Maui's cowboy town, keeps up its "Machowao" image through periodic rodeos. Maui's own Ikua Purdy stunned the mainland cowboy establishment when he won the 1908 world championship in steer roping—the first time Hawaiian *paniolos* had competed in a mainland event. While the ranchhands twirled their lariats, their bosses played polo with the plantation aristocracy, a tradition also maintained in Makawao. Matches are played in July and November; call 283–1930 for exact dates and times. Most cowpokes work at the surrounding ranches during the week, leaving Makawao to a more precious set. No longer selling rawhide and rope, many of Makawao's shops have gone yuppie, stimulated not only by a boost in tourism but also by a rash of Upcountry subdivisions. The main streets are choked with fashionable boutiques and art galleries. Note the store selling fireplaces and chimneys—an indication of Upcountry's chilly nights.

Start your browsing amid the former Makawao Theater complex at the lower end of Baldwin Avenue. Yet another artists' collective exhibits here, and in back, **Hot Island Glass** (572–4527) displays its own form of artistry. Watch colored lumps of glass being shaped in the 2,000-degree furnace. Open daily 9:00 A.M. to 5:00 P.M., with glassblowing starting at 10:30 A.M. (except on Saturday), but call to confirm there will be glassblowing during your visit. The complex also has a very pleasant courtyard cafe.

A number of alternative-lifestyle people live here, too, close to the spiritual "power source" of Haleakala Crater. Seekers, or those merely curious, can enter **The Dragon's Den** (572–2424), at the corner of Baldwin and Makawao Avenues. This Asian lair has shelves filled with jars of exotic herbs, teas, and medicines. William Malik grew up in China and acquired a formal education in Chinese healing. He opened this shop as the pharmaceutical wing of his adjacent practice. Other alternative practitioners have joined him.

As for restaurants, Makawao has plenty. **Kitada's** (572–7241), across the street from the theater complex on Baldwin, serves a mean bowl of *saimin* (a kind of ramen in broth) to a mostly local clientele. Open Monday through Saturday 6:00 A.M. to 1:30 P.M. Old-timers also favor the cream puffs from **Komoda Bakery** (572–7261) and head to **Polli's** (572–7808), at the top of Baldwin, for their Mexican fix. Across the street **Casanova's Italian Deli** (572–0220) embodies Makawao's new upscale persona. The deli was established by four Italian school friends from Milan who moved to Makawao because they heard it had horses. Casanova's has expanded into an adjacent property to operate a *ristorante* and *discoteca,* but it's cheaper to order from the deli counter. Park yourself on the front porch and watch life in Makawao pass by. The deli is open daily from 8:00 A.M. to 6:00 P.M., but call first to confirm they're open. The restaurant is open for lunch Monday through Saturday 11:30 A.M. to 2:00 P.M. and nightly 5:30 to 9:00 P.M.

Above Makawao Avenue, Baldwin Avenue becomes Olinda Road, which leads past the 1843 coral-block **Po`okela Church** and climbs steeply through lush hills. Eucalyptuses line the narrow road, along which designer homes alternate with rustic farmhouses. Gaps in the tree cover offer dramatic vistas of the coast far below. Higher up, you'll pass the state's Captive Rearing Project for endangered `alala crows and nene geese. To stretch your legs at the top of Olinda, follow the dirt road that continues from the gate through rolling pastures. If you take the left fork, you can follow a large irrigation pipe east through several miles of variegated forest to end up in Haleakala's moss-covered watershed.

Just before it dead-ends, Olinda connects with Piiholo Road, which winds through a pine forest to loop back to Makawao. On the way down, look for **Aloha o Ka Aina,** a plant nursery that specializes in ferns. Turn left at the bottom of Piiholo to return to town.

Makawao Avenue continues southwest as Route 365 to Pukalani. Here, amid this elevated wasteland of shopping malls and suburban homes, one of Maui's few authentic Hawaiian kitchens lurks in an unlikely place, the Pukalani Country Club. To reach it, go a half mile downhill on Haleakala Highway from Makawao Avenue, turn left onto Pukalani Street past the shopping center, and follow the street to its end. The **Pukalani Country Club** (572–1325) serves all your local favorites, such as squid in coconut milk. Large picture windows overlook the golf course with views of West Maui beyond. Open daily 7:30 A.M. to 9:00 P.M. Inexpensive.

Ever since its opening in a forgotten plantation camp, a stampede of savvy locals have flocked to the **Haliimaile General Store** (572–2666). To follow their footprints, turn from Haleakala Highway onto Haliimaile Road, just south of Pukalani. Beverly and Joe Gannon have forsaken a background in show business to team up with two local chefs and convert this 1929-vintage plantation store into a gourmet restaurant. The partners share cooking duties and collaborate on recipe ideas to maintain an ever-changing menu of eclectically blended dishes based around "fish, pasta, duck, lamb, and a smoked something." Delicatessen-style lunches command moderate prices, while dinners approach the investment-caliber range. Open Monday through Friday 11:00 A.M. to 2:30 P.M. and nightly 5:30 to 9:30 P.M. If you're here during the day, stop by *Maui Fresh Fruit Store and Farmer's Market* (573–5129) next door to sample Maui produce and peruse Maui Pineapple Company memorabilia. Open Monday through Friday 10:00 A.M. to 5:30 P.M. and Saturday 9:00 A.M. to 2:00 P.M.

Beyond Pukalani, the Haleakala Highway splits off to the left as Route 377, while Route 37 continues south as the Kula Highway. These parallel routes traverse the Kula District, some of Maui's most fertile farmland. Kula onions are prized throughout the state for their sweet, mild flavor. Kula potatoes, first planted to feed hungry forty-niners during the California Gold Rush, now appear in island markets as Maui-style potato chips. Kula's flower farms have blossomed into a multimillion-dollar business, thanks largely to the commercial success of the South African protea. Like the Greek god Proteus, for whom they are named, these striking flowers take many forms; dressed in metallic hues, they have a texture ranging between feathers and stiff felt and form exotic bouquets that retain their beauty fresh or dry. There are five major types: the regal powderpuffs of the king protea, the spiky bristles of pincushions, the featherlike minks, the silvery foliage of leucadendrons, and the odd-looking banksias, resembling an acorn on a stick. Although primarily a winter crop, some varieties bloom year-round. Many of Kula's flower nurseries post signs welcoming visitors and will sell retail.

Most of the farms lie alongside roads running between the two highways. Plot your own course on these steep country lanes, perfect for a lazy Sunday drive. If you take Copp Road, one such connector, uphill from the Kula Highway, turn left onto Mauna Place two intersections up to reach *Proteas of Hawaii* (878–2533), at the north end of Mauna Place. More than one hundred shape-morphing varieties await your inspection here Monday through Thursday 8:00 A.M. to 4:30 P.M. and Friday 8:00 A.M. to 3:00 P.M. To see new varieties-in-the-making, you can also visit the experimental *University of Hawaii Maui Agricultural Research Center* (878–1213), across the street, open Monday through Thursday 7:30 A.M. to 3:30 P.M. There's a self-guiding map you can follow, or call ahead and someone may be able to escort you. Calling ahead (preferably the day before) will also get you a tour of *Kula Vista* (878–3251; 888–878–3251), the state's largest protea farm, at the 5-mile point of the Haleakala Highway; their eighty acres could fit the rest of Kula's protea farms put together. Open Monday through Friday 8:00 A.M. to 3:30 P.M.

Immediately before Copp Road, on your way down the Hula Highway, look for the silver roof of the *Holy Ghost Church* on the uphill side of the Kula Highway. Portuguese Azores islanders built this unusual octagonal structure in 1894. To reach it, turn left from Copp onto confusingly named Lower Kula Road, which runs above and parallel to the highway. Inside the church,

Holy Ghost Church

you'll find a lovely gilded altar and bas-relief sculptures depicting the Stations of the Cross. Notice the statue of Saint Antone with a pig underfoot. Volunteers bake *pao doce* (Portuguese sweetbread) every Monday and Thursday morning for sale in the adjacent hall. Church members also throw an annual free luau in a tradition stemming from the old country. Their ancestral village had faced a severe drought, and the villagers had vowed that if God brought forth rain, they would feed the entire island. Centuries later, on a new island, in a faraway land, this vow is still remembered.

If you took Copp Road to reach Lower Kula Road, on the way to the church you'll pass *Cafe 808* (878–6874). It has a menu as local as its clientele. At $9.95, the fresh-catch special is the most expensive item on the menu. Grab a table inside this former plantation store or carry out to enjoy the sumptuous hilltop views from the parking lot. Open daily 6:00 A.M. to 8:00 P.M.

The high road is worth taking too, either coming or going, not for moral reasons, but because the scenery's better. Chrysanthemum and carnation farms decorate the surrounding hillside. In spring the jacaranda trees erupt in a blaze of lavender/periwinkle blossoms. A mile farther, the Haleakala Highway turns uphill again, becoming Route 378, while Route 377 continues as Kekaulike Avenue and soon begins to descend. About 2.5 miles along and just after the

Copp Road junction, the **Kula Botanical Gardens** (878–1715) on the left might merit a visit. In case you're planning a vendetta, the "taboo garden" near the top features an assortment of some of the world's most poisonous plants. Open daily 9:00 A.M. to 4:00 P.M.; small admission fee.

The next left is Waipoli Road, which narrows to a single lane as it climbs 10 miles of switchbacks through cattle land to reach **Polipoli State Park** (984–8109). The last few miles are unpaved and require four-wheel drive. If you can make it to the top, the combination of serenity and scenery can't be beat. Tall stands of redwood mingle in an experimental forest composed of trees from around the world. A variety of hiking trails beckon, and campers can enjoy the park's unearthly views overnight by booking the state-owned cabin (587–0300) well in advance. Immediately past Waipoli Road, Route 377 rejoins the Kula Highway.

As you continue south along the Kula Highway, moving farther around the volcano's flank, Moloka`i disappears from the north and reappears behind the south end of West Maui. Every mile brings you farther into Haleakala's rain shadow. In contrast with the lush hills of Olinda, *panini* (prickly pear) cactus carpets the lower elevations. A couple of miles south from the second junction of Routes 37 and 377, you reach tiny Keokea, a onetime community of Chinese immigrants. Downtown Keokea has four stores, two of them rival gas stations. **Keokea Gallery** (878–3555) takes its ties to local art seriously; many of the paintings depict scenes in or around town, while owners Sheldon and Elizabeth Wallau paint new ones in the back of the room. Open daily 9:00 A.M. to 5:00 P.M. A real treat awaits you in **Grandma's Coffee** (878–2140), where owner Alfred Franco roasts his homegrown beans just like Grandma taught him, using a century-old roaster that her family may have brought when they fled Puerto Rico after the Spanish-American War. Peek through the counter window to see the original machinery he uses. Grandma's also serves breakfast and lunch, with local specials such as sweet-and-sour spareribs. Paintings of Upcountry rodeos by local artist Sharon Shigekawa decorate the walls. Open daily from 7:00 A.M. to 5:00 P.M.

To tour Keokea's "Chinatown," backtrack to Cross Road, near the town entrance, which angles above the park. A half mile uphill, the **Kwock Hing Society Building** serves as a solitary reminder of the immigrant farmers who flocked to the area. Among the village's early residents was Sun Yat-sen's brother. The future Chinese leader often visited Keokea while studying in Honolulu. He sent his family here for safety while plotting his revolution and was funded heavily by Hawaiian Chinese through societies such as Kwock Hing. A mile and a half past Keokea town on the highway, look for **Dr. Sun**

Yat-sen Memorial Park. Two enormous mock-stone lions face off in opposing corners, while a statue of the great man gazes down the hill to the site of his brother's former home.

From here, Route 37 begins a gradual, bumpy descent as it continues south across miles of cactus-studded pastureland partitioned by crumbling walls of lava stone. Most of Moloka`i swings out of view as the island of Lana`i seizes center stage on the horizon. Farther along, uninhabited Kaho`olawe appears with tiny Molokini in mid-channel. Five miles out of Keokea, the highway reaches the headquarters of the vast Ulupalakua Ranch. James Makee, a whaling captain turned gentleman planter, founded the ranch in 1856 to complement his sugar ventures. Makee's lavish social life included the entertainment of royalty; King Kalakaua was a frequent visitor.

Across the street, the ***Ranch Store*** boasts the oldest Levi Strauss account in the world. Bags of swine and horse feed have yielded shelf space to tourist bric-a-brac as well as a deli. Sitting on a porch in front of the store, two life-size sculptures impersonate a pair of old-timers who actually hung out on this very porch. Ulupalakua resident Reems Mitchell immortalized the duo in his trademark caricature style. The cowpoke standing next to them is Ikua Purdy, a world-champion roper from the ranch's early history. Mitchell's better-known works on exhibit elsewhere include the "old salts" fronting the Pioneer Inn in Lahaina. The artist makes his home inside the ruins of the old Makee Sugar Mill, a quarter mile up the road.

Across the street from the mill, you can visit ***Tedeschi Vineyards*** (878–6058) and reward yourself with a glass of bubbly for coming this far. Emil Tedeschi has brought family know-how from Napa Valley to open Hawaii's first vineyard and winery, in cooperation with Ulupalakua Ranch. You can take a free tour of the winery to learn the painstaking steps through which grapes and pineapples become bottled wines and champagne. Almost everything gets done by manual labor according to traditional methods. Despite its founder's credentials, the winery likes to boast that "this is not Napa Valley." After the tour, stop at the visitor center to sample the final product. It is housed in a cottage built for King Kalakaua's use during his visits. An adjacent gallery filled with historic photos chronicles a century of ranching life. Open daily 9:00 A.M. to 5:00 P.M.; half-hour tours are offered at 10:30 A.M. and 1:30 P.M.

Beyond the winery, the highway deteriorates further. A narrow, winding road rattles its way east to Kaupo across 22 miles of old lava flows covered by scrub bushes that barely sustain the scattered cattle that graze here. Consider going at least the first couple of miles to experience the bleak solitude of the landscape. As you round the corner to Haleakala's southern slopes, the ink-black path of the Cape Kinau lava flow below draws the eye, in vivid contrast with the tree-covered cinder cones higher up.

Those who wish to devote more than a day to Upcountry or position themselves midway to Haleakala's summit for a predawn ascent have several options. *Gildersleeve's B&B* (878–6623; 2112 Naalae Road, Kula), in lower Kula, offers perhaps the most outstanding value. A retired couple from Alaska, Murray and Elaine, spent five years building their dream home on this small Upcountry farm. Resplendent with natural woods, the split-level home enjoys breathtaking views across the isthmus. The three guest rooms on the lower level have a private entrance and share separate cooking facilities and living space. Murray still tends the pineapple fields and harvests other fruits and vegetables, of which guests can partake. Rooms go for $75 double and the cottage for $125 as a quad, with a surcharge for stays of less than three nights. The hosts prefer that smoking and drinking be done elsewhere.

Olinda Country Cottages & Inn (572–1453; 800–932–3435; mauibnb cottages.com) offers a variety of lodging spread across a seven-acre former protea farm with hilltop views. The owners, who also own the Hamoa Bay House and Bungalow in Hana, have decorated the property with an abundance of country charm. Two rooms in the upstairs of the main country manor rent for $140, with a studio for $140. A pair of secluded, fully equipped cottages rent for $195 and $245. Two- or three-night minimum depending on room.

Malu Manu (888–878–6161; www.mauisunrise.com) offers two options: a two-bedroom house and a log-cabin studio, each nestled within a wooded seven-acre lot, with views spanning three islands. The cabin, built in the 1920s as a writer's retreat, rents for $150; the house goes for $185. Both feature simple Hawaiian decor, with wood-burning stoves. An outdoor Japanese *ofuro* (wooden bathtub) and paddle-tennis court await use by guests. Other Upcountry bed-and-breakfast cottages with hilltop views include Bloom Cottage (878–1425), Moonlight (878–6977), and Kula Cottage (878–2043).

Located just below Makawao, the *Banyan Tree* (572–9021; www .banyantreehouse.com) offers historical charm and leafy tranquillity in lieu of unobstructed views. Built in the 1920s as a plantation manager's home abutting the pineapple fields, the property became the residence of Ethel Baldwin, one of Maui's early patrons of the arts. Ethel painted here daily and even got her chauffeur to join her. The main, three-bedroom house combines antique furnishings with an understated island decor. It rents for $390; individual rooms are occasionally rented on a last-minute basis. If not, you'll have to make do with the servants' quarters, which, refurbished as studios, rent for $110 to $135. A swimming pool is on-site. Another Makawao home of similar vintage, *Hale Ho`okipa* (572–6698; 877–572–6698, www.maui-bed-n-breakfast.com) was built by a Portuguese financier who raised thirteen kids here. Remnants of the original twenty-two-acre estate (since subdivided) include a small Madeira vineyard, Portuguese bread oven, and water tower. Bed-and-breakfast rooms in this antiques-filled craftsman-style home rent for $100 to $165. Owner Cherie Attix also offers hiking tours.

The voyage to the top of **Haleakala Crater** provides in every way the crowning experience of a Maui visit. After driving to the volcano's 10,023-foot summit, you peer over the rim of the 3,000-foot-deep crater inside. Measuring 7.5 miles long by 2.5 miles across, this mind-boggling space could swallow Manhattan, skyscrapers and all. Erosive stream action cut the original basin during a lull between eruptions, after which subsequent flows filled in the floor and restored the crater's volcanic appearance. Rust-streaked colors paint a lunar landscape of cinder cones and crusted lava flows. Mark Twain called it "the sublimest spectacle" he had ever seen.

To receive the quintessential Haleakala experience, purists insist you must arrive at the mountain early enough to watch the sun rise above the far rim of the summit wall. Shadows creep along the crater-pocked floor as the first rays ignite the smoldering embers of the volcano in a blaze of colorful light. Such a vision entertained the demigod Maui, who waited here in ambush and used a magic lasso to snare the sun's legs as they poked above the crater rim. Threatened with its life, the sun promised to travel across the sky more slowly, giving Maui's mother time to dry her kapa cloth. Almost as impressive as the show itself is the number of pilgrims willing to brave frigid early-morning temperatures to follow in Maui's footsteps.

The Art of Maui

The unsurpassed beauty of the Hawaiian Islands has always attracted a steady stream of artists. Maui has made a cottage industry out of "art tourism" as a means of exploiting the synergy between local talent and tourist pocketbooks. The hotbed of such activity is undoubtedly Lahaina, which claims more art galleries per capita than any other American city. Local galleries promote Friday night as Art Night, with special shows, featured artists-in-residence, and free refreshments offered from 7:00 to 10:00 p.m. The weekend outdoor showings of the Lahaina Arts Society beneath the central banyan tree provide another chance to get acquainted with local artists. The art on Maui should not be dismissed as only made-for-tourists kitsch. The many artist cooperatives scattered around the island nurture some genuine talents. Moreover, the Maui Arts and Cultural Center in Kahului showcases rotating exhibits and performances from throughout the world. Call 242–2787 for details or visit www.mauiarts.org.

Putting the Hawaiian Back in Hawaii

The closest most tourists come to experiencing Hawaiian culture is at a commercial luau, where a "Polynesian Review" blurs Hawaiian hula with other Polynesian dancing in an elaborate showbiz production that is more Vegas than Hawaii. Maui offers a number of unique experiences that help to fill this gap.

To raise funds for the restoration of Moku`ula Island (see page 203), the nonprofit group *Maui Nei* (661–9494), at 505 Front Street, conducts cultural tours of historic Lahaina. Visitors are welcomed by a *malo-* ("loincloth") clad islander and escorted on a narrated journey through Lahaina's past that includes archaeological explanations, costumed role-playing, Hawaiian *oli* ("chanting"), and *mo`olelo* ("storytelling"). Learn the medicinal uses of native plants; admire authentic reconstructions of double-hulled sailing canoes; and understand the special significance of Lahaina's location and, of course, that of Moku`ula. The two-hour tours are offered Monday through Saturday 9:30 to 11:30 A.M., snack included; cost is $37.

For a very different, but no less moving presentation of Hawaii's story, `*Ulalena* (661–9913; 877–688–4800) relies on imaginative costuming and innovative choreography to take a whirlwind ride through Hawaiian history and myth told through a combination of traditional hula, Japanese Butoh theater, and modern dance. The people behind Montreal's Cirque de Soleil account for the show's sophisticated showmanship, but its emotional power draws on the deep wellsprings of Hawaiian culture. Read the program beforehand because there is little or no narrative, and the story is often told at an abstract, almost archetypal level. The seventy-five-minute show plays Tuesday through Saturday in the specially built Maui Theater off Front Street in the Old Lahaina Center. Tickets cost $49, $59, or $70 for the meet-the-cast Producer's Package.

Another way to get a taste of old Hawaii is by visiting *Hale Kahiko* (667–5758), in the Lahaina Center at 845 Wainee Street and Papalaua. This reconstructed "Hawaiian village" is centered around three authentic Hawaiian hale, built from native

Those preferring to rise at a more civilized hour will be pleased to know that Haleakala's sunsets claim a following of their own, even though clouds that descend into the crater during the day sometimes linger after dark, obscuring the view. Call 877–5111 for the exact times of sunrise and sunset and general weather conditions. Allow an hour and a half for the drive up.

From the junction of Routes 377 and 378, a series of switchbacks ascends 6,800 feet over 20 miles, reaching the summit a total distance of 38 miles from Kahului. You'll pass a number of biking groups cruising "the world's steepest downhill ride." If that sounds impressive, how about the autumn "Run to the Sun," an annual footrace going up! The road quickly ohia wood lashed with coconut fiber twine, thatched with pili grass, and floored with stream and shoreline pebbles. Planted around each hale are plants used in traditional Hawaiian life: The *wauke* (a Polynesian mulberry) tree grows beside the *hale kuku,* in which its bark was pounded into kapa cloth. Men had their own *hale mua* to eat in (mixed-sex dining was forbidden), an injustice partly mitigated by the fact that they did all the cooking at the *imu* ("fire pit"). The village is open daily 9:00 A.M. to 6:00 P.M. Guided tours of the village are offered weekdays 10:00 A.M. to 4:00 P.M.; at other times, a self-guiding map is available. Free hula performances and/or Hawaiian craft lessons are offered on weekdays; call for schedule.

Meanwhile, in South Maui, the Fairmont Kea Lani in Wailea offers visitors the chance to paddle a Hawaiian canoe. Canoes were the automobiles of ancient Hawaii: the fastest way to get from point A to point B, and a symbol of personal freedom. Giant voyaging canoes carried the first Polynesians to Hawaii, perhaps refugees from political strife or simply overcrowded islanders seeking a brighter future across the horizon. Canoes also enabled fishermen to access the ocean's bounty and kept communities connected before modern means of communication. Today most boating activity aimed at visitors involves modern powered craft, and chances are if a tourist paddles anything during his or her Maui visit, it'll be a kayak. The Fairmont teaches visitors the basics of canoe paddling, as well as its cultural significance, in part through native chants associated with canoe travel. Weather permitting, canoe trips depart four times each weekday morning. The whole experience lasts about forty-five minutes and is free and open to all; reservations are required; call the hotel concierge at 875–4100, ext. 290.

Finally, for your Hawaiian cultural fix in East Maui, check out the Kipahulu `Ohana's ongoing programs of cultural activities at the Kipahulu District of Haleakala National Park. Under the guidance of their *kupuna* ("elders"), Native Hawaiians who reside locally provide demonstrations and hands-on activities for visitors. Call for a schedule: 248–7375.

climbs above the tree line through open cattle land. Signs advise you to TURN ON LIGHTS IN CLOUDS. The **Haleakala National Park** boundary and turnoff to the **Hosmer Grove** campground arrive at roughly the halfway mark. A brochure available at the campground will guide you along the quarter-mile nature trail nearby. Just ahead you can pay the $10 entrance fee and proceed to the **Park Headquarters** building. Inquire here about the morning schedule of ranger-led talks and hikes, and collect camping permits, if desired. Call 572–4400 for live bodies 7:00 A.M. to 4:00 P.M. A small collection of displays chronicles the natural history of the park. You can learn about the campaign to restore the nene goose, Hawaii's state bird, to the unique habitats of Hawaii's tall volcanoes. Somewhat-tame nene often hang out in the parking lot; don't encourage them with food.

As you continue zigzagging up the barren rubble that covers Haleakala's upper slopes, you will come to two crater overlooks that deserve a stop on the way up or down. *Leleiwi Overlook*, at 8,800 feet, offers the chance to view the elusive "specter of the brocken." During late afternoon on cloudy days, you may see your own rainbow-shrouded shadow reflected in the mist. *Kalabaku Overlook*, at 9,320 feet, features a patch of silversword plants, which thrive atop Hawaii's highest volcanoes. These exotic bushes resemble metallic porcupines. After growing for five to twenty years, they erupt once in a spectacular display of tiny flowers and then wither and die. Because silverswords have fragile, shallow roots adapted to the volcanic soil, take care not to walk within 6 feet of any plant.

Near the summit, the Park Service operates another visitor center, open from 6:30 A.M. to 3:30 P.M. daily. In addition to natural history exhibits, the center houses a much-reproduced painting by Paul Rockwood depicting Maui's encounter with the sun god, La. The metallic domes of Science City, an off-limits research center, gleam nearby. From the visitor center, the road climbs a half mile to *Red Hill*, the actual summit. Most people watch the sunrise from the small shelter here. The 360-degree windowpanes allow you to view every island except Kaua`i on a clear day.

No one with the legs to carry them should pass up the chance to explore Haleakala Crater on foot. Short of space flight, it's the closest thing to walking on another planet. Those who would rather ride than walk can contact Pony Express Tours (667–2200) or Maui Crater Bound (878–1743) to ask about crater trail rides. The *Sliding Sands Trail* from the visitor center provides the main access to the crater floor. The trail gets its name from the loose cinders it traverses, so watch your footing. As you descend, you pass a procession of cinder cones, some of which rise as high as 700 feet; when clouds roll in, these poke through the mist like islands in a sea. The crater floor below is wracked by crevices and lava caves. Hawaiians threw the umbilical cords of their newborns into one such pit called *Keanawilinau.* This practice prevented rodents from making off with the cords, which would have given the grown child ratlike qualities.

The Sliding Sands Trail connects midway with the *Halemauu Trail*, which loops back up the crater walls, emerging near the highway at the 8,000-foot level for a hardy 11-mile daylong hike. A third trail allows backpackers an overnight route through the *Kaupo Gap*, descending to Maui's remote southeastern coast. Hawaiians often made such a trek as a shortcut across the island. Except for kahuna in training, Hawaiians did not live in the crater itself. If you're not a kahuna, camping in the crater's two campgrounds requires a permit. If you write at least three months in advance and are flexible about your dates, you can book one of the three cabins here. Address requests to the Cabins, Haleakala Park, Box 369, Makawao, Maui 96768.

In a hurry to get back to the beach? ***Proflyght Hawaii Paragliding*** (874–5433) launches tandem flights from atop Haleakala, weather permitting; more often they'll leave from the 6,000-foot level, where you may see other para/hang gliders launching as well. Prices vary by flight time.

Places to Stay in Maui

HANA

Hamoa Bay House & Bungalow
P.O. Box 773, 96713
248–7884
www.hamoabay.com
Balinese bungalow nestled in tropical jungle estate. $195 per night.

Hana Accommodations
248–7868, (800) 228–4262
www.hana-maui.com
Rent a cottage on the beautiful Hana coast. Rates start at $80 for a studio.

HUELO

A`apali Cliffhouse
Pali Uli Estate
P.O. Box 1059, 96708
573–0693, (800) 861–9566
One-bedroom Balinese pleasure palace perched above dramatic waterfall gorge along Hana Coast. $445 per night.

KULA

Gildersleeve's B&B
2112 Naalae Road
878–6623
A product of a retired couple's dream. Views and accommodations are wonderful. Rates start at $75.

Haikuleana B&B
555 Haiku Road
Haiku 96708
575–2890
www.haikuleana.net
Consists of three rooms in an elegantly restored plantation home. Rates start at $130.

LAHAINA

Lahaina Inn
127 Lahainaluna Road
661–0577, (800) 669-3444
www.lahainainn.com
A wonderfully restored mansion in the center of town, with twelve rooms decorated with period antique furniture. Rates start at $140.

MAKAWAO

Olinda Country Cottages & Inn
2660 Olinda Road
572–1453, (800) 932–3435
www.mauibnbcottages.com
Hilltop protea farm offers bed-and-breakfast rooms and secluded cottages, decorated in country elegance. Rates start at $140.

WAILUKU

The Old Wailuku Inn at Ulupono
2199 Kaho`okele Street
244–5897, (800) 305–4899
www.mauiinn.com
Offers gracious hospitality in a nostalgic old Hawaii setting. Rates start at $140.

Places to Eat in Maui

HAIKU

Hana Hou Cafe
810 Haiku Road
575-2661
A mix of island ethnic specialties served in a former Haiku cannery cookhouse. Live music on Monday and Saturday nights. Moderate to expensive.

HALIIMAILE

Haliimaile General Store
900 Haliimaile Road
572-2666
Neither "general" nor a "store." Offers a wide-ranging selection of great regional dishes and wines. Expensive but worth it.

KAHANA

Roy's Kahana Bar and Grill/Roy's Nicolina
4405 Honoapiilani Highway
669-6999
www.roys-restaurants.com
Hawaii superchef Roy Yamaguchi opened these twin venues to cope with the demand for his inventive Pacific Rim cuisine. Expensive.

KAPALUA

Sansei Seafood Restaurant & Sushi Bar
115 Bay Drive
669-6286
www.sanseihawaii.com
Top-rated sushi venue thrives on East-West culinary fusion. Expensive.

LAHAINA

Chez Paul
820 Olowalu Village Road B
661-3843
Offers classic French cuisine in a one-horse town. Investment-caliber.

David Paul's Lahaina Grill
1127 Lahainaluna Road
667-5117
Award-winning Pacific Rim cuisine with southwestern accents. Investment-caliber.

Plantation House
2000 Plantation Club Drive
669-6299
www.theplantationhouse.com
Romantic hilltop dining with views across three islands. Expensive.

MA`ALAEA

The Waterfront Restaurant
50 Hauoli Street
244-9028
"The local's Mama's" serves fresh fish in an oceanfront venue on the South Shore. Investment-caliber.

MAKAWAO

Makawao Cafe
3673 Baldwin Avenue
573-9065
For lunch only; innovative island cuisine. Inexpensive.

PAIA

Mama's Fish House
799 Poho Place
579-8488
www.mamasfishhouse.com
Offers fresh seafood in a romantic oceanfront setting. Investment-caliber.

WAILUKU

Saigon Cafe
1792 Main Street
243-9560
Serves delicious Vietnamese fare in a no-nonsense setting. Moderate.

TO LEARN MORE ABOUT MAUI VISIT THE FOLLOWING WEB SITES:

www.maui.net

www.visitmaui.com

Glossary

Hawaiian words are used for most place names in Hawaii and are sprinkled throughout the everyday speech of islanders. With a little practice, you too can speak like a *kama`aina*. The Hawaiian language has only twelve letters: seven consonants—*h, k, l, m, n, p, w*—and five vowels—*a, e, i, o, u*. Pronounce the consonants as you would in English, except for *w*, which is pronounced as a soft *v* after *e, i,* or *a*. (Yes, some people say Havaii.) Vowel sounds are more like Spanish: *a* as in *father, e* as in *acorn, i* as in *macaroni, o* as in *solo, u* as in *union*. Always pronounce each letter separately. Special cases are *ao* or *au*, which are usually pronounced "ow"; *ae* and *ai*, which sound like "eye"; and *ei*, which becomes "ay." A ` symbol before or between vowels indicates a slight pause or separation in the sounds. Give each syllable an even stress. When you see an eye-popper such as *humuhumunukunukuapuaa* (a tiny fish), don't panic. Just take it one group at a time: humu–humu–nuku–nuku–a–pu–a–a. It's easy!

Here is a selected list of Hawaiian terms used in this guide.

alii *(ah-lee-eee):* Hawaiian chief or royalty

aloha *(ah-loh-ha):* greetings, love

hala *(hah-lah):* pandanus, screwpine, or tourist pineapple; a Polynesian introduction, this tree has stiltlike aerial roots, pineapple-like fruit, and long fibrous leaves used for weaving (*see* lauhala)

hale *(hah-leh):* house

haole *(how-leh):* Caucasian; originally the word for foreigner

heiau *(hay-ow):* ancient Hawaiian temple

hula *(hoo-lah):* Hawaiian dance

kahili *(kah-hee-lee):* a feathered standard held on a pole as the symbol of royalty

kahuna *(kah-hoo-nah):* "one who knows the secrets"; Hawaiian priest, healer, or other skilled "professional"

kalua *(kah-loo-ah):* steam-cooked in leaves in an underground oven

kama`aina *(kah-mah-eye-nah):* longtime island resident

kane *(kah-neh):* man; also the name of one of the principal Hawaiian gods

kapu *(kah-poo):* taboo, forbidden

kokua *(koh-koo-ah):* help, cooperation

konane *(koh-nah-neh):* Hawaiian game similar to checkers

kukui *(kookoo-ee):* candlenut tree; a Polynesian introduction with light green leaves whose oil-rich nuts were strung together and burned as candles

lanai *(la-nye):* large open-air veranda

lauhala *(laow-hah-lah):* "leaf of hala"; woven to make mats, sails, and so on

lau-lau *(laow-laow):* Hawaiian specialty featuring pork, fish, and taro leaves wrapped and steamed in a ti leaf bundle

lei *(lay):* garland or necklace, most often made of flowers

loco moco *(loh-coh moh-coh):* a local dish based on rice, a fried egg, a hamburger patty, and plenty of gravy

luakini *(loo-ah-kee-nee):* sacrifice; describes large state temples where human sacrifices were offered

luau *(loo-ow):* traditional Hawaiian feast; also decribes a specific dish cooked in coconut milk

mahalo *(mah-hah-loh):* thank you

makai *(mah-kye):* toward the sea, coastal

mana *(mah-nah):* spiritual power, prestige

mauka *(maow-kah):* toward the mountains, inland

Menehune *(men-eh-hoo-nay):* legendary race of "little people"

ono *(oh-noh):* delicious

pali *(pah-lee):* cliff

paniolo *(pah-nee-olo):* cowboy

poi *(poy):* mashed vegetable paste, usually made from taro tubers

tapa *(tah-pah):* Polynesian bark cloth; called *kapa* in old Hawaii

taro *(tah-roh):* traditional food staple, source of poi

tiki *(tee-kee):* carved idol

wahine *(wah-hee-nay):* woman

As noted in the Introduction, much of the foreign-sounding speech you'll hear in the islands isn't Hawaiian but pidgin, a unique vernacular that grew out of the mongrelized vocabularies of multiethnic plantation workers. It continues to thrive today as a "locals only" slang. A glossary to pidgin is impractical, as word usages are nonstandard; you just have to get a feel for it. Just remember to say "howzit"—it's the way locals say hello.

Index

About the Author

Sean Pager first came to Hawaii at the age of six months. It didn't make much of an impression at the time, but he enjoyed growing up in the islands and appreciated them even more when he continued to travel and live elsewhere. Sean did his first paid travel writing for the *Let's Go* series as a summer job while in college and liked it enough to stick with it after graduation. *Hawaii: Off the Beaten Path* is his first book-length publication. In his free time, Sean likes to go off the beaten path in the islands by hiking the hills or sailboarding the coast. He currently lives with his wife, Sheryl and daughter, Sophie.